# JUDAISM AND MODERN MAN
## An Interpretation of Jewish Religion

## Will Herberg

### New Introduction by Neil Gillman

A JEWISH LIGHTS
CLASSIC REPRINT

D0062486

JEWISH LIGHTS Publishing
Woodstock, Vermont

# To Anna

Judaism and Modern Man
A JEWISH LIGHTS Classic Reprint
©1997 by Donald G. Jones, executor of the estate of Will Herberg
Copyright © renewed 1979 by Donald G. Jones
Copyright © 1951 by Will Herberg
Introduction © 1997 by Neil Gillman

Originally published by Farrar, Straus and Young.

*Library of Congress Cataloging-in-Publication Data*

Herberg, Will.
Judaism and modern man : an interpretation of Jewish religion / by Will Herberg ; new introduction by Neil Gillman.
p.      cm. — (A Jewish Lights classic reprint)
Originally published: New York : Farrar, Straus and Young, 1951.
Includes bibliographical references and index.
     ISBN 1-879045-87-7 (pbk.)
     1. Judaism.   2. Judaism—20th century.   I. Title.   II. Series.
BM565.H335   1997
296—dc21                                         97-35990
                                                 CIP
                                                 r97


10 9 8 7 6 5 4 3 2 1

Manufactured in the United States of America

Published by Jewish Lights Publishing
A Division of LongHill Partners Inc.
P.O. Box 237
Sunset Farm Offices, Route 4
Woodstock, VT 05091
Tel: (802) 457-4000      Fax: (802) 457-4004

# CONTENTS

# INTRODUCTION

I remember my first encounter with Will Herberg as if it were yesterday. It was in January, 1952. I was a second year undergraduate at McGill University in Montreal, sitting in a class in English Romantic Poetry, awaiting the arrival of the professor. Sitting next to me that day was a young woman whom I had come to know through that course. We were chatting when she suddenly asked me what I was doing for lunch. I replied in my most gallant manner, "Whatever you're doing for lunch!" She was going to a lecture at Hillel. "Who is lecturing?" Will Herberg. "Who is Will Herberg?" "He's a Jewish theologian who just wrote a book and is on a cross-country tour speaking about his book."

After class, we walked over to Hillel. I grabbed a sandwich and a Coke, and settled myself in the lounge. A few moments later, Rabbi Samuel Cass, the Hillel Director at that time, walked in, accompanied by a short, stocky man, a bulldog-shaped head set firmly on his shoulders, with thinning grey hair, thick jowls, a face pockmarked with nicks from his razor, and a deadly serious, passionate mien.

He was properly introduced, rose to the podium and without the introductory pleasantries that public speakers typically use to put their audience at ease, launched into what I subsequently realized was a forty-minute summary of his book. His very first sentence was something along these lines: "There is only one real philosophical problem: How to counter the absurdity of our existence. On this, there are only two possible answers: God, or an idol."

I was entranced. My friend left for her next class, but a few of us stayed behind, throwing questions, arguing and challenging. Soon I was the only one left. He took my arm and together with his devoted wife Anna (who, I later discovered, never left his side and who carried his leather briefcase, stuffed with books, papers, and a Bible), he suggested, "Let's go for a drink." We talked for another few hours. I spent most of the next three days with him, accompanying him to his lectures at various Montreal synagogues and at McGill's Divinity School. In between, the three of us ate, drank, walked and talked.

When we parted, he gave me his itinerary for the next month, urged me to read his book and to write to him. I did and he never failed to respond—sometimes with a postcard from places like Fort Dodge, Iowa, with notes such as "No. Read *I and Thou*, p. 67."

I spent another ten days with him later that summer at the Hillel Leadership Institute in Starlight, Pennsylvania. (My encounter with the riches of McGill Hillel had led me to assume a leadership role in the Foundation.) My fondest memory of that experience was the moment when Herberg ran on to the basketball court in the middle of a game, pulled me aside, and expostulated: "You just don't understand Rosenzweig on that point!" (I had challenged him on Rosenzweig's notion that revelation was never legislation.) "I'm in the middle of a game," I shouted. "So what! What's more important? A game or Rosenzweig?" I left the game.

What entranced me? Partly, this was the first time anyone had convinced me that there was something in Judaism that was intellectually challenging and worth taking seriously. I had had no serious Jewish education in my younger years. I came to McGill, majored in Philosophy and French literature, and I was comfortably and guiltlessly on my way out of any serious Jewish involvement. I was going to practice law in Montreal.

Suddenly, Judaism became integrated into my studies in philosophy and in 20th century French literature where I had learned a good deal about existentialism, though little about Buber and Rosenzweig, or about Herberg's other teacher,

Reinhold Niebuhr, and still less about existentialist expressions in the Bible and in other Jewish texts.

Even more, this was a man who cared passionately about his issues. This was not a dispassionate academic. For Herberg, Judaism was the ultimate risk—the faith that lent meaning to his existence. The alternative was equally ultimate absurdity.

There must have been much more in that initial encounter. I was living a typically rootless undergraduate existence—lectures, classes, bookstores, frat parties and those night-long, intellectualized schmooze sessions with friends and classmates. I had no real passion for the law; it was safe, comfortable, well-paying, conventional—essentially a fallback career. I was awaiting something that would galvanize my intellectual energy, some ideal vision, a cause that would enable me to save the world—nothing less.

Months later, I found myself a tutor (there were no Jewish Studies at McGill, or for that matter, at any major university in those days), began to study Hebrew, Chumash and Rashi, First Prophets, and to build a Jewish library. I went to Israel for the summer of 1953, applied to Rabbinical School at The Jewish Theological Seminary, and began doctoral work in philosophy at Columbia. I have been teaching and writing on Jewish philosophy and theology ever since. Never for a moment have I regretted those decisions.

I subsequently discovered that I was but one of a number of young undergraduates around the country who had been hooked by Herberg. I discovered some of those at the Seminary. Most of the Seminary faculty disdained Herberg—he had never mastered Hebrew, never studied Talmud in the original, he was not an academic, he had never earned a doctorate in course, etcetera....

But there were exceptions to that rule. My first professor of Talmud and Jewish theology, the late Seymour Siegel, was a friend and fan of Herberg's and invited him—somewhat surreptitiously I recall—to meet informally with small groups of

JTS students in the evenings. I later discovered that the Seminary community had played a critical role in Herberg's own discovery of Judaism after his break with Communism in the '40s. The late Professor Gerson Cohen, who taught me Talmud and Jewish history and subsequently served as Chancellor of the Seminary, had been one of Herberg's tutors. So had Rabbi Milton Steinberg, then rabbi of Park Avenue Synagogue, whose death in 1950 at the tragically young age of 47, robbed the Jewish community of one its most thoughtful and eloquent teachers. *Judaism and Modern Man* was published in 1951, and Herberg devotes an entire paragraph of his Foreword to expressing the debt he owed to Steinberg.

Herberg was born in Russia in 1901 into a family of convinced socialists. Essentially self-taught, he imbibed the heady socialist intellectualism of his family's circle of friends, mastered several languages and studied at CCNY and Columbia without ever completing an academic degree. He formally joined the Communist party in the 1920s and wrote for a host of publications on the intricacies of Marxist theory.

Herberg's disenchantment with Marxism and Communism progressed apace during the '30s. The final break was precipitated by the Stalin-Hitler nonagression pact of 1939. But Marxism was much more than an intellectual exercise for Herberg. It was in fact a religion, a faith, a total, life-encompassing system which he used to ground his very existence. When this collapsed, he needed another faith, and he found it in the work of the eminent liberal Protestant theologian, Reinhold Niebuhr. Niebuhr gave Herberg a new center for his faith, a combination of realism and radicalism without illusion, and a theology which grounded Herberg's long-standing interest in political activity. So taken was Herberg with Niebuhr that he petitioned his teacher to convert him to Christianity. Niebuhr urged him, instead, to pursue his own Judaism, and directed him across Broadway—Niebuhr was then teaching at Union Theological Seminary in New York—to The Jewish

Theological Seminary.

At the Seminary in the '40s, Herberg found a circle of friends and tutors who fed him Judaism. He earned a living as educational director of the International Ladies Garment Workers Union, began to write on his personal journey from Marxism to Judaism, and eventually, on what was to become *Judaism and Modern Man*. But academic recognition eluded him until the publication of his *Protestant-Catholic-Jew* (1955), which Niebuhr hailed as "...the most fascinating essay on the religious sociology of America that has appeared in decades." He then received a full-time appointment at Drew University in New Jersey where he taught until his retirement in 1976.

As the '50s wore on, Herberg's political loyalties changed dramatically. He became identified with a group of neo-conservative ex-Communists, served as religion editor of William F. Buckley's *National Review*, wrote passionately on the threat of Marxism which he understood as a uniquely modern idolatry, and pleaded for a reassessment of the prevailing liberal consensus on issues such as the separation of church and state. After the death of his beloved Anna, he drifted more and more into his private world, isolating himself from friends and colleagues. He died in 1977.

I have read and re-read *Judaism and Modern Man* many times since 1951, and I still assign significant portions of the book as required reading for courses I teach here at the Seminary. I am always surprised at how well it has held up over the decades. Its opening chapters remain one of the clearest and sharpest expositions of modern existentialism, both in its critical and its constructive phases. The chapters on the Jewish philosophy of history and on eschatology are simply brilliant. His unpacking of biblical eschatology and its Marxist parallels are startling. It plays a major role in my own *The Death of Death: Resurrection and Immortality in Jewish Thought* (Jewish Lights, 1997). Herberg was the first thinker to convince me to take the doctrine of bodily resurrection seriously, though not literally, which is the central thesis of my book.

Herberg subtitles his book "An Interpretation of Jewish Religion," which it is. But it is also a very personal interpretation. He calls it "a confession of faith." "To stand witness to one's faith...is at bottom all that theology can pretend to do without falling into the delusion that it is speaking 'objectively' from the throne of God." It is personal in two ways: first, in its selection of issues—there is little here, for example, on prayer in Judaism—and second, in its presentation of Judaism as testimony, one man's version of how Judaism has provided a grounding for his life in this world.

Of course, I now know much more about Jewish theology than I did in 1951, and I can appreciate why my Seminary teachers questioned his book as an authentic Jewish theological statement. Herberg is uncritical in his use of biblical and rabbinic texts. For the latter, he relies heavily on secondary sources such as Solomon Schechter's *Aspects of Rabbinic Theology* and George Foot Moore's three-volume *Judaism in the First Centuries of the Christian Era: The Age of the Tannaim.* Beyond this, the on-the-edge, sharply individualistic quality of existentialist thinking has always irritated more conventional Jewish thinkers.

Herberg was also criticized for using the writings of Christian theologians such as Pascal, Kierkegaard, Paul Tillich, Reinhold Niebuhr and his brother, H. Richard Niebuhr. But Herberg's range is far wider. There are also copious references to the writings of Plato, Bertrand Russell, Sigmund Freud, John Dewey, Thomas Hobbes, Karl Marx of course, and Arnold Toynbee. On this issue, my sense is that Herberg is fully in tune with the great Jewish philosophers of the ages, whose common aim was the integration of Torah with the best of the intellectual world outside of Judaism.

But Herberg's most significant teachers remain Martin Buber and Franz Rosenzweig. We today enjoy a plethora of writings by and on Buber and Rosenzweig, but in 1951, this was far from the case, particularly in the case of Rosenzweig.

Nahum N. Glatzer's first monumental anthology of Rosenzweig's writings, *Franz Rosenzweig: His Life and Thought,* was published only in 1953. Herberg was one of the first thinkers—Milton Steinberg and Jacob Agus are two others that come to mind—to have presented the thought of this figure in English and to make it accessible to the modern American reader.

*Judaism and Modern Man* is an apologia for Judaism, in the sense that Herberg's goal is to make the case for Judaism for those readers of a time and a setting in which identification with Jewish religion does not come naturally or intuitively. In this, Herberg is again fully within the tradition of great Jewish philosophical statements. His teachers, Buber and Rosenzweig, and his contemporaries, Mordecai Kaplan and Abraham Joshua Heschel, had the same goal.

Jewish philosophy is inevitably written for the marginal Jew, for the Jew who stands on the edge of Jewish identity, who is tempted by the competing ideologies of the surrounding culture, but is also sufficiently intrigued by the richness of this ancient tradition to wonder whether it may speak again in a new voice. Herberg understood that marginal state very well. He had been there. In fact, he, together with the thinkers whom he followed, wrote primarily for himself. In the process, he invites us to look over his shoulder. The enduring value of this book is that so many young American Jews took up the invitation and were convinced.

This remains, then, a disturbing book—disturbing to those Jews who are already there, comfortably within Judaism, and are unaware of any tension with their Jewish identity, and even more disturbing for those of us who are prepared to follow Herberg's path. Herberg's interpretation of Judaism offers no panacea, no easy path into faith, no comfortable way-stations on the journey.

This is not Herberg's way. His Judaism demands total commitment, and he acknowledges, early and frequently, that this kind of faith is filled with risk, venture and decision. The leap of faith which he champions is, he warns us, never secure, never a permanent acquisition. It is, rather "...a never-ending battle against self-absolutization and idolatry; it is a battle which has to be refought every moment of life because it is a battle in which the victory can never be final."

But, he also assures us, "...the outstretched hand over the abyss is always there for us to take hold of." It is this certainty of God's enduring grace that provided him and countless other Jews with the grounding that gave new and ultimate meaning to their lives.

With the republication of this book, Herberg's path can now challenge a new generation of Jewish readers. I envy them this encounter.

Neil Gillman
August 1997

*Dr. Gillman is the Aaron Rabinowitz and Simon H. Rifkind Professor of Jewish Philosophy at The Jewish Theological Seminary of America in New York.*

# FOREWORD

This book is in the nature of a confession of faith. It is an attempt to make explicit what I take to be the truth about my religious existence. To stand witness to one's faith and to try to communicate a sense of its meaning, power and relevance: that, it seems to me, is at bottom all that theology can pretend to do without falling into the delusion that it is speaking "objectively" from the throne of God.

The whole burden of my "confession of faith" is that I find the truth of my existence as man and as Jew illumined by historical Judaism in a way that directly compels acceptance—not merely intellectual affirmation but total acceptance as the very foundation of life. As Franz Rosenzweig and the religious existentialists of all ages have emphasized, it is an acceptance which involves one's whole being and upon which one stakes one's entire existence. My "confession of faith" is, therefore, meant as a declaration of total commitment.

When I speak of historical Judaism, I mean the religious affirmation embodied in the biblical-rabbinic tradition. I am well aware, of course, that there are various readings of this tradition, differing widely in important respects. What I try to do, and all that I can presume to do, is to present my reading, together with some suggestions as to why I find it valid. That is why I call my book "An Interpretation of Jewish Religion."

The attentive reader will note that the approach shifts as the book goes on. In the first part of the book (chaps. 1 - 5), the viewpoint is that of existential analysis and criticism. In the second part (chaps. 6 - 16), the attempt is made to present the basic teachings of Jewish faith in their relevance to individual and social life. In the final section (chaps. 17 - 19), dealing with "The Mystery of Israel," Jewish faith is presented as *Heilsgeschichte*. This repeated

Foreword

shift of approach may perhaps prove distracting, but I have found
it to be the only way in which I could communicate what I wanted
to say about Jewish faith in its relation to the perennial condition
of man, on the one hand, and to the particular perplexities of our
time, on the other.

To make an adequate statement of my indebtedness to men and
books is utterly beyond my power. What I owe to Reinhold Niebuhr
in the formation of my general theological outlook, every page of
this book bears witness. To the writings of Solomon Schechter, I
owe my first appreciation of how vital and relevant, how contemporary, the rabbinic tradition can be. I have almost without exception
followed his interpretation of that tradition. To Martin Buber and
Franz Rosenzweig, I owe not only my basic "existentialist" approach
but also—and here I can never sufficiently express my gratitude—
my understanding of how to establish my religious existence in
Jewish terms in the modern world.

I must now speak of Milton Steinberg. I don't know how I can
possibly convey to the reader what my three years of close friendship with Milton Steinberg, the three years immediately preceding
his death, meant to me in the making of this book. I can say this:
that had it not been for Milton Steinberg, this book might not have
come into being and almost certainly would not have been completed. He read my original manuscript through the fifteenth
chapter with a care, concern and critical insight that one does not
ordinarily bestow on the work of another. I took every one of his
many suggestions and criticisms, as they emerged out of our vigorous
discussions, with the utmost seriousness and have followed virtually
all of them. On some points we differed, but our differences were
as nothing in comparison with the common commitment and common understanding that bound us together.

To Solomon Grayzel, editor of the Jewish Publication Society,
I owe many thanks for his original invitation to write this book and
for his unfailing patience at my long delays. To Dr. Grayzel and to
Gershon Cohen, I must express my appreciation for the help they
gave me in checking and establishing rabbinical sources. Gershon
Cohen, Hershel Matt, Monford Harris, Max Ticktin and other of
my friends read the manuscript, in whole or in part, and made

many valuable suggestions. And finally, I must state, though I cannot conceivably state adequately, what I owe to my wife. Her advice and assistance at every stage in the making of this book amounted to virtual collaboration. To her the book is dedicated.

A word on the usage of certain terms. I have employed the term "Hebraic religion" (or "biblical faith") to express the fundamental religious affirmation and commitment held in common by Judaism and Christianity. For the specific structure of Jewish spirituality, I have generally used the terms "Jewish religion" or "Jewish faith."

WILL HERBERG

*New York City*
*May, 1951*

# 1. THE PLIGHT OF MODERN MAN

In 1871, Algernon Charles Swinburne, the poet of the "new freedom," hailed man in words that brought a thrill of pride to the "emancipated" minds of the day:

> Glory to Man in the highest,
> The maker and master of things.
> (*Hymn to Man*)

Today, not much more than three-quarters of a century later, poets and publicists are proclaiming the "end of the human race." In his brief reign as "master of things," man has brought himself and his universe to the brink of destruction. The world of twentieth-century man is going out with a "whimper" *and* a "bang." Never in all recorded history has the collapse of the hopes of a civilization taken place so suddenly, almost in the sight of one generation. The "decline and fall" of the Roman Empire, stretching over centuries, was slow by comparison. In its chaos, insecurity and all-pervading sense of disaster, the world of today is more akin to the world of 912, to the Dark Ages a thousand years ago, than to the world of 1912, which some of us can still remember.

No wonder that the prevailing mood of our time is frustration, bewilderment, despair. Horrors which only yesterday we all believed had been banished once and for all from human society—slavery and despotism, vile superstition, famine and torture, persecution for opinion—have come back in the most virulent form. The problems with which mankind is confronted have suddenly regressed to a primitive level. Our fathers were concerned with fashioning the good life; for us today, the all-absorbing problem is life itself, bare survival.

Before our very eyes, within the past fifteen years, six million Jews were exterminated by the government of the culturally most advanced country of Europe. Before our very eyes, almost as many peasants

3

were destroyed in state-engineered famines by the rulers of a regime that spoke in the name of socialism. In 1903, at the outset of our century, the Kishinev massacre—in which forty-seven Jews were killed and ninety-two severely wounded—aroused a storm of indignation throughout the world. Today, less than half a century later, millions of men are wiped out, millions more are enslaved, while we stand by silent, dumb—yes, let us confess it—too callous and indifferent even to glance at the record. Three decades of unbroken violence have done their work.

With the feverish irresponsibility so characteristic of our times, we speak of "one world" as a discovery and achievement of our own. Yet what we have actually done in the past generation is to shatter the beginnings of world community into a thousand jagged fragments. In 1912, anyone could travel anywhere—aside from "backward" Russia, Turkey and China—without so much as a passport. Today, the greater part of the inhabitants of "enlightened" Europe cannot go to a nearby town without permission from the police. In 1912, a displaced persons camp would have been unthinkable in any Western nation. Today, scores of thousands of men, women and children are without home or fatherland, happy if they can find a grudging refuge in some corner of the earth.

In 1912, progressive thought was preoccupied with the problem of developing adequate social control over modern industrialism so as to assure a greater measure of freedom and economic justice than seemed possible under an unregulated capitalism. This problem is, of course, still with us; indeed, in a larger and considerably changed context, it remains one of the crucial problems of our time. But over a large part of Europe and Asia, capitalism—whatever there was of it—has disappeared; it has given way to a regime that in its normal operations is simply industrial serfdom resting upon outright slavery. The forced-labor system of the totalitarian states, in which millions upon millions toil their lives away as mere chattels, has reintroduced human bondage on a scale unknown since the days of Rome. And even the "free" workers in these countries are indistinguishable in status from serfs tied to their place of work and at the mercy of their overseers. The economic problem, too, has been reduced to the most primitive level.

In 1912, parliamentarism and the constitutional state were in some form accepted as normative throughout the civilized world; the only task seemed to be the speedy elimination of the "remnants" of "feudalism" and special privilege that were still to be found in political life. Today, less than forty years after, parliamentary democracy is almost nonexistent outside the borders of a few countries of the Western world, and even there it is in many cases fighting for its life. Vast areas—most of Europe and Asia—are dominated by authoritarian regimes, which, for sheer ruthlessness and despotism, can find few parallels in history. In these areas, political and civil liberty, which is in retreat everywhere, has become an almost utopian goal.

Of nothing were our fathers so proud as of the cultural emancipation they and their ancestors had won. By 1912, freedom of thought, of inquiry, of conscience, had been formally acknowledged everywhere, however grossly the principle was violated in practice. Because of such freedom, the men of those days could look with untroubled confidence to the spread of literacy and popular education for the final achievement of democracy. Nowhere has the reversal been more tragic. In most of the world today, any claim to freedom of thought is regarded as an intolerable presumption by the holders of power. Thinking—in science, philosophy, art and religion, as well as in politics—is the monopoly of the totalitarian state. Through its agencies of "education" and "popular enlightenment," the state tells its subjects what to think, what to feel, what to say and do, and through its vast network of control it makes sure that the totalitarian patterns pervade all of life. In the most literal sense, the problem of intellectual survival has been reduced to a desperate effort to find some nook or cranny overlooked by the state in which one may think a thought of one's own.

In 1912, the world had not known a really large-scale war for almost a century, although conflict in the Balkans was already sounding a warning for those who had ears to hear. Since then, two world wars have overwhelmed mankind and a third looms in the offing. In the face of the approaching catastrophe, we stand utterly helpless. The very survival of mankind has become problematical, and there seems to be nothing we can do about it.

All this in one brief generation! Everything modern man has touched has turned to ashes; every achievement of his has been transformed before his very eyes into a demonic force of destruction. His miracles of science and technology have led to industrial exploitation and to the construction of instruments of self-annihilation. His grandiose schemes of universal enlightenment have found realization in the sway of the gutter journalist, the propagandist and demagogue, or in the monopoly of state indoctrination. His marvels of organization have taken form in organized despotism, organized slavery, organized mass-murder; his visions of permanent peace, in a succession of world wars; his fervent hopes of freedom, in universal regimentation and totalitarian dictatorship; his dreams of brotherhood and social justice, in the reign of terror, naked and unashamed. . . . Only yesterday man proclaimed himself "master of things"; today he considers himself lucky merely to survive. What has happened?

There are still those among us who, like their spiritual ancestors of the eighteenth and nineteenth centuries, feel they can meet the problem by laying the blame on wicked kings, priests or capitalists and the evil institutions they produce—or are produced by. There is much in this view. Wicked, tyrannical, power-lusting men there are aplenty, and the havoc they work is incalculable. Social institutions, too, necessarily reflect and tend to perpetuate oppression and injustice. But institutions are men writ large, and the wicked, tyrannical, power-lusting man, at whose door the responsibility is to be laid, is—everyman. Whatever be the line of inquiry, the thread leads back to man. Man is the problem.

The events of the past generation have brought mankind to the brink of the abyss. But the horrors we glimpse are not merely the horrors of the hell without; they are also—and primarily—the horrors of the hell within, the chaos and evil in the heart of man. It is this glimpse of the hell within that so frightens us; our philosophy has done nothing to prepare us for it. Whatever it is that has gone wrong, it is obviously not merely something in the external machinery of life; it is something within the soul of man.

We are all deeply involved in this spiritual confusion. We stare with horror at the demonic obsessions, the power-mad cults, that have seized upon millions of men in the past generation; we stare with horror, but also with fascination. For what have we to offer against these obsessive cults? What have we to offer not merely to others who may have succumbed but to ourselves, who are always on the verge of succumbing? Have we anything to preserve us against the sorcery of nihilism? Have we any faith, any "philosophy of life," that can give meaning to existence and save us from being driven headlong down the path of destruction?

Modern man is beginning to lose the arrogance, the self-assurance, which speaks to us through Swinburne's verse in a tongue already strange though less than a century old. If the men for whom Swinburne wrote were "modern" men, we of this generation are no longer so: our world, our age, is, let us say, *post*-modern. There are those who tell us that this is nothing but a "failure of nerve." Be it so; "nerve," in American English, has a double meaning, and to lose one's "nerve" may well be the first step to recovering the sense of reality without which there is no finding one's way again.

Our post-modern generation, shocked out of its illusions by three decades of unbroken horror, is trying to find its way again; that is the meaning of the "return to religion" which so many have noted as the sign of our times. Much, almost everything, is still in confusion, but one thing seems to be emerging as the foundation of the new consciousness: the realization that the collapse of our civilization, the disasters of our time, are somehow the fruit of the fatal Prometheanism of modern man. In the historical period whose ending in a whimper and a bang we are now witnessing, man tried recklessly to dispense with the transcendental and to fashion his life and culture entirely in human terms, in implicit and often explicit denial of any reality beyond the merely human. In his incredible arrogance, he imagined himself entirely sufficient unto himself. The astounding expansion of natural science and technology fostered the illusion that human welfare was simply a matter of increasing economic productivity and industrial power. "Progress" became the new catchword, replacing the older, now obsolete, notion of salvation. In morals and philosophy, in social life, even in religion, man—omnipotent man—became the "master" of all things. Intoxicated with his success, he denied God because he could imagine no power superior to his own. Or rather he transformed himself into God and began worshiping himself and his power. It was an appalling idolatry, and its consequences could hardly have been otherwise. If man is indeed the "master of things," then everything, literally everything, is permitted to him—to him as individual, as collectivity, as dictator or state: there is nothing he need reverence, nothing he need fear, if only he has the power. Out of this self-idolatry was generated the demonism that has taken possession of humanity and driven it to the brink of the abyss.

Our post-modern generation is beginning to understand this. It is beginning to see that in the process of establishing his autonomy and gaining mastery over the instruments of living, Western man has managed to lose his grasp of the meaning of life, his control over the dark destructive forces within himself and society. In gaining— or rather in trying to gain—the world, he has come very close to losing his soul.

Our post-modern generation understands this, for it sees how the earthly paradise that man, in his delusions of grandeur, was to erect through his own unaided efforts has come to assume the aspect of one vast universal hell. Now we of this generation want to find our way back. But how? Where shall we turn? We have lost our direction and all but lost the ability to read the map that might show us how to regain it.

## 2.  AT THE BRINK OF THE ABYSS: THE PERMANENT CRISIS OF LIFE

No word is more common in our mouths or more familiar to our ears than the word "crisis." Every enterprise, every institution, every phase of modern life, stands under this ominous sign. A "philosophy of crisis" would seem to be not merely the most natural but actually the only intelligible, the only possible, philosophy for our time.

Yet one may wonder whether in becoming such a humdrum, everyday affair, the word has not lost its meaning. Is not our constant, almost affectionate use of the term a device to escape its impact? Our first task—if we are ever to understand the condition of man— is to recover the full and living sense of the word "crisis."

Crisis means insecurity, peril, threat of destruction; crisis means conflict, movement, urgency. But crisis also means judgment, "turning," decision: it also points to the new reality beyond—for the eyes of faith to discern.

In all of these senses, human existence—individual and collective— stands under the sign of crisis; or, better put, human existence *is* crisis, *is* insecurity, peril, conflict, urgency, judgment and decision. Not merely human existence today, in this period of war and social convulsion, but human existence as such, the existence of man.

It is, of course, true that the time we live in is pre-eminently a time of troubles. History seems to have taken our age by the throat and forced it to recognize the bloody reality of crisis and judgment. But the particular crisis of our time, for all the agony it has brought us, will sooner or later pass away; nothing in history is eternal. If suffering is to bring knowledge, as the Greek poet tells us it can, we must find a significance in our experience that transcends the passing historical phase. We must learn to discern the *permanent* crisis of life, the existential crisis which no time or history can cure.

Whether we look outward or inward, we descry a restlessness, a dynamism, in human existance that drives life in all its phases to the brink, to the "boundary" or "limit," where the question of ultimate meaning suddenly arises and demands answer. But answer there is none—certainly not on the level on which the question is asked. There is no turning back; yet ahead there is nothing but a yawning gulf of meaninglessness, absurdity and despair. Only on the other side of the abyss, only on a plane in which the natural conditions of life are transcended, can the answer be found and the meaning of existence regained.

Most obvious to us—the generation of the mid-twentieth century— is the tragic absurdity of existence in its social and collective aspects. We have fought two world wars in our generation, the second against a monstrous tyranny that threatened to overwhelm us. We had no alternative, we had to fight, but before that war was over, another, startlingly similar in the threat it held out for us, was already looming on the horizon. We may have to fight again—a third world war in one generation—but will that bring us out of the darkness? Will it not rather drive us yet further into the abyss? Our freedom of action is reduced almost to nothing, but we are compelled to make a decision. And upon this decision hangs our fate, insofar as fate can be enacted in history.

In domestic affairs, almost all of us realize that some sort of reform of the economic order is necessary so as to bring the centers of wealth and industrial power under social control. But does not social control bring with it the peril of state regimentation and totalitarian enslavement? Is not this one of the "lessons" history has impressed upon us so painfully in the course of the past generation? Act we must; yet how shall we act when all action seems doomed to self-defeat?

In our political faith, the values of democracy and civil liberty seem fixed and secure. But are they? Can democracy stand the pressures of the contemporary "ice age"? What shall we do with those who shamelessly, brazenly, attempt to use our democracy in order to smash it and enslave us all? Can we exclude them from its operations without destroying democracy itself? Again we are up against a blank wall; our certainty has vanished; every course we take seems perilous and self-defeating.

In our social life, we erect vast institutions and organizations—beginning with an all-engulfing industrialism—in order to implement the various enterprises we have initiated for the purpose of enhancing the quality of life. But these institutions and organizations, by an iron logic of their own, generate bureaucracy and privilege, accelerate depersonalization and hasten the destruction of organic community between man and man. What shall we do? Without large-scale organization we cannot live; yet large-scale organization threatens our very existence.

These problems are not brought forward for the purpose of social diagnosis. They are brought forward because, although they are social and therefore historical problems, they point to something that is, at bottom, neither social or historical but existential: *the self-defeating,*

*self-destroying dynamic of human life conceived in its own terms.*
The political events and historical developments of our time hammer
this fact home with shattering force, for, in our time, political events
and historical developments are the outcropping of final existential
realities. We live in an age when ultimate questions have, quite un-
accountably, become immediate questions.

These questions—the final questions of existence—arise and demand answer once we gain the courage to face them. The questions
have always been there, but as long as we could comfort ourselves
with flattering illusions and easy solutions, we could avoid seeing
them. This is no longer possible today.

What do we find when we look inward? The same relentless existential pressure that drives us forward, by means of our very achievements, to the brink of nothingness, to an abyss of meaninglessness,
contradiction and unreality.

Human existence is nothing if it is not personal—concrete, individual, irreplaceable. "Man stamps many coins with the one seal and
they are all like one another; but the King of Kings, the Holy One
blessed is He, has stamped every man with the seal of the first man;
yet not one of them is like his fellows."[1]  This uniqueness is the ultimate, the "real" reality of life. But what becomes of it once we turn
our glance upon it? What—in our science, our philosophy, our thought
—can this intractable, irreducible, indestructible uniqueness of ours
mean? Objective thought, philosophical or scientific, knows nothing
of the absolutely concrete, absolutely unique; all thinking is necessarily
in terms of abstractions, universals. How then shall I grasp the real
"I" of my existence, the concrete, individual person that I am? If I
cannot grasp it in objective thought, how shall I ground its existence?
It is not merely the "I" who is in peril; it is also the "Thou" with whom
the "I" enters into genuinely personal relations. Both are concrete,
unique, personal existences and both are therefore thrown into question. Personality becomes utterly problematical; what we had taken
to be the very rock of our existence threatens to vanish into meaninglessness.

The magnificent creative achievement of the human mind in comprehending the universe in thought, in subjecting all things to the uni-

form laws of reason and causality which nothing can escape, has evoked the very understandable admiration of man himself. We owe all our science and most of our philosophy to this enterprise. But like so many other aspects of human creativity, it no sooner triumphs than it turns upon and consumes itself. Analytical thought threatens not merely man the person but also man the thinker. What is man in the light of the science that has penetrated the universe? What is he but part of nature, a bit of matter, a structure of energy, an organism, an animal, a cell of society? Are not his actions, his beliefs, indeed his very thoughts—like everything else in the universe—determined by antecedent causes? "What man thinks, feels and does is determined by his culture," a professor of anthropology tells us in a leading scientific journal. "Human beings are merely the instruments through which cultures express themselves. . . . Neither as groups nor as individuals do we have a choice of roles or fates."² Not all contemporary scientists would put it so crudely, and many would dispute the all-determining role of culture in favor of some other causal determinant. But all would have to affirm, insofar as they remain scientists, that man is simply a natural object, subject to the same natural determinism as the rest of nature. But note the self-destructive force of this logic. Is not the scientist, the philosopher, himself a man? Is not his science, his philosophy, even his very principle of determinism, as inevitable and determined a consequence of antecedent causes as the rumbling of thunder, the murmuring of the leaves or the chirping of a cricket? A natural event is fully taken account of when its antecedent causes are given; no other question need arise. On what ground then does the philosopher or scientist claim that the natural event called his "thought" should be "judged" in terms of "standards" of "truth" and "falsity"? Indeed, what can these terms mean in his deterministic system? Nothing whatever. But if these terms have no meaning, his thought loses its claim to truth, even its significance as thought. And if it abandons its claim to truth and significance, it destroys itself as philosophy or science.

What shall we conclude? There is but one answer: the science and reason that have enabled man to "comprehend" the universe—*if taken as ultimate*—destroy themselves and man along with them. Blank absurdity meets us at the end of this road, too.

Man finds the meaning of his human existence in his capacity for decision, in his freedom of choice. It is a dreadful freedom, for it also means responsibility, but without it man would be as nothing. Yet is not decision likewise merely an illusion? Can we speak of freedom of choice and responsibility within the limits of natural human existence?

The more we examine this vaunted capacity of ours, the more dubious it becomes. Our character, our habits, our sentiments, our motives, are they not all fixed and conditioned by a whole variety of factors—some rooted in heredity, others going back to infancy and childhood, still others reflecting the external social, economic and cultural circumstances of life? Even our mental life, we are reliably informed, is in large, and determinative, part unconscious.

What sense then is there in speaking of "decision"? Is not the "decision" made for us by the totality of conditioning circumstances? Yet without decision, without freedom, what is left of man, what is left of human existence?

Even if we somehow succeed in retrieving our freedom from the peril of annihilation, we have merely carried the existential problem to another and more critical phase. Freedom means anxiety and guilt; that is why anxiety and guilt so pervade the whole of human existence. Is not our existential anxiety, in fact, generated out of the feeling of the immeasurable consequence yet ultimate groundlessness of every act of decision? Does not our sense of guilt reflect the frightening discrepancy between the infinite obligations under which we stand, on the one hand, and the finiteness of our capacities and perversity of our impulses, on the other? We must choose—but in what shall our decision be grounded? We must act—but how can we possibly act responsibly? We must live up to our obligations—obligations laid upon us by whom? We must somehow master the guilt that overwhelms us—but where shall we find the power to do so? In terms merely of our limited being, there is no answer; yet the dynamic of human existence—decision, responsibility, guilt[3]—drives us to the point where unless an answer is forthcoming, there is no escaping the bottomless pit.

But surely the final verdict on human life comprehended in its own terms is given by—*death*. Death is the final "boundary situation";

it rips off all deceptions and self-deceptions. Seen in the perspective of that decisive moment, what is any man's life but a record of folly, futility and frustration? What is history but a chaos, a jumble, a senseless conglomeration of senseless events? For death not only brings all our enterprises to an abrupt end; it reduces them all to nonsense. One man sows, another reaps; one man builds, another inhabits. All that we have constructed, so laboriously, so conscientiously, so hopefully, a breath of air, a turn in the tide of history, may wipe out—or, what is even more dismaying, may pervert to uses abhorrent to our heart. The work which the pioneers of bourgeois individualism began ended in the mass-society. The work which the pioneers of Russian socialism initiated with such high hopes ended in totalitarian slavery. Is this not the pattern of all things? If there is no fulfilment more than human life or history can give, what is life but "a tale told by an idiot, full of sound and fury, signifying nothing"? Everything becomes "questionable in the face of death. Essential to man can be that which retains its value only in the face of death, while that which does not stand this ultimate test reveals itself in its utter delusiveness."[4] But on the level of the merely historical, the merely human, the merely natural, what is there that can stand this test?

Death is the final judge and critic: it is the *crisis* of life. And the verdict? Long ago the Preacher pronounced it:

> What profit has a man of all his toil beneath the sun? One generation goes and another comes but the earth is forever unchanged. . . . I have seen all the works that are done under the sun and behold all is vanity and chasing of wind, a crookedness not to be straightened, a void not to be filled. . . . Wisdom and knowledge are madness and folly. . . . The wise man is no more remembered than the fool, for already in the days that follow everything is forgotten. . . . Vanity of vanities, all is vanity (Eccles. 1:3-4, 14-15; 2:16; *passim*).

From this verdict there is no appeal—unless death, unless life itself, is transcended and left behind.

Whatever line we take, we are relentlessly driven into the same predicament. Face to face with the ultimate questions of existence, we have nothing to say. We stand confounded, perplexed, consumed with anxiety. Everything has become problematical, everything has turned into meaninglessness, absurdity, nothingness. But that everything is our existence, our very life.

What does it all signify? It signifies that, deceive himself as he may, man is never entirely at home in the natural universe of which he is part—and he knows it. The essential homelessness of the human spirit is the theme of much of recent philosophy and imaginative literature. Buber[5] speaks of the "special solitude" that is the mark of man. The world which we inhabit affords us no resting place, no security: "We are the incommensurable idiots of the universe."[6] Pascal expressed this terror of existence in unforgettable words:

> When I consider the brief span of my life, swallowed up in eternity past and to come, the little space that I occupy, lost in the immensity of space of which I know nothing and which knows nothing of me—I am terrified.[7]

Perhaps only a philosopher would ever feel impelled to express himself in such ultimate form. But any man—every man—is bound to be stirred by this metaphysical dread once he brings himself to the point of asking for the meaning of things, even if he does not go beyond the social institutions of which he is part; for even on this level, perhaps especially on this level, the precariousness, the instability, the utter unintelligibility of existence is overwhelming.

Insecurity is notoriously the common lot of men, permeating every sphere of life. What is more, every move we make to overcome our insecurity on some particular level not only never quite achieves its purpose but only too often merely succeeds in transferring the insecurity to another and more critical phase of existence. The means we employ to gain security in material life become the institutions that are responsible for the economic insecurity which is so perplexing a problem for our time. Against this insecurity we try to protect ourselves by programs and devices which create the politico-moral ambiguities of collectivism and state planning. The security men and nations seek, and do indeed to an extent find, in preponderant power is never final; it only drives them to deeper insecurities. And so it is in every aspect of life. As long as we try to find—or rather to establish—the center of our being, the meaning of our existence *within ourselves,* we are bound to fail. And this failure is not merely intellectual; it is existential through and through: it strikes at the foundations of life.

Human existence, individual and social alike, is radically incomplete, fragmentary. The attempt to comprehend life in its own terms, to live it in and for itself, must necessarily prove self-destructive. Human existence, through its own dialectic, drives relentlessly on to its ultimate limits, where it is suddenly brought face to face with a chaos of insecurity and meaninglessness. From this chaos there is no escape except by breaking through the natural conditions of life and seeking completion in something beyond. Along this self-transcending dimension of life, the reality, the meaning, of human existence is to be found—if anywhere.

NOTES TO CHAPTER 2

1. *M.* Sanh. 4.5.
2. Leslie A. White, "Man's Control Over Civilization: An Anthropocentric Illusion," *Scientific Monthly,* Vol. LXVI (March, 1948), No. 3.
3. Freud points out that "even though man has repressed his evil desires into his unconsciousness and would then gladly say to himself that he is no longer answerable for them, he is yet compelled to feel his responsibility in thé form of a sense of guilt for which he can discern no foundation." *Introductory Lectures on Psychoanalysis* (Allen and Unwin: London, 1922), p. 279.
4. Erich Frank, *Philosophical Understanding and Religious Truth* (Oxford: New York, 1945), p. 10.
5. Martin Buber, "What is Man?" *Between Man and Man* (Kegan Paul: London, 1947), p. 134.
6. James Rorty, "Words for a Young Woman," *Nation,* Vol. CXXIII, No. 3192.
7. Pascal, *Pensées,* No. 205.

3.   THE DEVALUATION OF LIFE

Human life, individual and collective, is a dynamic structure of values. Without existential commitment to some system of values which, despite an inescapable element of relativity, is felt to be some-how anchored in ultimate reality, human life in any significant sense is simply impossible. Man lives by values; all his enterprises and ac-tivities, insofar as they are specifically human, make sense only in terms of some structure of purposes which are themselves values in action. The first requirement that a philosophy of life adequate to human existence must meet is that it vindicate the full reality and significance of values in the universe.

This the philosophy of modern man cannot do. Indeed, its main tendency through recent decades has been to drain the universe of value and thus to devaluate human life. Since life void of value is, however, ultimately impossible, the positivistic devaluation of life that lies at the heart of the modern world-outlook has in effect opened the door to the surreptitious introduction of every variety of folly and superstition, which is sure to find welcome if only it holds out the promise of restoring some unity and significance to life.

The devaluation of life in the modern world has proceeded along two closely related lines: (a) the extrusion of value from the uni-verse through the premature identification of science and reality; and (b) the reduction of value to semi-illusory "subjectivity" through the corrosion of relativism. In each case, a valid and important in-sight has, through failure to observe its necessary limitations, been converted into a dangerous fallacy. In their total effect, the two ten-dencies have combined to create a picture of the universe in which man, his hopes and aspirations, his interests and enterprises, are rele-gated to a mean and paltry place. The drift of modern thought, as expressed in naturalism and relativism, has not simply made man a stranger in the universe, which in some sense he inescapably is, it has reduced him to a mere nonentity, utterly insignificant amidst the vast play of natural forces, which constitute his only reality and yet know nothing of him or his values.[1]

The history of modern science from the days of Galileo and Des-cartes is a record of the systematic extrusion of value from what is conceived to be the reality of the universe. This process can best be described in the vocabulary which, though brought into use by Locke two and a half centuries ago, still governs the "scientific" thinking of modern man. Locke distinguished between "primary" qualities, which —like extension, motion and geometrical shape—are supposed really to belong to the external object, and "secondary" qualities, which— like color, sound, odor and taste—are obviously not in the object itself but are the result of the effect of the stimulation of the human senses. Every person today with the least pretension to scientific understanding knows that "greenness," for example, does not inhere in the grass as physical object. The grass as physical object sends forth light waves of a certain frequency; when these light waves impinge on the proper sensory organ—the eye—they bring about the sensation of green in the mind. This applies to sound and the other sense qualities as well. Physical reality, therefore, is *really* something without color, odor, taste or sound; all of these qualities, which seem to us to be the very substance of things, are "merely subjective," occupying an altogether secondary, indeed almost illusory, status in the scheme of reality. What this "scientific" conception of the universe comes to has been well described by Whitehead: "Nature is a dull affair, soundless, scentless, colorless; merely the hurrying of material, endlessly, meaninglessly."[2] This is the world, this is the reality, in which modern man must somehow try to lead a significant existence.

But the difficulty goes deeper. If even "secondary" qualities, such as color, taste or sound, are "merely subjective" and not there at all in the real world, what shall we say of *values*, which have often been called "tertiary" qualities? Surely these have even less claim to lodg- ment in the "real world" that is revealed by science. Value qualities— like truth, beauty, goodness—must be even more subjective than the data of the senses, even more remote from any reality as conceived by science. In fact, they seem to be little more than figments of the mind, somehow projected upon an alien reality: "purposeless, . . . void of meaning, blind to good and evil, reckless of destruction, . . . is the world which Science presents for our belief."[3]

The world of science, whether of Newton or of Einstein, is a world of objective process describable in terms of factual statements, which remain factual no matter how abstract. Into this world, no *values* in the proper sense can enter.[4] It is thus a world that is not merely color- less, soundless and scentless but also *meaningless* and *valueless*. No merely scientific picture of the universe can possibly find a place for the values upon which significant human life depends. This conclusion is incontrovertible.

It is also fateful—*if* the world of science is taken, as it is in modern thought, to be simply identical with the world of reality. If science reveals the "real reality" of things, reality is void of value. Scientism —by which name we may designate the conversion of science into a revelation of ultimate reality—inevitably leads to the utter devaluation of the universe.

What then are these "values" about which so much ado is made? They are, to the positivist devotee of scientism, part of the strange illusory world of "subjectivity" outside the scope of scientific fact. Some hold "values" to be nothing but emotional outbursts; others regard them as the verbalizations of the vagaries of personal taste; still others, as a queer "inner" reflection of folkways or class and community standards. But all agree that values *as values* have no status in reality and therefore no normative significance in terms of reality. "Values" may help to describe how people do in fact behave; they can have absolutely no meaning as norms beyond and distinct from facts.

Modern positivism has not hesitated to carry this devaluating logic to its final conclusion and has thereby brought the problem of value in all its urgency to the fore as a problem for modern man. It is not the philosopher alone who is concerned; it is also, and above all, the mass of modern-minded men, who may not be acquainted with the technical vocabulary or the latest aspects of positivist speculation but who are, nevertheless, thoroughly permeated with its basic concepts and attitudes. They know that value no longer has any place in the universe of science—which they take to be the only *real* universe— and they are therefore no longer able to orient their human existence in terms of reality.

The push of scientism toward devaluation has been reinforced by a simultaneous drift toward relativism, which also set in with the rise of modern thought. Relativism is, at bottom, the view that value-embodying ideas or activities are in reality nothing but a reflection or product of some particular empirical context and therefore possess neither meaning nor validity apart from that context. Right and wrong, good and evil, true and false, it is held, make no sense unless they are "relativized," unless *true* is made to mean "true from this particular point of view"; *right,* "right by the standards of this particular culture"; *good,* "good according to the ethics of this particular class or society." Nothing is absolute; everything is relative.

The experience to which relativism appeals is widespread and familiar; relativism as a philosophy has assumed many forms in its long history. Already the sophist Protagoras proclaimed that "man is the measure of all things." Ancient skepticism rang all possible changes on this theme, and in early modern times it became the recurrent subject of Montaigne's reflections. But the relativism that has proved so corrosive in the contemporary world is scientific rather than philosophical: it looks for inspiration not so much to skeptical speculations about the fallibility of human reason as to recent scientific evidence of the bewildering variety of customs and attitudes among men.

Already Pascal noted how strange it was that "three degrees of latitude reverse all jurisprudence; a meridian decides the truth: . . . truth on this side of the Pyrenees, error on the other."[5] This kind of anthropological relativism, which calls attention to the wide variation of customs and attitudes among men, is at once the earliest and the most recent type. Herodotus resorted to it, and it is still the chief stock in trade of the contemporary anthropologist who strives to reduce the value-embodying ideas and activities of a group simply to its "pattern of culture." During the nineteenth century, historical relativism—historicism—came to the fore. It was now the stage or phase of historical development that was held to be determinative; each period had its own characteristic outlook, its own ideas and values, restricted in meaning and validity to that period. At about the same time, sociological relativism made its appearance and insisted that everything was really the expression of social situation or class interest; the latter was especially stressed by Marx. Most recent —largely the work of this century—is the psychological relativism associated with the teachings of Freud: ideas, values and standards are regarded as at bottom merely the expression of unconscious desires striving for fulfilment and of the various mechanisms by which these desires are diverted or checked. In the thinking of modern man, all of these varieties of relativism are commingled and fused; what emerges is a deep though rather vague feeling that right, truth and justice are, at bottom, merely a matter of ideology or opinion; that no one can help feeling the way he does about those things; and that there is no rational ground for holding to one set of values or standards rather than to another.

It is necessary to acknowledge explicitly the important elements of validity in scientism and relativism; but it is also necessary to insist with at least equal emphasis on their utter inadequacy. The world of science is indeed very much as it is pictured by modern positivism— but the world of science is very far from being the world of reality! The world of science, Whitehead points out:

> is an abstraction, arrived at by confining thought to purely formal relations which then masquerade as the final reality. This is why science, in its perfection, relapses into the study of differential equations. The concrete world has slipped through the meshes of the scientific net.[6]

The error of scientism consists, not in taking science seriously— science is one of the enduring achievements of the human spirit—but in mistaking the nature of science and taking it to be somehow a revelation of the "real reality" of things. It is not that at all, and responsible modern scientists and philosophers are the first to say so. "The most general definition of reality for science," Victor Lenzen says, "is that it is the universe of discourse of a conceptual system that serves to correlate and predict the data of experience."[7] When a physicist affirms the existence of an electron and denies the existence of the ether, he is simply asserting that the *conceptual construction* called an electron serves effectively to "correlate and predict the data of experience," whereas the concept of the ether does not. It is of such entities that the world of science is in large part composed. From this world—which is not the world of experience but merely symbolic of it[8]—value is indeed excluded, but this world is not the concrete world of human existence; it is a highly abstract "world" constructed for a special purpose and quite adequate to that purpose. The fault, in short, lies not with science but with the "naive belief that science represents an absolute and exclusive view of reality."[9] It lies with the

22    *Judaism and Modern Man*

utterly illegitimate positivist conversion of science into an ultimate philosophy, or metaphysic, of reality.

Very much the same may be said of relativism. That attitudes, ideas and activities do not pursue a disembodied existence but are always somehow related to men and their situation in life is an important truth—indeed, as we shall see, it is an important *religious* truth—and we have to thank the anthropologists, sociologists and psychologists for hammering this truth home in the face of a blind and uncritical absolutism. But from this truth one may not infer that values are "nothing but" the reflection of something else; above all, may one not infer that relativity pervades the entire realm of value and leaves nothing untouched. Such *thoroughgoing* relativism not only goes beyond empirical fact,[10] it is philosophically self-destructive; if seriously entertained, it threatens to turn around and destroy the very principle of relativism. For this principle is but an "idea," and ideas, we are assured by the relativist, have neither meaning nor validity apart from their particular context. How then does the relativist presume to apply his principle, his "idea," to *all* contexts, to *all* situations, without regard to time, place or circumstance? How does the anthropological relativist presume to apply his principle of relativism, which is an outgrowth of and relative to his own particular cultural pattern, to all other societies and cultures? How does the Marxist relativist, for whom the principle of class relativism is part of the proletarian class ideology and hence "true" only from that class point of view, presume to apply it to the ideology of other classes from whose point of view it may not be true? How does the Freudian relativist, who "explains" conscious ideas and conceptions as reflections of determinative unconscious processes, presume to apply his own conscious principle of psychological relativism without reducing it also to some unconscious process? How, in short, does the relativist presume to relativize everybody and everything except himself and his ideas? Apparently what the relativist is actually doing is to grant himself and his particular principle of relativism a special exemption from the corroding skepticism of the doctrine he preaches—thereby in effect rejecting its sweeping pretensions. "All philosophies based on universal relativity," Carl Becker says, "must be prepared at the appropriate moment to commit hara-kiri in deference to the ceaseless change which they postulate."[11] Thoroughgoing relativism—the denial of anything beyond the reach of relativity—is simply self-destructive.

This point is of crucial importance in the refutation of the devaluating philosophy of relativism. Without some fixed point of support beyond relativity, no system of standards or values, no matter how relative, is possible. Everything would collapse, and in the collapse science itself would be inescapably involved, for science—strange as it may sound—is founded on values.[12] To save science, and indeed to save every other enterprise of the human spirit, some point of lodgment for value in the world of reality must be found. But where is this point to be found if reality is made identical with the world of science and nature?

The philosophical refutation of scientism and radical relativism is thus not very difficult, but formal arguments, however valid, are far from sufficient. The philosophy that has become normative for modern man is part of an entire spiritual complex which paradoxically combines a practical Prometheanism with a world-outlook that is nothing short of nihilism. If, indeed, values cannot claim some lodgment in reality, and right and wrong, true and false, good and evil, are no more than merely a matter of ideology or conditioning, then clearly nothing is ultimately better than anything else and everything is permitted.[13] But man, in thus becoming a law unto himself, loses the ground of his existence and the dynamic of his activity. Utter moral chaos results.

The world-outlook of modern man, compounded of relativism and scientism, can find no place for value in reality. But without a secure foundation in value, human life and all its enterprises are deprived of sense and meaning. Decision is paralyzed; judgment is rendered void and empty. Along this road, too, modern man has been driven to the brink of the abyss.

## NOTES TO CHAPTER 3

1. D. W. Gotschalk, himself a naturalist in philosophy, calls attention to "the perplexing situation that confronts naturalism, today even more urgently than ever before, stemming from the persistent paradox of com-

bining an optimistic humanism with a paltry, even dismal, conception of human life and destiny" ("The Paradox of Naturalism," *The Journal of Philosophy*, March 14, 1946). This "paltry and dismal conception" is well formulated by Bertrand Russell: "Man, with his knowledge of good and evil, is but a helpless atom in a world which has no such knowledge." "A Free Man's Worship," *Mysticism and Logic* (Norton: New York, 1929), pp. 49-50.

2. A. N. Whitehead, *Science and the Modern World* (Macmillan: New York, 1941), p. 80.

3. Russell, "A Free Man's Worship," *Mysticism and Logic*, pp. 47, 56.

4. Although, of course, the *fact* that particular human beings hold certain things to be "good," "true," "beautiful," etc., and other things not to be so, must be taken note of in science simply because it is a fact.

5. Pascal, *Pensées*, No. 294.

6. A. N. Whitehead, *Modes of Thought* (Macmillan: New York, 1938), p. 25.

7. Quoted by D. S. Robinson, *The Principles of Reasoning* (Appleton: New York, 1948), 3rd Rev. Ed., p. 388.

8. "The exploration of the external world by the methods of physical science leads not to a concrete reality but to a shadow world of symbols, beneath which these methods are unadapted for penetrating." A. S. Eddington, *Science and the Unseen World* (Macmillan: New York, 1929), p. 73.

9. Benjamin Ginsburg, "Science," *Encyclopedia of the Social Sciences* (MacMillan: New York, 1930-34), XIII, 592b.

10. "Contrary to widely held views, comparative studies reveal a considerable uniformity in the moral judgments regarding the fundamental relationships." Morris Ginsberg, *Reason and Unreason in Society* (Harvard University: Cambridge, Mass., 1948), p. 25. Professor Ginsberg quotes (p. 73) from Westermarck to the same effect: "When we examine the moral rules laid down by the customs of savage peoples, we find that they in very large measure resemble the rules of civilized nations."

11. Carl Becker, "Progress," *Encyclopedia of the Social Sciences*, XII, 499a.

12. "Judgments of worth are no part of the texture of physical science but they are part of the motive of its production. . . . Without judgments of value, there would have been no science." Whitehead, *The Aims of Education* (Macmillan: New York, 1938), pp. 228-29.

13. What contemporary relativism leads to is well described by Arthur Child in *Ethics*, Vol. LVIII (July, 1948), No. 4, p. 319. "Some anthropologists. . . claim to have learned from their science and proclaim to their students with the authority of Science that no society . . . is better than another but is only preferred by some people over another, or that there is no reason a widow should not be burnt alive on her

husband's funeral pyre, provided she lives in a society which practices and approves this treatment. Whether in class these anthropologists draw out the further consequences of their teachings, I do not know, but their students will draw some—will conclude, say, that the United States is no better than Nazi Germany but only happens to be preferred by ourselves; that there is no reason Hitler should not have murdered six million Jews except as the murders may have led to unpleasant results for himself, although of course the murders do happen to offend our own sentiments. . . ."


# 4. DELUSIVE SECURITY: THE SUBSTITUTE FAITHS OF OUR TIME

The burden of the earlier chapters has been to indicate "what man has made of man," what modern man has made of himself and the conditions of his existence. The account, however summarily put, adds up to a fundamental criticism of modernity.

In his effort to refashion himself and the world in autonomous terms, modern man has disrupted the age-old continuities of life—religion, the family, the community—and has reduced the individual to a forlorn, fragmentary existence in which he is no more than an insignificant cell in the vast impersonal organism of society.[1] He has drained the universe of value and thus deprived himself of all possibility of finding a secure anchorage in reality for the ideas and purposes that constitute significant human life. He has maneuvered himself into a position where the basic and irreducible realities of human existence—will, personality, freedom—simply make no sense in his philosophy. In short, modern man no longer possesses any unity or orientation in life. He stands lost, bewildered, unable to understand himself or to master the forces of his inner and outer life. Despairingly, he confronts a universe that is bleak, empty and hostile: "a stranger and afraid, in a world [he] never made."

But life without orientation, existence without unity or meaning, is ultimately impossible and so modern man strives desperately to relate himself to some overall principle or power that promises to provide spiritual security and yet not violate the basic presuppositions of his thought. This enterprise cannot prove successful; it is doomed to failure precisely because it refuses to make the basic challenge to modern culture, and in its failure it but deepens the spiritual crisis it cannot allay.

Many are the ways in which men endeavor to achieve the unity and meaning they must have in order to live. They may identify themselves with some larger whole—such as nation, class or race—and, by absolutizing that, strive to give universal validity to their fragmentary lives. Or they may place their faith in some man or movement to relieve them of the increasingly intolerable burden of existence. Or again they may see the promise of deliverance in some doctrine or idea that somehow holds out the hope of fulfilment without seriously calling into question current prepossessions and prejudices. Perhaps the most influential of contemporary faiths cherished by modern man are those that look to science, psychoanalysis and Marxism for salvation.

The science to which men of today look with such hope is not science as a theoretical system but science as a wonder-working technology, the science that has given mankind the airplane, the radio, penicillin and the atom bomb. It is this science that, in the fervid imagination of its publicity men and devotees, promises to usher in the "world of tomorrow" in which all the tasks of life will be performed by their appropriate devices and man left free to fill his vacuous existence with mechanized entertainment. The utopia displayed so luxuriously in the advertising pages of the "slick" magazines may seem too stupid for criticism, but let us not forget that it is but the logical culmination of the view of life that underlies the modern outlook and constitutes the dominant motif in contemporary culture— the conception of the good life as simply and solely a life of carefree ease amidst material plenty. It is this conception which has led us to exalt large-scale industrialism and to accept as normal the thing-centered, gadget-ridden culture in which we live.

The idolization of scientific technology, which pervades so much of our thinking, has deeper roots than we know or imagine. It has been noted more than once that in the lower recesses of the mind—

yes, of the "modern" mind—the laboratory scientist takes on the shape of the archetypal wizard or miracle man who has at his disposal the magical means of solving our problems and relieving us of all the difficulties of life. This unconscious imagery, compounded with the popular philosophy of scientism, to which reference was made in the last chapter, expresses itself on the conscious level in an attitude that regards all problems of life to be, at bottom, merely *technical* problems capable of solution simply by the application of "scientific method." That ends and values lie in a realm beyond positive science, whose usefulness is limited to devising means for ends already established, and that therefore the fundamental problems of life are in their very nature incapable of scientific solution, is something that seems to be utterly incomprehensible, as much to the modern-minded pragmatist philosopher as to the modern-minded votary of the prefabricated life.

The cult of science is obviously a delusion. It means more of the same thing that has driven mankind into the ghastly predicament in which it finds itself today: further depersonalization, further atomization, further spread of mass standardization, further stultification of man's aspirations toward a worthy and significant existence. Science may prove an invaluable servant, but when it turns master and savior, it inevitably becomes a brainless mechanical monster, imperiling life.

Marxism—not so much the thinking of Karl Marx as the doctrine that has passed into Marxist tradition—has had a pervasive influence on the Western world. For all its "scientific" pretensions, its appeal has been almost entirely religious: it has offered modern man an absolutist faith, a world-view in which the cosmic force of the Dialectic is seen as realizing the ends and sustaining the values that give meaning to life. To the believer who, through his belief, aligns himself with the "movement of History," it grants the feeling of security and self-esteem that comes from identification with omnipotent power as well as the confidence that is the result of the assurance of ultimate victory. In this sense, Marxism is one of the most potent religions of modern times.

But it is a religion that has failed most disastrously. The events of the past thirty years have shown that it is sheer folly to look to history, in whatever form, for the solution of our problems. History cannot solve our problems; history is *itself* the problem. The faith that has counted on the indwelling Dialectic to bring salvation has proved utterly delusive: man, whom it was to liberate and exalt, it has ended by dehumanizing; the human values it was designed to realize and sustain, it has ended by destroying. We need not identify Marxism with the distorted antihumanistic form it has assumed in Soviet Russia to realize the truth of this statement.

The failure of Marxism is directly due to the fact that it has proved incapable of transcending the limitations of the bourgeois culture to which it is ostensibly so uncompromisingly opposed. Its criticism of the bourgeois outlook is by no means radical; in fact, it shares some of the most characteristic presuppositions of "modern-mindedness." It may bitterly excoriate the more obvious excesses of contemporary society, but in its fundamental view of life it differs little from its "class enemy." The glories which the naive "bourgeois liberal" sees as the gift of present-day industrialism, Marxism simply postpones to the "new social order" on the other side of the Revolution: the same externality, the same worship of technology, the same conception of the good life as a life of effortless ease in a machine-run paradise.

Uncritically Marxism takes over the cultural outlook of bourgeois civilization; uncritically, too, it absolutizes the socialist society that comes with the Revolution. This absolutization of what is, after all, the work of man's hands is reinforced by the sociological relativism of values that lies close to the heart of the Marxist philosophy and leads to the double conclusion that right and wrong, good and evil, are determined by the "interests of the proletariat" and that everything—literally everything—is permitted if it is necessary for the victory of socialism. The attrition of all moral standards and the utterly shameless exaltation of power to which this has led are notorious.

The chief defect of Marxism and scientism from the point of view of the modern mind which has gained some sophistication from contemporary experience is their externality. They both see man from the outside and seem utterly incapable of penetrating to what is within. Here is where psychoanalysis makes its chief appeal as a truly modern vehicle of salvation—not so much the psychoanalysis of Freud and other explorers of the deepest recesses of the human psyche as the psychoanalysis of the swarm of cult-priests and panacea-mongers spawned out of the troubles of our age. Where the scientist is the wizard and the revolutionary leader the redeemer in the mass imagination, the popular psychologist is the priest and father-confessor of our time. It is he who promises to give us "peace of mind," to relieve us of our anxieties, guilts and insecurities, to "adjust" us to our environment and to convey us into the blissful heaven of normality. He, it seems, is certainly in possession of the magic formula.

Precisely because of the potency of the genuine article, this kind of quackery has proved one of the most delusive and dangerous of the substitute faiths of our time. The "peace of mind" it seeks to achieve is not the "peace that passeth understanding"—which no practitioner can give—but the "peace" that comes from the dulling of the conscience, the blunting of moral sensitivity and the shameless encouragement of an almost lascivious preoccupation with self. It reduces all of man's problems to problems of "mental hygiene" and then proceeds to solve them as if they were so many problems of bed-wetting or thumb-sucking.

The "peace of mind" therapy that constitutes the cult of popular psychoanalysis is essentially an effort to extinguish the anxiety, the restlessness, the disquiet, that is the heritage of man as a creature of freedom; it is therefore, at bottom, an effort to dehumanize man and reduce his life to the level of subhuman creation which knows neither sin nor guilt. The poet's outburst—"I am sick and tired of all these humans with their eternal whining about conscience and sin; I am going out to the cattle in the barn"—just about expresses the way it looks at man and his problems.

This type of popular psychoanalysis does not see that behind and beyond the particular empirical disquiets and anxieties of life, which it is indeed the business of genuine psychoanalysis to relieve, there is the metaphysical, the existential anxiety that is the mark of man's paradoxical status in the universe. It does not see that while morbid guilt feelings are an ailment to be removed, "total lack of a sense of guilt is a disease which would necessarily make man a beast."[2] It does not see that while neuroses are illnesses requiring medical treatment, without "maladjusted" personalities at odds with their environment there would be no civilization or culture.[3] It does not see that while inner harmony is always a possibility for one who has succeeded in making his peace with God, the "inner harmony" that can be achieved through psychological devices is no more than a delusion born out of, and serving to inflate, one's smugness and self-complacency. It does not see that the human predicament—the malady of life—far transcends the medical.

Psychoanalysis—even the authentic kind, not to speak of the popular cult of "peace of mind"—has no salvation to offer modern man. It can provide no genuine unity, no lasting security, to his life. It cannot really relieve him of his burden of anxiety or save him from the discord and chaos that imperil his existence. It cannot do this because, for all its insight, it operates on too superficial a level of human life. Its naturalistic presuppositions prevent it from plumbing the full depth or comprehending the full significance of the spiritual dimension of personality. Its inwardness is not true inwardness, for it cannot penetrate to the inner core of human existence. It is after all restricted to the naturalistic level of science, while man, though rooted in nature, is human precisely because he transcends the natural conditions of existence. Like scientific technology, psychoanalysis has its undoubted utility for human life as an instrument of analysis and as a therapeutic device. But again like scientific technology, it can never be more than means; when it pretends to define ends or show the way to salvation, it too becomes a snare and a delusion.

Science, Marxism, psychoanalysis, along with the currently discredited cults of nationalism and racism, are—as ways of salvation— all attempts to erect "systems of thought and belief [as] comforting little houses to shelter the mind of man from the great winds that blow between worlds and the cold darkness of outer space."[4] As such they have all proved failures, and there are hardier spirits who are not afraid to admit this failure and to face the fact that such systems are not to be erected by the hand of man. And yet such is the complexity of the human spirit and its unquenchable thirst for what is beyond that this very abjuration of the quest for security is itself transformed into a "comforting little house" outfitted with all the latest devices for protection against the "cold darkness of outer space." This is the significance of contemporary "atheistic" existentialism. In this type of existentialism—which, despite the common name and a certain resemblance of ideas, is radically different from the religious existentialism of a Kierkegaard or a Buber—in this type of existentialism, the forlornness and despair of existence are strangely transmuted into a kind of self-satisfied, rather cozy, defiance of the universe. "Man," we are told, "is forlorn because neither within him nor without does he find anything to cling to."⁵ But is he *really* forlorn, *really* without support? Has he *really* renounced all gods, all absolutes? Well, not quite. "To be a man," says Sartre, "means to try to be God." "Human reality is a pure effort to become God, to become *ens causa sui*."⁶ And so this sober, self-possessed disillusionment culminates in the most monstrous illusion of all—in man's deification of himself!

Can we deny that much the same is the outcome of Bertrand Russell's magnificent manifesto, "A Free Man's Worship"? Despite its fine sensitivity, despite its subtle assimilation of some of the deepest insights of authentic religion, this, too, manages to convert a bleak, proud stoicism into an idolatrous cult.⁷ Its "atheism," its renunciation of all gods, turns out, after all, to be no more than clearing the ground for the deification of man and the absolutization of his creative spirit. It is a desperate measure, but it is not any the more effective in breaking through the impasse: even the flattery of self-deification cannot forever seduce the human spirit; there are moments when man, looking within, knows that he is the last thing on earth worthy of worship. The gospel of nihilism—even when it is called existentialism—leads nowhere.

The substitute faiths of our time are failures, and a failure, too, is the attempt to do without absolutes, without "anything to cling to within or without." What then?

NOTES TO CHAPTER 4

1. Cf. Martin Buber, "What is Man," *Between Man and Man* (Kegan Paul: London, 1947), pp 157-58.
2. F. Wittels, *Freud and His Time* (Liveright: New York, 1931), p. 343. "There is nothing more profoundly human than the sense of guilt; nothing in which the lost image of God manifests its presence more clearly." Emil Brunner, *Man in Revolt* (Westminster: Philadelphia, 1947), p. 178.
3. "Those [neurotic personalities] who do not [develop neuroses] are the chief contributors to the advance of civilization. In fact, one might say that the neurotic personalities contribute to the advance of civilization at the expense of their own peace of mind. . . . Civilization itself is a neurotic product." Karl Menninger, *The Human Mind* (Garden City: Garden City, N.Y., 1930), pp. 116-17. See also Freud, *Civilization and its Discontents* (Hogarth: London, 1930).
4. Ralph Linton, address at Herald Tribune Forum, New York *Herald Tribune*, October 26, 1947.
5. Cf. Ralph Harper, *Existentialism* (Harvard University: Cambridge, Mass., 1948), p. 102.
6. Harper, *op. cit.*, p. 104; Jean-Paul Sartre, *L'être et le néant* (Gallimard: Paris, 1943) p. 655.
7. "Man creates God, all-powerful and all-good. . . . In this lies Man's true freedom: in the determination to worship only the God created by our own love of the good, to respect only the heaven which inspires the insight of our best moments. . . We must build a temple for the worship of our own ideals. . . . In this way, Man's mind asserts its subtle mastery over the thoughtless forces of Nature." Bertrand Russell, "A Free Man's Worship," *Mysticism and Logic* (Norton: New York, 1929), pp. 49-53.

# 5.   DECISION: THE LEAP OF FAITH

Man's existential predicament, which it has been my purpose to describe, assumes many shapes, but in the last analysis it all comes down to the fundamental fact that the attempt to comprehend life in its own terms, to live it in and for itself, must necessarily prove destructive. It must prove destructive intellectually, reducing life to unreality and contradiction. It must prove destructive morally, undermining the very presuppositions of the moral life—freedom and responsibility. It must prove destructive in our individual and collective enterprises, for it leads inexorably to dilemmas which it gives us no power to meet or overcome. On every level, existence is threatened with dissolution. Unity and meaning are utterly impossible to achieve because, simply within the natural conditions of life, there is no center about which life may be securely built and a stable structure of meaning established. In the endless flux of relativity which confronts modern man as the ultimate reality, no fixed center can be found; yet without some secure anchorage in the absolute, everything—relativity itself—must collapse into nothingness. Life, if only to save itself, must find fulfilment in something beyond, in something more than life.

To live a human life, men must have grounding in something, "in some sense outside of human life, . . . [in] some end which is impersonal and above mankind, such as God or truth or beauty."[1] These words are from Bertrand Russell, whose hostility to traditional religion has never entirely obscured his deep sense of man's existential crisis.

> In order to promote life [Russell goes on] it is necessary to value something more than mere life. Life devoted to life is. . . without real human value, incapable of preserving men permanently from weariness and the feeling that all is vanity. . . Those who best promote life do not have life for their purpose.

But having posed the problem in all its urgency, Russell has no better suggestion to offer than that men find their strength and support, the meaning of their life, through contact with an "eternal world" of their own imagining! Surely it must have occured to Russell himself that this heroic effort at make-believe salvation could not possibly succeed: men cannot find fulfilment by worshiping a god they know they have themselves constructed, even though the materials going into the making of the idol be the very highest ideals humanity has achieved. Even such ideals are the ideals of men, of men of flesh and blood, and are therefore hopelessly infected with relativity; they neither deserve nor can stand absolutization. None of them, not even "truth" or "beauty" or a "god" thought up for the purpose, can really take us out of our own life with all its fragmentariness and ambiguity; none of them, therefore, can provide us with the anchorage in the absolute without which there is no meaningful existence. More; the very attempt to attribute absolute significance to powers, institutions or ideals that, however excellent, are after all not absolute, results in the corruption of their excellence and their transformation into forces of destruction. Idols, we have it on good authority, are not merely hollow frauds; they are havoc-working demons—and all of recent history is there to prove it.

The full depth of the contemporary crisis is measured by the fact that all of our idols—our own splendid ones as well as the hideous ones of the enemy—have been weighed and found wanting; they have all been exposed in their utter vacuity and destructiveness. It is no longer possible for us who have learned the lesson of our generation to deceive ourselves. The props of existence that served in other days have collapsed. We stand at the brink of the abyss with all our supports swept away. Science, History, Culture, Economic Progress, Socialism—yes, even conventional ethics and religion—how vain and powerless they have shown themselves to be amidst the cataclysms of our time! Who can look to them for deliverance today? The conclusion is inescapable: only by breaking through and transcending the natural limitations of life, only on the *other side of the abyss,* can the Absolute which is the eternal ground of existence be reached. Against the relentless drive toward chaos that forms the dynamic of autonomous human life, the miserable idols we have erected, the false absolutes we have exalted, are utterly helpless. Nothing in this world can save us; nothing *within* life can sustain life. Only from what is *beyond* life, only from the transcendant source of life, can come the power to deliver us from our desperate plight. In more traditional language, only the God whom we know to be the Creator of heaven and earth, the Lord of life and history, can help us.

We must break through the natural limitations of life and establish vital contact with what is beyond. But how? How shall we cross the abyss? Not by the power of science or abstract-objective thought, certainly. The efforts of contemporary scientists to "prove" that God is to be inferred from the course of organic evolution or the strange phenomena of subatomic physics is on a par with the efforts of the older philosophers to deduce God from the nature of pure being or the requirement of cosmology. These "proofs" are dubious at best,[2] but even if they were to succeed in making their case, it would be a case irrelevant to our purpose. For what such arguments, granting them all they claim, prove is no more than the probable validity of some ultimate metaphysical principle—a Principle of Perfection, a First Cause, an Unmoved Mover, a Demiurgic Power, Pure-Thought-Thinking-Itself; in any case, nothing of any vital significance to man in his existential crisis. If the word "God" is to have any relevance to our problem, we must recognize that God is not a "something" the existence of which can be established by the simple expedient of pushing scientific investigation or metaphysical speculation just a bit further. The very attempt to do so is a mistaken and delusive enterprise, for, at bottom, it treats God as just another object in the world of objects, not as the transcendent Subject who cannot be encompassed within the material of reason and experience. Very much the same may be said of the attempt to "deduce" God from history or the inner depths of the human consciousness, in which, after all, are mirrored our own confusions and limitations. God creates and sustains nature; God works in and through history; in the human mind we come upon something that points beyond itself to the dimension of God—but all this is visible only to the eyes of those who have *already* found and affirmed the God of faith. "God cannot," Buber concludes, "be inferred in anything—in nature, say, as its author, or in history as its master, or in the subject as the self that is thought in it. Something else is not 'given' and God then elicited from it."[3] That is not the way.

Nor is the way, however promising at first sight it may seem, that of mysticism. Mysticism offers us a doctrine and a technique for penetrating the "curtain" of finiteness and achieving identification with the Infinite. This self-deification—for what is *identification* with the Infinite but self-deification?—is purchased at a heavy price, the price of self-annihilation, of the extinction of life and personality in some vast, formless, impersonal All-Soul. Mysticism begins and ends in a "colossal illusion of the human spirit."[4] Whatever may be the "absolute" reached through mysticism, it is not the God who gives life and sustains personal existence.

No; neither science nor abstract reason nor mysticism can help us cross the abyss. The abyss can be crossed in one way and in one way only—by the "leap of faith." It is a leap beyond experience, beyond science, beyond objective logic. Experience, science, philosophy can bring us to the edge of the precipice and point beyond; they cannot help us cross: only the decision of faith can do that.

The decision of faith is beyond the abstract reason of science and philosophy because this latter type of reason, however adequate for dealing with the world of objects, is simply not capable of penetrating to the inner core of existence. For this purpose the only thinking that will serve is the thinking which is not content with the disinterested judgment of a spectator but insists on the total commitment of the personality; the thinking that is inward and concrete rather than outward and abstract, concerned rather than detached; the thinking that seeks not to discover external facts or to establish universal truths but to "make sense" of existence. This is the thinking that has come to be known as *existential*; it is a logic of choice, of decision, of commitment. "The man who thinks existentially," says Buber, following Kierkegaard, "[is] the man who stakes his life on his thinking."[5] And Franz Rosenzweig expands the conception of the "new thinking" in these words:[6]

> From those unimportant truths of the type "twice two equal four," to which men lightly assent with the expenditure of no more than a trifle mind energy—a little less for the ordinary multiplication table, a little more for the theory of relativity— the way leads to the truths for which a man is willing to pay something, on to those which he cannot prove true except with the sacrifice of his life, and finally to those the truth of which can be proved only by staking the lives of all the generations.

This is the kind of thinking that can provide a grounding for the decision that is the "leap of faith."

But let us be clear as to what this decision really involves. It does *not* involve an option between placing one's faith in something beyond empirical or rational "proof" and in refusing to do so; it is not, in a general sense, a choice between faith and no-faith. Man cannot live without placing his faith in *something* as the source of the meaning and value of his existence, in something that for him is absolute,

ultimate; in something that he "loves," according to the profound
Scriptural formula, "with all his heart, with all his soul, with all his
might"—and that "something" can never be justified in terms of fact
or reason.[7] Every man, therefore, has his faith, whether he recognizes it or not, whether he avows it or not; the beliefs which a man
really holds, it is well to remember, are not necessarily those he affirms with his mouth but those that are operative in his life.[8] The real
decision is thus not between faith and no-faith but between faith in
some false absolute, in some man-made idol—the construction of our
hands or heart or mind—and faith in the true Absolute, in the transcendent God. This is the decision, and it is a decision that wrenches
man's whole being. For it means a decision once and for all to
abandon all efforts to find the center of existence within one's self,
a decision to commit oneself to God without qualification or reservation. It is not easy for us to abandon confidence in self, in ourselves,
in our ideas and enterprises; it comes only after a desperate inner
struggle in which the victory is never final. That is why the decision
of faith is not merely an intellectual judgment but a total personal
commitment reaching down to the foundations of existence.

It has often been charged, from Feuerbach to Freud, that such
faith is mere "wish-fulfilment" and therefore rationally untenable. In
its crude sense, this criticism falls obviously wide of the mark. For
the authentic decision of faith is not something that is pleasant to
natural man or flattering to his ego; on the contrary, it challenges the
self in all its claims and voids it of all its pretensions. In that sense,
therefore, it is the very opposite of "wish-fulfilment." Yet the charge
of wishful thinking is sometimes intended to go deeper. Religious
thinking is rejected because it is held to be based on presuppositions
themselves not susceptible to empirical verification or rational proof.
On this level, too, the rationalist criticism is misconceived. For all
thinking, not to say all life, is grounded in unproved postulates that
may well be condemned as "wish-fulfilments." Presuppositionless
thinking is impossible. The affirmation of an external world beyond
sense impressions is surely something upon which all science, formal
and informal, depends and yet this affirmation is reached not by
reasoning but by a kind of "will-to-believe." It is, indeed, as Bertrand
Russell points out, not even "susceptible to argument."[9] In exactly

the same way, according to Whitehead, "there can be no science unless there is an instinctive conviction in the existence of an order of things and, in particular, of an order of nature. . . This faith in the order of nature cannot be justified by any inductive generalization;"[10] it is again a *salto mortale* of reason, a decision of the "will-to-believe." From fact to value requires another "leap"; that gulf, too, cannot be bridged by reason or science. Even reasoning itself is ultimately groundless, for obviously "the laws of reasoning cannot themselves be established by reasoning, they must be intuitively perceived to be true."[11]

This kind of "will-to-believe" is the dynamic factor in every enterprise of the human spirit: it must be there before reason can begin operating or experience make sense; it must be there to bridge the inevitable gaps left by reason and experience; and it must be there to carry the mind beyond their limits. Of course, we may *in words* pretend to withhold assent and declare any and every nonempirical affirmation to be a mere "wish-fulfilment." But such skepticism can never be more than merely verbal.[12] "All knowledge," so good a skeptic as Bertrand Russell assures us "must be built on our intuitive beliefs; if they are rejected, nothing is left."[13] Whether we employ the intuitionist terminology or not—and I myself do not find it very useful—the conclusion is the same: an antecedent postulation is necessary before we can begin thinking or acting in any sphere of reality, and the volitional form of such postulation is plainly the "will-to-believe."

In all of the cases I have mentioned, the affirmation of faith, as it may be called, is related only to a particular area and is meant to meet merely a particular need. But the affirmation of faith demanded in religion is something different and something more, infinitely more: it is a *total* commitment, relating to and underlying *all* of existence. On the ultimate question of religion, the agnostic withholding of belief is thus even more obviously impossible. In the totality of existence, something must be affirmed as ultimate; some primary commitment must be made; some attitude to the universe must be taken; some answer to the question of existence must be given—and whatever it may be, it cannot in the nature of the case be susceptible to rational proof or scientific verification. Whatever we may say, we affirm an external world and an order of nature whenever we engage in action or indulge in expectation. Whatever we may say, we affirm some system of values whenever we make conscious choice among alternatives. Whatever we say, there is something that we take as our absolute, as our anchorage in reality, as our "god." The only question—but it is a great, decisive, shattering question—is: *What* shall we acknowledge as absolute—some man-made god, in fact ourselves writ large, or the God beyond the abyss, the God who is Lord of all? This is the decision which each of us must make every moment of our lives. Trying to avoid the necessity of choice through an impossible agnosticism simply means to have the choice made for us below the level of vital personal decision. Feuerbach's skepticism did not keep him from a gross idolatry of Man, nor did Freud's keen insight into the mechanism of rationalization and "wish-fulfilment" save him from the incredible banalities of nineteenth-century science-worship that we find in *The Future of an Illusion*.

Shall we then say, in the language of the philosophers, that we "postulate" God? Only in the sense that "[we] need God in order to be."[14] In other words, it is not so much that God is a "postulate"—this again would make God into an object—but that the "postulation," the affirmation, of God is an existential necessity.

This affirmation—the "leap of faith" that springs out of the decision for God—is not a leap of despair but rather a leap in triumph over despair. It is a leap made not in order to search blindly for an unknown God somewhere on the other side; it is a leap that is made because—wonderfully enough—God has *already* been found. Faith is risk, venture, decision:[15] so it is for us while we are still on this side of the abyss. We must dare the leap if the gulf is ever to be crossed; but once the decision of faith has been made, it is seen that the leap was possible only because the gulf had already been bridged for us from the other side.[16] The reality of the decision remains, but we now see that what we had to decide was whether or not to accept the outstretched hand offered us over the abyss as we stood bewildered, anxious and despairing at the brink.

The existential achievement of faith is never secure. Faith is not a particular psychological goal, intellectual or emotional, which, once attained, may be expected to remain a permanent acquisition. Faith is a never-ending battle against self-absolutization and idolatry; it is a battle which has to be refought every moment of life because it is a battle in which the victory can never be final. But although never final, victory is always possible, for the outstretched hand over the abyss is always there for us to take hold of. The resources of divine grace are always available in the spontaneity of faith.

Faith is not mere "feeling"; nor is it intellectual assent to a creed. It is orientation of the whole man; it is a total existential commitment that brings with it á new way of seeing things, new perspectives and categories in the confrontation of reality. Through faith, existence is transposed into a new key. Everything—the universe, man, human life—is transfigured. Even faith itself takes on new meaning: our attitude to God, as Buber has well noted,[17] is something very different from our relation to the "finite goods" we idolize. The idol—even if it be an exalted idea or a noble cause—is always an object, something to be "enjoyed" or used; God—if it is the true God we affirm— is always the eternal Subject beyond human possession or employment. Our way of worship is different: "It is blasphemy when a man wishes, after the idol has crashed behind the altar, to pile up an unholy sacrifice to God on the desecrated place. . . [Man] cannot serve two masters—not even one *after* the other; he must first learn to serve *in a different way.*"[18]

In the transcendent perspective of faith, the entire universe is transformed. All the existential problems of life assume a new aspect. The world is no longer empty and God-forsaken; it has found its Creator and Sustainer. Human personality acquires a secure grounding in the eternal Person that is ultimate reality. Freedom and responsibility take on vital meaning. Life acquires unity, direction, significance. All the problems of life are not, of course, automatically solved; indeed, many of them now for the first time reveal their depth and poignancy. But through faith we gain access to spiritual resources for dealing with life. And life itself emerges as something very different when seen under the aspect of eternity, in the perspective of a transcendent goal and fulfilment beyond all relativity.

For those who possess it—or rather for those whom it possesses— faith is a force, an energy. When we abandon our fatal pretension to autonomy, to being a law unto ourselves, and face God in the self-emptying of true humility, we gain a new strength, a new sense of power, that we know is not ours but comes from beyond. It is this power that sustains and carries us through the darkness into the light.

The affirmation of faith is existential in its dynamic: it emerges out of the crisis of existence, which is always a crisis of the "now." Yet this affirmation of faith is also something historical, for it has no reality or meaning apart from the tradition through which it reaches the individual. The structure of faith in its dimensions of thought, feeling and action is historically given in terms of actual religion. To understand a faith means to understand this historical structure. It is, therefore, my purpose at this point to attempt to describe the *Jewish* structure of faith and to relate it to the various phases of the human situation.

## NOTES TO CHAPTER 5

1. Bertrand Russell, *Principles of Social Reconstruction* (Allen and Unwin: London, 1916), p. 245.

   "The nature of man as a conscious creature" is such, Professor Carl Becker tells us, that he "finds existence intolerable unless he can enlarge and enrich his otherwise futile activities by relating them to something more enduring and significant than himself". *Encyclopedia of Social Sciences*, p. 495b.

2. Hume's argument showing the dubiousness of all such "proofs" and Kant's brilliant demonstration of their inherent fallacy may still be read with great profit by anyone seriously concerned with religious thinking. In this sense, modern logical positivism has also performed a useful service by showing what science and scientific reason really are; this must be recognized even though the logical positivists, by absolutizing science and empirical thinking, in effect destroy the *critical* power of their own doctrine.

3. Martin Buber, *I and Thou* (T. & T. Clark: Edinburgh, 1937), p. 80.

   "Obviously that which is acknowledged to be superior to Nature cannot be proved to exist in the way existence is proved or disproved in Nature. Could it be, it would cease to be supernatural. Its existence must be supernatural existence. . . ." F. J. E. Woodbridge, *An Essay on Nature* (Columbia University Press: New York, 1940), p. 306.

4. Buber, *ibid.*, p. 93. See also Buber's comments on mysticism in *Between Man and Man* (Kegan Paul: London, 1947), pp. 24, 25, 43, particularly significant in view of his own earlier leanings in that direction: "From my own unforgettable experience I know well. . . ." (p. 24).

5. Buber, "The Question to the Single One," *Between Man and Man*, p. 81.

6. Franz Rosenzweig, "Das neue Denken," *Kleinere Schriften* (Schocken: Berlin, 1937), pp. 395-96. See also Jacob Agus, *Modern Philosophies of Judaism* (Behrman's: New York, 1941), chap. iii, "Franz Rosenzweig"; and Will Herberg, "Franz Rosenzweig's 'Judaism of Personal Existence'," *Commentary*, Vol. X (December, 1950), No. 6.

The "naturalist" philosopher, F. J. E. Woodbridge, expresses a strikingly similar thought: "Knowledge which would give us security. . .must not be like physics, biology or history. . . .The desired knowledge requires a light which would reveal something totally different, something that would satisfy personality instead of cognitive curiosity" (*op. cit.*, p. 279).

7. If only because no logical inference from scientific fact to value is possible, as indicated in chapter 7, above.

In his remarkable *Essay on Nature*, to which reference has been made, F. J. E. Woodbridge emphasizes that such "ultimates," often called "ideals," "are not ideas of anything disclosed in Nature's history, nor does she forecast their realization" (p. 336). He also indicates that in this usage " 'the ideal' is an alternative word for 'the supernatural' " and deplores the "word-phobia" that prefers the former term to the latter, despite its many inadequacies.

8. "The beliefs that are implied by his actions are the beliefs which a man really holds. The beliefs that are implied by the actions that he cannot avoid are the beliefs which a man *must* hold". Eli Karlin, "The Nature of the Individual," *Review of Metaphysics*, Vol. I (December, 1947), No. 2, p. 84.

9. Russell, "A Reply to My Critics," *The Philosophy of Bertrand Russell*, ed. by Paul Schilpp (Northwestern University: Chicago, 1944), p. 719

10. Whitehead, *Science and the Modern World*, pp. 5, 27.

11. C. E. M. Joad, Guide to *Philosophy* (Dover: New York, 1936), p. 152.

12. Such "insincere skepticism" is what Russell calls "professing disbeliefs we are in fact incapable of entertaining." *The Philosophy of Bertrand Russell*, p. 683.

13. Russell, *The Problems of Philosophy* (Holt: New York, 1912), p. 39.

"All our reasoning reduces itself to yielding to feeling." Paschal, *Pensées*, No. 274.

14. Buber, *I and Thou*, p. 82.

15. "Faith is . . . the venture pure and simple." Buber, "What Shall We

Do About the Ten Commandments?" *Israel and the World* (Schocken: New York, 1948), p. 86.

16. "The person who makes a decision knows that his deciding is no self-delusion; the person who has acted knows that he was and is in the hand of God." *Ibid*, p. 17.

17. Buber, *I and Thou*, pp. 104-05.

18. *Ibid.*, pp. 105-06.

# II.

# GOD AND MAN

# 6. FUNDAMENTAL OUTLOOK OF
# HEBRAIC RELIGION

An initial understanding of what the Jewish religious commitment really signifies as an attitude to life may perhaps best be obtained by comparing the Hebraic world-outlook with the outlook of the very different type of religion manifested in Greco-Oriental spirituality. This comparison is not arbitrary, nor is it merely conceived as an explanatory device. It really goes to the heart of the matter. For whatever may be thought of the so-called primitive religions, it seems to be the case that the higher religions of mankind fall into two main groups distinguished by widely different, often diametrically opposed preconceptions and attitudes. One group we may quite properly call Hebraic, for it includes Judaism, Christianity and Islam. The other group consists, as Moore points out, of "the soteric religions and philosophies of India and of Greece and the native and foreign mysteries of the Hellenistic-Roman world."[1] Perhaps the most appropriate designation for this type would be Greco-Oriental; Buddhism and Yoga are its best-known modern representatives.

It is not suggested that these religious types are manifested in pure form in any existing empirical religion; every existing religion would probably show, in its doctrine and practice, a varying mixture of elements stemming from both sources. But it is maintained that normative Judaism through the centuries has remained remarkably close to its Hebraic center, and that its "essence" can best be understood from this point of view. A brief presentation of the nature of the Hebraic religious outlook, in contrast to the outlook we have called Greco-Oriental, will therefore serve as our point of departure for an account of the structure of faith in Judaism.

Hebraic and Greco-Oriental religion, as religion, agree in affirming some Absolute Reality as ultimate, but they differ fundamentally in

47

48    *Judaism and Modern Man*

what they say about this reality. To Greco-Oriental thought, whether mystical or philosophic, the ultimate reality is some primal impersonal force. To call it God, as so many have done, would be misleading; it is more nearly "godness" than God, an all-engulfing divine quality, the ground and end of everything. Whether one names it Brahma or the All-Soul or Nature (as Spinoza does).or nothing at all (as is the way of many mystics) does not really matter; what is meant is very much the same in all cases—some ineffable, immutable, impassive divine substance that pervades the universe or rather *is* the universe insofar as the latter is at all real. This, of course, is pantheism: the All is "God." Greco-Oriental religion, whatever its specific form, irresistibly tends towards a pantheistic position.

Nothing could be further from normative Hebraic religion. To Hebraic religion, God is neither a metaphysical principle nor an impersonal force. God is a living Will, a "living, active Being. . .endowed with personality."² As against the Greco-Oriental conception of *immanence*, of divinity permeating all things and constituting their reality, Hebraic religion affirms God as a *transcendent* Person, who has indeed created the universe but who cannot without blasphemy be identified with it. Where Greco-Oriental thought sees continuity between God and the universe, Hebraic religion insists on discontinuity. "Hebrew religion," Frankfort declares, "rejects precisely this doctrine [that the divine is immanent in nature]. The absolute transcendence of God is the foundation of Hebrew religious thought. God is absolute, unqualified, transcending every phenomenon. . . . God is not in sun and stars, rain and wind; they are his creatures and serve him."³

This radical difference in the conception of God makes for an equally profound divergence in attitude to life and the world. Both Greco-Oriental and Hebraic religion draw some distinction between the Absolute Reality that they affirm as ultimate and the empirical world of everyday experience. To the Buddhist theologian, the Hindu mystic or the Platonic philosopher, the empirical world is illusion, an unreal, shifting flux of sensory deception: only the Absolute, which is beyond time and change, is real. Life and history are therefore essentially meaningless; as temporal processes, they are hopelessly infected with the irrational and the unreal. True knowledge—saving knowledge—consists in breaking through the "veil of illusion" of empirical life, in sweeping this shadow world aside, in order to obtain a glimpse of the unchanging reality which it hides. This is the way of salvation.

To the Hebraic mind, on the other hand, the empirical world is real and significant, though not, of course, self-subsistent since it is ultimately dependent on God as Creator. Life and history, too, are real and meaningful, though again not in their own terms. As against Greco-Oriental otherworldliness, Hebraic religion strikes an unmistakably *this*-worldly note: this world, the world in which we pass our lives, the world in which history is enacted, the world of time and change and confusion, is the world in which the divine Will is operative and in which, however strange it may seem, man encounters God. Depreciation of this world in favor of some timeless world of pure being or essence is utterly out of line with the realistic temper of Hebraism.[4]

Since man is of course in some sense part of the empirical world, one's fundamental attitude to the world will find reflection in the conception one has of man and his nature. The drift of Greco-Oriental thought is quite clear: it affirms a body-soul dualism according to which the body—that is, matter—is held to be the principle of evil, and the soul—the mind or reason—the principle of good. In the Platonic figure, the body is the "prison-house of the soul";[5] as a result of its confinement in its carnal dungeon, the soul is confused and stupefied and dragged down into the mire of immorality. "For the Greeks," Moore writes, and what he says applies to all within the sphere of Greco-Oriental spirituality, "the soul is a fallen divinity . . . imprisoned in a material mortal body . . . [In earthly life] the soul is subject to physical and moral defilement; the body is the tomb of the soul or its prison-house, its transient tabernacle, its vesture of flesh, its filthy garment."[6] Death, which releases the immortal soul, is liberation.

However familiar and plausible this dualistic view may seem to many religious people today, it is nevertheless utterly contrary to the Hebraic outlook. In authentic Hebraism, man is not a compound of two "substances" but a dynamic unity. It is indeed necessary to distinguish between the natural and the spiritual dimensions of human life, but this is not a distinction between body and soul, much less between good and evil. The body, its impulses and passions, are not evil; as parts of God's creation, they are innocent and, when properly ordered, positively good. Nor, on the other hand, is human spirit the "fallen divinity" of the Greeks. Spirit is the source of *both* good and evil, for spirit is will, freedom, decision. It is impossible to imagine a more profound difference in orientation and outlook than is here revealed.

Equally profound is the divergence between the two religious outlooks in their view of man's spiritual condition and need. They agree, of course, in finding men in this world to be lost, forlorn, sunk in evil from which they must be saved. But they are poles apart in their conception of the nature of the evil and the way of salvation.

Greco-Oriental religion finds the evil besetting men to be error and illusion. Men are so bedazzled by the empirical world that they actually take it for reality. They thus become involved in the world and attached to it; they develop cravings for its illusory "goods," thereby inviting pain and suffering. All the ills that afflict men are, in the view of Plato and the Buddha alike, the result of the benightedness that mistakes illusion for reality.

Perhaps the most dangerous of the errors that bedevil mankind, in this view, is the notion of individuality. Individuality is born out of illusion since the separateness of one man from another is simply an aspect of the world of empirical unreality; in its turn, individuality generates craving and greed, a grasping after things, a clinging to personality, which effectually blocks the hope of liberation from evil. "Individuality," Moore says, describing this type of religion, "is the great error, the cause of all man's ills . . . The real self, mistakenly imagined to be individual, is identical with the All-Soul and the end of man's being is to realize this identity."[7]

When we approach the same problem through Hebraic eyes, we move in an entirely different universe. Man's personality is taken as the inexpugnable reality of his being; it is because man is a person that he can hear God's word and respond to it. Nor, as we have seen, is the world itself unreal. That is not the source of evil. The evil condition, the lost state, from which man seeks salvation is, in the Hebraic view, his alienation from God. Man's proper condition is fellowship with God in faith and obedience. It is when man denies his faith and forgets his obedience, when he falls into egocentricity and self-absolutization, that he brings disorder to his own soul and confusion to the world. This self-absolutization in rebellion against God is *sin,* a concept central to Hebraic religion but, in its proper sense, quite unknown to Greek and Eastern thought.

We shall, of course, discuss in detail below this basic conception as well as the doctrine of salvation which it implies. But it may be said here that in Hebraic religion salvation for the individual consists essentially in repentance and reconciliation, in his abandoning his sinful pretensions and thankfully accepting the privilege of walking humbly with his God. Salvation is thus not the denial of personality but its enhancement through the power of personal communion in which all barriers of alienation are removed.

To the Yogi, Buddhist or neo-Platonic philosopher, this goal must seem both fantastic and delusive. How can personal relationship be established with the Ultimate Reality when personality itself is unreal and illusory? And what sort of salvation would it be, even if it were possible, since it would leave man actively involved in the things of this world? No, to Greco-Oriental religion, salvation is first of all "nonattachment," the breaking of all ties with the world of desire and body and matter, the annihilation of personality and ultimately its dissolution in the All-Soul as a drop of water is dissolved in the ocean. Only in the East, however, where there is no Hebraic heritage to restrain it, has mystic religion gone that far; but even where it stops halfway and speaks of salvation as the "beatific vision" or the "vision of God" after death, the tendency toward flight from the world and personal self-annihilation through "nearness to God" is unmistakable.[8]

If the question were put to the Buddhist or Hindu: "What am I? What shall I do to be saved?" his answer would be: "You are a fragment of the All-Soul whose effort it must be to find its way back to the Divine Whole." But if the same question were asked of one who holds to the biblical standpoint, the answer would be very different indeed. Man is a person, so the answer would run, a dynamic center of action, yet at the same time a creature, brought into being to serve his Creator in faith and love and thus achieve his salvation.[9] In one case, salvation is *from* life and *from* the world; in the other, it is *for* life and *for* the world.

There is still another radical distinction. For the Greek philosopher, as for the Hindu mystic, salvation is essentially self-salvation. "Primitive Buddhism and some other contemporary and cognate religions," Moore states, "acknowledge no power whose aid man can enlist to deliver him from the endless round of rebirth . . .; he alone can be his own deliverer and by his own effort attain release in Nirvana. . . . They lodge in man the power to emancipate himself from the bondage of empirical humanity and the cycle of mundane existence."[10] The role of philosophy as conceived in neo-Platonic tradition is not essentially different.

To the Hebraic mind, such confident claims to self-salvation are nothing short of blasphemy. They amount to self-absolutization in its most presumptuous form. For man is thus held to be entirely self-sufficient; he does not need God, not even for his eternal salvation. What is this but outright atheism?[11]

The good life for man is life ordered to the Absolute. But what does this life imply? In the Greco-Oriental view, the good life is a life of contemplation, in which all attachments to the empirical world are broken and all illusions as to its reality dissipated; it is a life of total self-absorption, with illumination and finally mystic union as its goal. To the Hebraic mind, the good life is the life of action in the service of God and therefore of one's fellow-men. Nowhere is the contrast sharper than between the passionless quietism of the one and the active service of love of the other. The mystic or philosopher "sees and enjoys"; the man of the Bible "hears and obeys."[12]

Greco-Oriental religion is "beyond good and evil." In its view, ethics is instrumental, useful to clear the way for higher things. Obviously, no man can regard himself as "detached" from the world and free from craving if he still harbors hate or anger or envy; these therefore must be removed to start with. But the higher stages of the mystic way transcend ethical considerations of every kind: compassion and loving concern are likewise obstacles to self-liberation since they, too, are bonds that tie the aspirant down to the world of change and desire.

In Hebrew religion, ethics is central and ultimate for man, though God himself, of course, transcends ethical categories as he does all others. For man, the moral life, the life of personal concern and loving service, is not something to be left behind at any stage of spiritual development: man stands ever active in the service of the Absolute who is Lord of life.

That there is and must be a fulfilment beyond immediate life is an insight common to all higher religion. But as to what this fulfilment is and how it is related to our present life there is the very sharpest disagreement. Greek and Oriental religions contemplate not so much the fulfilment of life and history as escape from it. What is passionately longed for is the liberation of the soul from the body, from time and empirical existence, and its translation to an immaterial aboveworld out of time: "the emancipation of the soul," as Moore puts it, "from bondage to matter and sense and the realization of its divine nature."[13] The immortality of an immaterial soul by virtue of its own imperishable quality is the characteristic doctrine of the more familiar varieties of this type of religion.

In the Hebraic scheme, the great goal is not escape from life but its fulfilment. The prophetic proclamation of the Messianic Age and the "end of days" speaks of "a new heaven and new earth" in which all the possibilities of life will be realized and all human enterprises judged and fulfilled. The Hebraic outlook, which in its attitude to the world is so pronouncedly this-worldly, is here deepened and completed in a *trans*-worldly, *trans*-historical vision—a vision in which the ultimate meaning of life is revealed in terms of an "end" which ever confronts it. And this fulfilment is conceived as the fulfilment of the *whole man,* not merely of a disembodied soul; that is why rabbinic tradition is so insistent on the dogma of the resurrection of the dead, to the scandal of all modern minds. As in the beginning, so in the end: like the affirmation of a transcendent personal God, this hope of a "last day" on which life and history will achieve their fulfilment defines the unbridgeable gulf between Hebraic and Geco-Oriental spirituality. Here there can be no reconciliation, no compromise.[14]

Let us now summarize briefly the picture thus hastily sketched. Greco-Oriental religion affirms an impersonal immanent reality; Hebraism proclaims its allegiance to the Lord of life and history, the Creator of the universe, a transcendent Person with whom man can establish genuinely personal relations. Greco-Oriental thought negates the empirical world and urges that it be brushed aside as unreal and delusive. It finds the principle of evil in the body and in personal "separateness," which it associates with the body. It has no sense of sin or guilt, since it finds the root of man's trouble in the benighted state that leads him to take illusion for reality. It can assign no meaning to life or history since both are immersed in time while only the eternal is real. It assures man that he can achieve salvation—liberation from the world—through his own efforts without God. It holds out mystic illumination, the contemplative "vision of God" and, in its extreme form, even absorption in the All-Soul as the final goal. In the strictest sense of the term, it is self-annihilating and life-denying.

Hebraic religion, on the other hand, is self-affirming and life-enhancing. It sees in human personality the "image of God" and the source of spiritual creativity. "It is not the I that is given up," Martin Buber declares, speaking of Judaism, "but the false self-asserting impulse. . . . There is no self-love that is not self-deceit, but without being and remaining oneself, there is no love."[15] It does not split man into body and soul, but sees him whole, as a dynamic unity immersed in nature, yet transcending it by virtue of his freedom. Evil it finds not in matter or body or the natural impulses of life, but in a certain spiritual perversity which tempts man to try to throw off his allegiance to the Absolute and to make himself the center of his universe. From this sinful self-absolutization stems the disorder and misery of life, individual and collective. There is no salvation except return to God in faith and repentance, no salvation except through the grateful acceptance of the divine forgiveness that alone can heal the soul rent with guilt and despair. Hebraic religion declares the life of moral action, the life of service to God in this world, to be the ultimate duty of man. It knows how to prize the inexhaustible resources of authentic communion with God in prayer, contemplation and study, but it never sees in this experience the ultimate end of human existence. It sees it rather as a never-failing source of spiritual power in the struggle of life and a sure refuge for the weary soul amidst the futilities and frustrations of existence. The "end" of life and history Hebraic religion envisions as the Kingdom of God, in which all our efforts, all our hopes and enterprises, will come to fruition and judgment.

Greco-Oriental spirituality is selfcentered and individualistic: "Salvation is in the strictest sense an achievement of the individual for himself and by himself."[16] Hebraism, on the other hand, holds salvation, like life itself, to be communal, and sees man's self-transcending service to fellow-man as the true service of God. Yet such is the ultimate paradox of life, that the self-absorption of the Buddhist or Yogi culminates in self-annihilation, while the sacrificial service enjoined by prophet and rabbi turns out to be the way toward personal fulfilment: "Identify your will with the will of God, that he may identify his will with yours."[17]

Such are the two world-outlooks. At bottom, they are irreconcilable, for what one affirms the other denies, and what one denies the other affirms. Between them, too, in their various forms and combinations, they exhaust the field of significant religious expression. How, then, is one to choose between them? By what criterion are we to make our choice? In the last analysis, there is no such criterion, for since these world-views are in fact ultimate orientations, there is nothing beyond in terms of which they can be judged. Affirmation of one or the other is concretely a matter of total existential commitment, a staking of our life and the "lives of all the generations" on the truth-for-us. Yet even here a less ultimate consideration may be allowed some weight. After explaining that, in the Greco-Oriental view, "salvation is an achievement of the individual for himself and by himself," Moore adds: "Buddha discovered the way and taught it to men." But *why?* Why, having discovered it, did he teach it to others? This question would seem to constitute an insurmountable stumbling block to Buddhism and to lead it to what in effect is a repudiation of itself. For if the highest good is, as Buddhism affirms, liberation of the self from empirical existence and the attainment of the "endless peace" of Nirvana and if, as Buddhism further affirms, the Buddha had acquired the knowledge necessary to achieve this goal, why then did he not make use of this saving knowledge "for himself and by himself"? Why, instead of liberating himself immediately as he might have done, did he suspend or postpone his liberation and go about preaching to his fellow-men? What was his concern with his fellow-men? In the Buddhist system, such behavior on the part of the Buddha and countless Buddhist preachers after him simply makes no sense; indeed, it seems to amount, as I have suggested, to a fundamental repudiation of Buddhism. It looks very much as if, at the crucial moment of decision, the Buddha acted not in accord with the imperative of Buddhism: "Save yourself by your own effort," but in accordance with the Hebraic imperative: "Thou shalt love thy neighbor as thyself." The very first act of Buddhism was thus in a basic sense a refutation of itself. In this self-contradiction, which permeates Greco-Oriental spirituality in all its forms, may perhaps be found the clue for a final judgment between the two irreconcilable religious world-views.

## NOTES TO CHAPTER 6

1. G. F. Moore, *The Birth and Growth of Religion* (Scribner's: New York, 1923), pp. 126-27.
2. Meyer Waxman, *A Handbook of Judaism* (Bloch: New York, 1947), p. 134.
3. Henri Frankfort, *Kingship and the Gods* (University of Chicago: Chicago, 1948), p. 343.
4. "To the Hebrew, the world of phenomena, so far from being illusion, is the field of values. . . . And from this flows a correlated diversity in their fundamental conceptions of the role of religion. To the Indian, this is the attainment of peace; to the Jew, it is the realization of value." B. H. Streeter, *The Buddha and the Christ* (Macmillan: New York, 1933), p. 49.
5. Plato *Phaedo* 66B, 67C, 67D; *Cratylus* 400C; *Phaedrus* 250C.
6. Moore, *op. cit.*, p. 120.
7. Moore, *op. cit.*, pp. 160, 99.
8. "If at first he [Buber] regarded himself as a mystic, he later came to the conclusion that mysticism, which seeks through 'nearness to God' to submerge and efface man's individual character is essentially anti-religious and therefore non-Jewish." A. Steinberg, "The History of Jewish Religious Thought," *The Jewish People: Past and Present* (Central Yiddish Culture Organization: New York, 1946), I, 305.
9. See the very significant article by John A. Hutchison, "The Biblical Idea of Vocation," *Christianity and Society*, Vol. XIII (Spring, 1948), No. 2.
10. Moore, *op. cit.*, p. 19.

11. Indeed, original Buddhism and many varieties of present-day Yoga must be regarded as explicitly atheistic. Speaking of Yoga and associated cults, Moore writes: "They worship no gods and they own no Lord (personal supreme God) . . . they undertake to show a man what he must do to achieve his own deliverance from the round of rebirth and its endless misery, to be his own savior without the aid of god or man." Moore, *op. cit.*, p. 149. "Nor [in primitive Buddhism] was there any god who could further a man in his pursuit of salvation, much less bestow it upon him." p. 153.

12. "For the Bible, the fundamental religious encounter is God's call to man—a call not primarily to communion or contemplation but to action. . . . God calls us, puts us under orders, and sets us tasks in such a way that we become his servants, the instruments by which the divine purpose is accomplished in the world. And for us men, the meaning of our existence consists in responding to this call." Hutchison, *ibid.*

13. Moore, *op. cit.*, p. 125.

14. Sikhism, which makes a deliberate effort to combine Hinduism with Chrstianity and Islam, has gone far in the direction of Hebraism but has stopped short at these two points: (1) it affirms an "Impersonal Formless God," and (2) it "looks to no decisive Day of Judgment with eternal reward and punishment, but rather to the continued development of the soul through countless rebirths, as in Hinduism, until it becomes at last ready for absorption in the Infinite Soul." H. W. Boulter, "Sikhism," *Religion in the Twentieth Century* (Philosophical Library: New York, 1948), pp. 197-98. On these two points there could be no syncretism.

15. Buber, "The Question to the Single One," *Between Man and Man* (Kegan Paul: London, 1947), p. 43.

16. Moore, *op. cit.*, p. 153.

17. *M.* Abot 2.4.

# 7. THE "GOD-IDEA" AND THE LIVING GOD

One of the greatest obstacles in the way of modern man's appropriating or even understanding the religious tradition to which he is heir is the fact that the only "God-idea" made available to him by contemporary culture is one that can possess very little significance for his life or for the larger destiny of the world he lives in. We are all of us more or less involved in this strange situation. Even when we have succeeded in breaking through current secularist prejudice to the point of being ready to think seriously about God, we only too easily fall into a conception of the divine that has virtually no power or meaning in human existence. That is the only conception, apparently, of which we, in our modern-mindedness, are capable, and yet it is a conception that leads nowhere. The biblical teaching about God, even when we read and ponder the Scriptures, seems somehow to elude our comprehension, but it is the only teaching that can make our affirmation of God a potent transforming force in our lives.

The "God-idea" that comes, so to speak, naturally to modern man is an idea out of Greek metaphysics and medieval scholasticism, recast here and there by the rationalism of the past two centuries. It sees "God" as, on the one hand, a sort of all-embracing cosmic force or "soul of the universe" and, on the other, as the "divine in us," the exalted ideals toward which we strive. Religion then becomes indeed what Matthew Arnold called it, "morality touched with emotion"—a kind of sentimentalized ethic afloat in a vague, heart-warming sea of cosmic piety. But if that is God and that is religion, of what possible significance can either be? No wonder so many today who are earnestly searching for something beyond the prevalent secularism can make nothing of religion. The religion that reaches us is somehow too tenuous to be relevant to the burning interests of our time, too etherealized to give us an understanding of the permanent crisis in which we find ourselves or the resources with which to cope with it. Something very different is required.

And something very different is available. The "God-idea" of contemporary spirituality is not the God of Hebraic religion. The God of Hebraic religion is not a philosophical principle, an ethical ideal or a cosmic process. The God of Hebraic religion, the God of the Bible, is a *Living God*. In this tremendous phrase—the Living God—which has become so strange to our ears but which occurs repeatedly in the Bible and continues right through rabbinic tradition,[1] is concentrated the full potency of the Hebraic "God-idea." Only, it is no longer a mere "God-idea"; it is the Living God himself.

When Judaism speaks of the Living God, it means to affirm that the transcendent Absolute which is the ultimate reality is not an abstract idea or an intellectual principal but a *dynamic Power* in life and history—and a dynamic power that is *personal*. The God of Judaism is thus best understood as a transcendent Person whose very "essence" is activity, activity not in some superworld of disembodied souls but in the actual world of men and things.

Attribution of personality to God is a scandal to modern minds. The religiously inclined man of today can understand and "appreciate" a God who—or rather, *which*—is some impersonal process or metaphysical concept. But a God who is personal, a person: that seems to be the grossest "anthropomorphism" and therefore the grossest superstition. Who can believe in any such thing?

The embarrassment of modern man when confronted with a personal God casts a revealing light on his entire outlook. In a certain sense, of course, every statement we make about God is bound to be both misleading and paradoxical. For the language we employ is of necessity the language of nature, while that to which we apply it is beyond nature; such usage must therefore necessarily be in some sense figurative and burdened with a heavy load of ambiguity. The transcendent Absolute obviously cannot be comprehended in any formula devised by the mind of man. Attempting to express or communicate what one wants to say about God is very much like trying to represent three-dimensional reality on a flat surface, by perspective drawing or projection. The representation is both true and false, significant and misleading: true and significant if taken in terms of the symbolism employed, false and misleading if taken literally. In speaking of God and religion, the words or phrases we use are symbols in a very special sense: they serve to point to a super-dimensional reality that cannot be grasped in idea or perception. They do more; if they are adequate to the purpose, they serve also to reveal some of its reality and meaning for us. We thus express what is beyond nature in terms of the natural, what is unconditioned in terms of the conditioned, what is eternal in terms of the temporal, what is absolute in terms of the relative.[2] No wonder that every such expression of ours ends up in paradox; paradox can penetrate where the self-consistent speculations of reason can never reach.

In whatever way we speak of God, whether we speak of him as a cosmic force or as a transcendent Person, we are making use of religious symbols. Everything depends upon the kind of symbols we use, for the symbols we use indicate not only the kind of God we affirm but also—what is very much the same thing in the end—our entire outlook on the universe. What do we mean when we speak of God as a Person? We mean that we meet God in life and history, not as an object, not as a thing, not as an *It*—to use Buber's pregnant distinction[3]—but as a Thou, with whom we can enter into genuine person-to-person relations. Indeed, it is this I-Thou encounter with God that constitutes the primary life-giving experience of faith: God, as Buber points out, can never be expressed; he can only be addressed.[4] This personal encounter with God—"the Being that is directly, most nearly and lastingly over against us"[5]—is not "merely" subjective, as naturalistic oversimplification would have it; it is an immediate self-validating encounter which transcends the ordinary distinction between subject and object, just as does any genuine encounter between man and man. For there are two ways of "knowing": knowing a *person* by *encounter* and communication, and knowing a *thing* by *using* it. When one man meets another as person to person, is it not absurd to speak of this encounter as either subjective or objective? Is it not absurd to speak of it as if the encounter itself, as well as the person we meet, were no more than a state of mind of ours or, on the other hand, as if the other person were an object about whose existence we have to assure ourselves through the objective procedures of scientific method? Is not this a total falsification of the real meaning of the I-Thou encounter, which is primary and self-revealing and prior to all distinctions of the understanding? What is true between man and man is true equally, or rather pre-eminently, between man and God.[6]

The ascription of personality to God is thus an affirmation of the fact that in the encounter of faith God meets us as person to person. It means, too, that the divine Person we meet in this encounter confronts us as a source of free dynamic activity and purpose. It is this freedom and purpose that, within limits—for the human spirit is conditioned by all the circumstances of life—exhibits itself in our own existence as an essential part of the meaning of personality. In God, these limitations are, of course, stripped away, and the free activity of personality manifests itself in consummate form. The Scriptural writers—whether legalist, priestly or prophetic—simply take the full personality of God as axiomatic. God speaks and is spoken to; he is jealous, angry, compassionate and forgiving; he acts and is acted upon; he has aims and purposes which he executes in history: he is, in short, a "decision-making person who has communication with and care for decision-making persons on this earth."[7] Later philosophers and to some extent even rabbinic writers were embarrassed by biblical expressions reflecting this "conception" of God and tried to explain them away as merely figurative or poetical;[8] modern apologists have generally followed the same line. But this will not do. Remove the "anthropomorphic"—or rather anthropo*pathic*—features from the biblical account of God and nothing whatever is left, not even a philosophical concept. "The divine reveals itself," writes A. J. Heschel, discussing the prophetic experience, "in a characteristically conditioned manner. . . . It reveals itself in its 'pathetic,' that is, emotional-personal bearing. God does not merely command and require obedience, he is also moved and affected; he does not simply go on ruling the world impassively, he also experiences it."[9] The God of Hebraic religion is either a living, active, "feeling" God or he is nothing.

Why is it that we, modern-minded men, are so scandalized when we are seriously asked to think of God as personal? To some extent, it is probably due to the fact that we have inherited the Greek metaphysical conception of God as Pure Being, incapable of change, modification, affection or outgoing action; after all, as Brunner points out, are not the Greeks the "tutors of our age" so that "even the thinking of the common man . . . is thoroughly pervaded by their thought"?[10] But fundamentally, it seems to me, this embarrassment of ours is to be traced to the pervasive antipersonalistic bias of our culture. The whole tendency of mechanistic science and technology in the past two centuries has been to "dehumanize" our thinking and to imbue us with the conviction that personality is "merely subjective" and therefore unreal, since *real* reality, the reality presented to us by science, is impersonal. It is not seen how ambiguous, how dangerous, this term "impersonal" is, implying, as it does, both what is above and what is below personality. It may be proper to hesitate to attribute personality unconditionally to the divine because God's superpersonal being takes in and transcends all aspects of personality, but it is sheer stultification to relegate the divine to a *sub*personal level.[11] How far must the depersonalization, the dehumanization, of our culture have gone that we have come to regard it as a mark of enlightenment and sophistication to picture the highest reality in terms of such subhuman concepts as a tendency of development or a field of force!

To deny personality to God, as the modern mind is prone to do, is thus, at bottom, to deny the reality and worth of personality in man. On the other hand, the affirmation of God as personal is not only dictated by the reality of the divine-human encounter but is also a vindication of the pre-eminence of personal being as we find it in human existence over the nonpersonal categories of science and philosophy. This conclusion is significant of a general relation we shall find repeated in various contexts: the denial of God leads inexorably to the devaluation and destruction of man.

God is thus not some "spiritual" abstraction or principle for man to reach through intellectual illumination; God, in Hebraic religion, is an active, living "decision-making" Being who plunges into human history and personally encounters men in their activity. But this God, let us not forget, is a transcendent God never to be simply identified with, or found inside of, the world of nature and man. This paradox of a God who is beyond everything in nature and history, and yet is ever actively involved in both, goes to the heart of Hebraic religion, especially as revealed in the prophetic writings. It is the dialectical paradox of the Wholly Other/Wholly Present that we meet on all levels of life and experience.[12]

This paradox is most profoundly expressed in the biblical teaching on creation, which is in more than one sense the beginning of all that follows. According to the Scriptural account, God creates the world, and, in later interpretation, creates it *out of nothing*. All existence that is not God is thus affirmed to be conditioned by and dependent upon God, the Unconditioned: God as Creator is Lord over all. This is the foundation of biblical theology.

Modern man finds it difficult to understand this or any other concept of creation because science seems to him to teach the infinity of time and space, the beginninglessness and endlessness and therefore the essential changelessness of things.[13] But the pronouncements of science in this regard are not only dubious but irrelevant, for what the biblical doctrine of creation is intended to express is not so much an event in time as the presupposition of all temporal existence. Creation is thus in the first place an affirmation that "nature" or the world is not self-subsistent and autonomous but owes its being to its transcendent source. The Creator God, however, is not the absentee divinity of deism, who, having once completed his work, retires from the universe. God re-creates the universe at every moment, rabbinic tradition tells us,[14] and this is meant to express not only the pregnant insight that creation continues but also the fundamental fact that, even after it has come into being, the created universe can make no claim to self-subsistence. Creation continues because the universe remains open and novelty ever emerges, because no system of closed mechanical determinism can ever be final. For the same reason, the universe can never lay claim to autonomy unless "Nature," as with Spinoza and other pantheists, is taken to be divine. It is precisely this type of idolatry—the worship of the world, its powers and "laws"—that the biblical doctrine of creation protects us against.

Between the Creator God and the world that is his creation there is a vast gulf that can be bridged only from the side of the divine: all significance, all value, all power is an endowment from God. This, in the last analysis, is the meaning of the holiness of God which the Scriptural and rabbinical writers are never tired of exalting.[15]

The absolute transcendence of God [H. Frankfort declares] is the foundation of Hebrew religious thought. God is absolute, unqualified, ineffable, transcending every phenomenon, the one and only cause of all existence. God, moreover, is holy, which means that all values are ultimately his. . . . To Hebrew thought, nature appears void of divinity. . . God is not in sun and stars, rain and wind; they are his creatures and serve him. Every alleviation of the stern belief in God's transcendence is corruption. In Hebrew religion, and in Hebrew religion alone, the ancient [pagan] bond between man and nature is destroyed. . . . Man remains outside nature. . . .[16]

As Waxman puts it, in Judaism "man is freed from subjection to nature."[17] And indeed faith in the transcendent God who is Lord of nature saves man from standing in superstitious terror before the powers of nature or from being swallowed up in sentimental-mystical ecstasy by its mysterious rhythms. Nature is neither divine nor corrupt; sustained in this belief, man can confront it without fear and master it.[18]

The traditional doctrine of creation *out of nothing* expresses the conviction that there is no ultimate principle in the universe aside from God. It is thus an utter rejection of the dualism or polytheism that underlies all religions but those stemming from Hebraic sources. Because God created the universe, existence as such must be good;[19] indeed, the Scriptural account presents God as making this pronouncement at every stage of the creative process. Hebraic teaching has no place for the Greco-Oriental notion, so influential in our thinking, that matter is the eternal source of evil. There is nothing eternal but God; moreover, the created universe, the natural, the "material" universe in all its aspects, is not evil. Evil, of course, there is, but this evil cannot be inherent in existence. It cannot be part of the eternal order of creation but must rather represent a disruption of it. How that is brought about we shall have occasion to discuss.

Taking it in its larger meaning, the biblical doctrine of creation can thus be seen to be the indispensable ground for any conception of nature that does justice to its reality and value without losing sight of its contingent and conditioned character.

The affirmation of God as Creator is associated with the affirmation of the divine sovereignty. No appellation for God is more common in biblical-rabbinical literature or in Jewish liturgy than the term King; no concept is more characteristic of the Hebraic outlook than the Kingdom—that is, the kingship—of God. David's prayer, as recorded in Chronicles, communicates something of the intensity and exaltation of spirit behind these phrases: "Thine, O Lord, is the greatness and the power and the glory and the victory and the majesty; for all that is in the heaven and in the earth is Thine; Thine is the kingdom, O Lord, and Thou art exalted as head above all" (I Chron. 29:11). The formula introducing virtually every prayer in the liturgy is: "Blessed art Thou, O Lord our God, King of the Universe. . . ."[20]

What does the kingship of God mean in the context of Hebraic religion? Its implications are inexhaustible, but above everything else it means that the God who created the universe is the absolute Lord over nature, life and history. No aspect of existence escapes his sovereign rule: *"All* men must bring *all* their lives under the whole will of God."[21] Life cannot be departmentalized into secular and sacred, material and spiritual, with the latter alone falling under divine jurisdiction. No such distinction is recognized in Hebraic religion; the attempt to withdraw anything, no matter how seemingly insignificant, from divine rule is branded as an attempt to set up a rival, an idolatrous, claim against the sovereignty of God: "I am the Lord thy God . . .; thou shalt have no other gods before me" (Exod. 20:2-3). All life, all existence, is governed by one ultimate principle and that principle is the will of the Living God.

The affirmation of the divine sovereignty taken seriously means, of course, that *only* God is absolute. This simple statement has the widest ramifications. It implies immediately that everything which is *not* God is "relativized." Nothing but God possesses any value in its own right. Whatever is not God—and that means everything in the world, every society, institution, belief or movement—is infected with relativity and can at best claim only a passing and partial validity. This God-centered relativism does justice to whatever is valid in the relativistic emphasis of modern thought without falling into the self-destructive nihilism to which the latter invariably leads. It makes available a perspective that transcends the immediacies and partial interests of life and is thus a most potent force for sanity in individual and social existence.

Moreover, if God is the sovereign Lord of existence, it follows that the whole duty of man is comprised in single-minded obedience and service to him. God is master; man, his servant—with all that this implies. This exaltation of the absolute sovereignty of God and the unrelieved emphasis on man's utter subjection and dependence, so characteristic of Hebraic spirituality, comes rather as a shock to the modern mind, which finds such notions "archaic," not to say offensive to democratic decency. Indeed, one very popular writer on religion finds it un-American. "A religion that will emphasize man's nothingness and God's omnipotence, that calls upon us to deny our own powers and glorify his," he proclaims, "may have fitted the needs of many Europeans but it will not satisfy the growing self-confident character of America. . . . We Americans have had little of the feeling of helplessness and dependence that characterizes so much of Oriental and European religion."[22] There is no occasion here to examine what the religious tradition of America really is; it is obviously something very different from the brash and superficial chauvinism this writer makes it out to be. What is much more important is to bring to light the utter confusion as to the nature of religion and the nature of man involved in this type of criticism. For the democratic idea makes sense only in a society of equals and not even the most zealous liberal would venture to assert such a relation between man and God. As a matter of fact, as we shall see later, the very concept of human equality has no meaning and democracy no validity except in terms of the common subjection of all men to the sovereignty of God. It is through loyal and devoted acknowledgment of this sovereignty that man finds his true freedom and personal dignity. Pretensions to self-sufficiency and attempts to measure himself against his Maker can only lead, as they have always led in the past, to utter chaos within the soul of man and the community he attempts to create. Denial of the divine sovereignty leads directly and inexorably to the disruption of human life. No one should know this better than the man of today who is heir to all the devastation that the fatal Prometheanism of the modern age has brought upon the world.

## NOTES TO CHAPTER 7

1. See, e.g., Deut. 5:23; Jer. 10:10, 23, 36; Hos. 2:1; Pss. 42: 2-3; 84:3. —The term is particularly frequent in the liturgy.
2. "Religious symbols always use a finite reality in order to express our relation to the infinite. But the finite reality they use is not an arbitrary means for an end, something strange to it. It participates in the power of the ultimate for which it stands. A religious symbol is double-edged. It expresses not only that which is symbolized but also that through which it is symbolized." Paul Tillich, "Religion and Secular Culture," *The Journal of Religion,* Vol. XXVI (April, 1946), No. 2.
3. Martin Buber, *I and Thou* (T. & T. Clark: Edinburgh, 1937), *passim.*
4. Buber, *op. cit.,* p. 81.
5. Buber, *op. cit.,* p. 80.

6. That is what makes attempts to "prove" the existence of God such an impertinence. "So rather let us mock God out and out," says Kierkegaard; "this is always preferable to the disparaging air of importance with which one would prove God's existence. For to prove the existence of one who is present is the most shameless affront, since it is an attempt to make him ridiculous. . . . How could it occur to anybody to prove that he exists unless one had permitted oneself to ignore him and now makes the thing all the worse by proving his existence before his very nose? The existence of a king or his presence is commonly acknowledged by an appropriate expression of subjection and submission; what if, in his presence, one were to prove that he existed? . . . One proves God's existence by worship." *Concluding Unscientific Postscript* (Princeton University: Princeton, N. J., 1944), p. 485.

7. J. P. Hyatt, *Prophetic Religion* (Abingdon-Cokesbury: Nashville, Tenn., 1947), p. 154.

8. The efforts of Philo, Maimonides and other philosophers to get rid of or explain away the anthropomorphisms of Scripture are well known. Even Judah Halevi is so far carried away by the philosophic conception of the impassive, immutable deity that he actually denies God the attribute of *mercy*: "They attribute to him mercy and compassion, although this is, in our conception, surely nothing but a weakness of the soul and a quick movement of nature. This cannot be applied to God, ordaining the poverty of one individual and the wealth of another. His nature remains quite unaffected by it. He has no sympathy with one nor anger against another." *Kitab Al-Khazari*, tr. by Hartwig Hirschfeld (Bernard G. Richards: New York, 1927), ii. 2.

9. A. J. Heschel, *Die Prophetie* (Polish Academy of Sciences: Cracow, 1936), p. 131.

10. Emil Brunner, "Die Bedeutung des Alten Testaments," *Zwischen den Zeiten*, Vol. VIII (1930).

11. "The depth of being cannot be symbolized by objects taken from a realm which is lower than the personal, from the realm of things and subpersonal living beings. The supra-personal is not an 'It,' or more correctly it is a 'He' as much as it is an 'It' and it is above both of them. But if the 'He' element is left out, the 'It' element transforms the alleged suprapersonal into a sub-personal, as it usually happens in monism and pantheism." Tillich, "The Idea of the Personal God," *Union Review* (November, 1940).

12. Buber, *I and Thou*, p. 79.

13. It is significant, as E. Frank points out, that "although modern man does doubt creative power in God, he certainly does not doubt the possibility of such a creative power in himself. And how could he doubt the possibility of a free will and of the power of self-determination in himself if without it his own thinking would be without truth and meaning?"

68     *Judaism and Modern Man*

"Time and Eternity," *Review of Metaphysics,* Vol. 1 (September, 1948), No. 5.

14. "God is not only the sole creator of the world, he alone upholds it and maintains in existence by his immediate will and power everything that is. This universal teaching of the Bible is equally the doctrine of Judaism: 'God created and he provides; he made and he sustains.' The maintenance of the world is a kind of continuous creation: God in his goodness makes new every day continually the work of creation." G. F. Moore, *Judaism* (Harvard University: Cambridge, Mass, 1927), I, 384; Moore provides the documentation.

"[The Prophets] proclaimed God's work in nature in the creation as sustaining of the cosmos. . . Second Isaiah did not believe that Yahweh's work in creation was an absolutely finished thing; Yahweh was ever creating in history that which could be proclaimed as *new.*" J. P. Hyatt, *Prophetic Religion,* p. 158.

15. E.g., Lev. 19:2 : "I, the Lord your God, am holy"; Isa. 6:3 : "Holy, holy, holy is the Lord of Hosts." *The Holy One Blessed is He* is one of the most familiar appellations of God in rabbinic literature. — See Moore, *Judaism,* II, 101 ff., 109 ff.

"According to this attribute [the "Holy One of Israel," as used by Isaiah], YHVH is not only holy but *the* Holy, that is to say, everything in the world which is to be named holy is so because it is hallowed by him." Buber, *The Prophetic Faith* (Macmillan: New York, 1949), pp. 206-07.

16. Henri Frankfort, *Kingship and the Gods* (University of Chicago: Chicago, 1948), pp. 342-44. Some tenses have been changed in the quotation.

17. Meyer Waxman, *A Handbook of Judaism* (Bloch: New York, 1947), p. 136.

18. E. A. Burtt shows how conceptions of God and his creative work derived from Hebraic tradition served to provide the metaphysical foundations of early modern science. *The Metaphysical Foundations of Early Modern Science* (Harcourt, Brace: New York, 1932), esp. pp. 148, 256, 293.

19. Waxman, *A Handbook of Judaism,* p. 140.

20. Particularly significant are the *Malkuyot* (Kingdom verses) in the liturgy for Rosh Hashanah. — Rosh Hashanah, echoing the ancient festival of the enthronement of Yahweh, is in fact the celebration of the Kingship of God.

21. J. P. Hyatt, *Prophetic Religion,* p. 51.

22. Joshua Loth Liebman, *Peace of Mind* (Simon & Schuster: New York, 1946), p. 173.

# 8. GOD AND MAN

In the universe created and sustained by the divine power, man enters as an anomalous element. Man is, of course, a creature, a part of the natural order, yet he obviously cannot be confined to the limiting conditions of nature. He alone of all creation is somehow capable of assuming a standpoint outside of creation. Bertrand Russell, whose feeling for man's uniqueness is so strangely at odds with the general cast of his thought, has expressed this aspect of the human situation in the following words:

> A strange mystery it is that nature, omnipotent but blind, has brought forth at last a child, subject still to her power but gifted with sight, with knowledge of good and evil, with the capacity of judging all the works of his unthinking mother . . . Man is yet free, during his brief years, to examine, to criticize, to know and in imagination to create. To him alone in the world with which he is acquainted, this freedom belongs and in this lies his superiority to the resistless forces that control his outer life.[1]

It is this capacity to see, to judge, to criticize, to create, that points to the spiritual dimension of human life and lifts man above the plane of natural causality. "Man," says Pascal, "surpasses himself infinitely."[2] He is the "undefined animal" of Nietzsche. Even the "materialist" Engels finds him to be "the sole animal capable of working his way out of the mere animal state—his normal state being one appropriate to his consciousness, one to be created by himself."[3] Self-transcendence is the mark of man. Every aspect of his finite life opens up with infinite possibilities.

The Scriptural account of the creation of man conveys the profound truth of his paradoxical status in the universe. Man is in nature, yet transcends it; he is subject to the rule of natural necessity, yet retains an irreducible freedom of self-determination within the conditioning factors of nature and history. He is fixed at the juncture of time and eternity.

An adequate philosophy of man must do justice to both of the in-

69

separable aspects of his nature. The Hebraic conception avoids alike the pitfalls of naturalism and of body-soul dualism. Naturalism considers man as merely a natural object, part of the order of nature in a way not essentially different from "other" animals. It does not, therefore, hesitate to insert him into a scheme of causal determinism that leaves no room for freedom, reason or moral responsibility. It deprives him of his character as man. Dualism, on the other hand, the dualism that vitiates so much of Greek and Oriental thought, looks upon the body as a prison-house of the soul from which the latter is constantly striving to escape. It sees man as essentially immaterial.

Judaism refuses to adopt either view. It refuses to exalt nature as self-sufficient or to disparage it as inferior and unreal. It unreservedly accepts it as the condition of life and finds the distinctive human note in the transfiguration of life and nature by spirit. In the age-old vision of the resurrection, it is the *whole* man, not his "soul" alone, that is revived to share in the fulfilment of human destiny. It is the whole man, man as a natural organism transfigured by spirit, that Judaism sees and with which it is concerned.

Because dualism thinks of man as essentially immaterial, it sees the essence of human existence in the contemplative life proper to a disembodied spirit. Naturalism, on the other hand, attempts to reduce human existence to the interaction of organism and environment. The Hebraic view differs from both in its realistic and dynamic emphasis. It finds the "essence" of man in his will and activity. How we will and what we do, that we are. It is not that man exists and then acts. He exists in that he wills and acts. His activity is explicit, forthgoing existence; his existence, implicit activity. In a sense far more profound than ever pragmatism conceived it, man *is* what he *does*.

To those accustomed to think of man in dualistic terms stemming from Greek philosophy or Oriental mysticism, the Hebraic conception of man as dynamic and unitary[4] must seem insufferably materialistic. And indeed in a sense it is. For in the Hebraic view, there is no aspect of life so exalted, so spiritual, that it is without its roots in material nature. But, on the other hand, there is nothing, literally nothing, that is simply and exclusively material in man. In man, every natural impulse is transformed, every organic vitality is transmuted, into a spiritual force that operates in indeterminate forms along a new dimension of freedom.[5] Sex becomes love or lust; kinship becomes racialism or fraternity; gregariousness becomes free community or totalitarian regimentation; the will-to-live becomes the service of love or the drive for power. Nothing is merely given or fixed in nature; yet everything, however transfigured in spirituality, is grounded in the natural conditions of life. Such is the paradox that is man, a natural organism that is more than nature because it is transformed through spirit and is thus able to achieve a new level of freedom.

"Spirit," says Kierkegaard,[6] "is self," personality. But a human self isolated and alone could never come into being: without a "Thou" there could be no "I".[7] It is in the encounter between the "I" and the "Thou," between the one and the other, that the human self is born. In the ordinary commerce of life, the other is, of course, one's fellow-man; but this relationship cannot be ultimate since neither party to it is self-subsistent. The reality of the human self is grounded in its relation as a "Thou" to the absolute "I" which is God. It is the word of God that calls it forth and maintains it in being.[8] Thus its very structure is *responsive,* since it depends for its existence upon the Absolute Subject to whom it responds. In this relation is expressed both the creatureliness and the personality of man: he is not merely spoken to; he answers, and in answering he has his being. The "word of God" is thus no mere arbitrary figure; it is a true symbol since it points to the intrinsic nature of human existence and of the divine-human relationship in a way which is somehow congruent with the reality itself.

We can now see why Buber so often speaks of spirit as "the word,"[9] or rather the capacity of the word, the capacity to hear and respond. For whatever may be one's relation to an object, the word alone is a suitable means for establishing relations between two subjects, not only between man and man but also between man and God. Man's personal relationship to God, as indeed his personal relationship to his fellow-men, baffles reason and outstrips interpretation; but in opposition to mysticism, we must emphatically affirm that it takes place only on the level of the *dialogic life,*[10] on the level of personal communion through the word. The centrality of the word in Scripture and later Jewish tradition[11] reflects the decisive fact that the "point of contact" between God and man—the *that* in man which raises him above the level of nature—is his "capacity of the word." It is this capacity that opens before man the infinite and indeterminate possibilities of his freedom. It is this capacity that endows him with responsibility as a moral being. In the inwardness of responsive freedom is grounded the power of decision that sets man apart from the rest of creation.

This is the aspect of man's nature—his capacity of the word, his personality, his freedom and responsibility—which Jewish tradition holds to be the mark of the divine likeness impressed upon him. Man. in the words of Scripture, is created "in the image of God." From this conception of the divine image in man flow all those aspects of life that we speak of as the spiritual dimension of existence.

The "image of God" in man establishes an affinity between man and God without in the least obscuring the vast gulf between creature and Creator. It makes possible personal fellowship, a genuine I-Thou relation, between the two. Man is meant for this fellowship and he is constantly striving for it, often against his knowledge and conscious intent. "With emphasis primarily on the *person*," Woodbridge writes, "man seeks kinship not with animals and the rest of nature but with the divine."[12] For it is the divine to which he is ordained. That is his "essential nature," if by that term we understand his original being and the vocation for which he is meant.

With such an exalted destiny open to him, it is no wonder that man is hailed by the Psalmist as "but little lower than the divine" (Ps. 8:6).

But to whatever heights Judaism may raise man in recognition of the potentialities of the "image of God" within him, it never forgets that he is but man. It never forgets that he is but a creature; it never confuses him with his Creator. "For the Israelite consciousness," Heschel writes, "the divine being is unapproachable. Its holiness is set in polar opposition to human limitations."[13] The contrast between God and man is not merely a contrast between infinity and finiteness, power and weakness, wisdom and ignorance, although, of course, it is that, too; the fundamental and devastating contrast is, as Heschel notes, between the holiness of God and the "limitations," the unworthiness, of man. Extolling man's freedom and his capacity to transcend self in decision as evidence of the divine image impressed upon him, Judaism does not overlook the dark side of human existence. It does not overlook the fact of sin.

Sin has long been a word repugnant to a certain type of modern mind, more concerned with evading responsibility for the horrors of the world than with facing the facts of life. Contemporary thinking, however, is beginning to take a much more realistic view of the problem of evil. It is beginning to see that we cannot do without the concept of sin or its equivalent if we are serious about trying to understand the nature of man. With E. A. Burtt, many to whom the word was once anathema are coming "to see some very profound truths in the theological doctrine of sin."[14] A mere reading of modern psychology would be enough to lead one to this conclusion, even if the entire experience of the twentieth century had not driven it home with tragic emphasis.

Facing unflinchingly the darker aspects of human existence, Jewish tradition, following in the line of the prophets, recognizes that there is in man something making for evil, which it knows as the *yetzer ha-ra* (impulse to evil). But authentic Jewish tradition refuses to take the easy way of identifying this aspect of man's nature with his body or flesh, in the manner of Greek and Oriental philosophy. The flesh and its impulses, being part of God's creation, are in themselves innocent, though they may be perverted by an evil "heart." For the source of the evil and unreason in human life, prophet and rabbi look elsewhere and deeper. And what they find is as fresh and pertinent to the facts of today as if it had just been discovered.

Moral evil—the dreadful ills inflicted by man upon himself and his fellow-men—they find to be the fruit of the same spiritual freedom that constitutes his glory and makes possible his fellowship with God: it is the fruit of the wrong use of that freedom. Man alone possesses the power to defy and frustrate his "essential nature." Such is the paradox of man that it is precisely his powers of spirit, the powers that raise him pre-eminent in the scale of creation, which enable him to upset the harmonies of creation and bring untold misery upon himself and his fellows. It is the divine image impressed upon him, as manifested in his freedom and capacity for decision, that gives him power to make or mar life, to serve God or to defy him.[15]

For that is just what sin is—revolt against God, turning away from the source of life, renunciation of allegiance to the Absolute.[16] This is the theme of the Scriptural account of "man's first disobedience," a profound symbol of the predicament in which every human being finds himself.

Man is a creature—relative, finite, incomplete. But he is also a creature endowed with a capacity to know and to resent his finiteness, relativity and incompleteness. In his efforts to surmount his limitations, he is ever tempted to forget his Creator and to insert himself at the center of all his enterprises, to make every activity of his life serve not the glory of God but his own self-glorification and aggrandizement. He is ever tempted to exalt himself and the work of his hands into the god of his own little universe. When man thus runs amok in the pride of his spirit, the devastation he leaves in his wake is fearful indeed. The divine image in him is obscured,[17] his reason is warped, his natural instincts are perverted, his relations with his fellow-men are poisoned: a tragic wall of alienation is erected between himself and the divine source of his life. Man is then lost indeed, desolate and forlorn in a hostile universe.

The impulse to the aggrandizement and exaltation of the self is, at bottom, the consequence of man's insecurity. Not merely the ordinary insecurities of life are here implied but the underlying existential insecurity, the cosmic anxiety, in which man is involved simply because he is man and of which he can free himself only through the self-forgetting love of God. Its source is the tension arising out of the conflict between man's self-transcending freedom and the inherent limitations of his creatureliness.[18] Striving to overcome this tension and to allay the anxiety gnawing at his heart, he is constantly under a double temptation: either to deny his *freedom* and lose himself in a welter of organic impulse, which is sensuality, or to deny his *creatureliness* by attempting, in his pride, to play the god and assert his power over his fellow-men.[19]

It is not mere finiteness, be it noted, that constitutes the "misery" of man, just as it is not simply the infinity of self-transcendence that constitutes his "grandeur." What is at the root of the human predicament is the paradox of *finite infinity*—or better, of finiteness "infinitized." Man is finite and knows it. Therefore he can never remain content in his finiteness, as can the rest of creation. The "infinity" he craves he may hope to achieve by an all-engulfing, all-transcending love of God—or else by making infinite pretensions for his finite impulses, ideas and enterprises. The former is faith; the latter, sin—the sin of sins: pride, self-absolutization.

The prophetic-rabbinic teaching reveals a profound understanding of the roots of human evil in man's sinful pretensions. "Pride," Solomon Schechter tells us, summarizing the traditional doctrine on the subject, "is the root of all evil, man setting himself up as an idol, worshipping his own self, and thus forced to come into collision with God and his fellow-men."[20] There is no limit to the havoc man works once he begins to exalt himself and usurp the place of God, and nowhere is the devastation greater than in his own soul.

Through sinful self-absolutization, man builds a barrier between himself and God and thus forfeits the divine fellowship which alone can bring him peace and fulfilment. He condemns himself to frustration and despair, to a life that cannot escape the emptiness of futility, to an anxious insecurity that grows more intense with every effort to overcome it. There is only one way out. By repentance and repentance alone—by "turning back" to God, as the Hebrew phrase so significantly puts it—can man remove the wall of alienation and regain his fellowship with the divine. Only thus can we establish a secure foundation for existence. Not by the denial of sin or an attempt to evade responsibility for it, but by a contrite recognition of the true source of our guilt in the self estranged from God, can we hope to find a path that will lead us back to the Lord of life from whom alone ultimate security and fulfilment can come.

The Hebraic view of man is thus irreducibly ambivalent, hinging as it does upon a dramatic tension both in the nature of man and in his relations with God. Man's "essential nature"—that is, the nature with which he is endowed by his Creator—is such as to require and make possible a life of self-giving fellowship; his actual sinful existence, however, stands in stark contrast to the law of his being. We have it within ourselves to transcend self in reason, imagination and moral freedom, but this capacity of ours for self-transcendence is limited and corrupted by the radical egotism of our sinful nature.

Even when we do succeed in rising above the self and its interests, our very achievement, as we well know, is only too prone to become the instrument of the self on a new level of self-assertion. In Jewish tradition, this insight into the dual nature of man is expressed in the doctrine of the two "impulses," the good and evil *yetzers*, with which he is endowed. This is a profound insight and it should not be reduced, as it sometimes has been, to the simple affirmation that man is both originally good and originally evil, as if the two were coordinate and paired off to balance each other. "The more conspicuous figure of the two *yetzers*," Solomon Schechter says, "is that of the evil *yetzer*"; indeed, "by *yetzer* without any specification is often meant the evil *yetzer*."[21] Moreover, and this is crucial, the evil *yetzer* is held to be something inherent in man as he exists in this world: "The Scripture," Moore says, "unqualifiedly declares man's native impulse to be evil."[22] The power for good, on the other hand, is described as coming to man through the Torah—that is, through divine grace—when man is in condition to receive it.[23] "Every day," we are told, "the *yetzer* of man assaults him and but for the Holy One blessed be he, who helps man, he could not resist it."[24] Man does indeed possess a capacity for the good, but for this capacity to become operative in his life, he needs the grace, the help, of God and the faith to receive it. He who would do evil—so runs an important rabbinic teaching—finds the means ready at hand; but he who would do good requires the assistance of the heavenly power.[25] The weakness and evil in man operate out of the freedom of his own nature; his capacity for good, though grounded in his nature, needs the grace of God for its realization. Ethics thus passes over into religion.

The full dimensions of human sin are represented symbolically in the biblical account of Paradise and the fall of man. In the primal perfection ("rightness") of his essential nature in Paradise, Adam (the man) was at one with his Creator, with himself, with the woman and with nature. Through his sin, through his turning away from God in self-willed disobedience, we are told, he disrupted all of these harmonies and brought self-contradiction into his own being and into his relations with his environment. He thus lost Paradise and was obliged henceforth to pursue his existence amidst conditions of inner conflict, social discord and an external nature that was "cursed" because of his sin. Yet despite his sin, we are given to understand, the structure of being in which he was created was still his. He was still man, and the regret and remorse he felt may be taken as a sign that his original perfection had not been totally destroyed by his lapse. Man left Paradise under the dominance of sin, yet with something within him that testified to the fact that the original power of the divine image with which he had been endowed in creation was still somehow operative in his nature.

Thus understood, man's fall is not an historical event in the life of the first man, nor is "original sin" a stain transmitted biologically to his descendants. Both "original sin" and "original perfection" are aspects of the existential moment, true of every point in history but not themselves historical. The original perfection of Paradise is the perfection of the idea; the fall occurs in the transition to action:

> Between the idea
> And the reality
> Between the motion
> And the act
> Falls the Shadow.[26]

In idea, the self is capable of achieving a position in which its own anxieties and interests are transcended, but when idea gives way to action, the self always manages to insinuate itself again at the heart of the enterprise. Yet however "inevitable" the corruption of the act may be, it is never "natural," for it runs counter to our essential nature, given in creation. That is why we are never content with sinning, but must always attempt to justify ourselves by an appeal to some universal principle. The guilt we feel and the justifications to which we are driven are striking evidence that the original perfection or "rightness" of our nature is still there operative within us, though now no longer sufficient of itself to save us from sin. The dominion of sin can only be broken by a power not our own, the power of divine grace.

Recognizing this polarity at the heart of man's moral nature, the Hebraic conception refuses to countenance either the fatuous optimism of the Rousseauistic[27] doctrine of the "natural goodness" of man or the hopeless pessimism of the ultra-Calvinistic doctrine of his utter depravity.[28] Nor can it accept either idealism, which pretends that man is still in his unfallen state and therefore capable of apprehending in reason the ultimate truth of things, or naturalism, which takes the fallen state as normal, ignores the divine image in man and treats him as if he were nothing but an animal organism. The Hebraic conception is at once more realistic and more complex, for it sees man in his duality and conflict, in the tension of struggle out of which is generated that tragic sense of life which is the mark of high religion.

As man faces God in obedience, rebellion and repentance, so God confronts man as Judge and Father. These two terms, drawn from our earthly experience, have been found to be most adequate for expressing the ever-threatening judgment and the never-failing love that meet us in the divine-human encounter. The rabbinic doctrine of the twin "attributes" of justice and mercy[29] is rooted in and is continuous with the teachings of Scripture about the God who is the righteous "Judge of all the earth" (Gen. 18: 25) and yet is "merciful and gracious, slow to anger, . . . forgiving iniquity and transgression and sin" (Exod 34: 6-7). The righteousness of God places all our enterprises, all our ideas, interests and activities, under a pitiless and inescapable judgment. It is a judgment under which we stand every moment of our lives and before which all our inadequacies and perversities are laid bare. It is a judgment that is partially executed in the course of life and history but which always hangs over us as a final judgment-to-come in which a full reckoning will be required and given. We of today should not find it so hard to recapture some of this sense of the urgency and immediacy of judgment if we bethink ourselves of the precariousness of our life and the abrupt end to which all our activities, individual and collective, may be brought at any moment. How large, how significant, how pure, how decent, will we and our enterprises appear in the perspective of that moment? But that moment is *every* moment, is *now*.[30]

The consciousness of God as Judge brings to focus the perennial crisis of life. For what is crisis, even in the popular sense, but a crucial event demanding decision and entailing judgment? In the more ultimate sense, it is the divine demand breaking through the routine of life, the response to that demand in decision, and the judgment that follows. The demand may come directly to us in the inner life of the spirit or it may arise out of the context of the social and historical situation—here the two meanings of crisis converge; but in whatever way it comes, it comes as a call and an obligation. Our response is decision: we may, like Adam, run and try to hide or, like Abraham, reply, Here am I. In making our decision in response to the call, we bring ourselves and our works under the judgment of a power that is not ours but which we cannot help but acknowledge. This is the crisis situation—call, decision, judgment—in which each of us stands at every moment of life.[31] It is a situation in which man would be utterly lost were it not for the resources of divine love.

The affirmation of God as Father is one of the oldest expressions of Hebraic spirituality and it remains the pervasive and underlying conception of rabbinic Judaism through the ages.[32] The fatherhood of God implies both authority and protection, and originally, it seems, both were equally stressed. But as, with time, the aspect of authority came to be associated with the divine kingship, fatherhood came to mean primarily love and mercy, and this in an absolute sense: God loves all men, all creatures, even the wicked. Not even sin can annul or destroy this relation; on the contrary, it is precisely when man is lost in sin and alienated from God that the divine fatherhood means so much to him, for it then means the ever-available possibility of repentance and return. When Jeremiah, at God's command, bade the Israelites repent, a rabbinic commentary tells us, [33] they exclaimed out of the depths of their despair: "How can we repent? With what countenance can we come before him,  steeped as we are in our wickedness and sin?" Whereupon God commanded the Prophet to return and say to the people in the Lord's name: "If you come near to me, is it not your Father in heaven that you approach? Will I not give ear to you, my children?" The fatherhood of God, with the unfailing love and tender concern that it implies, is the one sure resource we possess against the oppressions of the world and the crushing burden of guilt that we in our perversity bring upon ourselves.

In the liturgy, which so well reveals the profoundest aspects of Jewish religion, the appellation of Father is frequently linked to that of King, without mitigating the love and tenderness of the one or the awe and majesty of the other. It is the final paradox of the transcendent yet always available God, the God who is "supramundane, throned high above the world" but never "aloof or inaccessible in his remote exaltation."[34] The invocation "Our Father, Our King" thus embodies the ultimate reach of Hebraic spirituality: the affirmation of the Living God as the supreme power in the life of man.

It is precisely this ultimate affirmation of God as Father and King that has been taken by many modern psychologists, following in the tradition of Freud, as their point of vantage for the deflation of religion. "Psychoanalysis," Theodor Reik tells us in his significant work on ritual, "has proved that the idea of God in the life of the individual and of the people has its origin in the veneration and exaltation of the father. . .Psychoanalysis has proved the deity to be the deified father."[35] And indeed we must recognize that the connection to which the Freudians point is a very real one: who can deny that our thinking about God is in some sense related to the father-image built up in infancy and childhood? But while the connection is real, the relation is in actuality something very different from what the Freudians assume.

Taking Freud's and Reik's findings at their face value, what do they actually prove? Do they prove that God is simply the "deified father," that "the idea of God. . .has its origin in the veneration and exaltation of the father"? A moment of sober thought is enough to show how unwarranted is such a conclusion. At most, what the findings of psychoanalysis show is that *when man comes to think or feel about God, he does so in terms of a superfather,* transferring to the deity the now unconscious images and emotions which in childhood arose in relation to the father. This is an important but not particularly subversive conclusion; it is, in fact, no more than is implied in the use of Our Father as an appellation for God. In trying to express our ideas and feelings about God, we must, as we have already seen, necessarily employ a vocabulary borrowed from the natural relations of life; to use this fact as evidence that God is *nothing but* what our vocabulary literally means is very crude reasoning. A king, too, is a father-substitute; so is some very wise and stern teacher. Shall we therefore conclude that the "idea of King" or the "idea of Teacher" has its origin in "the veneration and exaltation of the father" in the sense that Teacher and King are nothing but figments of the unconscious imagination? Is everything that becomes the object of a father-projection to be reduced to illusion simply on that account? Absurd as it is, this is precisely the logic of the Freudian argument against God. The fact of the matter is that Freud and many of his followers, in their positivistic, even materialistic, philosophy of life, which has nothing to do with the findings of psychoanalysis, simply *assume* that God is unreal and then, of course, have no difficulty in extracting that conclusion from their argument. They do not see that no findings of theirs can possibly have any bearing on the reality of God since the reality of God is affirmed and has meaning on a level that empirical inquiry cannot reach. They do not see—and that is even more remarkable, for psychoanalytic thinkers are generally men of insight and penetration—that the very tendency to project the father-image as God already *presupposes* an impulse in man toward the divine and cannot therefore be used to explain its origin.[36] How could man ever come to invent an entirely fictitious entity upon which to project the father-image? Is not the universal human propensity to do so itself evidence of something in the human mind that points beyond itself? One would have thought that the psychoanalyst, with his sensitivity to 'he involutions and subtleties of the human psyche, would be the first to see this; yet, as a matter of fact, he has rarely done so. His failure, it seems to me, is very largely due to the stultifying effects of the pitifully inadequate philosopy that Freud took over from nineteenth-century materialism and passed on to his disciples as part of his legacy.

C. G. Jung is a depth-psychologist who has explicitly rejected the materialistic philosophy of earlier days and has taken a positve attitude to religion, to which he grants considerable place in his system. Yet Jung's vindication of religion is strangely ambiguous and equivocal. This great psychologist relates religion to the "racial archetypes" or "primordial images," which he holds to be more basic than rational thought. "Thinking in primordial images," he writes, "[is thinking] in symbols which are older than historical man, which have been ingrained in him from earliest times and, eternally living, outlasting all generations, still make up the groundwork of the human psyche. . . Wisdom is a return to them. . ."[37] Religion is rooted in these "primordial images" of the soul and is for that reason psychologically justified. Science can raise no objection since, as Jung emphasizes, "science and these symbols are incommensurable."

We need not here inquire as to the validity of the "racial unconscious" and the other concepts upon which Jung's doctrine seems to depend. What is much more important for our purpose is to note that the Jungian vindication of religion in terms of "primordial images" serves equally well to vindicate any religion, the most pagan and idolatrous as well as the purest. The heathen abominations of Canaan against which the prophets stormed were presumably as deeply and authentically rooted in the "primordial images" of the race as the religion of the prophets themselves. And today, Jung's psychological profundities provide the apologetic for a loose and undisciplined neo-pagan mysticism that is becoming increasingly fashionable as sophisticated religion for disillusioned moderns. It is, in any case, profoundly repugnant to the Hebraic spirit, which looks with deep suspicion on the obscure promptings of "natural" religion as essentially pagan and grounds its faith not in "racial archetypes" but in the revelation of the Living God.

No, our religious affirmation neither needs nor can make use of such vindication. Psychology, both Freudian and Jungian, can throw a great deal of valuable light on the various aspects of the religious "problem." But the fundamental affirmation of faith comes into being on a level of existential reality that not even the deepest of depth-psychology can reach.

In this existential affirmation of faith, which shatters and reconstitutes our very being, we learn with a sureness which no merely empirical knowledge can give that there is no reality more potent, more pervasive, more directly operative in human life than the power of the Living God. It is this power that creates and sustains the universe, that calls man into being and endows him with the spirit which transforms him from a natural organism into a creature "gifted with sight, with knowledge of good and evil," with the capacity for responsibility and decision. It is this power which calls us to fellowship with the divine in humility, faith and obedience and at the same time stands in judgment over every human enterprise that is not single-mindedly ordered to the service of God. It is this power that, as divine anger, condemns us to wretchedness and despair whenever, out of sinful pride, we defy God and deny his sovereign will. But it is also this power that, as divine mercy, offers us the unfailing resource of grace by which we may, if we will, be saved from the utter forlornness of a life cut off from God. It is this power that gives meaning and promise of fulfilment to life amidst its confusions, frustrations and defeats and thus provides us with a transcendent security that nothing can shake. The Living God, in the Hebraic faith, is indeed the beginning and end of everything. Without Him, there is no life, no hope, no meaning; with Him—in love and obedience to Him—life is transfigured and begins to assume the quality and dimensions which belong to it in the order of creation.

## NOTES TO CHAPTER 8

1. Bertrand Russell, "A Free Man's Worship," *Mysticism and Logic* (Norton: New York, 1929), p. 48.

2. Pascal, *Pensées*, No. 434.

3. Friedrich Engels, *Dialectics of Nature* (International Publishers: New York, 1940), p. 87.

4. "For the Hebrew, man is not a being composed of two distinct and separable entities—body and soul—but an unanalyzed complex psychophysical unity . . . The Hebrew conception of the personality of man is that of an unbroken integrated unity which is identified with the animated body . . . The Hebrew, unlike the Greek, recognizes no antithesis between flesh and soul . . . Soul and body are interfused with a completeness which it is difficult for us to understand . . . For the Hebrew, there is no antithesis between the outward and the inward, the physical and the psychical, the material and the spiritual . . . The psychical is unknown apart from the physical centers through which it is manifested . . . Man's personality is always identified with the animated body; hence it is always conceived as an indivisible organism functioning as an integrated unity . . . ." Harold Knight, *The Hebrew Prophetic Consciousness* (Lutterworth: London, 1947), pp. 8, 10, 11, 51, 67, 125. See also Otto J. Baab, *The Theology of the Old Testament* (Abingdon-Cokesbury: Nashville, Tenn., 1949), pp. 65, 66, 68, 214, 264.

5. This many psychoanalytic writers, following Freud, seem to forget when they tend to picture all "drives" emerging from the id as instinctual impulses of a simple biological character. In man, there are no simply

biological, instinctual impulses; in man, every natural impulse is transformed into a spiritual force.

6. Sören Kierkegaard, *The Sickness Unto Death* (Princeton University: Princeton, N. J., 1941), p. 17.

7. Martin Buber, *I and Thou* (T. & T. Clark: Edinburgh, 1937), p. 20: "Through the *Thou* a man becomes an *I*." "The 'I' can be personal . . . only when it is confronted by a 'Thou.' To live personally means to live in responsibility and love." Emil Brunner. *The Divine Imperative* (Westminster: Philadelphia, 1947), p. 191.

8. "It is only through God's calling Adam, 'Where art thou?', that the latter's 'Here I am' reveals to man, in the answer, his being as related to God. The ego is at the outset wrapped up in itself and dumb; it waits for its being called—directly by God and indirectly by the neighbor." Thus Karl Löwith summarizes the teaching of Franz Rosenzweig on man's responsive nature. "M. Heidegger and F. Rosenzweig," *Philosophy and Phenomenological Research*, Vol. III (September, 1942), No. 1.

9. Buber, *I and Thou*, p. 39.

10. Buber, *I and Thou*, pp. 6, 75 and *passim; Between Man and Man* (Kegan Paul: London, 1947), pp. 43, 50, 97 and *passim.* "He to whom and by whom the word is spoken is, in the full sense of the word, a *person*. . . .In order to speak to man, God must become a person; but in order to speak to him, he must make him too a person. This human person not only adopts the word; it also answers." Buber, *The Prophetic Faith* (Macmillan: New York, 1949), pp. 164-65.

11. Ernst Simon refers to the "salient point which distinguishes the people of the ear and obedience from the people of the eye and imitation, Israel from Hellas." "Notes on Jewish Wit," *Jewish Frontier*, Vol XV (October, 1948), No. 10.

12. F. J. E. Woodbridge, *An Essay on Nature* (Columbia University: New York, 1940), p. 279.

13. A. J. Heschel, *Die Prophetie* (Polish Academy of Sciences: Cracow, 1936), p. 50.

14. E. A. Burtt, "Does Humanism Understand Man?" *The Humanist*, Vol. V (Autumn [Oct.], 1945), No. 3; "Humanism and the Doctrine of Sin," *The Humanist*, Vol. V (Winter [Jan.], 1946), No. 4.

15. "The unformulated primal theological principle of the Garden of Eden story about the divine-human relationship [is] . . . that created man has been provided by the Creator's breath with real power of decision and so is able actually to oppose YHVH's commanding will . . . ." Buber, *Prophetic Faith*, p. 103.

16. "In its inner aspects, sin is [held by the prophets to be] revolt against the authority of God, failure to recognize his sovereignty, disobedience to a higher will, because man places his own will or the sovereignty of someone else above the sovereign power of Almighty God. In its outer aspect, sin is a deviation from a moral standard set up by God." J. Philip Hyatt,

*Prophetic Religion* (Abingdon-Cokesbury: Nashville, Tenn., 1947), pp. 162-63.

17."This image [of God in man] is defaced by sin." Solomon Schechter, "The History of Jewish Tradition," *Studies in Judaism:* First Series (Jewish Publication Society: Philadelphia, 1945), p. 199.

18. "It is the condition of the sailor climbing the mast (to use a simile), with the abyss of the waves beneath him and the 'crow's nest' above him. He is anxious about both the end toward which he strives and the abyss of nothingness into which he may fall." Reinhold Niebuhr, *The Nature and Destiny of Man* (Scribner's: New York, 1941), I, 185.

19. See Reinhold Niebuhr, *The Nature and Destiny of Man*, I. chaps. vii and viii, esp. pp. 178-79.

20. Schechter, "Saints and Saintliness," *Studies in Judaism:* Second Series, p. 167.

21. Schechter, *Some Aspects of Rabbinic Theology* (Macmillan: New York, 1909), pp. 243, 262.

22. George Foot Moore, *Judaism* (Harvard University: Cambridge, Mass., 1927), I, 484.

"From the moment a man is born, the evil *yetzer* clings to him." Abot de Rabbi Nathan, 32; Schechter, *Some Aspects*, p. 255.

"The inclination of man's heart is evil from his youth." Gen. 8:21.

"The criminal," says David Abrahamsen (*Crime and the Human Mind* [Columbia University: New York, 1944], p. 59), "acts as the child would act—if the child was permitted to."

23. Schechter, *Some Aspects*, pp. 254-55.

24. *B.* Sukkah 52.

25. *B.* Yoma 38; C. G. Montefiore and H. Loewe, *A Rabbinic Anthology* (Macmillan: London, 1938), p. 293.

"The underlying idea of these [rabbinic] passages, which can be multiplied by any number of parallel passages, is man's consciousness of his helplessness against the powers of temptation, which can only be overcome by the grace of God." Schechter, *Some Aspects*, p. 280.

26. T. S. Eliot, "The Hollow Men," *Collected Poems* (Harcourt, Brace: New York, 1936), p. 104.

"The act shows forth its essence beyond itself. However free it may be in its intention, however pure in its appearance, it is at the mercy of its own consequences. The most exalted act, entering the world without the slightest regard for causality, is dragged along in its wake just as soon as it sees the light." Buber, *Der heilige Weg* (Literarische Anstalt Rütten & Loening: Frankfort, 1920), pp. 23-24.

27. "Rousseauistic" and "Calvinistic" are here used conventionally. Rousseau himself apparently had a rather more complex view of human nature (A. O. Lovejoy, "The Supposed Primitivism of Rousseau," *Essays in the History of Ideas* [Johns Hopkins: Baltimore, 1948]), while Calvin, though

## 86    Judaism and Modern Man

believing that *all* aspects of the human spirit were corrupted by sin, does not seem to have asserted that sinful man was *utterly* depraved (*Institute of the Christian Religion*, II, iii, 3;I, xv, 1-6).

28. Freud quite properly deplores the damage done by the utopian idealization of human nature in the education of children: "The upbringing of young people at the present day . . . offends too in not preparing them for the aggressions of which they are destined to become the object . . One clearly sees that ethical standards are being misused in a way. The strictness of these standards would not do much harm if education were to say: 'This is how men ought to be in order to be happy and make others happy, but you have to reckon with their not being so.' Instead of this, the young are made to believe that everyone else conforms to the standard of ethics, i.e., that everyone else is good. And then on this is based the demand that the young shall be so too." *Civilization and Its Discontents* (Hogarth: London, 1930), pp. 123-24, footnote. This criticism is valid when directed against secular humanism and "liberal" religion, which have so strongly obscured the biblical doctrine of man. But Freud himself sometimes tends to lapse into an attitude very close to an affirmation of man's utter depravity (pp. 79 ff.).

29. "The two aspects of God's character which are here displayed, his mercy and his justice, are the essential moral attributes on which religion in Jewish conception is founded . . . In the Palestinian schools, justice and mercy are frequently coupled as the primary 'norms' of God's dealing with men individually and collectively." Moore, *Judaism*, I, 386-87, with documentation.

30. The sense of standing constantly under judgment is powerfully conveyed in the saying attributed to R. Akabya b. Mahalalel: "Keep in view three things . . . Know whence thou comest and wither thou goest and before whom thou art to give strict account. Whence thou comest—from a fetid drop. Whither thou goest—to the place of dust, worms and maggots. Before whom thou art to give strict account—before the King of Kings, the Holy One blessed is He." *M.* Abot 3. 1.

31. "To be religious [Agus writes, describing Buber's view] is to be actual, to live in perpetual conversation with God—a conversation which, coming from God to us, is expressed in the needs of the situation as understood by man . . . and which, returning from us to God, is concretized in the form of deed performed to meet those needs." Jacob Agus, *Modern Philosophies of Judaism* (Behrmans: New York, 1941), p. 260.

32. Moore, *Judaism*, II, 201-11.

"The idea of the Fatherhood of God is very ancient, older even than the idea of God as King." Millar Burrows, *An Outline of Biblical Theology* (Westminster: Philadelphia, 1946), p. 72.

33. Pesikta de-Rab Kahana (ed. Buber), 165a.

34. Moore, *Judaism*, I, 368. "The sense of God's majesty is combined

with an equally strong sense of his nearness and goodness" (Burrows, *op. cit.*, p. 65).

35. Theodor Reik, *Ritual: Psychoanalytic Studies* (Farrar, Straus: New York, 1946), pp. 73, 76.

In the preface to Reik's book, Freul writes: "God the father at one time walked incarnate on the earth and exercised his sovereignty as leader of the hordes of primitive men until his sons combined together and slew him" (p. 11). This view underlies Freud's psycho-anthropological conception of religion as presented particularly to *Totem and Taboo* and *Moses and Monotheism*.

36. A very similar line of argument reveals the fallacy of the familiar Freudian reduction of the conscience via the Super-ego to the Oedipus complex. See chap. 9, note 7, below.

37. C. G. Jung, *Modern Man in Search of a Soul* (Kegan Paul: London, 1933), p. 234.

# 9. THE DIVINE IMPERATIVE: ETHICS AND RELIGION

## I

One of the most familiar aspects of the contemporary cult of "scientism" is the conviction that science, and science alone, can afford a secure foundation for our moral standards. Ethics must become scientific, is the watchword of our time, or at least it was until we began to have our doubts about science itself.

As a matter of fact, the idea behind this slogan is by no means new. In another form and in another vocabulary, it was the idea that dominated much of Greek philosophy and that has persisted in the thinking that derives from the Greek tradition. But it is not an idea that can find lodgment in authentic Hebraic religion. For the Hebraic conception of the role of ethics, of the source and sanction of moral obligation, is such that is brings Jewish teaching into significant opposition to rationalist philosophy while keeping it close to the facts of existence.

In their basic presuppositions, the two approaches to ethics—and to religion as well, for Judaism insists that religion and ethics are not ultimately separable—represent two radically opposed attitudes to life and the world. All attempts to combine and reconcile them must in the end prove futile. We in our time still use much of the religious vocabulary derived from Hebraic sources, but, at bottom, our ethical thinking, insofar as it is systematic and reflective, is dominated by the Greek-rationalist tradition. This is true even for modern positivism, which makes such a violent gesture at repudiating "metaphysics."

What is the essential Greek-rationalist view and how does it differ from the ethics of Hebraic religion? Despite all secondary variations, Greek thought, and the thought that follows in Greek paths, holds to the fundamental idea that ethics—the principles of right and wrong, of good and evil—can be deduced by reason from the nature of things, including the nature of man. Nature reveals to the mind the true values of human life and therefore also man's duties and responsibilities. "Follow nature" seems to be the first and last word of Greek ethics, however variously nature is interpreted. The true prescriptions of morality are conceived to be essentially "laws of nature" and it is for human reason to discover and obey them.

In this rationalist scheme, religion is only incidental. Reason teaches man his duties and responsibilities, among which are certain duties he owes to the gods: these constitute religion in its formal aspect. Religion in Greek thought, if it is not altogether ignored, is thus relegated to the status of a rather minor subdivision of ethics.

Greek ethical rationalism may therefore be said to exhibit two crucial features. On the one hand, it relies upon reason to derive moral principles from the nature of things, or, as we would put it, to extract values and obligations from what are held to be facts, metaphysical or empirical. On the other hand, it converts religion into a mere branch of the ethical system thus derived. In effect, human reason is omnipotent and autonomous; it is a law unto itself. Both of these aspects of Greek rationalism have had a powerful influence on Western thought; even Kant, who challenged the former, only the more emphatically reiterated the latter.

Modern criticism has called into question the possibility of deducing value from fact. From mere facts nothing but facts can ever be derived. The distinction between that which *is* and that which *ought to be* is the starting point of all ethics; no one, however, can possibly infer the latter from the former. Earlier thinkers who claimed to be able to perform this intellectual miracle can be shown to have accomplished their result by a kind of logical sleight of hand.[1] Not only did they use the word "nature" ambiguously, sometimes to designate how things actually are and at other times to imply how things ought to be; they also unwittingly introduced affirmations of value in a line of argument supposedly dealing only with fact. Strangely enough, they did not see that had they really succeeded in proving that moral principles could be derived from the facts of existence, they would have destroyed the *imperative* nature of these principles. Fact are facts; they must be acknowledged as facts, but no one is obliged to *approve* of them unless he starts with the principle that "whatever is, is right."

Boas has well formulated the conclusion of modern critical thought in this respect. "That one cannot argue from existence to value," he says, "has become almost a philosophic dogma and the break between the two realms would seem to be absolute as far as deduction is concerned. . . .We could theoretically state the conditions under which evaluations are made and explain psychologically why they are made. But that does not 'reduce' values to facts. . . ."[2] If this is the case, and it is hard to see how this conclusion can be disputed, not only is traditional rationalism deprived of the ground it stands on but the attempts still being made to validate ethics "scientifically" are called into serious question. For exactly the same fallacies and confusions are involved. Not so long ago the "social Darwinists" tried to justify imperialism and capitalism on the ground that these were in line with the "struggle for existence" in biologic evolution. At about the same time, Kropotkin turned the argument around and built up a case for libertarian socialism from the tendencies to "mutual aid" that he found in nature. In both cases, the argument proved nothing. The course of biologic evolution may conceivably show us how life has developed hitherto but it cannot possibly prove that any line of human action is right or wrong, good or evil. We are back again to the old fallacy: "nature" is simply fact, and not all fact, obviously, is to be morally approved simply because it is fact. Nature may be "red in tooth and claw," as Thomas Henry Huxley thought,[3] or it may be quite peaceable and co-operative, as Kropotkin urged, but that does not tell us how *we* ought to be. No amount of evolution will evolve an *obligation* out of the story of how things have developed in the past or are developing today. This is as true for social as for biological evolution. Socialism cannot be validated simply by pointing to the "inherent" tendencies of social and economic development; such an argument may prove that socialism is bound to come but not that it is right and good. "Whatever is, is right" does not become any more cogent by being turned into "whatever will be, is right." Facts, whether past, present, or future, cannot claim moral status simply because they are facts; moral judgment must somehow transcend factuality if it is to make any sense at all.

There are not lacking bolder spirits among contemporary thinkers who accept this conclusion, but in negative form. Since moral judgment cannot be reduced to a factual statement, they argue, moral judgments simply do not make sense. They are meaningless as statements because they are, at bottom, merely the verbal expression of private emotions. To say that slavery is "wrong" is in the last analysis no different from making a wry face and exclaiming in disgust over some unpalatable food. This is the point of view of consistent positivism. It is based on the premise that, aside from the rules of logic, only scientific statements, only statements of fact, have any meaning. This premise is a gratuitous assumption affirmed as a dogma; it is, moreover, self-destructive. Not only does it sweep away as so much nonsense virtually all human thinking—all, that is, but what has been devoted to logic and empirical science; in the end, it turns upon and destroys itself. For the basic doctrine of positivism, as thus defined, is itself obviously neither a principle of logic nor the conclusion of any particular empirical science; it is therefore, by its own criterion, nonsense. "The fundamental conviction of this school," it has been well said, "is that philosophy has but one task to perform—to undo all the harm it has created and then quietly commit suicide."[4]

The "Greek" way, whether rationalist or positivist, thus leads nowhere. Neither nature nor science will yield ethics. Science, Bertrand Russell points out, "is ethically neutral; it assures men that they can perform wonders but does not tell them what wonders to perform."[5]

Even Julian Huxley, who ordinarily worships at the altar of science, comes to much the same conclusion.[6] Science is without a scale of values. Where then shall we look for the spring and source of the moral life?

In religion, is the answer of Hebraic thought. Man's moral nature—his capacity for judgment and decision, his responsibility—is itself, as we have seen, a manifestation of the "image of God" in which he is made, and thus ultimately intelligible only in religious terms. "Conscience and every moral consciousness," Kierkegaard concludes, "presupposes God, for to have a conscience is to relate oneself to God."[7] Conscience is, in fact, a mark of the original perfection in sinful man and thus points beyond the mere factuality of existence to the divine order of creation. Hebraic thought, therefore, starts not with self-sufficient nature or reason from which everything relating to human life is to be deduced, but with the will of God. Ethics, dealing with man's duties and responsibilities in the world of men, is developed as an aspect of the religious obligation. Instead of religion being relegated to the periphery of ethics, one's moral outlook is seen to be the consequence and reflection of one's fundamental religious affirmation, of the kind of god one serves. Ethics is not merely central to Jewish religion; it is, in fact, inseparable from it as one of its most essential manifestations. Long ago, Josephus, who undertook the task of interpreting the Jewish outlook to the Greek world, put the matter in succinct and pregnant form. "Moses," he said, "did not make religion a part of virtue [i.e., ethics], but he saw and ordained the virtues to be part of religion. . . , for all our actions and all our words have a reference to piety towards God."[8]

The moral principles of Western civilization are, in fact, all derived from the tradition rooted in Scripture and have vital meaning only in the context of that tradition. The attempt made in recent decades by secularist thinkers to disengage these values from their religious context, in the assurance that they could live a life of their own as a "humanistic" ethic, has resulted in what one writer has called our "cut-flower" culture. Cut flowers retain their original beauty and fragrance, but only so long as they retain the vitality they have drawn from their now severed roots; after that is exhausted, they wither and die. So with freedom, brotherhood, justice and personal dignity—the values that form the moral foundation of our civilization. Without the life-giving power of the faith out of which they have sprung, they possess neither meaning nor vitality. Morality ungrounded in God is indeed a house built upon sand, unable to stand up against the vagaries of impulse and the brutal pressures of power and self-interest.

## II

Judaism relates the ethical obligation to man's free obedience to God. Man's freedom—his capacity for genuine decision—is taken as fundamental, for without it there could be neither religion nor ethics. Even under the bondage of sin, man does not lose this freedom; even God's providence is no denial of it. "All is foreseen," we are told, "yet freedom of choice is given." "Everything is in the hand of Heaven except the fear of Heaven."[9]

Human freedom has always been a great paradox for philosopher and theologian. Neither Plato nor the modern naturalist can find a place for it in his system. As we have seen, contemporary naturalism regards man as simply part of nature and therefore does not hesitate to insert him into a scheme of causal determinism that leaves no room for freedom, reason or moral responsibility. For all its "idealism," the Platonic tradition leaves man in but little better plight. In this tradition, it will be recalled, the body is the principle of evil, while the mind, or reason, is the principle of good. The two are in perpetual conflict. It is a struggle in which "the victory of reason over the passions, or its defeat by them, depends entirely upon the relative strength or weakness of these two contestants. If, therefore, we had a gauge by which we could measure the relative strength or weakness of mind and body, we could at any given moment predict the outcome of the conflict between them . . . For man there is no choice in the matter . . . There is no such third factor as a will, conceived as something autonomous . . ."[10]

If man is to have a "choice in the matter," some very different frame of reference is required, and that frame of reference we find in the religious philosophy of Judaism. Man possesses freedom and the power of decision because he is more than merely part of nature and therefore transcends the limitations of causal determinism, not simply the scientific determinism of naturalist philosophy but also the "ideal-istic" determinism of Plato. In the Jewish view, there is no situation in which man finds himself that is without some margin of freedom of decision and responsibility. Man possesses a will which, however conditioned by external factors of nature and society, however distort-ed by sin, is yet, in the final analysis, free and self-determining.[11] As Philo puts it—and here Philo is true to his Judaism and at sharp vari-ance with his master, Plato—God gave to man a portion "of that free will which is his most peculiar possession and most worthy of his ma-jesty." Man's freedom, the power by which he is raised above natural determinism, is thus "nothing but a part of God's own freedom, with which man is endowed by God."[12] It is the "image of God" in man, full of infinite potentiality for good or evil.

Whether this freedom operates for the one or the other depends, in the Jewish view, upon man's basic orientation, upon the direction of his will, upon the placement of his love. Man is meant for fellowship with God; that is his "essential nature" in creation. He is meant to walk with his Creator in humility and love. He is meant to conduct his life in the ever-present awareness of the divine source and center of his being. This, as we have seen, is the significance of the Scrip-tural account of the blissful life in Paradise before the Fall. It is the *normative* condition of human existence, bringing peace and harmony within and without.

This peace is lost and this harmony disrupted the moment man, in the exercise of his freedom, turns away from God and thus denies his own essential nature and the law of his being. Such is the meaning of sin—the "original" sin of Adam (man) in Paradise and the sin of each of us throughout our lives.

But man cannot go on without some ultimate to give substance and meaning to life. Having, in the wilfulness of sin, turned away from the Living God, he is driven to seek for a ground of existence in what is not God. This is idolatry.

Idolatry, in Jewish thinking, is the root source of all wrongdoing and moral evil.[13] But to grasp the full scope and significance of this principle it is necessary to understand the essential meaning of idolatry. Idolatry is not simply the worship of sticks and stones, or it would obviously have no relevance to our times. *Idolatry is the absolutization of the relative;* it is absolute devotion paid to anything short of the Absolute. The object of idolatrous worship may be, and in fact generally is, some *good;* but, since it is not God, it is necessarily a good that is only partial and relative.[14] What idolatry does is to convert its object into an absolute, thereby destroying the partial good within it and transforming it into a total evil. Jewish tradition tells us that idols are both "vanities" and "demons." They are "vanities" because they are foolishness, illusory in their unreal and unwarranted claims to independent being. They are "demons" because, as the objects of such absolute worship, they become sources of corruption and chaos, of violence and perversion, in human life. No wonder Judaism has always had such a horror of idolatry and has made rejection of it central to all its codes, even to those which, like the so-called Noahite laws, were conceived as binding upon non-Israelites as well.

Contemporary life is idolatry-ridden to an appalling degree. Man, it cannot be too often repeated, must fix his devotion and anchor his being in something ultimate, and if it is not the Living God, it will be some spurious substitute. "It is impossible to be a man and not bow down to something," Dostoevski says in *A Raw Youth.* "Such a man could not bear the burden of himself . . . If he rejects God, then he bows down to an idol . . . fashioned of wood or of gold or of thought. . . ." The vacuum created by the decay of traditional religion in our time has been filled by the influx of a legion of devils demanding idolatrous worship.

Even the ancient nature cults find their representation in modern idolatry. What is the cult of "life" as we find it under various guises in the Romantics, in Nietzsche, in the ecstatic worship of sex and the "dark forces" of instinct, and most crassly perhaps, in the Nazi religion of "blood and soil," but an orgiastic exaltation of the powers and vitalities of nature that recalls the frenzied "nature" rite of long ago? But the dominant idolatries of our time are not so much the primitivistic cults of "nature" as the cults of collective man and objectified ideas. Race, nation, empire, class, state or party, even church and humanity, these are among the gods who claim the allegiance of modern man; so are science, culture, social reform, progress. Each of these things represents a significant and valuable aspect of human life; each of them, however, becomes delusive and demonic once it is absolutized and exalted into the god of our existence.

Even so useful a thing as scientific research may be idolized and turned into a demonic force of destruction. When "scientific truth"—which is, after all, no more than the accurate reporting of what happens under specified conditions—is held to be the only or the ultimate truth, and its acquisition is exalted into the be-all and end-all of existence, what is there to inhibit anyone from treating the rest of mankind as so much material to be manipulated or expended as science may dictate? How, in terms of the value-system of science *taken as ultimate,* can we condemn or criticize such overzealous devotees of pursuit of "scientific truth"? The squeamishness that recoils from treating human beings as guinea pigs is felt to be nothing more than irrational sentimentality obstructing the progress of science, and if science and scientific method are, indeed, absolutes, all such obstacles must obviously be brushed aside. The horrible barbarities practiced under the Nazi regime by German scientists in the name of scientific research arise to remind us that the logic of science absolutized is not merely theoretical but possesses a monstrous actuality in the present-day world.

Our modern world is as filled with idolatry as the world ever was, but our modern idolatry differs from the idolatries of the pagan world in a way more fundamental than mere difference in what we tend to idolize. Pagan idolators worship their idols directly and unashamedly; they know no higher law. We, on the contrary, whose entire culture is permeated with the "God-idea" of Judaism and Christianity, cannot simply convert our false absolutes into acknowledged idols. We generally carry idolatry a step further. We convert God himself into an idol, or rather we make God into the sanctifier and protector of the idols we really love with all our heart and all our might. We speak of God and honor him, but the god we are really honoring, what is he but the god whom we look to to promote our interests and guarantee our ideals? Our modern idolatries are thus like the Baal practices of the Israelites in Canaan, modes of everyday life rather than explicit confessions of faith.[15] They are, perhaps, all the more dangerous on that account.

It is this idolatry that is the root source of our sin and wrongdoing.

Ultimately, all idolatry is worship of the self projected and objectified:
all idolization is self-idolization, individual or collective. In exalting
the natural vitalities of life, we exalt and lose ourselves in the vitalities
of our own nature. In absolutizing the collectivities or movements of
which we form part, we but absolutize ourselves writ large. In proclaiming as ultimate the ideas and programs to which we are devoted,
we are but proclaiming the work of our minds to be the final truth
of life. In the last analysis, the choice is only between love of God and
love of self, between a *God*-centered and *self*-centered existence.[16]
Sin is *ego*centricity as against *theo*centricity. It is, in effect, denying
God and making oneself, in direct or indirect form, the god of one's
universe.[17]

The ultimate imperative of Jewish ethics is, therefore, the affirmation of the Living God and the repudiation of idolatry. It is an imperative that is not really ethical at all, but religious: "Thou shalt love
the Lord thy God with all thy heart, with all thy soul, with all thy
might" (Deut. 6:5). With the love of God thus enjoined, love of self
is entirely incompatible.[18] Love of God is love exclusive in its claim
because God cannot be made to share his ultimacy. The universe of
our existence can have but one source and center, and if that source
and center is not *entirely* God, it is not God at all but the self.
Exclusive love in the absolute sense is the claim that God makes
upon man. It is a claim that we perceive only in faith and can meet
only because we are empowered with God's gracious love for us. The
exclusive love which the Bible requires is a responsive love, a love of
which we are capable only when we come to realize how infinite is the
lovingkindness which God manifests to us. The claim is thus a claim
of love; but once acknowledged in faith, it calls for unfaltering loyalty
and obedience: "And now, O Israel, what does the Lord your God
require of you but to fear the Lord your God, to walk in all his ways,
to love him and to serve him with all your heart and all your soul"
(Deut. 10:12). This obligation under which man is placed is a great
and fearful one, for it is nothing less than a call to perfection. "Walk
before me and be perfect" (Gen. 17:1), are the words in which Scripture records God's injunction to Abraham, and his words to Abraham
are his words to all of us. It is a call to holiness: "You shall be holy

for I the Lord your God am holy" (Lev. 19:2). It is, in short, a call to the imitation of God.[19]

The imitation of God may be taken as the operative formula of Jewish ethics. But imitation of God, walking in his ways, is never to be confused with the sinful and presumptuous effort to be "like unto God." It is to be imitation, no impersonation. The difference, rabbinical sources suggest, is like the difference between loving and obedient subjects who conform their will to the will of their king, on the one hand, and rebels who strive to set themselves up as rivals or even to usurp his throne, on the other. The primary condition—indeed, the presupposition and yet at the same time the final flower—of a life acceptable to God is humility.

All Scripture, all tradition, unite in extolling humility and in denouncing pride and presumption as the cardinal sin. Pride means "man setting himself up as an idol"; "it is tantamount to a defiance of God . . . and this corresponds to idol-worship"; it is "the mortal sin."[20] On the other hand, humility is proclaimed in the Talmud to be "the greatest of the ten steps in the ascent of the righteous."[21] Even Maimonides, who is otherwise so taken with the Aristotelian ethic and the "golden mean," draws the line when it comes to this most characteristic of Hebraic virtues. "There are," he states, "some dispositions in regard to which it is wrong to pursue a middle course, but the contrary extreme is to be embraced, as for instance in respect to pride. One does not follow the proper path by merely being humble. Men should be very humble and extremely meek. To this end Scripture says of Moses our Teacher that he was 'very meek' (Num. 12:3) . . . Therefore the command of the Sages is, 'Be thou very humble' (*M*. Abot 4.4), and they say furthermore that all who are proud-hearted deny an important principle of our faith. . . ."[22]

Humility is so central in Jewish ethics that "the man who has a taint of pride or insolence, though he be righteous and upright in all other respects," is held to be "worth nothing."[23] On the other hand, "whosoever abases himself, him God will exalt."[24] Self-righteousness —that is, righteousness without humility—must therefore be regarded as the most insidious and most dangerous form of pride: "Even if thou art perfect in all other respects, thou failest if thou hast no humility in thee."[25] When it reaches such a stage, humility is no longer simply a moral virtue; it transcends ethics, it is the shattering aware-ness of one's utter nothingness in the face of a holy God.

Walking in the ways of God in faith and humility means the love of fellow-man. Abba Saul expounds Exodus 15:2, which he reads "I will imitate him," as meaning: "As he [God] is gracious and merciful, be thou gracious and merciful."[26] With the injunction to love God is linked the command to love our neighbor as ourself, and the two are not two but one.[27] It is the love of God that, in its fulness, gives us the power to love our fellow-men in the radical sense required by the commandment:[28] we love with the love wherewith we are loved. On the other hand, as Buber points out, [29] it is only by achieving a "legiti-mate relation" to our neighbor that we can achieve such relation to God. The self that defies God by exalting itself into the center of all life is necessarily driven to wrong other men by striving to debase them into instrumentalities of its own paramount interests. It is from these insights, crucial to Hebraic religion, that the humanitarian and social-reform impulse of Western civilization is derived.

But why can we not affirm the law of love of fellow-man on its own ground without involving ourselves in any commitment about God? This is the question which the humanists of all ages have converted into the basis of their ethic without religion. It is, however, a basis that will not hold the superstructure erected upon it. For what ground is there for the affirmation of the love of fellow-man simply as such? *Why* love one's neighbor as oneself, especially when one's neighbor frequently turns out to be so unlovable? Because, says the humanist who has seen through the folly of the argument from self-interest, we are all human and are therefore as such entitled to the same treatment. But in virtue of what are we all human? Humanists have given vary-ing answers to this question, but, by and large, these answers may be grouped under two heads: (a) we are all human because we are all rational; and (b) we are all human because we all possess a moral sense. It is reason, moral sense or both that are felt to define human beings as human and to distinguish them from the rest of creation. But note, although we may all be rational, we are not all *equally* rational; although we may all possess a moral sense, we are not all *equally* endowed with that faculty. Some of us are more rational than others, some morally more sensitive and cultivated than others. From which it follows that even if we are in the abstract all human, some are in fact more human than others. And this is true no matter what attribute is taken ás defining humanness. An ethic grounded in humanistic premises thus leads inescapably to the conclusion that human beings are entitled to treatment in accord with the law of love *only to the degree* that they exhibit or embody the human-making quality. But this, of course, is the very denial of the law of love. There is no avoiding the conclusion that only in relation to the transcendent God who is our Father —a relation which humanism can make nothing of —do men come to possess the human character that binds them in love.

The incompatability of the law of love with the humanistic scheme of ethics would be much more obvious were not our contemporary humanists so thoroughly imbued with the moral values of the Judeo-Christian tradition which they have taken over with their cultural heritage; yet occasionally we do get a glimpse of what humanism in its pure form implies. Thus, Julien Benda, the eminent French publicist, writes:

> I speak of the person insofar as he presents the moral characteristics of the human species. My position—and here I am in opposition to the Church and to a certain type of democracy for which any man is sacred by reason solely of the fact that he presents the anatomical characteristics of the species—my position is that the human person has a right to this designation, and in consequence to the respect it implies, only if he has been capable of raising himself to a certain level of morality, one that consists precisely in respecting this personality in others—let us say if he has been able to rise to the conception of the rights of man. This amounts to saying that while I do not admit the concept of biological races, I do admit that of *moral* races.[30]

To hold a human being to be human only "insofar as he presents the moral characteristics of the human species"—in other words, the affirmation of the insufferably self-righteous doctrine of "moral races" —is precisely the logic of humanistic ethics, but it is utterly repugnant to the meaning of love as that is understood in Hebraic religion. In the great Hillel's understanding, "love of man . . . was an ideal only if it was universal in intent and extension; otherwise it was cant of the worst sort.[31] To the rabbis, it implies not merely loving one's neighbor (Lev. 19:18), not merely loving the "stranger" (Deut. 10:19), but also loving one's enemy. It means long-suffering, forgiveness and the return of good for evil. "They shall see the majesty of God," the Talmud tells us, "who meet with humiliation but do not humiliate, who bear insult but do not inflict it on others, who endure a life of suffering for the pure love of God."[32] The passage in Proverbs 25:21-22, which enjoins us to give our enemy food and drink, R. Hanina interprets to mean that even if the enemy come to our house to slay us and he is hungry and thirsty, we are to give him food and drink![33] There is no break in this tradition. The great moral teacher of the last century, R. Israel Salanter, insisted on the same doctrine and grounded it in the same principle. "Imitation of God is explicitly commanded in the Torah"—thus Professor Ginzberg reports Salanter's teaching [34]—"and accordingly it is our duty not only to confer an act of kindness upon those who have done harm to us but to do it at the very moment we are wronged. God is kind to the sinner at the time of his sin, since without the kindness of God that gives him life and strength he would not be able to sin, and we are to imitate him and so be like him. We must be kind to those who sin against us at the time of their wrongdoing."

Love of one's fellow-man, in Jewish tradition, is associated with an abiding sense of the dignity and worth of every individual human being as a person. It is a dignity and worth that man can claim not by virtue of his own merit but as the gracious gift of God. The worth and quality of the individual person are proclaimed in the Mishnah in a passage, part of which I have already quoted:

> Therefore but a single man was created in the world, to teach that if any man has caused a single soul to perish Scripture imputes it to him as though he had caused the whole world to perish; and if man saves alive a single soul Scripture imputes it to him as though he had saved alive the whole world . . . For man stamps many coins with the one seal and they are all like one another; but the King of Kings, the Holy One blessed is He, has stamped every man with the seal of the first man, yet not one of them is like his fellow. Therefore every one must say, For my sake was the world created.[35]

Every man is thus proclaimed—to use the Kantian formula obviously derived from the Hebraic tradition—to be, in relation to other men, an end in himself, though all men are ordained to God. Every man is a self, a subject, a person, a Thou[36]—and it is an offense against God to attempt to convert him into a thing, an object, an It, to be used for another's advantage.

Every man, as the bearer of the divine image, is endowed with freedom, self-determination and responsibility. Because every human being is of infinite worth in God's love—"A single person is equal [in value] to the entire universe," R. Nehemiah says[37]—men are essentially and intrinsically equal. Judaism knows nothing of the blasphemous doctrine of racialism, regardless of whether the lines along which mankind is alleged to be divided are biological, as in Nazi doctrine, or "moral," as in the teaching of certain self-righteous "democrats." All men have been created in the divine image and are therefore equally entitled to our love and respect: that is the unshakable principle of Jewish ethics.[38]

If man is enjoined to subordinate the self in love of God and fellowman, it is not because personality is evil and deserving of repression. On the contrary, the self really comes into its own only when, through transcending its own obsessive concerns and interests, it has achieved fellowship with God. It is in perfect abnegation that human personality attains its highest reach. "Is it thy wish not to die? Die; so that thou needst not die. Is it thy wish to live? Do not live; so that thou mayest live."[39] Life—self-fulfilment—like "peace of mind," cannot be gained by being directly striven for; it comes as the fruit of devoted, selfless service to God and man.

Jewish ethics is an ethic of perfection, for its goal and standard is nothing short of the perfect love of God and the perfect imitation of his ways. It is also an ethic of inwardness. It distinguishes carefully between the inward aspect of the moral act—the intent, the disposition of the heart or direction of the will—and the outward part. *Kavvanah,* intention or inwardness, is held essential for every act directed toward God, and it is this intention that gives the act its *moral* quality: "Alike are he who does much and he who does little if only the heart be directed to Heaven."[40] What is true of actions to be performed is also true of sin. Sinful "thoughts"—that is, sinful intentions, a perverse will—are regarded as constituting the sin itself.[41] It is the direction of the will toward or away from God that is decisive.

Yet this fundamental truth must not be so interpreted as to imply that it makes no difference whether the sinful impulse is or is not given free play in action, or in what kind of action it is expressed. It makes a vast difference, not only from the point of view of society but from the point of view of the inner moral life of the individual as well. The capacity for self-control, the ability to master one's sinful impulses and deal with them constructively, is itself a crucial moral power. It may not represent the highest reach of the moral life and it is only too easily converted into a source of self-righteousness, but it is an indispensable factor in any ethical system which permits discrimination between one course of action and another.

Purity of heart is solely dependent upon love of God, which alone can purge the heart of evil "thoughts" and impulses. From this absolute point of view, envy is theft, anger is murder, and looking at another woman with desire is adultery. But in the relativities of life, a distinction must be made not only between the evil impulse that is kept under control and the evil impulse that is carried out into action but also between the various ways in which the same impulse may find expression in human behavior. Impulse and action, inwardness and externality, are organically related but they are not the same thing. If it is mistaken to separate the action from the "thought" and hold the former alone to be morally relevant, as some utilitarian systems do, it is no less mistaken to identify the two in such a way that action becomes morally indifferent. Jewish ethics, with its emphasis on the motives of the heart and its concern for the actions of men, has shown itself able to preserve the tension between the inner and the outer, the absolute and the relative.

## NOTES TO CHAPTER 9

1. "No sense of obligation can be evolved from the actual constitution of humanity without some logical sharp practice. It is impossible to define

what man ought to be from that which he actually is." Emil Brunner, *The Divine Imperative* (Westminster: Philadelphia, 1947), p. 40.

2. George Boas, "The Irrational," *Journal of Philosophy*, Vol. XLIV (February 13, 1947), No. 4.

3. T. H. Huxley, "Evolution and Ethics" (1893), republished in *Touchstone for Ethics*, ed. Julian Huxley (Harper: New York, 1947). But from the "ruthlessness" of nature, the great evolutionist thinker does not conclude that man, too, "following" nature, must be ruthless. "Social progress," he emphasizes, "means the checking of the cosmic process at every step and the substitution for it of another which may be called the ethical process".

4. Morris Weitz, "Philosophy and the Abuse of Language," *Journal of Philosophy*, Vol. XLIV (September 25, 1947), No. 20.

5. Bertrand Russell, *A History of Western Philosophy* (Simon & Schuster: New York, 1945), p. 494.

6. See Julian Huxley, "Religion and Science," *Essays of a Biologist;* "Science, Natural or Social," *Man in the Modern World.*

V. F. Lenzen, in his paper "Philosophy of Science," *Twentieth Century Philosophy* (Philosophical Library: New York, 1943), p. 120, emphasizes the same point: "Except insofar as knowledge is sought for its own sake, science is an extrinsic value. Natural science, at least, does not determine the intrinsic value of ends that are to be achieved by its application. Science may indicate how to realize an end but does not furnish the test whether it is intrinsically good or bad."

7. R. Thomte, *Kierkegaard's Philosophy of Religion* (Princeton University: Princeton, N. J., 1948), p. 111.

"An ethical decision is itself an act of faith." Dorothy M. Emmet, "Kierkegaard and the 'Existential' Philosophy," *Philosophy*, Vol. XVI (July, 1941), No. 63.

Naturalistic attempts to reduce ethics to science by a genetic account of the development of conscience are all based on the device of equating a phenomenon with the conditions under which it occurs. This, as Boas points out, "makes for simplicity of technique but for . . . confusion of thought" (Boas, *op. cit.*). Thus Freud, for example, identifies the conscience with the superego and traces the latter to the Oedipus complex. But it is clear that the Oedipus complex—that is, the child's early relations to his parents—could never have developed into a mental agency issuing moral judgments were not man *already* possessed of the need and capacity for moral judgment. Thus the Freudian "explanation" of the conscience really *presupposes* conscience in man. Freud seems to recognize this difficulty (*Civilization and its Discontents* [Hogarth: London, 1930], p. 119), but his efforts to extricate himself from it (p. 120) are by no means impressive. Edmund Bergler, though an orthodox Freudian, is more circumspect. "The religious and scientific approaches to the genesis of conscience," he writes, "start of necessity at different points. The religious approach assumes a manifestation of God as the basis of conscience. The scientific approach describes clinically observable facts. There is no contradiction between the two approaches." *The Battle of the Conscience* (Washington Institute of Medicine: Washington, D. C., 1948), p. 1.

8. Josephus, *To the Hellenes* (*Against Apion*), ii, sec. 18.

9. *M.* Abot 3.19; *B.* Berakot 33b (cf. *B.* Megillah 25a).

"In creating his creature, God, who is Omnipotence, gave it freedom of action, by virtue of which it can turn to or from him, act for or against him." Martin Buber, "In the Midst of History," *Israel and the World* (Schocken: New York, 1948), p. 79.

10. H. A. Wolfson, *Philo* (Harvard University: Cambridge, Mass., 1947), I, 430-31. Wolfson is here describing the Platonic view.

11. Even Augustine, with all his emphasis on the bondage of sinful man, recognizes this: "Who of us, however, would like to assert that, through the sin of the first man, free decision has disappeared from the human race? . . . Free decision has been so little lost in the sinner that it is precisely by its aid that men sin" (quoted in Brunner, *Man in Revolt* [Westminister: Philadelphia, 1947], p. 268).

12. Quoted by Wolfson, *op. cit.,* I, 436, 455.

13. "According to Jewish tradition, the basis of all moral evil is idolatry" (Wolfson, *op. cit.,* I, 16). Wolfson supplies the documentation.

14. This insight is well brought out in the familiar rabbinic tale about the "[Jewish] elders in Rome" who were asked: "If God has no pleasure in an idol, why does he not make an end of it?" To which they replied: "If men worshipped a thing of which the world had no need, he would make an end of it; but lo, they worship the sun and the moon and the stars and the planets: shall God destroy the world because of fools?" (*M.* Abodah Zarah 4.7).

15. Buber, *Prophetic Faith* (Macmillan, New York, 1949), p. 74.

16. The "evil impulse" in man is often likened to a "foreign god within." Thus *B.* Shabbat 105b: " 'There shall not be in thee a foreign God' (Ps. 81:10). What is the foreign god (idol) within the human being? The evil impulse." (See also *J.* Ned. 9:1, 41b.) Note the suggestion that the power of sin, though generated out of the self, confronts us as a power *against* the self.

17. "The sin of Adam, we are told in the biblical myth, is not merely *a* sin but the *original sin,* the archetype from which all sin, the source of all human suffering springs . . . the attempt of man to *play the part of a god,* to set himself up as a deity, to usurp God's role as law-giver and to become a law unto himself. . . ." M. M. Kaplan, *The Future of the American Jew* (Macmillan: New York, 1948), p. 274.

18. Solomon Schechter, *Some Aspects of Rabbinic Theology* (Macmillan: New York, 1909), p. 68.
19. Schechter, *op. cit.*, p. 199; Buber, *Prophetic Faith*, pp. 102, 114.
20. Schechter, *Studies in Judaism* (Jewish Publication Society: Philadelphia, 1945), Second Series, p. 167; Max Kadushin, *Organic Thinking: A Study in Rabbinic Thought* (Jewish Theological Seminary: New York, 1938), p. 305; Isadore Epstein, *The Jewish Way of Life* (Goldston: London, 1946), p. 22.
21. *B.* Abodah Zarah 20b.
22. Hilkot Deot 2:3.
23. Schechter, *Studies*, Second Series, p. 167, quoting Horodetsky.
24. *B.* Erubin 13b.
25. Kallah rabbati 3.
26. Mekilta, Shirata chap iii.
27. "The Torah commands one to love God (Deut. 6:5, 10:12, 11:1); only in that connection does it enjoin heartfelt love of the sojourner who is also one's 'neighbor' (Deut. 10:19—because God loves the sojourner. If I love God, in the course of loving him, I come to love the one whom God loves too." Buber, "The Love of God and the Idea of Deity," *Israel and the World*, p. 61.
28. "The love between a man and his neighbor flows from the love of God." Buber, *Prophetic Faith*, p. 161.
29. Buber, "The Question of the Single One," *Between Man and Man* (Kegan Paul: London, 1947), p. 76.
30. Julien Benda, "The Attack on Western Morality," *Commentary*, Vol. IV (November, 1947), No. 5. Precisely the same concept of "moral races" is to be found, explicitly or by implication, in Greek ethical thinking, including Stoicism, in Confucianism, and in modern humanism, to the degree that it has succeeded in emancipating itself from the Judo-Christian tradition.
31. Judah Goldin, "Hillel the Elder," *Journal of Religion*, Vol. XXVI (October, 1946), No. 4.
32. *B.* Yoma 23a.
33. Midrash Prov. 25:21 (ed. Buber, p. 98).
34. L. Ginzberg, *Students, Scholars and Saints* (Jewish Publication Society: Philadelphia, 1928), p. 192.
35. *M.* Sanh. 4. 5.
36. Buber interprets the injunction to love one's neighbor "as oneself" to mean loving one's neighbor "as one like myself," i.e., as a *person*. "The Question to the Single One," *Between Man and Man*, p. 51.
37. Abot d. R.N. chap. 31.
38. Sifra on Lev. 19.18.
39. Abot d. R. N., ed. Schechter. version B. chap. 32, p. 71.

40. *M*. Menahot 13. 11
41. *B*. Yoma 29a.
"Do not think that he alone is an adulterer who by his sinful act has sinned; he is equally an adulterer who lusts with his eyes." Pesikta rabbati 124b; cf. Midrash r. Lev., chap. xxiii, No. 12. "When a man has the intention to sin, it is as though he betrays God." Midrash r. Numb. 8.5.

# 10.  THE DIVINE IMPERATIVE:
## THE ABSOLUTE AND THE RELATIVE

Jewish ethics is an ethic of law; but beyond that it is an ethic of love. The relation between law[1] and love is one of the most profound and perplexing paradoxes of the moral life. It confronts us with the task of finding our way amidst perils and pitfalls of opposed but equally dangerous character—legalism, on the one hand, and antinomianism, on the other.

Without law, social life would be impossible; without justice, relations among men would not reach the human level. Yet however advanced the law, however exalted the level of justice, it can never be anything more than relative—relative to the wisdom and insight of men, as well as to the balance of social forces and interests. Even if the laws are received from God in divine revelation, no absolute position is achieved, for the laws have to be applied by men to changing human conditions. Even the best system of justice is thus bound to contain an element of injustice simply because of the inescapable relativity of everything human. The injustice that is inherent in our best efforts at justice can only be overcome in a love that transcends law.

Law and justice are the foundation of social existence, but the commandment of love demands that we go beyond them. Would we not fall under condemnation if God did not allow his love and mercy to prevail over his justice?[2] Are we not then required, in imitation of God, to go beyond the limits of the law in our dealings with our brothers? Indeed, this very concept—*lifenim mi-shurat ha-din, beyond the line of the law*—is one of the most important operative ideas in Jewish ethics. "A Jew who acts *lifenim mi-shurat ha-din,*" Epstein explains, "is a man who forgoes his rights which the 'letter' of justice accords him. . . . [He is one] who submits to the rule of love [and] will therefore refuse to take advantage of the letter of justice."³ Rabbinical literature is full of examples of such transcendence of law in love. Every man has the *right* to exact what is his under the law— that is, to deal with his fellow-men in purely legal relations; but woe unto the generation composed of such men. Jerusalem fell, we are told, precisely because the men of the time insisted on their rights under the law.⁴ The commandment of love is not only the source of all justice but is also the ultimate perspective from which the limitations of every standard of justice may be perceived.

It is thus an error to identify law or justice with the highest principle of Jewish ethics, for beyond them is love. A legalism that absolutizes law as ultimate must therefore be rejected. But so also must the antinomianism that rejects law as unnecessary in human life on the ground that relations among men should be "regulated" in the spontaneous freedom of love. If *all* men could achieve as a *permanent* condition the love that purges one of self-centeredness and sin, then indeed might such spontaneous harmony without law become the way of life of men in society. But the slightest acquaintance with men should be enough to teach us that such sanctification is not to be sought for in history and that it is the sheerest folly to base one's ethical philosophy on the expectation that men will in fact behave as saints. No responsible thinker will venture to foresee human conditions within history in which faith will be so perfectly realized in love that law can be dispensed with and all action take rise in spontaneous freedom. The transcendence of law in love is the divine imperative that confronts every man in his relations with his fellow-men but it is an imperative that only the most sentimental utopianism can identify with the realities of social life at any stage of history. Law may not be the final word of the will of God, but so long as men remain sinful—that is, so long as they remain human—it is the will of God in a form that is indispensable and authoritative for the everyday conduct of life.

The paradox whereby the commandment of love is recognized as governing all human conduct and yet as incapable of replacing law in the ongoing process of social life is a paradox that goes to the very heart of Jewish ethics and is the source of its depth and power. In its ultimate reach, Jewish ethics is an ethic of perfection: it calls upon men to be holy and perfect in imitation of God. On this level, it will accept no excuse or compromise. Love of fellow-man must be universal and unconditional. Schechter tells us of a Jewish saint who "declined to be considered as one of the righteous of his generation, saying that he had no right to this distinction so long as he felt that he loved his children better than the rest of mankind."⁵ We must acknowledge the utter validity of this absolutist affirmation and yet we cannot help recognizing that all life within history involves persistent violation of the divine imperative and the obligations derived therefrom. We know, we cannot deny, that all men are brothers whom we should treat with the same benevolence as we do ourselves. Yet who of us can transact the business of a day without transgressing this law a thousand times? Every time we eat a full meal while others anywhere in the world go hungry we offend the law of our moral life.⁶

We are called to perfection in imitation of and fellowship with God. But our very finiteness stands in the way of our fulfilling the infinite obligation thus incurred. Our limited resources do not absolve us of the responsibility. "Just as no man can claim that his poverty frees him from the duty to repay a loan," Paul Weiss tellingly points out, "so no man can claim to be without guilt because unable to fulfill [his] infinite obligation."⁷ Nor is it merely that we fall short of our duty. Much more portentous is the fact that the moment we begin to translate intention into deed we become involved in all the relativities of expediency and all the ambiguities of actual life. Evil means, we know, cannot achieve good ends. Such means necessarily tend to vitiate the ends they are instituted to serve. In the first place, they, in a very real sense, enter into the composition of the ends they bring into being and thus impart to them something of their own moral quality. In the second place, perhaps even more importantly, their employment tends to corrupt the human agents resorting to them and therefore to corrupt the end itself, which is, after all, made up of the actions of these very men. So far, therefore, from a good end sanctifying evil means, evil means actually operate to destroy the good end.

But is action in this world possible without using means that are at best equivocal? "He who acts is always to some degree unjust," Goethe somewhere says; "only the spectator can preserve his conscience." There is no level of life that is free from this tragic dilemma. The Midrash portrays Abraham as expostulating with God: "If you want a world, you will not have justice; if it is justice you want, there will be no world. You are taking hold of the rope by both ends—you desire both a world *and* justice—but if you don't concede a little, the world cannot stand."[8] Activity of men in history, even in pursuit of the best ends, carries with it not only the promotion but also the violation of the highest imperatives of the moral life.

But we have still not gotten to the bottom of our moral predicament. Not only do we always fall short of our obligations: not only do we always tend to imperil the ends we pursue by the means we employ; but we are always under the temptation of perverting even the partial good we do manage to achieve by making it the vehicle of our pride and self-glorification. There is no ideal, however pure, that is not compounded to some degree with the self-interest of those who promote it. The great statesman devotes his life to the welfare of his people, but is he not also serving his self-esteem and love of power? The selfless revolutionary dedicates himself to the struggle for social justice, but is he not also finding an outlet for his obscure hates and resentments? The philanthropist showers benefits on his less fortunate brothers, but is not his generosity a display of superiority as well as an expression of pity? Even the saint in his humility, does he not exalt himself in the pride of his humility? When even these best of men are judged in the scale of the divine imperative—perfect and undivided love of God—is not the verdict bound to be condemnation? Does this sound severe, unreasonable, impossible? That is just what Jewish ethics is. "As for him who does not fulfill the Torah for its own sake," we are warned, "it were better had he never been created."[9]

In its most practical aspect, the dilemma of the moral life we are trying to understand reveals itself in the fact that in the actual course of social existence, the choice we are confronted with is not between a line of conduct that is absolutely good and another that is absolutely evil, but between courses of action all of which are ambiguous, equivocal and to some degree infected with evil. That this is a fact no one, I think, with any experience of life will care to deny. The practical problem of the moral life is, therefore, how to make a choice among evils without losing for a moment the living awareness that they *are* evils from among which we are compelled to choose. It is the problem of relating the absolute to the relative, of making the ideal imperative relevant to the conditions of actual life. Cynicism denies that ideal imperatives, since they are impossible of actual enactment in life, can have any meaning or relevance to human existence; it thus falls into utter moral unscrupulousness. Perfectionist utopianism, on the other hand, insists that the absolute ideal, because it is relevant and binding, must somehow be capable of complete realization in history; it escapes cynicism only to fall into a delusive self-righteousness. A realistic ethic must avoid both pitfalls. It must know how to relate the ideal to reality without deceiving itself as to the actual distance between them. It must know how to choose from among evils without obliterating the distinction between good and evil.

The absolute imperatives calling to perfection acquire their potency precisely through the fact that they transcend every actuality of existence. They are regulative, not constitutive, principles of the moral life; they cannot themselves be directly embodied in action but they operate as a dynamic power within it. They serve, first, as principles of criticism of existing conditions. They serve, next, as principles of guidance in the struggle for better conditions. And they serve, finally, as principles of discrimination and action in the choice among relevant possibilities under any conditions. These three functions are most intimately related. Serious criticism of existing conditions is possible only in terms of a standard that transcends these conditions, and since there are no conditions of life that can claim exemption from criticism, this standard must be such as to transcend all possible conditions. Precisely the same is true when we consider the ideal in relation to action. It is the absolute ideal beyond any existing reality which alone is capable of moving men to defy the limitations of the actual and to overcome them. Moral action which lacks some reference to an absolute standard inevitably falls short of satisfying even the limited necessities of life; its ends are always too immediate and its perspectives too narrow. It is bereft of vision and drained of dynamic power.

In no connection is the "impossible" ideal more pertinent, indeed indispensable, than in relation to the decisions that constitute the ongoing process of our moral life. When we are confronted with a number of alternative courses of action, none of which is simply right or wrong—and that is the permanent predicament of human life—how shall we make our choice? Clearly no choice is possible unless we are able to measure the alternative courses against some standard that transcends them. Once we have such a criterion, it becomes possible to say—*after a responsible estimate of consequences*—that one course constitutes a lesser evil than another, but without a criterion no judgment at all is possible. Decision, choice, is always in terms of an ideal standard: that is what the cynics cannot understand. But this standard, though practically operative, remains transcendent and ideal; it can never be simply identified with any course of action possible under the circumstances: this the perfectionist utopian refuses to see. Jewish ethics grasps both sides of the complex reality and is thus able to make moral ideals relevant to actual life without falling into sentimentality and illusion. It is able to make pragmatic and utilitarian judgments without taking either pragmatism or utilitarianism as final. It is able to employ all the resources of science for co-ordinating and implementing ends without falling victim to the delusion that empirical science can *set* the ends of human life.

Amidst the intractable realities of existence, our choice is thus only too often a choice between different degrees of evil. The real moral peril consists not so much in choosing what in our best judgment seems to be the lesser evil; such choice is entailed by the very process of living. The real moral peril consists in trying to make a virtue out of necessity, in converting the lesser evil we choose, merely because we choose it, into a positive good. The course we fix upon may, in our considered opinion, fall less short of the moral law than any alternative possible under the circumstances, and we therefore choose it. But it still falls short of the moral law; it still represents to some degree and in some way a violation of the ideal imperative we recognize as the law of our moral life. With a heavy heart, we may decide that going to war is the only course open to us in the world of today, but killing does not thereby become right and good. What is essential to moral sanity in any situation is that we never refuse to call the policy or course of action we decide upon by its right name in the light of our absolute standard, that we never try to deceive ourselves as to the real moral quality of what we do. For once we permit such self-deception, once we yield to the easy temptation of proclaiming the lesser evil, because it is lesser, to be right and good, we have taken the first fatal step toward wiping out all distinction between good and evil. Any course of action, no matter how repugnant to the moral law, may then be embraced without scruple of conscience and passed off as unqualifiedly good. It is the end of all ethical discrimination, of all significant moral life. "It is true," Buber writes, summarizing the biblical outlook, "that we are not able to live in perfect justice, and in order to preserve the community of men, we are often compelled to accept wrongs in decisions concerning the community. But what matters is that in every hour of decision we are aware of our responsibility and summon our conscience to weigh exactly how much is necessary to preserve the community, and accept just so much and no more."[10] This is possible only if we acknowledge the moral law even when we are compelled to violate it.

However involved we may become in the relativities of life, we can never deny our responsibility to the Absolute. Incapable of achievement amidst the intractable forces of life and history though they may be, the ideal imperatives of the Jewish ethic are directly pertinent to all action. They constitute transcendent principles of aspiration, criticism and judgment. They point to goals of moral striving and generate the dynamic of moral effort. They provide a touchstone by which we may discriminate the better from the worse, while recognizing the imperfection of all our alternatives. Above all, they stand over us as an eternal judgment reminding us that the best we can do is none too good and warning us against converting the inescapable necessities of practical life into standards of right and good. Allegiance to the absolute imperatives of the moral law is the ethical aspect of the worship of a holy God. It saves us from taking final satisfaction in anything we do in a situation where everything we can do is qualified by the relativities of time and circumstance. It inculcates a wholesome spirit of humility which gives the soul no peace in any achievement while a still higher level is possible.

Because it views the moral life in this way, the Jewish ethic is an ethic of decision. The call to decision comes to us in the midst of life, in the existential context of life. It is always concrete and always different, always in terms of some particular situation or problem. That is why we are so prone to think of it in impersonal terms. "The situation demands," we say; "conditions require . . ." But situations cannot demand, nor can conditions require. It is God who calls us through the particular situation and who sets us a task within the particular conditions. To that call we must respond in action. No system of fixed absolutes, no authoritative code, not even mystic illumination, can absolve us from the appalling duty of making responsible choice among relevant possibilities. Light and guidance we may receive from these and other sources, but the ultimate decision is always ours to make. We cannot escape this responsibility, and in the responsibility of decision we come face to face with God.

The Jewish ethic is at bottom an ethic of vital tension, of tension between the absolute good we ought to do and the relative possibilities open to us in any actual situation. It is this tension that generates the dynamic of moral action, which is, in the last analysis, the pull of the ideal that always transcends reality and yet is always relevant to it. But the significance of this tension is more than ethical; indeed, on the moral plane alone, the dilemma out of which this tension grows can never be resolved. The resolution of the heart-rending, existence-shattering conflict between that which we know we ought to do and that which in fact we do do is possible only on the religious level, on the level of repentance, grace and forgiveness. At this point, ethics transcends itself and returns to its religious source and origin.

Having done our best amidst the harsh realities of existence, we realize that the very best we do always falls short of, if indeed it does not pervert, the absolute standard which we recognize as the law of our life. Looking within ourselves, we can no longer deny that if divine justice were meted out, we would all stand condemned and there would indeed be "no world," as the midrash above quoted points out. We owe our very existence to divine grace, to God's merciful decision to "concede a little." Jewish religion understands this with

114    *Judaism and Modern Man*

every fiber of its being. Every morning the observant Jew repeats the prayer that, if existentially appropriated, must indeed shatter all human pretensions and leave man in humble dependence upon the grace of God:

> Sovereign of all the worlds! Not because of our righteous acts do we lay our supplications before thee but because of thine abundant mercies. What are we? What is our life? What is our piety? What is our righteousness?

## NOTES TO CHAPTER 10

1. As used in this context, "law" means neither the so-called "ritual law," which will be discussed below, nor the legislative enactments of the state; the term refers to what is usually known as the moral law.
2. *B.* Berakot 7a.
3. Isadore Epstein, *The Jewish Way of Life* (Goldston: London, 1946), pp. 30, 93.
4. *B.* Baba Metzia 30b: "R. Johanan said: Jerusalem was destroyed for nothing but that . . . they were wont to establish justice in accordance with the strict law of the Torah and did not operate *lifenim mi-shurat ha-din.*"
5. Solomon Schechter, *Studies in Judaism* (Jewish Publication Society: Philadelphia, 1945), Second Series, p. 169.
6. "According to Israel's law," Schechter says, "no man has a right to more than bread and water and wood as long as the poor are not provided with the necessaries of life." *American Hebrew,* January, 1916; quoted in N. Bentwich, *Solomon Schechter* (Jewish Publication Society: Philadelphia, 1938), p. 229.
7. Paul Weiss, "God, Job and Evil," *Commentary,* Vol. VI (August, 1948), No. 2.
8. Midrash r. Gen. chap. XLIX, No. 20.
9. *B.* Berakot 17a.
10. Martin Buber, "Hebrew Humanism," *Israel and the World* (Schocken: New York, 1948), p. 246.

# 11. THE QUEST FOR SALVATION

"Consciousness of sin and assurance of grace are the two great motive powers in the working of religion."[1] Why is it that these words of Solomon Schechter seem to have so little meaning to the modern-minded man of our time? Is it because we have finally abolished sin and no longer need salvation? Hardly so; we of today are more anxiously concerned with "saving" ourselves than men have been for centuries. Salvation cults multiply. Every bizarre quackery finds its horde of devotees; every panecea that promises deliverance in up-to date terms is hailed with eager hope by thousands of lost souls. Our generation is literally obsessed with the search for salvation, and yet we seem utterly incapable of understanding what it is we are searching for or of turning in the only direction in which it is to be found.

The decades of secularism have left their mark. They have blunted our spiritual sensitivity and obscured our vision of the basic facts of human life. We are in a position where we have to begin painfully to regain the capacity to see things as they really are. This is not easy, for the things we are bound to see once we open our eyes are not things we want to see. They are not things calculated to flatter our self-esteem or grant us "peace of mind" on easy terms. Yet there is no other way. No short cuts will do. We must try to get to the bottom of the human situation as it presents itself to us in our own existence and see if we can pick up the thread by which men of past generations found their way out of the maze of confusion and frustration that is human life. We cannot relive their lives nor can we simply take over their answers verbatim. But man's existential condition and essential needs remain ever the same, and perhaps the experience of former ages embodied in our religious tradition may provide the clue for which we are seeking. Perhaps the resources of Scripture and rabbinic thought may possess the power and relevance that the up-to-the-minute "scientific" gospels of our day so obviously lack.

What shall we do to be saved? What is it that we want to be saved from? On this there is but one thought. The salvation we crave is

115

salvation from the fears, the futilities, the frustrations of existence. The salvation we crave is a security able to withstand the defeats and failures of the world, a validation of life capable of preserving it from the chaos of meaninglessness by which it is threatened on all sides.

The insecurity and meaninglessness from which we strive to be saved invade life at every level. At every level, in every field, in every enterprise from the seemingly trivial concerns of private life to the great movements of history, the partial meanings on which we try to build our lives are never enough to sustain us. The limited aims and incentives that motivate so much of our conduct—pleasure, wealth, reputation, power—are bound to prove inadequate in the long run. Sooner or later, they collapse under the pressure of existence, and we are left helpless, forlorn, without support in the vast emptiness that engulfs us. Nothing makes any sense, no structure of life can be depended upon, no undertaking seems capable of leading to anything. And at the end of everything there is death, the final absurdity of life.

The events of our generation have driven these facts home to us with the hammer blows of catastrophe. The comfortable illusions of the past are no longer available to us. We can no longer pretend that life fulfils itself, that history is gradually solving all our problems for us, that evil and irrationality are merely remnants of lower stages of development to be speedily overcome with the evolution of mankind. We know that life taken in its own terms can yield no meaning, that history of its own power can solve none of the perennial problems of existence. We know that *anomie*—the demoralization and atomization of society, to which sociologists have called attention—has now come to pervade all of life. We know that the abysses of nothingness from which the men of another age might conceivably have turned their eyes away now open up before us in every direction. Modern man may or may not understand the meaning of the words in which traditional religion describes the human situation, but of the realities of that situation he knows with the knowledge that only suffering can bring.

*Anomie* in the ultimate sense pervades all of human existence. Isolation, fragmentariness, "lostness" is man's everyday condition. It is this, this frightening vacuity within and without, from which we want to be saved. It is this state of dereliction, of being abandoned in a vast and crushing emptiness, that drives us to despair and makes life so intolerable if there is no vision beyond life.

But why? Why is it that this "metaphysical" anxiety, this terror of existence, this yawning gulf of futility and meaninglessness, confronts us at every step of life? Why is it that we are, in the stark literalness of the term, *lost souls?* Is it the inherent nature of life and man? Is life so evil, is essential human personality so utterly worthless, that nothing good can come of it? Is salvation, if possible at all, to be salvation *from* the world, escape from life, as Buddhism, Platonism and their modern variants aver? Jewish religion definitely rejects this world-denying, life-denying philosophy. Not that it refuses to face the hard facts of life. Jewish tradition is starkly realistic—pessimistic, even, some would say—in its estimate of the actual condition of man in this world. "For two and a half years," the Talmud tells us, "the school of Shammai and the school of Hillel debated the question of whether it were better for a man not to have been created. . . . Finally they voted and concluded: It were better for a man not to have been created—but now that he has been created, let him search his deeds."[2] Clearly, man's lot in life is not idealized, but clearly, too, human life is not despaired of or given up as lost beyond redemption.

The dereliction of human life Jewish religion attributes not to the nature of life itself or to the nature of things in general, for all creation was pronounced good as it left the hand of its Maker. The dereliction of human life Jewish religion traces to man's tragic division within and against himself. Actual human existence it finds in conflict with the essential law of our being. It is the essential law of our being, that which we were created as and for, to live in true love of God as the source and center of life. But our actual existence, is it not permeated through and through with *self*-love, is it not lived out as if we ourselves and not God were the center of our universe? Is not our actual existence an existence without God, in alienation from God? Estranged from God, we are torn out of the very texture of being and left a mere fragment, cut off from the only real source of security available to us. Is it any wonder that thus isolated from what is real within and without, our existence loses its foundation and we are compelled to live out our lives in restless frustration, forever trembling at the brink of chaos and dissolution?

118 Judaism and Modern Man

Because the plight of our human existence is thus rooted in a denial of the essential law of our being, we experience this plight not merely as fate but as *guilt*. The dereliction that overwhelms us is at once the despair of being abandoned in the universe and the agonizing consciousness that we are ultimately responsible for our own condition. The meaninglessness and vacuity in which life is involved confront us not merely as an external danger but as inner culpability. This sense of guilt is the mark of our human condition. It is the inward manifestation of the utter emptiness, the hopelessly fragmentary character, of existence without God, and it reflects our unwilling, perhaps even unconscious, confession that this isolation is not our original condition but somehow the result of our own doing. And indeed it *is* of our own doing. It is the consequence of our defying the essential law of our being. It is the consequence of sin.

Sin is one of the great facts of human life. It lies at the root of man's existential plight. In the last analysis, it is sin and the fruits of sin from which we require to be saved.

We have seen in earlier chapters that sin is not simply the violation of some particular moral or ritual injunction. It is that and much more. At bottom, sin is man's anxious effort to escape the ambiguities and responsibilities of his creaturely condition, either by trying to sink below the human level, as in sensuality, or by striving to rise above it, in pride and self-exaltation. Put in a different and perhaps more fundamental way, sin is a frantic attempt at self-absolutization, whether it is the absolutization of our organic powers, such as sex, or of our spiritual potencies, such as intelligence, knowledge and the force of will. The structures thus built up possess the entire personality and extend to every aspect of social life; they manifest themselves on every level of human behavior, unconscious as well as conscious.

Sin is plainly born of anxiety and therefore ultimately out of lack of faith. Were we possessed of true and steadfast faith in the divine source of our being, each of us would live out his life in confident fellowship with God and his fellow-men. Our paradoxical status in the scheme of things—our "finite infinity"— would then be a source of self-realization and creativity. This is the picture of life in Paradise, where, according to the Scriptural account, the untroubled harmony between the man and the woman, and between both and God, extended throughout all nature, which was at one with itself. But it is also the picture of the life that is possible for man at any time—if only by the power of his faith and love he were *really* to transfer the center of his existence from within himself to the Living God.

Born of anxiety, sin but deepens and spreads the anxiety that makes for the forlornness of life. In our anxiety—that is, in our distrust of God—we strive frantically to build up systems of defense, psychological and social, in which to ground our security without dependence on the divine. All the powers of mind and all the resources of personality we mobilize to establish the self in its self-sufficiency. It is a vain and delusive enterprise. Every attempt to achieve security on such a basis but deepens our insecurity and drives us into an ever-greater isolation without and contradiction within. These structures, which the soul alienated from God is impelled to build up to sustain itself, may give it temporary and illusory protection against the pressures of reality, but only at the expense of distorting it in ways that the psychoanalyst and the student of social pathology know so well.[3] The hard, defiant self-absorption, the mad straining for prestige and power, the feverish competition in conspicuous display, the restless hankering after novelty and distraction, the callousness, brutality and aggressions that characterize so much of life, what are they but ways in which the self tries desperately to ward off the threat of meaninglessness and insecurity with which it is beset? So also, for that matter, are the sentimentalities, the renunciations and repressions, of which the "good people" of the world, the virtuous, the puritanical and the self-righteous, are so proud. They are all structures by which the self strives to become sufficient unto itself, to overcome its misery through its own resources. And because man is social, these personality structures necessarily find their appropriate social expressions in the practices and institutions of society. The very texture of existence thus becomes permeated with the consequences of sinful egocentricity.

But the devices of man's heart, the protective and compensatory devices of sinful self-sufficiency, are bound to prove futile. Sooner or later, somehow, at some point, the divine claim breaks through.

Most immediately, we become aware of it in the forlornness and self-condemnation of guilt. Suddenly we find ourselves standing in hopeless contradiction to the divine imperative, which is also the law of our own life. The divine imperative is internalized and confronts us as a power from within. It is here that the profound insights of psychoanalysis become particularly relevant to a realistic theology.[4]

The experience of standing in guilt under judgment, to which psychoanalysis points without being able to exhaust its significance, is in its ultimate bearing the unconscious acknowledgment of the vision of a holy God before whom all our pretensions to self-sufficiency and righteousness crumble into dust. Isaiah's anguished cry—"Woe unto me, I am lost; I am a man of unclean lips . . . and mine eyes have seen the King, the Lord of Hosts" (Isa. 6:5)—is the cry that breaks out from the hidden depths of every one of us whenever the force of existence smashes through the hard crust of egocentric self-deception. At such moments, which none of us can escape, we stand confronted with the blinding, shattering power of the divine holiness. We may not know the vision we see. We may receive it in some fragmented and unrecognizable form. We may call it conscience or superego or perhaps even the command of society. We may think of it as the claim of reason or truth or social responsibility. But however we explain or explain it away, we feel its power. We stand lost in confusion and guilt, for the instant, at least, bereft of all our carefully constructed defenses against the Absolute. We stand broken in spirit, utterly devaluated, thirsting for a security beyond our own devising, reaching out for a salvation that will restore life and hope.

The salvation that alone seems capable of freeing us from the dreadful frustration of self-isolated existence is a salvation that promises to relate the self in faith to some larger whole beyond the self, to some superpersonal reality. It is precisely here that the last and perhaps the gravest peril lies. How easy it is, even when we are thus at the last extremity, to deceive ourselves and place our ultimate trust in what must, in the end, prove itself to be no more than the self projected and disguised. How easy it is to turn for salvation to the latest panacea, to the most advanced social movement, to the most fashionable philosophy, to the most recent "system of values," or even to the most "modern" religion. How easy it is to think that we have "tuned in on the Infinite" when we have found what we take to be the divine in ourselves, in our unconscious, in Beauty or Art, in Nature or Humanity. How easy but how disastrous. For it is not by such devices that we can be saved. Neither the cult of technology nor that of psychoanalysis, neither the worship of race and instinct nor that of science and reason, neither nationalism nor collectivism, neither the exaltation of democracy as a "common faith" nor the retreat into self-sufficient mysticism can really break through the isolation and fragmentariness of our sinful existence. On the contrary, in the last reckoning, they but feed our egocentricity and fortify the structures that the sinful self erects to shield itself against the divine claim. To turn to them for salvation is, in the long run, but to deepen the wretchedness from which we want to be saved.

It is true, salvation does indeed mean self-completion through relating oneself in faith to some greater reality beyond the self. But nothing short of the Living God will do. "Thou hast made us for thee and our heart is uneasy until it rest in thee."[5] Until we are ready to make a clean breast of it and abandon all our evasions and devices, salvation is not for us. Only when *all* our pretensions to self-sufficiency have been shattered, only when we have given up *all* our schemes of achieving security in some larger whole which is but the self writ large, only when we have finally realized that we cannot save ourselves even through our noblest aspirations and most exalted ideals, only when we come forward with empty hands but contrite heart and humble spirit, only then is there hope. Only the contrite self, sick of its pretensions, can find salvation.

The Hebraic concept of *teshubah*, so central to Jewish religion, expresses in consummate form the profound paradox involved in this return to God. *Teshubah*—"turning"—is the fusion of repentance and grace; it points at one and the same time to man's action in abandoning his delusive self-sufficiency so as to turn to God and to God's action in giving man the power to break the vicious circle of sin and turn to the divine source of his being. "Turn me, O Lord, that I may turn," pleads the author of Lamentations (Lam. 5:21) and this plea is the heart-rending prayer of sinful man at the end of his rope. It is a prayer that brings its sure fulfilment. "The Lord is nigh unto those of a broken heart and he delivers them that are crushed in spirit" (Ps. 34:18). "If you turn, I will restore you and you shall stand in my presence, says the Lord" (Jer. 15:19).

Only those of a broken heart can find God. For the broken heart— repentance, complete self-emptying before God—is the breaking of the stubborn isolation and self-sufficiency that is the root source of our troubles. It releases the stopped-up fountains of faith.

Because it is the delusion of self-sufficiency that must be overcome before the healing work of God becomes available to us, we obviously cannot hope to achieve our salvation through our own works, how-ever meritorious. To an earthly king, we are told a man comes full and returns empty; but to God he must come empty— that is, empty of pretensions and justifications and claims—and he will return full, full of grace and forgiveness.[6] It is not denied that man is called to obedience to God in works, or that his works in fulfilment of the divine law enter into God's judgment upon him. But it must be denied that any man can presume to count on his works to win him his salvation: good works are the fruit and evidence of a saving faith, but salvation is ultimately by faith and by grace received in faith.

A moment's reflection will show why this must be so. Pretensions to self-sufficiency are of the very essence of sin. Who of us, looking into his own heart, would care to assert that his works are enough to justify him in the sight of a holy God? If the world were ruled by the attribute of justice alone—authoritative rabbinic tradition tells us—that is, if each of us received his deserts according to his works, no one would escape destruction.[7] Therefore did God couple the attribute of mercy to that of justice.[8] If we are to be saved at all, if we are to be restored to fellowship with God, it must be through his mercy. It must be because we abandon all pretense to self-sufficiency, all claims and pretensions, and throw ourselves upon his grace. "Our Father, our King," so runs the daily *Tahanun* in the morning prayer, "be gracious unto us and answer us, for we have no works . . . Save us according to thy grace." All men need grace. Abraham needed it; it was for his sake, we are told, that grace came plenteously into the world.[9] And if Abraham the friend of God, how much more we? From the pit of sin we can be saved only by God's grace: it is grace which gives us strength to see the right and to persevere in doing it:

above all, it is grace which gives us the power to break through the vicious circle of egocentricity and return to the divine center of our being. Salvation is of repentance and faith, for faith is at bottom right relation to God and that *is* salvation. This is our side, the human side, of *teshubah*. "We are not the less serious about grace because we are serious about the human power of deciding:"[10] But while initiative is required of us, it is plainly not sufficient, and Jewish tradition is emphatic about telling us so. "The Pharisaic position," Israel Abrahams notes, "tried to hold the balance between man's duty to *strive* to earn pardon and his *inability* to attain it without God's gracious gift of it."[11] Indeed, like the decision of faith of which it is but the reenactment at every crisis of life, the turning to God in true repentance is already in a way a manifestation of divine grace. In the final analysis, despite the initiative and activity required of him, man cannot save himself; the assurances to the contrary of the self-redemptive cults, whether secularist, legalist or mystic, are dangerously delusive. It is God who saves. To the truly repentant, to the broken of heart who have disarmed themselves before God, the divine spirit goes out to meet and to purge. "Then came one of the seraphim unto me," Isaiah continues after his shattering confession of unworthiness and guilt. "Then came one of the seraphim unto me, with a red-hot coal in his hand, which he had taken from the altar, and he touched my mouth with it and said: Lo, this has touched your lips and your sin is taken away, your sin is forgiven." (Isa. 6:6). With the purging of guilt, the crushing load of fear[12] and anxiety is lifted from the heart. At last the peace for which we have been yearning comes to us, the "peace that passeth understanding": at last we have found our place in the supernatural order for which we are meant. "The religious," says the philosopher, F. J. E. Woodbridge, strangely recalling the words of the rabbinic scholar, Solomon Schechter, "are those who have a sense of the need and possibility of salvation. Only the saved can be genuinely happy and at peace. And what are they saved from? . . . Their sins. And what are their sins? . . . There is one sin which is unforgivable: the refusal of allegiance to the supernatural. One may be converted from that sin and then there is salvation."[13]

Repentence in the sense of *teshubah* opens up the heart to a new influx of strength and power. It is an activity of the entire personality and therefore affects the entire personality. It is the beginning of a new life. Out of the return to God in true contrition and humility of spirit, the new self is born.

This "new life" in God is the true life of man. It is, as Kierkegaard says, the life of the self that "wills to be itself" and that therefore "grounds its existence transparently on the Power which posited it."[14] Existence now becomes secure and meaningful. The fearful isolation of the self-centered life is broken and despair is dissolved in faith. Fellowship with God opens the way for fellowship with man in true personal communion. Life becomes whole again and what was vacuous and empty is now full of significance. The salvation that brings deliverance from the power of sin brings also the possibility of dissolving the distorted personality structures in which sin finds its embodiment and expression.

Salvation thus brings self-realization, but it is the self-realization that comes of self-giving. Anxious concern for the self and its fate leads, as we have seen, inevitably to self-isolation, frustration and defeat. It is by turning away from itself to God that the self may be saved: "Is it thy wish to live? Do not live; so that thou mayest live."[15] Life more abundant is the fruit of faith and love and repentance, not of any self-obsessed strategy of self-salvation.

Scripture and rabbinic literature never tire of assuring sinful man of the unfailing availability of redemption through repentance and of the transforming power of divine grace. Isaiah 57:19, read as: "Peace, peace, to the far and the near: to all who draw near to me I draw near and heal them," is used by a midrashic commentator to attribute to God the moving words: "My hands are stretched out toward the penitent; I reject no creature who gives me his heart in repentance."[16] No life is so derelict, so sin-hardened, so lost in self, that it is beyond redemption: "Though your sins be as scarlet, they shall be white as snow" (Isa.1:18).

That *teshubah*—turning to God in contrition and humility of spirit —creates a "new heart" within us and transforms us into a new self, Jewish tradition consistently teaches through prophet and rabbi. "I

will give you a new heart and place within you a new spirit; I will remove the heart of stone out of your flesh and give you a heart of
flesh; I will put my spirit within you" (Ezek. 36:26): these words of
God spoken to Ezekiel are taken to refer not only to corporate Israel
but to the personal existence of every man who sins and repents. "God
creates them [repentant sinners], as it were, into new creatures."[17]
"Atonement," Montefiore summarizes the rabbinic teaching, "becomes
the destruction of sin and sinfulness, the creation of a new being, a sort
of being who is born again, the breaking of the barrier between sinful
man and his Maker."[18] It is for this reason that he who repents is regarded as if he had never sinned and is even exalted above the conventionally righteous man.[19] It is for this reason that we are so often
admonished never to remind the sinner who has "returned" of his
former condition,[20] not only so as not to offend or embarrass him but
also and perhaps more importantly because such reminders reveal our
own lack of faith in the redemptive miracle of divine grace. The
sinner who "returns" *is* a new man, and as such he enters into new
relations of fellowship with God and fellow-man.

The "new self" that emerges once we achieve deliverance from self-
enclosed egocentricity brings a new power for life and introduces a
subtle transformation into every aspect of the personality. Our human
purposes, broken in the experience of guilt and repentance, are re-
directed. The self is opened to other selves in genuine community.
The entire scale of values by which we live undergoes a radical change;
new motives arise and what was once so prone to frustrate and dis-
tract now loses its power over us. Organized about its true center,
life regains its freedom and wholeness. The victory has been won.

But if the victory has been won, it is, let us remember, a victory
that is never final. Salvation, like faith, out of which it is born, can
never become a secure possession of ours. For at bottom, salvation
is reconciliation with God—*at-one-ment;* and such reconciliation is
predicated upon utter renunciation of the pretensions of the self to
autonomy. Yet so long as we live out our lives in this world, the
drive of self-absolutization will remain within us and the temptation
to find security in our own achievements, personal, social and spiritual,
will dog our every step. The battle of faith and repentance is thus one

that is never at an end but must be constantly refought lest the fruit be lost. It is the perennial struggle of life, and in this struggle, too, the resources of divine grace are available to all who "turn."

The same power that brings salvation to man by healing the wound of his "inner" existence brings him salvation also by giving validity and significance to his "outer" activities and enterprises. Indeed, the distinction between the two breaks down if carried beyond a certain point. The saving grace of God is one, though it operates along two dimensions: the *vertical* dimension of personal existence and the *horizontal* dimension of social life. Along the latter, salvation, collective and corporate, is embedded in the movement of history, yet is never entirely fulfilled within it.

In the religious life of Israel, the hope of corporate and collective salvation along the horizontal dimension of history emerged first and has continued to be the central emphasis of Jewish tradition. Individual salvation is comprehended within the grand sweep of the Messianic expectation and the promise of the "world-to-come." In the end, the two are one.

We of today no longer harbor the illusion so universal a few decades ago that history is the great redeeming power. We see what the prophets of Israel saw and proclaimed, that it is history itself which requires redemption. Just as individual life comprehended in its own terms and organized about itself as center can yield nothing but frustration, anxiety and despair, so the collective life of mankind in history, taken in its own terms, is nothing but a record of chaos and confusion, a "tale told by an idiot, full of sound and fury, signifying nothing." In the one case as in the other, fulfilment, completion, significance, can come only from the creative Power that is recognized as the transcendent sources of being and value. The grace of God which gives worth and meaning to personal existence endows history and all its enterprises with the promise of fulfilment. "Moral and social action is the road toward . . . salvation, [but] it is not true that man is his own savior: God alone can accomplish salvation through his grace."[21] These words of Albert Salomon, the distinguished sociologist, apply with the same force to history as to individual life.

In the salvation that moves along the vertical dimension of personal

existence, life is healed and restored in value by being related in faith
to the Living God.  In the social salvation that moves along the horizontal dimension of history, we are given the assurance that, despite
all the failures and frustrations of empirical events, the cause of freedom and justice will ultimately triumph, for with the eyes of faith we
discern that cause to be the cause of God.  By being related to a fulfilment beyond, though revelant to itself in the Messianic vision of
the Kingdom of God, human history is redeemed from the evil and
irrationality that infect it and is endowed with meaning in the larger
context of the divine purpose.  On this we shall have more to say in a
later chapter.

Salvation—individual and social, vertical or horizontal—is oriented
to eternity.  But eternity, in the Hebraic view, is not escape *from,* but
fulfilment *of* time.  It is both "now" and "hereafter."  It is *now* because, in fellowship with God, all the vicissitudes of time are overcome
and transcended.  Over the man bound to God in faith, and insofar
as he *is* bound to God in faith, time has lost its mastery.  He remains
in the world to work within it, for this world of life and history is, to
the Jew, the only field of service to God.  But in the new God-centered
life of faith, he has achieved a level of being in which value and meaning are assured beyond the power of time to destroy.  Nothing that
time can bring, neither failure nor defeat, neither sorrow nor calamity,
can separate him from the Eternal; only a resurgence of his own sinful
self-will can do that.  But that is precisely the battle of faith.

The eternity of salvation is also *hereafter.*  In the prophetic-rabbinic
vision, "this world"—the world of history, with its perverseness, in-
coherence and defeat—is destined to find fulfilment and rectification
in the "world-to-come," the "new heaven and new earth" in which
justice and power will finally be united in the kingship of God.  The
salvation that breaks through vertically into the *now* and redeems us
as individual persons from the vicious circle of sinful egocentricity is
the salvation that is *hereafter* to redeem all history in the consummation of the horizontal movement toward the Kingdom of God.  In the
Kingdom of God, the eternity that is ever present and the eternity of
the absolute future are one.

## NOTES TO CHAPTER 11

1. Solomon Schechter, *Studies in Judaism* (Jewish Publication Society: Philadelphia, 1945), Second Series, p. 178.
2. *B.* Erubin 13b.
3. Perceptive students of human ailments are coming to recognize the role of *decision,* and hence of *freedom.* "When their anxieties finally manifest themselves in some form of bodily illness," writes Flanders Dunbar of a certain type of patient (*Mind and Body: Psychosomatic Medicine* [Random: New York, 1947], p. 245), "they will say plaintively: 'I don't deserve to have this happen to me.' Actually, of course, *they do deserve it* in the sense that they have *earned* it by their own reluctance to progress" (my italics.—W. H.). The plight into which the victim of a psychosomatic or purely psychic illness has gotten himself is, in one way or another, to some degree traceable to wrong choices in action or attitude made at various critical points in the past. In other words, *decision*—in the total existential, not merely intellectual sense—is a constitutive factor in the formation of the disease. It is, of course, true that at a certain stage, the patient's freedom of action may become so restricted as to be almost if not quite nonexistent. But among the factors that have operated to destroy his freedom is the wrong use he himself made of it in the past when it was still operative. What is true of the genesis of the disease holds also for its treatment and "cure." The problem is to break through the hardened crust of determinism and restore some element of the patient's freedom. Hence the stress on building up the conscious self (the ego), which is regarded as the organ of freedom. See also Lewis J. Sherrill, "The Sense of Sin in Present-Day Experience," *Religion in Life,* Vol. VIII (Autumn, 1939), No. 4. Sherrill contends that personality disorders can be shown to involve sin, since in some way they all stem from unaccepted responsibility.
4. See, for example, Edmund Bergler's work, *The Battle of the Conscience* (Washington Institute of Medicine: Washington, D. C., 1948).
5. Augustine *Confessions* i. sec. 1.
6. Pesikta rabbati (ed. Friedmann), chap. 44, Shubah 185a.
7. "If thou, O Lord, shouldst mark iniquities, who could stand?" Ps. 130:3.
8. Midrash r. Gen. chap. xii, No. 15.
9. Midrash r. Gen. chap. lx, No. 2
10. Martin Buber, "The Faith of Judaism," *Israel and the World* (Schocken: New York, 1948), p. 18.

"We are dependent upon grace; but we do not do God's will when we take it upon ourselves to begin with grace instead of beginning with ourselves. Only our beginning, only our having begun, poor as it is, leads us to grace." Buber, "The Two Foci of the Jewish Soul," *Israel and the World*, pp. 32-33.

"The grace of forgiveness," Reinhold Niebuhr affirms, "is vouchsafed only to those who have consciously made the will of God their way of life." *Beyond Tragedy* (Scribner's: New York, 1937), p. 268.

11. Israel Abrahams, *Studies in Pharisaism and the Gospels* (Cambridge University: Cambridge, England, 1917), First Series, p. 147.

12. "When fear is mentioned as the origin of religion, it is not ultimately the shrinking fear of fire but the reverent or awful fear of being seen through and through with nothing concealed and with final judgment impending." F. J. E. Woodbridge, *An Essay on Nature* (Columbia University: New York, 1940), p. 321.

13. Woodbridge, *op. cit.*, p. 291.

14. Kierkegaard, *The Sickness unto Death* (Princeton University: Princeton, N. J., 1941), p. 19.

15. Abot d. R.N., ed Schechter, version B, chap. 32, p. 71.

16. Midrash Psalms on 120:7.

17. Midrash Psalms on 102:18.

18. Montefiore and Loewe, *A Rabbinic Anthology* (Macmillan: London, 1938), p. 230.

19. "Where repentants stand not even the very righteous can stand." *B. Berakot* 34b.

20. *Seder Eliyahu*, ed. Friedmann, p. 106; Max Kadushin, *Organic Thinking: A Study in Rabbinic Thought* (Jewish Theological Seminary: New York, 1938), p. 155.

1. Albert Salomon, "Natural Judaism," *Jewish Frontier*, Vol. XV (April 1948), No. 4.

# III.

# RELIGION AND SOCIETY

# 12.  RELIGION AND SOCIETY

Man, we are told, is a social animal, and however we may interpret that phrase, it is certain that human life is embedded in a social context. There is, of course, a dimension to human existence which transcends the social and in which the individual person stands alone, face to face with God. But the course of human life is normally run within society and is conditioned by the forces of society. Human needs and interests emerge within social life; human aspirations, however far-reaching, have to be realized, in part at least, through the means society makes available. Social institutions, on the other hand, obviously provide both setting and limiting conditions for human action. Man is not the product of society nor is he simply a cog in the wheel of the social mechanism, but human life altogether out of its social context is, even for the hermit, simply unthinkable.

If this is true, and it is hard to see how it can reasonably be denied, then the relevance of religion to social life is obvious and direct. For religion, as we have been using the term, is the relating of man's life to the Absolute, and man's life in this world is inescapably social. Only those who deny the reality of this world or else question God's power over it can possibly deny the bearing of religion upon every phase of social life. Once we recognize that the *whole* of life stands under the divine sovereignty,[1] we are unable to consent to the withdrawal of any area from the ultimate concern to which religion bears witness. The divine imperative is seen to be directly pertinent to every human interest, to economics and politics as much as to "private" morality and devotion. In political economy, Lord Keynes has testified, "there are practically no issues of policy, as distinct from technique, which do not involve ethical considerations." "If this is emphasized," he goes on to say, "the right of [religion] to interfere in what is essentially a branch of ethics becomes even more obvious."[2] The concern of religion extends to social life because no area of human existence can be withdrawn from the judgment and mercy of God.

133

These are surely commonplaces for anyone who has grasped the spirit of Hebraic religion. In Hebraic religion, as we have seen, time, history, the ongoing affairs of this world, possess the full reality and significance denied to them by Greek philosophy and Oriental mysticism. The God of Hebraic religion is a Living God, active in this world, endowing its concerns with meaning, yet keeping them under judgment through his activity. Social conditions really do matter for they are the conditions of life, and life is real. Indifference to social conditions must ultimately mean unconcern with life, with history, with the world; and this is altogether impossible for one who draws his religion from Scripture. Hebraic religion is social in its relevance and bearing, or it is nothing.

The Hebraic ethic, grounded in the law of love of God and fellow-man, is a social ethic par excellence. The very notion of an "individual" ethic distinct from man's outgoing obligations is a construction of Greek philosophy and without meaning or warrant in Scripture.[3] Rabbinic tradition, in accord with the double aspect of the law of love, first divides man's duties into those he owes to God and those he owes to his fellow-men, and then proceeds to bind the two in organic relation. "To love God truly one must love man. And if anyone tells you that he loves God and does not love his fellow-men, you will know he is lying."[4] The ethic of Judaism finds its source and power in the perfect love of God; *therefore* it is an ethic of total social responsibility. All institutions and practices of society fall within its scope, since social institutions and practices are, at bottom, no more than patterns of human behavior, and man is responsible for all his actions before God. The law of love—as embodied, however inadequately, in norms of justice—is ultimately the law of all social existence.

What does religion, in its effort to interpret the mercy and judgment of God, say to society? It says both *yes* and *no*, and then moves on to a synthesis of its affirmation and denial.

Religion says *yes* to society because the very being of society as such must be regarded as part of the divine order of creation. Man, according to the Scriptural account, left the hand of his Maker with his natural structure and impulses so ordered as to enable him to live the happy and harmonious life for which he was meant. His need for community which society makes possible must be taken as part of his God-given nature and therefore part of the creation which God saw and pronounced good. Community is not something external to man and alien to his essential nature. On the contrary, it is that through which man realizes his personality and in which he actualizes his being. If therefore we conceive of normative human life as life true to the intent of the Creator, we must necessarily regard community in society as part of the divine order of creation, as an "ordinance" of God for the proper ordering of human life. However much we may condemn any particular social institution—and no particular social institution is exempt from judgment—society as such must be basically affirmed. Hebraic religion cannot make any concession to that type of otherworldly, ultraindividualistic spirituality which sees the relation of man to man as simply an encumbrance on the human soul in its search for salvation. The perfection we are called upon to achieve in this life is a perfection of self-giving love and that is impossible without some structure of society. Even the ultimate I-Thou relation with God is, as Buber so insistently points out, a relation that involves also our fellow-man as the "other" in a community of love. To turn our back upon society in radical denial is to turn our back upon God's creation and upon the destiny for which we are meant in the totality of that creation.

In community and community alone, in the I-Thou communion of love which breaks down all barriers of sinful self-centeredness, is the full realization of personality to be attained. Self-enclosed existence is sinful and perverse; ultimately it destroys the very thing it strives to achieve. Now society is not to be identified with community, of course; in its actual functioning, it exhibits altogether too much of disharmony and conflict to make such simple identification possible. But if community is not society, it is certainly not to be achieved in this world outside of society. Society provides the possibility for the establishment of genuine person-to-person community on the human level and therefore opens the way for receiving and responding to the love of God. It is precisely as such that society is to be ultimately comprehended as part of the divine order of creation. As part of the divine order, it contributes to the end for which man is ordained by sustaining life and providing the matrix out of which true community may spring.

Religion, therefore, if it stands witness to the purposes of the Living God, must begin by saying *yes* to society. There is still another way in which the basically positive relation of religion to society becomes manifest. For whatever may be its overt attitude, religion enters integrally into society as the "spirit" of the culture of which society is the embodiment. That religion does play this role in culture is a commonplace of history, but it is a commonplace that needs to be reiterated today. For in no way is the inner disorganization of contemporary society more strikingly displayed than in the state of religion in our time.

In primitive societies, religion and culture are virtually identical. Even in the advanced societies of ancient times, this identity was not broken. City-state and empire were religious institutions as much as secular, if indeed the distinction can be intelligibly made. Conventions, laws and sanctions in social life were part of the texture of traditional religion, which was "official" simply because it was, so to speak, the sacramental aspect of the accepted way of life of the community. This was pre-eminently true of Jewish society, in principle and where possible in practice, throughout most of its history. Nor, despite the gradual emergence of autonomous interests and fields of activity, did it remain much less true of Western society until the dawn of modern times.

For the past four or five centuries, the overt connection between religion and society has been broken. But it would be well to look a little more closely into the meaning of this rupture and of the consequent secularization of modern life. Does it mean that religion no longer plays a central role in our culture? If we think only of the historical religions of the West, of Judaism and Christianity, then, of course, we must say that this is the case. In relation to these religions, Western society has indeed become largely secular. Vast areas of life have freed themselves from what we have been accustomed to call religion and have established their claim to autonomy. But we should not overlook how equivocal this secular emancipation actually is. Judaism and Christianity no longer dominate the life of Western society. But that is not because our social life has rid itself of religious influence; it is only because the traditional religions have been displaced, so far as influence on social life is concerned, by a legion of so-called "secular faiths," for which we have as yet no names but which we know only too well by their works. What expresses better the "spirit" of our social institutions and collective behavior than the latter-day cults of scientism, nationalism, fascism and communism? These are not ordinarily called religions, but under any functional definition of the term, they must be so regarded. No one observing the ways of modern man in the West, and increasingly even in the East, can ignore the fact that it is to science and technology that he looks for salvation and the solution of the problems of life. Nor can anyone observing, let us say, French or American society, with its round of patriotic festivals replacing the holidays of Church and Synagogue in all but name, with its elaborate patriotic ritual—flag-saluting, anthem-singing, wreath-laying—replacing the observances of the liturgical year, deny that the everyday religion of public life is really nationalism ("democracy," *"la Patrie"*). In all that goes to make up religion, the operative religion of Nazi Germany was a racist fascism and the operative religion of Soviet Russia is a totalitarian communism. Modern society has not rid itself of religion, as it fondly believes; it has merely replaced the historical religions by a host of idolatrous cults struggling for possession of the soul of man.

When Western society, at the dawn of the modern age, first raised its challenge to traditional religion, the immediate consequence was the fragmentation of life into a number of autonomous areas, each dominated by its own ultimate principle. Economics, politics, ethics, education, art, indeed religion itself, came to be regarded as distinct and independent spheres of life operating under their own peculiar laws. In effect, this meant the establishment of a kind of polytheism of ultimates, grouped together in a loosely organized pantheon. Insofar as he was recognized as having jurisdiction over the field called "religion," the Living God was graciously included in this pantheon along with the rest. For a time, this mild and tolerant polytheism proved culturally viable, even productive of some good; for one thing, it broke the grip of an oppressive and monopolistic ecclesiasticism upon the social and intellectual life of the West. But no such loose polytheism can be ultimately tenable. The various aspects of existence, each dissociated from the rest and each claiming to be a law unto itself,·tend to fly apart. Life, fragmented and distracted by conflicting allegiances, loses its unity and center of meaning; it becomes confused, anarchic, quite literally unlivable. Some center of meaning, some principle of unity, has to be found. Unity and meaning for life, however, can be established in only one of two ways: either in terms of the Living God who transcends yet embraces all life, or else in terms of some partial aspect of life elevated to absolute significance. The dominant secular spirit has hitherto blocked the way to a return to the transcendent source of our being. Is it any wonder, then, that modern man, in his craving for unity and meaning to life, has been turning in mass to the totalitarian cults of our time, among which nationalism, in its more extreme forms at least, must certainly be counted? A new "age of faith" seems to be in the offing, but whether or not it is to be an age of demonic idolatry, only the future—that is, we ourselves in our decisions today—can determine.

However that may be, it is plain that the modern world is no exception to what history reveals to be the relation between religion and society. In the modern world, as much as in the ancient or medieval, religion is not only a primary formative influence within society but its final expression as well. It is still true that the kind of society we build for ourselves depends fundamentally upon the kind of beliefs we entertain as to the nature and purpose of the universe and the place of man within it. It is still true, as Marx once said, though in a sense rather different from his, that the criticism of the religion of a society is potentially the criticism of the society of which it is the religion.[5]

Not perhaps since the decay of the Hellenistic-Roman world has Hebraic religion faced a greater challenge than it does today. If it is to make good its claim to be relevant to man's social existence, it must somehow find a way of overcoming the spiritual disintegration of contemporary life and of informing contemporary society with its intensely theocentric spirit. Religion, in the comprehensive sense in which we have used the term, supplies the cohesive force which unifies a society and its culture. Only the religion of the Living God

can drive out the legion of demons infesting our world and give it the
unity and power it needs for survival.

Religion, therefore, says *yes* to society both by affirming it as part
of the divine order of creation and by striving to reconstruct and unify
it in its own spirit. But it cannot stop at this point. It must go on
to say *no* as well. While society is to be affirmed as part of the divine
order of creation, no *particular* social order or social institution can
be so affirmed. And although religion strives to inform society with
its animating spirit, it can never sanctify any social order as being un-
equivocally the embodiment of the true faith. Social order may be
affirmed but every social order must be placed under judgment. Social
institutions may be upheld for what they do to promote and implement the divine imperative, but it must be understood that, from the
ultimate standpoint, no social institution can ever fully measure up
to or incarnate the law of love.

Hebraic religion says *no* to society whenever society, in its pride,
makes claims to absoluteness.[6] Society, in which men see themselves, their ideals and impulses writ large, is easily tempted into
making absolute claims because in doing so it merely serves as a
mask for that deep-rooted human drive to self-absolutization which
we have seen to be at the heart of sin.

Society is a necessary condition of life in this world and a necessary
medium of personal self-realization through community; that is why
we hold it to be part of the order of creation. But to assert this is
very far from asserting that man can achieve his true destiny only in
and through society. Such a claim would make society itself the ultimate end of man and thus turn it into a devouring idol. Personal self-
realization in faith and love needs society for its development,
but it possesses a dimension and a goal of which society knows
nothing. Ultimately, man stands related to God and fellow-man
in a bond which no society can comprehend or social institution
embody.

Community, let us remember, is not society. Community is a free
I-Thou relation of mutuality involving personal decision on both sides.
It is, as Buber puts it, the "between-man-and-man." It is the matrix
of true personality: "The meeting of man with himself can take place

only as the meeting of the individual with his fellow-man."[7] It is also in a sense a phase of redemptive communion with God.

Society, on the other hand, is objective. Man enters it as an "It" not as a "Thou." It involves, to some extent at least, institutionalization, bureaucracy and coercion. Institutionalization means objectification, depersonalization, the conversion of the unique and irreplaceable person into a unit, a number, a card in the file. Bureaucratization means social stratification, with its system of differential status, power and privilege. Coercion means the enforced subjection of man to man in violation of the law of love and the prerogative of God. All of these are necessary to society but they are all destructive of true community.

This ambiguity of relation between community and society determines the ambivalent attitude of religion to the sphere of social life. The divine imperative of love is realized in community, and society is therefore justified religiously insofar as it is necessary for and conducive to community among men. But, by the same token, those inherent tendencies of society, such as institutionalization, bureaucratism and coercion, which imperil community must necessarily fall under judgment as violations of the divine intent. Precisely in order to achieve free community, man must not permit himself to be totally engulfed in the social whole. For man—concrete, individual man— has a place in the divine order and an end in life which no society can contain.

The vindication of the uniqueness and significance of the individual was one of the great achievements of the Hebrew prophets, and with the prophetic tradition it passed into Judaism and Christianity. No ancient civilization had the least inkling of it, not even the Greek, to which we owe so much of our culture. The metaphysical category of the individual is utterly lacking in Greek thought. In the Greek scheme of things, the individual could find salvation only in and through the *polis* (city, state, society, culture).[8] He possessed no ultimate point of vantage on which he could take his stand to resist the total claims of society; he was, therefore, in the end bound to be absorbed by the all-engulfing social totality.

Modern totalitarianism is a monstrously exaggerated and far more effective reassertion of this philosophy. For totalitarianism is not merely a political system; it makes its claim as a spiritual regime, as a way of life. Everything is subjected to social control: no corner of existence is left free, not so much as a nook or cranny is overlooked. Everything is ordered and regulated by society—one's work and play, one's education and leisure, one's thoughts and emotions, one's loves and hates; yes, one's religion, too, for under totalitarianism no man can call his soul his own. There is no escape, no refuge, from the stifling omnipresence of society and state. There is no privacy.

Yet it is the freedom of privacy out of which true community grows and in which man meets God. "We can have dealings with God only as an individual person," Martin Buber says; "the collectivity cannot enter."[9] Against the total claim of society, religion must raise its voice in the name of community and man's true end.

Totalitarianism is not merely a particular regime restricted to some country or section of the world. It is an inner tendency of every society, in the sense in which society is distinguished from community. It is operative wherever society confronts the individual with the claim to being the whole of life. When society makes this claim, even though it is only by implication, Hebraic religion answers: *No!* Society is not the whole of life; man is meant for something more and something higher than society.

The *no* with which religion meets the total claims of society, it extends also to the absolute claims of any and every social institution. Hebraic religion proclaims the law of love to be the final rule of life. It is an imperative that on the social level impels toward ever greater effort for the "realization of life" (Buber) in terms of personality and community. It is an affirmation in terms of which social institutions are both justified and judged. They are justified insofar as they represent attempts to achieve some better balance of justice in society and to provide a more adequate social basis for true community among men. But however justified, they can never have more than a relative and transitory significance. Once they permit themselves to forget this fact, once they are tempted to deny their merely relative validity and begin to make pretensions to finality and absoluteness, they become structures of sin, the expression of self-seeking special interests and the instruments of injustice and oppression. As such, they fall under the judgment of God.

That is what is happening to the economic institutions of capitalism in our time. And that is what is bound to happen to every social institution and every social system at some point of its career. No social institution or system is absolute; none is eternal. Eternal only is the Living God and his law of love, which no social institution can ever fully embody and which every social institution must to some degree violate.

On this level, Hebraic religion must repeat its resolute *no*. It cannot mitigate its insistence that every social order stands under divine judgment and no social institution, no matter how necessary or useful, is exempt from criticism. The prophetic outlook is so radical because it refuses to accept as final the self-justifying claims and pretensions of any institution whatsoever, whether of civil society, church or state. All, even the best, are infected with relativity and injustice; all will at some point have to be transcended—and there can be no final stopping place within history.

No reader who has followed the argument thus far will have missed the affinity of the prophetic viewpoint to much that goes by the name of secular liberalism. For the prophetic affirmation, which is at the heart of Hebraic religion, is an affirmation of a God-centered relativism: God alone is eternal and absolute; all else is relative and passing and subject to judgment. It is easy to see how this viewpoint leaves room for the pluralism and social relativism upon which secular liberalism sets such store. But it escapes the pitfall of secular liberalism by refusing to absolutize any of the so-called "liberal values," whether democracy, "intelligence," or scientific method. Prophetic religion refuses to turn these ideas, institutions or practices, for all their acknowledged value, into idolatrous absolutes, and thus saves them from becoming the vehicles of destructive, ideologizing cults. It disengages what is enduring in the liberal tradition and preserves it from the corruption of false absolutism. And no wonder it can do this, for in the last analysis it is the source from which these liberal values are derived.

The *no* of religion to society is a *no* to the inordinate pretensions and self-absolutizing claims of society and the state. Hebraic religion cannot and will not admit that society is the whole of life or that any social institution whatever is above judgment and criticism in terms of the "higher law" revealed in the divine imperative. It says *no* to society or the state or the church when any of these dares to exalt itself and call for the worship of total allegiance. Only God can make total claims on man, and no institution of society, not even all together or society as a whole, is ever identical with God.

Religion informed with the Hebraic spirit, therefore, exhibits a double and basically ambivalent attitude to society. It affirms and even serves society so long as the latter is aware of its own limitations and is content to serve the purposes for which it was meant in the order of creation. But it is compelled to challenge society the moment the latter forgets its place in the scheme of things and pretends to be the whole of life beyond challenge or criticism. Under such conditions, religion is true to its vocation only if it rises in revolt against society, against the age, against what often appears to be the inescapable "wave of the future." For it is the vocation of religion ever to bear witness to the Living God against the idolatries of the world.

The *yes* and the *no* which religion speaks to society are not two separate words, separately uttered in isolation. The final word of religion to society is a fused, a dialectical *yes-no*. No social institution is ever so evil or corrupt that a vestige of the divine intent is not to be discerned in it. On the other hand, no institution or social order is ever so just or perfect that it can claim to be final. Amidst the relativities of social life, as amidst the relativities of life in general, we move under the obligation of making responsible choices. No absolutes, no infallible rules, no simple confrontations of good and evil, right and wrong, are available. We must judge and choose and act in terms of the relative. But we can so judge and choose and act only because we have in the divine imperative of the law of love an absolute criterion which, while it transcends the possibilities of social life, is also directly relevant to every social decision. Yet here, too, we cannot escape relativity. We judge and choose and act in the way that, in the humility of our faith, seems to us to come closest to the divine will. But we know that our judgment likewise is infected with fallibility and perverted by self-interest. We therefore decide and act, because act we must, but we do so "in fear and trembling," praying for divine mercy and trusting that divine grace will complete and purge the ambiguous enterprises that go to make up the life of man in history.

Hebraic religion does not, like Greek and Oriental spirituality, reject the world and human society as unreal, evil or beyond redemption; nor does it, like the secular cults of our day, take society as final and ultimate. Hebraic religion affirms the world without deifying it; it sanctions society but does not sanctify it. In the final analysis, what it does, in the social sphere as in every other, is to call men to total love of God and to warn them against the pitfalls of idolatry.

## NOTES TO CHAPTER 12

1. "The world of faith, the foundations of which are fixed in the wholeness of a community life subservient to God, guards against the division into two realms, the realm of myth and cult, heaven and the temple, subject to religion, and the civic and economic realm, the reality of everyday public life, subject to special laws of politics, civic politics and economic politics" (Martin Buber, *Prophetic Faith* [Macmillan: New York, 1949], p. 85).
"Man can fulfill the obligations of his partnership with God by no spiritual attitude, by no worship or sacred upper storey; the whole life is required, every one of its areas and every one of its circumstances." Buber, "The Two Foci of the Jewish Soul," *Israel and the World* (Shocken: New York, 1948), p. 33.
2. Letter of J. M. Keynes to Archbishop William Temple, quoted in F. A. Iremonger, *William Temple* (Oxford University: London, 1948), pp. 438-39.
3. Emil Brunner, *The Divine Imperative* (Westminster: Philadelphia, 1947), p. 308.
4. Buber, "Love of God and Love of One's Neighbor," *Hasidism* (Philosophical Library: New York, 1948), p. 168. Cf. I John 4:20: "If a man says he loves God and yet hates his neighbor, he is a liar."
5. Karl Marx, "Critique of the Hegelian Philosophy of Right," *Selected Essays* (International Publishers: New York, 1926), pp. 12-13.
6. In the ancient Yom Kippur ritual, the High Priest was wont to come

before the assembled multitude and confess first the sins of himself and his house and then the sins of the entire people. Thus he acknowledged that even the appointed ministers of the divine cult, even the covenant-people itself, stood guilty under the judgment of God. This part of the ritual is preserved in the *Avodah* of our present Yom Kippur service.

7. Buber, "What is Man?" *Between Man and Man* (Kegan Paul: London, 1947), p. 201.

8. "Greek rationalism had no organ for the free individual. The idea of the right of the individual to possess a sphere of his own was alien to the Greeks. The government was in total control of the community, and whatever freedom the individual might acquire he could gain only through participation in government. The Greek soul did not demand a field in life all to itself and beyond the social order" (Hajo Holborn, "Greek and Modern Concepts of History," *Journal of the History of Ideas*, Vol. X (January, 1949), No. 1.

9. Buber, "The Question to the Single One," *Between Man and Man*, pp. 43, 80.

# 13. JUSTICE AND THE SOCIAL ORDER

## I

However much they may differ in every other respect, all cultures known to history profess to prize justice as the paramount value of social life. Institutions, customs and traditions may vary, but all societies are alike in making this profession; even the modern totalitarian absolutisms have their Ministries of Justice! "To establish justice in the land" is the acknowledged responsibility of every organized society, and to act justly an obligation universally imposed upon every member of society. The content of justice may differ from group to group, the range of its application may vary quite widely, and the standards it imposes may be most grossly violated in practice, but the principle of justice is a principle almost synonymous with human society.

The universality of the concept of justice presents a problem to philosopher and historian. In Western tradition, this problem has been generally met by affirming justice to be innate in the human heart as a manifestation of "natural law" ("natural right"), which is itself conceived to be the deliverance of human reason contemplating the nature of man. This view, ultimately derived from Stoic philosophy and Roman law, holds a double difficulty: it can never convincingly show how justice or any other aspect of "natural law" may actually be deduced by human reason from the given nature of man, nor does it leave place for the wide variations in the content of justice that human societies do in fact display. It claims too much for human reason and therefore allows too little to the contingent factors of history.

In the traditional Jewish view, justice is held to be a divine commandment and its universality accounted for by the fact that it was given to the "sons of Noah" (or of Adam)—that is, to the entire human race. The command to do justice and to implement its enforcement is, in one form or another, included in all versions of the so-called Noahite, or Adamite, laws, and in some it stands first.[1] This view does not assert that human reason can of itself excogitate the concept of justice and fill it with rational content valid for all times and places. Such speculative pretensions are foreign to the Hebraic mind. What it does maintain is that the demand for justice confronts man not simply as a manifestation of his culture or a projection of his self-interest, but as a demand of the transcendent Power who is the Lord of life. And I think that this claim is far truer to the facts of existence than the rationalistic doctrine of "natural law."

The universality of justice is our point of departure. Yet for all its universality, justice seems strangely infected with relativity. It does not require much familiarity with history or anthropology to recognize that standards of justice are in fact greatly influenced by the general level of culture, by social structure and the balance of social forces, and by the pressures of group interest. This much, at least, of sociological relativism we all must grant, even though, following Westermarck and others,[2] we may emphasize the large element of uniformity amidst the seeming chaos of "folkways." We have not forgotten Pascal's ironic exclamation, "Three degrees of latitude reverse all jurisprudence";[3] and we have not forgotten Marx.

But granting relativity all it may legitimately claim, there still seems to remain an inexpugnable element of absoluteness. Quite apart from the particular social order, quite apart from the accepted system of standards, men may be just and unjust. It is even possible for a judge to enforce justly an obviously unjust law and, contrariwise, to enforce unjustly a just law. There thus seems to be a conception of justice that transcends the relative standards of any particular system and is the same for all systems. This is the conception of justice as the *unbiased, impartial* adjustment of conflicting claims in terms of some determinate standard. The just judge is he who applies this standard, whatever it may be, without fear or favor; the unjust judge is he who lets prejudice or interest or any other extraneous factor interfere with his judgment. It is this conception of justice as *evenhanded* that is proclaimed in the biblical injunction, "Thou shalt not wrest judgment; thou shalt not respect persons . . . Justice, justice shalt thou follow" (Deut. 16:19-20).⁴ And in such a sense, justice is indeed absolute.

We have, then, reached this conclusion: To act justly is a universal obligation laid upon man by God—the particular laws or standards of justice, however, vary greatly and are therefore infected with relativity—yet whatever the standards may be, there is a justice, a "righteousness" in judgment, that transcends them and is therefore, in a sense, absolute.

But this does not exhaust the dialectic of justice. The standards of justice of any social order—the content of the concept of justice in that particular society—are embodied in a complex of customs, laws and institutions. But unless we adopt a legal positivism which holds justice to be nothing more than the command of a deified society, we must recognize that it is possible to brand existing laws and institutions and standards of justice as unjust; it is even possible to denounce an entire social order as unjust and to demand one that is more just and equitable. No social order or institution is, in principle, exempt from this criticism and demand. There is, then, some criterion of justice, aside from unbiased enforcement, by which standards of justice, as embodied in laws, institutions and systems, may themselves be judged.

But how can that be? In terms of what standard can any particular standard of justice be judged? And is that standard itself relative? We seem to be caught up in an endless chain, a vicious circle, of relativity. Unless we can find something absolute in which to anchor our judgment, justice, for all its universality, is bound to collapse into a welter of incommensurable concepts and standards. It would then be impossible to use the words "just" and "unjust" at all in any normative sense.

A point of anchorage in the absolute we can find, but to do so we must go beyond justice. The ultimate criterion of justice, as of everything else in human life, is the divine imperative—the law of love.

Justice is the institutionalization of love in society. "The ideal of the religion of Israel," Moore states, "was society in which all the relations of men to their fellows were governed by the principle, 'Thou shalt love thy neighbor as thyself.' "[5] This law of love requires that every man be treated as a Thou, a person, an end in himself, never merely as a thing or a means to another's end. When this demand is translated into laws and institutions under the conditions of human life in history, justice arises. Because the demand of love is institutionalized, it is relativized and therefore in some measure violated and falsified. Yet that is the only way it can be made regularly operative in collective life. In its ultimate bearing, the commandment of love, of course, transcends all social arrangements, but unless it is to remain mere ideal and sentiment, it must find some way of enforcing itself in and through the institutions of society. This it does by establishing norms of justice.

We have already, in an earlier chapter, discussed the dialectic relation between love and justice, and everything we said there is directly relevant to the present problem. Justice is at once the outworking of love in social life and its denial. Let us note that whereas justice would be impossible did men give no acknowledgment whatever to the law of love, it would be unnecessary did the law of love prevail in the relations of men in society.[6] Justice calls for the impartial allotment to each of what is rightfully his of the goods that men in society have at their disposal. But in true community founded on love, such a problem could never arise, for in the self-giving of love, there is no "mine" and "thine,"[7] and all claims are merged in a genuine identity of interest. It is because love fails in the collective life of sinful men—and what does sinfulness mean except that love fails?—it is because love fails that justice is instituted among men. For without some structure of justice, the failure of love in social life would leave every man exposed to the unrestrained aggressions of every other and thus reduce society to utter chaos. In this sense, justice is indeed, as it is declared in tradition, the foundation of every social order, one of the pillars of the universe.[8]

The implementation of justice in laws and institutions brings with it all the ambiguities that inhere in collective life. It means institutionalization; it means bureaucratism; it means coercion. It means the adaptation of the norms and procedures of justice to the historical structure of the society and to the particular constellation of social forces. It means the inevitable compounding of the ideals of justice with expediency, power and self-interest. No system of justice is ever exempt from these corrupting influences, and therefore no system of justice, no matter how exalted, can ever claim to be final or perfect.

The tension of justice can be resolved only in love, but such resolution is not possible within history. Social life requires both freedom and order, both equality and subordination. In love, these contradictions are taken up and dissolved; under the rule of justice, however, they must remain ever in tension, in a precarious and constantly changing balance of claims and counterclaims raised by men in pursuit of their interests.

Justice is therefore no abstract formula of eternal validity through which the conflicts of men can be simply and fully resolved. To claim such an eternal and timeless quality for justice is the error of the doctrine of "natural law." The principle of a "just wage," for example, has no power to settle a dispute between employer and employee in the way that the rules of arithmetic can settle a dispute in computation; neither this principle nor any other is capable of establishing a suprapartisan truth to which both sides must submit out of sheer logical necessity. That is not how justice works in this world. Injustice, particularly social injustice, is, at bottom, due to inordinate disproportions of power in society, making it possible for some men to exploit and oppress others. Justice, therefore, requires an equalization of power; it strives to achieve a sort of moving equilibrium, a shifting adjustment of conflicting claims and interests, which themselves reflect and are conditioned by the given structure of society.

Jewish tradition, for all its exaltation of justice, does not fail to recognize its relative aspects. "Wherever there is strict truth," a remarkable passage in the Jerusalem Talmud tells us, "there cannot be peaceful judgment; wherever there is peaceful judgment, there cannot be strict truth. How then can one combine both? Only by an equitable settlement . . ."⁹ Both are satisfied, but neither fully. That is the nature of justice.

Because justice is so embedded in its social context, it will inevitably reflect the relativities and ambiguities—yes, the *injustices*—of the order in which it is involved. But because it is rooted in the law of love, it possesses the power of transcending its own limitations. For not only does justice require the impartial adjustment of claim and counterclaim *within* the framework of the social order; it requires also a criticism of the social order itself and of its system of justice in terms of a higher law, the law of love, the standard by which all human enterprises must ultimately be judged. Thus can justice rise above society and its institutions; thus can it bring society and its institutions before its bar for judgment; thus can it demand a more just, a more equitable, social order. But in doing so, it is no longer merely the institutional justice within society; it is the transcendent justice that ever stands under the sign of the eternal law of love.

Justice, which starts with love as its life-giving source, thus returns to it as its final law. Social justice will never be fully attained until men live as equals in free community. This means not only that it can never be attained in history but that, when it is attained, it is no longer justice that prevails but love. The law of love is involved in all the approximations of justice, not merely as the source of every particular set of norms but also as the standpoint from which the limitations of these norms are discovered and subjected to judgment.¹⁰ The regulative function of the law of love can be said to operate along two dimensions: in the first place, it requires us to go "beyond the limits of the law" in our dealings with our fellow-men, no matter how just the law may be, thus permitting love to temper the necessary rigors of justice; and, secondly, it requires us to place under judgment every historical embodiment of justice and to strive to achieve a higher level, less in conflict with the divine imperative. Deprived of this ultimate perspective, justice becomes a vehicle of power and oppression, a citadel of injustice. Only love can provide the leaven to keep justice fresh and ever changing and hence free from the corruption of idolatrous absolutization.[11]

Perhaps the most crucial area in the concern over social justice today is the realm of economic life. For economics is, in a very real sense, basic to social existence. Marx was not entirely wrong in this insight, however mistaken may be the general idea of "historical materialism"; and Freud has confirmed the emphasis from an entirely different direction. "Laying stress upon the importance of work," Freud says, "has a greater effect than any other technique of living in the direction of binding the individual more closely to reality; in his work he is at least securely attached to a part of reality, the human community."[12] The problem of "economic justice", of a "just" economic order, has always been of central concern to mankind, never more so than in the past century and a half.

But what is economic justice? Which economic system is *the* just one? Is it medieval corporatism, free-enterprise capitalism or collectivist socialism, or perhaps some other as yet unknown? Clearly, no answer is possible in the abstract. The problem of economic justice is a problem of the actual functioning of economic institutions under concrete historical conditions. Neither authentic Jewish nor authentic Christian religion endows any particular economic order with special sanctity. The prophets spared no detail in denouncing the economic evils of their time, which they traced to pride and idolatry, but they refrained from vesting any particular economic program with divine sanction; the only really "positive" note they struck was a call to repentance and return to God. All systems and programs were but the contrivance of men and therefore none could claim any final validity. What our religious tradition does give us is a basic attitude. The social attitude of Hebraic religion holds it to be the will of God that the resources of nature and the fruits of human creativity, which are a divine gift,[13] should be used for the satisfaction of human needs and the enhancement of human welfare. And the institutions arising out of economic activity are to be judged by how well they serve these ends and, even more comprehensively, by how they affect the total life of man in society

Since the conditioning circumstances of social life are in process of constant change, no institution, certainly no economic institution, can be finally evaluated once and for all. Judgments have to be made in the light of the particular conditions and always in terms of the balance of good over evil. But though the judgments may be relative and changing, the criterion is constant and absolute.

The ultimate criterion in economics is that which governs social life in all its aspects: the degree to which human persons are treated as ends in themselves, of equal worth and dignity as children of God and bearers of the divine image. This criterion demands true community and condemns the exploitation as well as the coercion of man by man. It condemns above all what Marx called *Verdinglichung* of the worker by the economic system—that is, his conversion into a thing, into a mere cog in the wheel of a vast impersonal mechanism.

By this criterion, all economic institutions and all economic systems must be found wanting, since all, being institutions devised and operated by sinful men, are bound to become in some degree vehicles of pride and greed. But not to the same degree. Some institutions may encourage the evils of economic life, whereas others may be so constructed as to check these evils and to divert or block the sinful impulses of men. On the other hand, institutions may promote or retard the capacity of society to produce, which is surely a basic factor in all economic calculations, since it is production which provides the indispensable condition for life itself and therefore for the good life. Indeed, material production—the conversion of the resources of nature to serve human needs—is part of man's vocation in this world, in pursuit of which he is said to imitate and continue the creative activity of God.[14] The essential problem of economic justice may thus be formulated somewhat as follows: What kind of economic institutions, under the given conditions, will best serve to sustain the values of personality-in-community, with due regard to the technical requirements of production?

The answer, of course, varies with time, place and circumstance, and to deal with the problem responsibly requires more than the repetition of moralizing phrases and doctrinaire slogans. Economics is indeed a branch of ethics, and ethics a branch of theology, as such eminent economists as R. H. Tawney and Lord Keynes have pointed out, but between the ethical and theological presuppositions, on the one side, and the economic conclusions, on the other, there is a vast middle ground in which special knowledge and experienced judgment are the prime requisites. That economics has ultimate ethical bearings does not imply that the economist is to be replaced by the moralist or theologian; on the contrary, specialized knowledge and technical competence are endowed with even greater significance in view of the ultimate issues to which they are related. But it must be a knowledge and training possessed by men aware of these issues and fully conscious of their moral responsibility.

All of these considerations are directly relevant to our own economic dilemma. The economic system known as capitalism today stands under judgment. Through the operations of this system, great accumulations of private wealth are piled up in society, giving rise to corresponding concentrations of social power in the hands of a few, those who own and control the economic process at its key points. The results are inescapable—want, insecurity and social dependence for large masses of people, and, only too often, economic chaos and social conflict as well. Very few responsible observers today would care to deny that the existing economic setup stands in need of far-reaching and thoroughgoing reconstruction. In order to meet the requirements by which all social institutions are judged, it must be transformed into a system designed for human welfare and controlled democratically, far more than today, by the people as producers, consumers and citizens.

This would seem to mean socialism, as the term has traditionally been employed. But here another consideration enters. Experience has painfully shown that the replacement of capitalist private property by collectivism may become the economic basis of an all-engulfing totalitarianism, in which the evils of even the most unregulated capitalism are far outdone. Such is the lesson of Russian communism and, in another way, of German nazism. The goal, therefore, cannot be a totally collectivized economy. It must be rather the kind of reconstruction of economic life that will enhance human freedom and avoid totalitarianism by developing an economy in which all economic power whether public or private is subject to effective institutional restraints and controls. As to which fields of economic life shall remain privately operated and which shall be transferred to public agencies, and to what degree, that, too, cannot be a preconceived dogma but must be determined by circumstances.

Once we have said this, we are again forced to recognize how relative and provisional our recipe for economic justice really is. We are no longer able to advance a doctrinaire system in which all the evils of life will be eliminated and pure justice attained. The best we can do is to put forward a program of social reform through which, we have reason to believe, a higher level of justice can be achieved in economic life.[15] But we can make no absolute claims, either for our program as such or for its permanent validity. No institutional setup, even if it is the very best under the circumstances, is ever the last word in social justice. The stabilization of any system, no matter how just and free, as *final* inevitably becomes the stabilization of the unfreedom and injustice within it. The absolute imperative of the divine law, precisely because it is binding and yet impossible of full realization in the course of history, places every economic and social achievement under judgment, and from that judgment none is exempt.

In a way, the prophetic principle here enunciated is more revolutionary than even the most revolutionary secular philosophy, for whereas secular philosophies are always expecting to build the perfect society in this world, after which there will no longer be any need or reason for change, the prophetic view holds that no social order within history can ever be regarded as final, so that men must *never* permit themselves to rest content with things as they are. On the other hand, just because all social institutions are so inescapably relative, there is none that is totally devoid of the divine intent: even Sodom had its justice; even a robber band cannot maintain itself without some semblance of mutual confidence and internal law. What we can achieve is never pure justice as against pure injustice; it is always no more than a somewhat higher measure of justice under the circumstances. But this "somewhat higher," this merely relative task, is of the greatest significance for the moral life.

What then of "true" justice? Is it nothing but a phrase, a mere illusion? No; it is a reality—but an *eschatological* reality. Perfect justice, which is identical with perfect love, cannot be realized in any historical society; it is, however, held out for us as the law of life in the "new heaven and new earth" for which all history is destined. "On that day," in the Kingdom of Heaven, justice and love will be finally reconciled for all creation, as they already are in God.

We shall, in a subsequent chapter, discuss the eschatological vision, the vision of "last things," that is so crucial to Hebraic religion. For our present purpose, it is enough to recognize that the Kingdom of Heaven is at once a promise, a demand and a norm. It is a promise in that it points to the fulfilment of life in a community of love in free obedience to the kingship of God. It is a norm in that it shows what life ought to be like if it is to fulfil the intent of the Creator and the vocation of man. But beyond promise and norm, the Kingdom of God is a *demand,* for by confronting us with the picture of life as it *should* be, it demands that we never rest until we have brought actual life into conformity with the divine intent. In the Kingdom of God we see the culmination of all things promised in faith, but in the Kingdom of God we also have an ever-present possibility and a never-failing reality. Wherever there is self-giving love, wherever there is true community, wherever men recognize, though perhaps only implicitly, the kingship of God and the divine imperative, there the Kingdom of Heaven is among us, there it is a reality in this world, in this our life. But it is a reality that drives men on to its ever-greater realization. "The *agapé* of the Kingdom of God," Reinhold Niebuhr tells us, "is a resource for infinite developments toward a more perfect brotherhood in history."[16] "Whatever God designs for the world-to-come," the rabbis teach, "he does by anticipation through the righteous in the present world."[17] The power of the Kingdom is the dynamic of the struggle for social justice; it is a dynamic born out of the tension between the always unsatisfactory actuality of history and the trans-historical perfection of the Kingdom of God.

This eschatological perspective is capable of generating a vital drive for social action while avoiding the pitfalls to which secular reform movements are always exposed. Secular reform movements, even when their intentions are of the best, are only too often hampered and confused by their utopianism, their lack of realism, their tendency to absolutize their particular program or blueprint. Only a religious realism informed with the power of the Kingdom and prepared to subject everything—every idea, institution and program, including one's own—to the criticism of divine judgment, in terms of the Kingdom, can make it possible for us to fight for a higher measure of justice in society without identifying our particular judgment with the absolute. Only a religious realism which understands that the Kingdom of God is ever present, and yet ever to be striven for, can generate a dynamic that will give us no rest in any achievement, no matter how high, so long as a higher level of achievement is possible—which it always is.

The power of the divine imperative to social justice reveals itself not only in the sacrificial idealism of those for whom the love of God implies love of their fellow-men. It operates also through the force of human self-interest. In the intricate dialectic of history, idealism and self-interest are so completely fused that only God, who is a searcher of hearts, can tell them apart.

Was it the economic self-interest of the industrial classes of the North or the devoted idealism of the Abolitionists that led to the eradication of Negro slavery in the United States? How much did each contribute to the final outcome and what part did each play in the motivations of the millions who had their share in the great struggle?

Or let us take an example from the experience of our own time. Not so long ago in this country, before trade unionism became a force to be reckoned with, industry was the preserve of what can only be described as absolutism. Management exercised a power in plant and factory that was virtually unlimited. Undoubtedly, most industrial magnates felt with George F. Baer[18] that the vast power they held over their fellow-men was a trust from God, vested in them because of their superior character and abilities, and employed not selfishly but in the best interests of all. We today can see what a large element of ideology and self-deception went into this idealism; we can see that what the industrial magnates were actually doing in the fulfilment of their "trust" was to enrich themselves, inflate their pride and enlarge their already exorbitant powers over their armies of workers. The gross injustice of it all was not visible to them, and they repelled with self-righteous indignation any question as to their motives or any challenge to their autocracy.

What was not visible to them was only too obvious to their victims. The workers, for whom the existing distribution of power meant poverty, insecurity and oppression, quickly saw the injustice and rose in rebellion. Painfully, at the cost of great effort and sacrifice, they formed their unions and were eventually able to confront management with a collective power that could not be brushed aside. Gradually, an element of democracy was introduced into industry; gradually, the absolutism of management was mitigated by the constitutional devices of unionism and collective bargaining. Gradually, a higher level of justice in terms of freedom, security and the material benefits of modern industry was attained. Few achievements in social justice are so impressive as what the trade unions have accomplished in Britain and America in the course of the past century. If, indeed, the industrial magnates were right in assuming that they had a commission from Heaven for the administration of industry, it has required a rather considerable effort on the part of labor to persuade them to exercise it with discretion.

Why was it that the workers were able to see so clearly the injustice to which so many of the most eminent men were blind? Is it not because the self-interest that closed the eyes and dulled the sense of justice of the one party had quite the opposite effect on the other? The victims of injustice are always more ready to perceive it than those who benefit by it. We need not believe that the workers, because they were so keenly aware of the injustice in the industrial relations of the time, were necessarily better men or gifted with a higher native sensitivity than the employers, who honestly could see nothing so very wrong. On the whole, they were about the same—well-meaning, respectable men, not without a touch of self-righteousness, men who wanted to be fair and certainly did not mean to do wrong if they could help it. But the workers had the inestimable advantage of being the victims of injustice rather than the perpetrators of it. Their eyes were opened and their sense of justice sharpened by their self-interest, the very same self-interest which had such morally devastating effects on their employers.

In this situation, which is so typical of the dialectic of social reform, self-interest served as the chief instrument of social justice. Yet not entirely, not finally. The oppressed workers would never have been able to take the first steps in organization, which often entailed great hardship and suffering, had they not been stirred by a handful of idealists, men and women for whom the organization of labor was a great cause which they were ready to serve in sacrificial devotion. But can we separate the idealists and the self-seekers so completely, so certainly? Was there not a ferment of idealism in every worker who went out on strike, and was there not an element of self-seeking, hidden from himself though it may have been, in the idealist whose leadership in the cause served so frequently to inflate his pride and extend his power over his fellow-men? The compounding of motives is beyond the power of man to descry. But this we do know, the divine will to social justice enforces itself through all the involvements and ambiguities of human nature and history.

## II

The passion for social justice runs through Judaism from the earliest writings to the present day. No modern attack upon economic exploitation can equal in earnestness and power the denunciations of the prophets against those who "grind down the faces of the poor."[19] No modern warning against the evils of authoritarianism is so arresting as the words of Samuel rebuking the people of Israel for desiring to subject themselves to the yoke of kingship.[20] And the numerous rabbinical provisions protecting workers against their employers and helping to mitigate the lot of the poor, the friendless and the underprivileged are a sign that the original biblical impetus was not lost in later Judaism.

The prophetic passion for social justice and the Scriptural emphasis upon the utter reality of this life of ours have had a powerful influence on our entire culture. Perhaps no aspect of biblical religion is more striking, particularly in contrast to the otherworldly quietism of Oriental spirituality, than its restless discontent with existing conditions and the perpetual striving for something better—indeed, for perfection. The social dynamic of Hebraic religion is certainly a dynamic of social progress. The serious concern with social justice, so characteristic of the West, is one of its fruits. The social activism of Western life and its sense of the reality of history constitute another.[21]

All the more strange, therefore, is it that the actual influence of religion in our culture, of religion not in its normative ideal but in its institutional actuality, has generally been exerted not so much to advance the cause of social justice as to hamper and retard it. Neither the Synagogue nor the Church can deny its share of responsibility for the fateful schism between religion and the movement for radical social reform that has come to be known as socialism.[22] In both Judaism and Christianity, the original prophetic-activist spirit at the heart of Hebraic religion came, in the course of events, to be vitiated by two factors of broad historical significance. On the one hand, institutional religion became more and more identified with the upper classes of society. On the other, the religious spirit became increasingly permeated with a life-denying otherworldliness stemming from sources far removed from Hebraic spirituality.

Throughout the Middle Ages and well into modern times, the Church and Synagogue, as social institutions, formed part of the privileged order in their respective communities. The alliance of "the altar and the throne" in Christian Europe is too notorious to require emphasis. The Jewish community was, of course, in a rather different position. It was itself outside the bounds of official society and at the very best maintained a precarious existence in the shadow of persecution, fear and insecurity. But within the Jewish community, the usual class distinctions and class antagonisms were rampant. The poor murmured against the power of the rich, which extended even to the Synagogue, for the Synagogue was only too often in the grip of the *parnasim*, the communal oligarchs. In its own way and under its own conditions, the Synagogue and the Church each alike threw its weight on the side of the status quo, sanctifying existing forms of economic exploitation and political privilege. The bitterness and inchoate resentment of the lower classes found expression on more than one occasion in open revolt, in sectarian movements and, with the rise of modern socialism, in an outright secession from the religious community.

The conservative, even reactionary attitude of established religion, reflecting its privileged status as a social institution within the community, was reinforced by the growing prevalence of an alien individualistic otherworldliness, which devaluated actual life and preached an ascetic indifference to worldly affairs. Within Judaism, which rabbinic tradition held close to everyday life, this tendency could not reach the extremes it sometimes did in Christian Europe, but no one at all acquainted with the ascetic aspect of medieval Jewish piety will care to deny that it was operative in the Jewish community as well.

In western Christendom, the Catholic Church for a time tried to maintain a middle course, which enabled it to find a place for ascetic otherworldliness while itself intervening actively to preserve and sustain the medieval social order. Protestantism, when it arose, upset the balance and strove to recapture the spirit of Hebraic-prophetic activism. But it was largely frustrated by its social and political involvements. Lutheranism, allied by corporate self-interest to the German princes, developed the famous doctrine of "orders," which was interpreted as entirely removing public life from the possibility of improvement and the operations of the moral law. Religion became an affair exclusively of private life, with no relevance to the larger concerns of society. Calvinism and the radical sects, particularly the latter, did manage to retain a good deal of the social dynamic of Hebraic religion and even developed significant theologies of social action. The ferment of Puritan radicalism in England and New England, the important contribution of British Protestantism to humanitarian reform and to the early labor-socialist movement, bear witness to this vital impulse. It is surely no accident that in Britain the schism between socialism and religion never developed very far, certainly never reached the point of irreconcilable hostility so characteristic of the Continent.

In the Jewish community, the same general forces were at work, though the historical pattern was naturally very different. Hardly a trace of the radical activism of the prophets was to be discerned in conventional religious life. Legalistic conformism and otherworldly quietism met and sustained each other. Forces of innovation and discontent could find only peripheral expression, further and further removed from the center of official religion. Amorphous lower-class revolt is to be detected in the various messianic movements and emphatically in Hasidism, while bourgeois reform interests came to the fore in the *Haskalah* (Enlightenment). But none of these impulses could find either understanding or adequate room for development within the established religious order. The breach became open and irreparable when labor socialism appeared on the scene in the latter half of the nineteenth century. For Judaism, far more than for Christendom, socialism came into being as a deep schism within the religious community, which had hitherto been virtually identical with Jewish society. The Synagogue, no more than the Church, proved able to find place for the new social forces that were coming to the fore and claiming their rights in community life.

On the whole, therefore, it may be said that established religion entered the modern world as a socially conservative force, systematically intervening on the side of the rich and powerful, whose self-seeking impulses it did not scruple to justify, while counseling the masses to patient resignation and submission to injustice. Neither its many charitable works nor its genuine spirit of dedication to what it conceived to be the true welfare of mankind can change this ominous fact.

But socialism, too, bears its heavy measure of historical responsibility.

The roots of socialism go deeper than its own philosophy would care to admit. Fundamentally, socialism is predicated on two convictions: on the conviction that life and history have meaning in terms of some fulfilment toward which they are heading, and on the conviction that men *can* change their social conditions for the better and are in duty bound to strive to do so. Both of these convictions are rooted in the Hebraic spirit—in the Hebraic passion for social justice and, even more profoundly, in the prophetic vision of the Kingdom of Heaven not simply as the negation but as the transfiguration and fulfilment of the actual world. The religious origins of the socialist idea are plain.

Nevertheless, for reasons we have noted, the socialist movement, outside of Britain, arose in modern times as an antireligious movement. On the social and political level, it was uncompromisingly anticlerical, waging bitter war against Church and Synagogue as bulwarks of reaction. On the spiritual level, it proclaimed a militant, atheistic materialism and thus came forward as the protagonist of a rival total philosophy claiming the allegiance of Western man. For socialism, as Dostoevski saw so clearly (*The Brothers Karamazov*), was "not merely the labor question." It was "before all things the atheistic question, the question of the form taken by atheism today, the question of the Tower of Babel, built without God, not to mount to heaven from earth but to set up heaven upon earth." On both levels, the social and the spiritual, socialism was the heir and continuator of the eighteenth-century bourgeois Enlightenment.

Socialism took the prophetic passion for social justice and the prophetic insight into the meaning of history and secularized them. It thereby stultified and corrupted their meaning. Driven on by the logic of secularism, which sees man as supreme and self-sufficient in the universe and believes him capable of fulfilling himself entirely in human terms, socialism placed the fulfilment of history *within* history itself and thus opened the door to a self-destructive utopianism. Its conception of human betterment exclusively in terms of man's material life in society betrayed it into a disastrous worship of industrialism and an exaltation of collectivism as an end in itself. Its secularist logic also drove it into an idolatrous moral absolutism, in which the interests of the "cause" (and only too often of the Party) became the final law of life, justifying everything. The other side of an old idolatrous moral absolutism is moral nihilism, and although socialism did affirm a set of humane values as the goal of its endeavors—values, incidentally, taken over from the Judeo-Christian tradition—these values were left ungrounded in anything really ultimate and therefore could not withstand the attrition of self-interest and the human lust for power.

Militant secularism very early became the dominant motif in modern socialism. In part, this was a justified protest against the failure of institutional religion and a judgment upon it, but in part only. Primarily, it was the unbridled Prometheanism that has brought modern man to the verge of destruction. This doctrinaire secularism not only robbed socialism of its legitimate source of moral power; it not only confused its insights and its understanding of the realities of human life; most fateful of all, it converted socialism into an idolatrous pseudo-religion and thus drove it into suicidal opposition to its own true source of being.

Thus arose the schism between socialism and religion in the modern world. The schism bears testimony to the fact that each, in a different way, has proved unworthy of its own best lights and has allowed itself to be perverted from its true course. It is a schism that has done much lasting damage to both sides, to socialism even more than to religion, but most of all, perhaps, to the internal stability of our culture, to its best hopes and aspirations.

Are there any prospects of an early end to this catastrophic schism? There are such signs. The time we are living in appears to mark the transition from the modern age, in which the schism arose and spread, to a new, "post-modern" period, in which a reconciliation between socialism and religion may prove possible. An entire historical epoch seems to be coming to a close with our generation.

The secularist culture of the past three centuries is in collapse. Perhaps most irreparably damaged is the materialistic socialism that was an integral part of this culture. Its metaphysical foundations are utterly gone: its stubborn denial of the spiritual dimension of human life, its uncritical faith in history as salvation, its crude economism and its fetishism of a thing-centered culture. Its utopianism has proved a snare and a delusion. Its moral principles have shown themselves incapable not only of sustaining the ends it affirms, but even more significantly, incapable of maintaining control over the means employed to achieve these ends. Its mystical exaltation of collectivism has generated a powerful drive toward a compulsive totalitarianism, completely engulfing and obliterating the individual human being.[23]

Within the movement that has its origins in Marxist socialism, there has taken place, in recent decades, a fundamental differentiation. Communism, relentlessly pursuing the logic of Prometheanism, has ended up as an ideology of total enslavement. The democratic elements in the socialist movement, on the other hand, aghast at this outcome, have shrunk back from the ultimate consequences of their traditional philosophy and are striving to reaffirm their humanistic, libertarian emphasis—at the price, however, of abandoning their metaphysical pretensions. With them, socialism is no longer a rival religion; it has been reduced to the rather more modest proportions of a program of social and economic reconstruction. On some socialists, indeed, the experience of the past generation has had an even more profound effect: it has led them, in the words of Ignazio Silone, to "go beyond [their] bourgeois limitations" and attempt to regain for socialism its religious grounding.[24] In any case, virtually all agree that the traditional antireligious bias of modern socialism has proved a disaster and must be eradicated if socialism is to have any future.

On the other side, there are new and significant trends in the world of religion. Under the impact of the crisis of our time, the historic alliance between institutional religion and the forces of reaction has been partly or wholly broken. There is a wide ferment under way in most religious bodies, Christian as well as Jewish, in favor of extensive social and economic reforms. Organized religion, moreover, has proved one of the most potent forces in the struggle against totalitarianism, against Nazi totalitarianism yesterday and against Soviet totalitarianism today. Whatever may be the factors involved, and no doubt a politic adaptation to new social realities is compounded with a more fundamental reorientation, it can no longer be said of most religious bodies—at least not in the democratic countries of western Europe and America nor, in the totalitarian countries, of the churches in opposition to the regime—that they are the bulwarks of political and economic oppression. When the Vatican denounces capitalism as "atheistic in its structure; gold is its god," when the World Council of Churches categorically condemns laissez-faire capitalism and communism and calls for a "third way," when rabbinical bodies reiterate almost as a matter of course their approval of programs that involve the most far-reaching reforms,[25] it is obvious that the old formulas will no longer do. "The ideas we [socialists] had about religion and clericalism fifty years ago cannot be maintained any longer today . . . Let us admit times have changed."[26] These words of Paul Henri Spaak, former Prime Minister of Belgium and an authoritative leader of Continental socialism, sum up in impressive fashion the change that has taken place.

Whatever the immediate future may bring, it seems clear that there is now emerging for the first time in two centuries a real basis for the reconciliation of the ancient foes, a real possibility for the end of a schism that has wrought such havoc in our civilization.

In order to preserve itself as a humane and democratic force in the present-day world, socialism has found it necessary to abandon its metaphysical pretensions. But in abandoning its metaphysics, it has had to abandon also the prophetic urgency of its call and its apocalyptic appeal. It can no longer summon the masses to the "final conflict" and it can no longer pretend that the program it fights for will usher in the Perfect Society. It has lost its revolutionary spiritual dynamic.

Basically, this loss is all to the good, for the only way in which a social movement can of itself develop a revolutionary spiritual dynamic is by absolutizing itself as an idolatrous cult, and the consequences of that we have already seen. Yet men cannot engage in any great and enduring work, involving frustration, hardship and sacrifice, without some sense of vocation and urgency, without some conviction in the lasting significance of what they are doing and without some promise of fulfilment beyond their own limited powers. The social movements of our day, disoriented and deflated by the horrors of the past three decades, do not possess such an ultimate standpoint and are therefore in constant danger of degenerating into visionless opportunism and futility. They can be saved only by being related to an ultimate concern beyond themselves, a concern that is truly ultimate and not simply the premature absolutization of something merely partial and transitory. The delusive utopian eschatology of Marxism, which believes it can bring history to a stop and establish perfection in this world, socialism is at last beginning to throw off. It now remains as the task of our time to reintegrate the socialist idea, the idea of militant action for social justice, into the transcendent eschatology of Hebraic religion. In the eschatological passion of the prophets, the social radicalism of our time can find the power and the vision to work within history for the fulfilment of history, while realizing that it is not in the time of man or by his hand that the work can be completed.

## NOTES TO CHAPTER 13

1. See, e.g., the formulations of the Noahite (Adamite) Laws in Midrash r. Gen. 16:9 and 34:8; *B.* Sanh. 56a and *Tos.* Ab. Z. 8 (9). 4-7 (ed. Zuckermandel, pp. 473f.), where justice is placed first.
2. See note 10, chapter 3, above.
3. Pascal, *Pensées*, No. 294.
4. "You shall do no unrighteousness in judgment; thou shalt not respect

the person of the poor nor favor the person of the mighty; but in righteousness shalt thou judge thy neighbor." Lev. 19:15. Exhortations to justice and "righteousness" in judgment form a dominant theme in rabbinic tradition.

5. G. F. Moore, *Judaism* (Harvard University: Cambridge, Mass., 1927), II, 156.

6. "Suppose that the necessities of the human race continue as at present, yet the mind is so enlarged and so replete with friendship and generosity that every man has the utmost tenderness for every other man and feels no more concern for his own interest than for that of his fellows; it seems indeed that the use of justice would in that case be suspended by an extensive benevolence. . . .Why raise landmarks between my neighbor's field and mine when my heart has made no division between our interests but shares his joys and sorrows with the same force and vivacity as if originally my own? Every man, upon this assumption, being a second self to another, would trust all his interests to the discretion of every man, without jealousy, without partition, without distinction. And the whole human race would form only one family." David Hume, *An Inquiry Concerning the Principles of Morals*, III, Part I.

7. "He who says what is mine is mine and what is thine is thine is the average type; some say it is the character of Sodom . . . He who says what is mine is thine and what is thine is thine is a saint. . . ." *M.* Abot 5.13.

8. "Rabban Shimon ben Gamliel said: Upon three things the world stands, on truth, on judgment and on peace." *M.* Abot 1.18.

9. *J.* Sanh. 1:1, 18b. A parallel passage, replacing "strict truth" by "charity," appears in *Tosefta* Sanh. 1.3.

10. Cf. Reinhold Niebuhr, *An Interpretation of Christian Ethics* (Harper; New York, 1935), p. 140.

11. "Any justice which is only justice soon degenerates into something less than justice. It must be saved by something which is more than justice." Reinhold Niebuhr, *Moral Man and Immoral Society* (Scribner's: New York, 1934), p. 258.

12. Sigmund Freud, *Civilization and Its Discontents* (Hogarth: London, 1930), page 34 note.

13. "The earth is the Lord's and the fullness thereof." Ps. 24:1.

14. Abot de R. N., version B, chap. xxi.

15. It follows, therefore, that there may well be several programs along different lines all aiming at the same general goal. It is not without significance that the advocates of a "controlled" capitalism and the champions of a limited or "democratic" socialism have been steadily converging, so that it is frequently difficult to tell them apart. Once the claim to absoluteness is abandoned, sweeping designations such as "capitalism" and "socialism" lose much of their meaning.

16. Reinhold Niebuhr, *The Nature and Destiny of Man* (Scribner's: New York, 1943), II, 85.
17. Midrash r. Gen. 77.1 (ed. Theodor-Albeck, p. 909).
18. Mr. Baer was spokesman for the anthracite operators in the great strike of 1903. He is best remembered for his pronouncement: "The rights and interests of the laboring man will be protected and cared for, not by the labor agitators but by the Christian men to whom God, in his infinite wisdom, has given control of the property interests of the country." Allen Nevins and H. S. Commanger, *History of the United States* (Pocket Books: New York, 1943), p. 409.
19. See, e.g., Isa. 1:15 ff., 5:8; Amos 2:6-7; Mic. 2:1-2. See also Moore, *Judaism*, II, 156.
20. I Sam. 8:4
21. "It is Jewish-Christian futurism which opened the future as the dynamic horizon of all modern striving and thinking." Karl Löwith, *Meaning in History* (University of Chicago: Chicago, 1949), p. 111.
22. By "socialism" in this general sense is meant the conviction that the welfare of the masses of the people is a prime social responsibility and that in modern society this responsibility is not likely to be met unless the masses of the people—the wage-workers, the farmers and other "functional" groups—themselves organize to act politically on behalf of their interests and the interests of the community.
23. Cf. Will Herberg, "The Crisis of Socialism," *Jewish Frontier*, Vol. XI (September, 1944), No. 9.
24. Ignazio Silone, *And He Hid Himself* (Harper: New York, 1946), "To the Reader," pp. v, vi.
25. A convenient summary of the authoritative Catholic position may be found in Benjamin L. Masse, "Pope Pius XII on Capitalism" and "Pope Pius XII Demands Economic Reform," *America*, Vol. 84 (December 2, 1950), No. 9 and No. 13 (December 30, 1950), respectively. The Protestant position is set forth in the statement, "The Church and the Disorders of Society," accepted by the Amsterdam Assembly of the World Council of Churches in 1948. For the Jewish position, reports of the conferences of rabbinical associations of this country may be consulted.
26. Reported from Brussels in the *Commonweal*, June 18, 1948.

# 14. SOCIETY, STATE AND THE INDIVIDUAL

## I

Every historical period has its characteristic problem which sets its mark on all phases of social life and endows all social issues with their measure of relevance. At one time, it was the problem of religious unity; at another, the problem of nationalism; at still another, the "labor" problem. These older problems still persist, of course, but they are no longer central. The central problem of today, as far as our social life is concerned, is the problem of totalitarianism—the problem of the relations between society, state and the individual.

What Judaism has to say on this problem is of basic importance, but it cannot be presented by trying to piece together a picture of a "true society" from the remarks of the rabbis or the laws and customs of ancient Israel, however illuminating these may prove in the proper context. The starting-point of authentic Jewish thinking on social and political questions is its underlying conception of the fundamental nature of man in his relation to society. Judaism, we have repeatedly noted, sees man as inescapably dual, the two sides of his nature involving and implying each other in all aspects of life. On the one hand, man is made "in the image of God"; he is a creature endowed with spirit, with the capacity to transcend nature and self through reason, imagination and moral freedom. But on the other hand, he is sinful, egocentric, perpetually driven to deny his creatureliness and make himself the center of his universe. His efforts at self-transcendence are thus limited and corrupted by his self-centeredness, by his pride and inordinate pretensions, which on the social level are manifested in the lust for power. As a creature endowed with freedom of spirit, man is capable of rising above immediate impulse and narrow self-interest to affirm the ideals of truth and justice. Yet no sooner does he achieve a standpoint outside of himself than he is tempted to convert his idealism into an instrument of his pride and self-aggrandizement. Between these two poles—between his self-transcending potentialities, on the one hand, and his sinful egocentricity, on the

168

other—man lives out his life and pursues his enterprises. They are the focal points for any really profound understanding of the problems of human existence.

It is in terms of this duality that we can formulate the paradox that pervades social ethics in all its aspects. As a child of God formed in his image, every human person is of infinite worth, an end in himself, never merely a means to some external end. Of course, this dignity which he possesses is not his own by "natural right"; it comes to him as an endowment from God and has no meaning or validity against God. But it does have meaning in relation to human society, and in that connection it implies freedom and equality—both in a radical sense. Because man is, within the order of creation, an end in himself, he possesses the freedom of self-determination and moral responsibility. On the same ground, we must affirm the essential equality of all men, not in any empirical respect—for in every empirical respect men are very far from equal—but as the children of a common Father. Liberty, fraternity and equality are not the mere watchwords of revolution; properly understood, they describe what belongs to every man by virtue of his unique relationship to God. Let us remember that, in the tremendous formula of the Mishnah, it is every individual person for whose sake the world was created.[1]

But this man for whose sake the world was created, and who is an end in himself within the order of creation, is also sinful man. Freedom and equality are his by divine endowment and these he is ready to claim as his right. But in his sinful egocentricity, he is only too prone to overlook that, if it was for his sake that the world was created, it was also and equally for the sake of his neighbor. In the infinite pretensions of his pride, he strives to elevate himself above his fellows and to subject them to his will. He sees himself as alone the true end, and all others as somehow instruments or means to his purpose. He strives to exploit every institutional advantage that may fall to him by virtue of his position in society in order to increase his power and to inflate his self-esteem. And all this he does with good conscience, for it is not himself he feels he is serving but some larger cause or goal beyond the self. The capacity of the human mind to deceive itself through ideology and rationalization is in itself startling evidence of the power of sin.

Man, who is entitled to and claims for himself the rights of personality that come to him from God, is driven by sinful egocentricity to deny them to others. In the light of this paradox, it can be seen why the traditional Jewish attitude to the political state is so radically ambivalent.

On the one hand, all earthly government is branded as sinful because it is usurpation—only God is the rightful king; and because no man has the right to coerce or dominate another—that is God's prerogative. Wellhausen has aptly described the Israelite ideal as a "commonwealth without [earthly] authorities"[2] in which all men are subject directly to God and his law. When the elders came to Ramah to demand that Samuel set up a king to rule over them "like all the nations," what they were really doing, Scripture makes clear, was rejecting God "from being king over them."[3] Earlier, Gideon had refused to take the kingship offered to him with the proud words: "I will not rule over you; neither shall my son rule over you. The Lord shall rule over you" (Judg. 8:23). This radical libertarian attitude remains a vital force in the rabbinic tradition, despite all vicissitudes of politics and history.[4] "Unto me are the children of Israel slaves (Lev. 25: 55)," the Talmud has God as proclaiming, "*not slaves unto slaves*":[5] men are unconditionally subject to God but not to other men. Normatively, all men are free; only God is above them. Coercion of man by man is thus inherently sinful, for it implies the exaltation of one man over another in flagrant defiance of the divine law that holds all men equal and equally subject to God.

Yet, on the other hand, earthly government, with all that it involves, is justified as necessary for the peace and security of society and the establishment of justice among men. "Pray for the peace of the government," we are enjoined in the Mishnah, "for were it not for the fear of that, we should have swallowed each other alive."[6] Coercive authority must be applied at some point if society and its institutions are not to be destroyed by the disruptive forces of individual and collective self-interest. The most elementary form of social organization, the barest rudiments of social justice, are impossible without the exertion of power. "In each pursuit and in each institution," the anthropologist Malinowski points out, "the element of authority and its hierarchical delegation are indispensable. Discipline and some means of enforcing this submission are essential to authority."[7] Justice is impotent and order impossible without the sword of the state ever ready to be drawn in their defense.

Earthly government is necessary for the preservation of society and the maintenance of justice, yet it is itself involved in sin and evil. This radical ambiguity reflects the paradox that, from the standpoint of Hebraic religion, earthly government is at once the consequence of human sinfulness, a protection against it and a vehicle which it employs. It is the consequence of human sinfulness because, normatively, men should live in fraternal and uncoerced harmony and their failure to do so, which makes government necessary, is the result of their sinful egocentricity. It is a vehicle of human sinfulness, because the powers and agencies of government only too often become instruments of self-aggrandizement on the part of those who wield them. It is a protection against human sinfulness because the might of the state is always to some degree a power against evildoers and a curb upon the lusts and aggressions of men. That an institution so dubious in its nature can serve as a protection against evil—that we must do violence to maintain order, engage in repressions to secure freedom and resort to coercion to establish justice—is a paradox involved in the final problem of ends and means.

In view of the ambivalence of all earthly government, only that state can be said to meet the test which is somehow able to sustain society and uphold justice by the use of its power and authority and yet is able also to guard against the excesses of arbitrary, uncontrolled power in its own operations. To put it another way, with a somewhat different emphasis, political and social institutions have a double function: the positive function of providing the best possible conditions for the free development of each individual person in community; and the negative function of setting up institutional curbs upon the human lust for power, which can convert even the most necessary institution into an instrument of self-aggrandizement. But this is essentially the democratic state. Democracy takes into account both sides of the human ambivalance. Man, in his idealism and imagination, possesses the capacity to transcend self and aspire to impartial justice: *this makes social order possible.* But man's capacity for self-transcendence is necessarily limited by the irreducible egotism of his nature: *this makes democracy necessary.* Both aspects are indispensable to any tenable theory of democracy: one as a protection against the pessimistic cynicism that leads to tyranny; the other, against the optimistic utopianism that leads to anarchy.

Particularly since Rousseau, belief in democracy has been associated with confidence in the "natural goodness" of man.[8] Human beings, we are assured, are by nature rational and virtuous but they have been corrupted by evil institutions, by the machinations of ambitious rulers, cunning priests and greedy exploiters. Free them of these, educate, enlighten and emancipate them, and their natural reason and virtue will reassert themselves. Given the opportunity, men will show that they can govern themselves in peace and wisdom. Democracy becomes at once the medium of emancipation and the final state of social harmony.

In one form or another, this naive optimism has permeated the democratic philosophy of the past two centuries. "Liberal" versions of Judaism and Christianity, Rousseau's romanticism, the rationalism of the Encyclopedists and utilitarians, Dewey's gospel of social intelligence, even the sophisticated millernarianism of the Marxists, are, at bottom, variant forms of an attitude that cannot be characterized as anything but a deceitful illusion. It is a deceitful illusion because it is manifestly untrue to the facts of life, because it fails to answer the critical question of how evil institutions could possibly have arisen if man is really good, but above all because it tends to betray us into a false security in a situation where only the utmost vigilance can promise safety. Democracy becomes in this view something very easy to achieve and, once achieved, still easier to maintain.

But by the same token, democracy becomes hardly necessary. Either anarchy or absolutism could be defended with equal plausibility. If the evil in man manifesting itself in social conflict is merely peripheral and accidental, merely the consequence of ignorance, obsolete institutions or "cultural lag," then one may reasonably look forward in the not too distant future to a state of uncoerced harmony in which "all need for force will vanish since people will grow accustomed to observing the elementary conditions of social existence without force and without subjection."⁹ Indeed, if democracy depends on the virtue of the "common man" for its realization and justification, then it is hardly possible as long as men continue in their benighted state and hardly necessary once they are truly enlightened.[10] Anarchism, not democracy, is the logic of the doctrine of the natural goodness of man.

But the same logic may be turned to very different purposes, to validate absolutism, whether of a despot or a majority. That natural goodness which is supposed to emerge once man sloughs off the encumbrance of ignorance and vicious institutions may very well permit the enlightened ruler to be the true guardian of the welfare and interests of his subjects. Hobbes, whose pessimism had curious lapses, used this alleged identity of interest to justify absolute monarchy.[11] Rousseau used it to justify the despotism of the "general will,"[12] and more than one apologist has used it to justify the Stalinist regime in Russia.[13] Their line of argument cannot be effectively met, at least not on the theoretical plane, so long as perfect rationality and goodness are held to characterize men and to be capable of realization or very close approximation in actual life.

Historically, as the French and Russian revolutions bear witness, the optimistic conception of human nature is closely associated with revolutionary terror and despotism. Robespierre and Lenin were both confirmed believers in the natural goodness of man. Each looked upon his revolutionary utopia as no more than an obviously reasonable, thoroughly practicable program bound to commend itself to all right-minded people. Opposition, where not the result simply of misunderstanding, they held to be due to incorrigible benightedness, to corruption by the old institutions beyond hope of repair. The only remedy seemed the merciless excision of the rotten, worthless flesh to permit the healthy growth of the newly emerging organism: revolutionary terror was obviously the proper instrument for this wholesome "surgical operation." In this way, the utopian revolutionary manages to make his idealistic theory serve to justify his bitter resentment at the shattering of his dreams on the hard rock of human recalcitrance. Rosa Luxemburg long ago warned that the revolutionary who "enters the arena with naive illusions" will be driven to "resort to bloody revenge when disillusionment comes."[14]

If the notion of the natural goodness of man makes democracy unnecessary, the doctrine of his utter depravity makes it impossible. Seizing upon the profoundly true insight that the state, in one of its aspects, serves as a protection against evildoers, thinkers such as Luther and Hobbes have elaborated a political philosophy which sees in the secular order simply the realm of evil and assigns to the state the sole function of repression.[15] Terrified at the destructive possibilities of human sinfulness, they find the only hope of social security, the only alternative to chaos, in an ironclad regime that will keep the inordinate egotism of human beings in strict check. The slightest relaxation of absolutism, in the view of these thinkers, would throw society into the abyss of anarchy at the brink of which it constantly stands.

But fear may be as delusive as hope, and the philosophers of unrelieved pessimism fall into a fatal error even in terms of their own system. If human nature is so utterly depraved that nothing but ruthless force from above can preserve society from self-destruction, what about the absolute ruler to whom the function of coercion is entrusted? He, too, is presumably human, hence totally depraved and bound to use his position of power to aggrandize himself at the expense of his subjects, thus in his turn destroying the social order. And this holds true whether the absolute sovereign is an individual, an aristocratic élite  or the "people." Hobbes's strange attempt to discover a community of interest between ruler and subjects is utterly out of line with his system. Luther does not seem to make even so much of an effort to achieve consistency. Because the doctrine of utter depravity denies man any capacity to transcend self, it renders not only democracy but even society ultimately impossible.

An adequate philosophy of the state cannot be grounded in either an oversimplified optimism or an oversimplified pessimism. It must seek its basis in a view of man more profound and many-sided, one that is capable of doing justice both to man's potentialities and to his limitations, both to his undoubted capacities for moral and intellectual achievement and to the inevitable deformation of his reason and will through inordinate self-love. There is no alternative to a recognition of the radical ambivalence of man's nature as posited in Hebraic religion.

II

The crucial point in the problem with which we are here concerned, the problem of man and the state, is the question of power— its nature, utilization and control.[16] The exercise of power by some men over others is implied in the very existence of society; yet power possesses its own compulsive dynamic. Those who possess power will seek to preserve, enlarge and exploit it in the interests of individual and collective self-aggrandizement. This conclusion emerges directly from our view of human nature and is the incontrovertible testimony of all history and experience. How can power be utilized, as it must, to preserve the social order from the chaos of anarchy, and yet be prevented from running wild and falling into the tyranny of absolutism? This is the problem which democracy claims it alone can deal with.

If there is any truth at all in the view we have presented, it should be clear that power cannot be tamed simply by enlarging the wisdom or fortifying the virtue of the holders of power, for there is no wisdom so broad or virtue so strong that it can completely escape the corruption of self-interest. Let us remember that the compounding of motives, so universal in the moral life, is particularly insidious on the social level. Men will do things in the name of their nation, their class or their party that they would shudder to do for their own advantage. It is not merely a question of falling short of ideal standards. There is no atrocity on the calendar that perfectly upright men will not commit to advance a cause to which they have given their total allegiance. This evil they do with good conscience, indeed with a glow of self-righteousness, for it is now stripped of the odium of selfishness and is sanctified by the holiness of their cause. Blinded by an idolatrous loyalty and deceived by the personal unselfishness of their conduct, they do not see that their idealism is but the service of a larger selfishness in which their own evil impulses find expression.

Nowhere are motives more mixed, nowhere are ideals more deeply entangled with interests, than in the power situation. And nowhere is the blighting effect of the impurity of means more disastrous. "Power tends to corrupt and absolute power corrupts absolutely," Lord Acton declares.[17] "Woe unto authority, for it destroys those who possess it," the rabbis teach.[18] Power corrupts the wielder and those upon whom it is wielded, feeding the pride and arrogance of the one and instilling hatred mingled with subserviency in the other. The lust for power easily penetrates the most idealistic cause, since all causes, even the most idealistic, require power for their realization in history. But power is not long content to remain a mere instrumentality. It has an obsessive logic of its own. Invoked to implement a higher purpose, it ultimately all but replaces that purpose. Power becomes its own end, pursued and cultivated for its own sake. The man who wields power, particularly unlimited power, however humane his impulses and idealistic his motives, falls gradually under its spell. Power becomes the god, the demon, he worships, at whose altar he is driven to sacrifice the best that is in him and in his ideals. "Love work, hate mastery," rabbinic tradition advises us,[19] and this advice reflects a profound insight into the sinful nature of man, who is not so made that he can wield power with safety to himself and his fellowmen.

The passion for dominance, which works such havoc in human life, is so rampant today because everything in our culture conspires to encourage it. Particularly insidious has been the effect of scientific technology and modern industrialism, which have given man almost incalculable power over nature. "The most important effect of machine production on the imaginative picture of the world," Bertrand Russell says, "is an immense increase in the sense of human power." As a result, "there arises, among those who direct affairs or are in touch with those who do so, a new belief in power: first, the power of man in his conflicts with nature, and then the power of rulers as against the human beings whose beliefs and aspirations they seek to control by scientific propaganda . . . Nature is raw material; so is that part of the human race which does not effectively participate in government . . . This whole outlook is new . . . It has already produced immense cataclysms and will undoubtedly produce others in the future. To frame a philosophy capable of coping with men intoxicated with the prospect of almost unlimited power and also with the apathy of the powerless," Russell concludes, "is the most pressing task of our time."[20] Such a "philosophy," however, need not be framed anew; it is already available in the fundamental affirmations of Hebraic religion—in the attitude of humility and mutual respect that is engendered by the recognition of our utter nothingness in the face of a transcendent God who, nevertheless, loves and cherishes us as his children. What is needed is to give these affirmations vital significance for modern life by making them relevant to the new cultural situation.

It is hard for us to grasp the meaning of power in its full dimensions, for we are all caught up in its temptations and involvements. It is only too easy to ignore the inner tensions· of the paradox and see power as something simple and unambiguous. It is only too easy to fall into either perfectionism or Machiavellianism.

Perfectionism, as we have had occasion to note, holds that the absolute imperatives of the moral law can be literally embodied in conduct if only the desire is present. It sees purely ideal possibilities as practical courses of action. It knows nothing of the clash of irreconcilable interests in social life and sees in strife and injustice little more than the fruit of a deplorable moral ignorance. To the perfectionist—to the "idealist," as he is called—the problem of power is therefore no more than a problem of moral enlightenment, a problem of replacing "force and violence," which he holds to be a remnant of barbarism, by the "civilized methods" of reason and goodwill. The perfectionist has no sense whatever of the depths of evil and unreason in sinful man; nor has he any understanding of the tragic predicament in which men find themselves in the real world, where the choice that confronts them in action is never simply a choice between an ideal good and an obvious evil but always a choice among relevant possibilities, all of them to some degree infected with evil.

At its best, perfectionism may serve as a needed protest against the corrupting relativities of practical life. But perfectionism has its less attractive side as well. Its utopianism too often degenerates into a fatuous optimism that expects all conflict and ill-will to disappear at the mere preaching of the word of love and therefore refuses self-righteously to countenance any "violent" resistance to evil. And when sad experience brings home the folly of these illusions, perfectionism only too easily turns into a blighting cynicism to which all courses are equally bad and all prospects equally hopeless. Cynicism is, after all, simply idealism gone sour.

Perfectionism logically implies nonparticipation in the decisions and

,activities of social life, all of which involve the exercise of power in some fashion and to some degree. Since it abjures power as simply evil, it can offer no guidance to the moral perplexities of men who find themselves inextricably involved in power situations.

Machiavellianism,[21] on the other hand, knows all about power and prides itself on its utter realism. It denies that moral standards, authoritative though they may be for private conduct, have any relevance to politics. The only valid criterion is success; power justifies power and everything necessary to attain and preserve it. Again, the real moral problem involved in power is ignored.

Traditional Marxism entertains a curious two-sided attitude toward power, compounded of both perfectionism and Machiavellianism. Its "interim" ethic—valid until the day when the true socialist society shall have been firmly and finally established—is frankly Machiavellian: power is the goal, everything is justified if it contributes to the "seizure of power," moral scruples are mere "bourgeois prejudices." But, since it asserts that all conflict and strife among men are the result merely of economic privilege, which will be wiped out with the triumph of socialism, Marxism concludes that in the socialist society of the future, perfectionism will prevail: mutuality, goodwill and universal harmony will be the rule of everyday life. Ultimate utopianism thus sanctifies and sustains a provisional Machiavellianism of unrestrained power politics.

Perfectionism demands that action, public as well as private, be the direct exemplification of ideal standards and therefore free from the corruptions of power. Machiavellianism denies the relevancy of such standards to politics and thus elevates power itself into the final good. Marxism's view is divided, agreeing with the one for the now and with the other for the hereafter. But nowhere do we find any sense of the complexity of the problem or any feeling for the tension generated out of the impact of power. Indeed, for perfectionism or Machiavellianism or Marxism there cannot be said to be a real problem of power at all. Their view of human life and its motivations is too simple to permit an understanding of the deep existential roots of the power drive in human life. Only the fulness of the biblical conception of man can provide the materials for such an understanding.

In the biblical conception, man is a creature uneasy and anxious in his creatureliness. He strives to escape the limitations of his condition by denying his dependence on the transcendent and claiming absolute significance for himself and his enterprises, in other words, by trying to play the god in his own little universe. What he is really striving for is security, but it is a security grounded in self. The lust for power over others—the power to subject others to one's will and to manipulate them as objects—is so universal among men because in the intoxication of power one may indeed imagine oneself the god of his own little world and blot out, for a time, the insecurity, the anxiety, gnawing at his heart. But security grounded in self is, as we have seen, a delusion. Every effort to establish it on such a basis but intensifies the radical insecurity it is striving to allay. Hence power requires ever more power to secure it, and to this devil's game there is no end. Thomas Hobbes was sufficiently close to his religious tradition and had a sufficiently clear eye for the doings of men to appreciate this fact and to express it in classical form.

> For the nature of Power [he writes] is, in this point, like to Fame, increasing as it proceeds; or like the motion of heavy bodies, which the further they go, make still the more haste. . . So that in the first place, I put for a general inclination of all mankind a perpetual and restless desire for power after power, that ceaseth only in death. And the cause of this is not always that a man hopes for a more intensive delight then he has already attained to; or that he cannot be content with a moderate power; but because he cannot assure the power and means to live which he hath at present without the acquisition of more.[22]

The drive for power is the root sin of pride in its social dimension. It is inherent in all men, however much it may be modified in its manifestations by social and cultural factors. Its operations pervade all levels of social existence in a bewildering multiplicity of forms and transmutations. It is at once the most fundamental reality and the most dangerous force with which man is confronted in his social life. How and to what degree may it be controlled?

There are easy solutions, but they cannot satisfy us. Simple moralism sees no great difficulty in drawing the fangs of power by appealing to man's "better nature." It has no understanding of the compulsions of the power situation. Simple rationalism and simple naturalism hope to render power-wielding man harmless, either by enlightening him or by removing his unfortunate fixations and complexes. They do not see that the thirst for power is rooted not in ignorance or the accidental frustrations of life but in the very conditions of man's creaturely existence. Equally futile is the simple "economism" of the Marxists, who are confident that once economic injustice and class conflict are abolished, no one will any longer have any interest in abusing power. They, too, do not see how deeply the power drive is rooted in the nature of sinful man, much deeper than the superficial layers of economic interest, nor does it seem to occur to them that power creates its own dynamic and feeds on itself.

Let us recognize that power of man over man can never be rendered completely innocuous. The best we can hope to do is to keep it under constant control, as one does with a dangerous natural force, such as fire or electricity—except that in this case the menace is within us, the very ones who are to control it. Ultimately, there is only one way in which power can be rendered safe and that is by diffusing it so widely through society that it becomes possible to pit power against power and block abuse in one direction by checks and balances in another.[23] The arbitrary power of management over workers, to take a contemporary example, can be mitigated only by raising against it the organized power of labor. But the very instrument thus developed to check the despotism of management—the trade union—itself harbors tendencies toward bureaucracy and authoritarianism, so that it ultimately becomes necessary to devise checks and balances upon the arbitrary power of the labor leader.[24] This process of check and countercheck, and further control, is one that never ends, for it is never safe to regard power, wherever vested, as in "good hands."

Not even when it is in the hands of the "scientists." Because physicists are able to be objective and impartial in the laboratory, we are asked to believe that they can somehow elevate themselves above the passions and interests of men and so be safely trusted with supreme power. Because the psychoanalysts and anthropologists have gone a little way in penetrating the superficial layers of human motivation, we are asked to accept them as the superguardians of society.[25] But the physicists and psychoanalysts and anthropologists, for all the pretensions raised in their name, are but human beings like the rest of us, subject to the same pressures and temptations of the human condition. If they are to be our supreme guardians, watching over the holders of power in society, who, we may ask, will watch the watchmen?

No, power can never be rendered harmless by placing it in "safe" hands, because in matters of power no man's hands are "safe."[26] The only way to tame power is to limit, restrict and counterbalance every delegation or exercise of it in society. This is really the heart of the democratic idea. The result is not impotence or paralysis, as the impatient advocates of authoritarianism declare, but a genuine mobilization of the resources of society for purposes sanctioned by broad agreement and effected with a minimum of coercion and regimentation. And in the long run, it has proved itself far tougher and more viable in the test of history than the superficially more efficient systems that the authoritarian principle has been able to devise.

Democracy, we may conclude, is predicated not on faith in man but on the conviction, so mercilessly inculcated by our experience of human nature and history, that no man is good enough or wise enough to be entrusted with irresponsible power over his fellow-men.[27] Under democracy, both rulers and masses are restrained and controlled for the security of the people against the rulers, on the one hand, and of minorities and individuals against both rulers and people, on the other. Democracy, in short, is the institutionalization of permanent resistance to human sinfulness in politics,[28] which, as we have seen, manifests itself primarily in the egocentric self-assertion of power. So thoroughly aware is democracy at its best of the inevitable moral dubiousness of all government that it embodies the principle of resistance to government in the very structure of government itself.

This conception of democracy as an institutional system for the control of power has immediate relevance beyond politics in the narrower sense. It is equally significant for economics. What it implies in this sphere is not merely economic security, however important that may be as a condition for the pursuit of the good life. Nor is it economic collectivism, however necessary some form of collectivism may be for the realization of freedom in the modern world. It is economic democracy, democracy in the sphere of economic life, the diffusion and control of economic power in the interests of freedom. It therefore implies the effective participation of the members of the community, producers and consumers alike, in the determination of the course, conditions and purposes of economic life. This I take to be the common element in all programs of economic reform in the interests of social justice.

What I have been trying to say should not be interpreted as meaning that, in my view, Judaism is identical with democracy or that democracy is the only political system compatible with Jewish religion. Jewish religion possesses a range and relevance to human life that far transcends the limited problem of the political order of society. And since democracy as a system is conditioned by social and cultural factors which are not universal in history, Judaism has found it possible to live with and give a degree of approval to many other types of political order—on the one condition, however, that they do not attempt to deify themselves and make total claims on man. The burden of the preceding discussion is simply this: that the complex yet realistic conception of the nature of man affirmed by Hebraic religion provides the framework in terms of which the idea at the heart of democracy may best be understood and justified and its inadequacies criticized.[29] In this way, it offers modern man a fundamental line to help guide him amidst the ambiguities and perplexities of political existence in the chaos of contemporary history. It does not, however, "solve" the political problem by constructing a blueprint of some ideal system in which the tensions and paradoxes of political life will be eliminated. These tensions and paradoxes still remain. Earthly government still remains a kind of usurpation of the divine prerogative, even though it may be necessary for social existence. Power of man over man still remains an evil, even though it may be an unavoidable instrument for the maintenance of justice and the preservation of society. The paradoxes and perils of man's collective life can never be completely eliminated in this world. But a religious awareness of their existence—particularly a contrite recognition that each of us is thoroughly involved in them, whatever be our station in life—may help arouse in us the uneasy conscience, the attitude of acting in repentance, that is our only safeguard amidst the corruptions of power and the endless relativities of history.

## III

Closest, perhaps, to the concern of Jewish religion in the sphere of political life is its stress on the inherent limitations of the claims of society and the state upon the individual person. Jewish religion, as we have seen, insists that genuine personality in man is developed through free community. Society is affirmed because and insofar as it serves to foster community among men, and the state is affirmed insofar as it is necessary to preserve society. But when the state claims to be identical with society and when society, on its part, sets itself up as a superperson, claiming superior reality and higher worth than the individual human being, both state and society become a force for evil and a danger to the moral life. The virtual deification of the collectivity, under the name of Society or the State, which runs through so much of Western thought from Plato to Hegel and the contemporary totalitarians, is utterly repugnant to the Hebraic outlook. Judaism affirms society to be more than the state, and the individual person to be more than either society or the state. It reserves for the individual basic rights and a sphere of life inviolate against all collective claims. It knows that society is more than the state because it can remember that its own "heroic" period—the period of the constitution of Israel as a "holy people" and its confrontation with God at Sinai—was a time without king or state. It knows that the individual is more than either society or the state because it knows that "the collectivity cannot enter instead of the person into the dialogue of the ages which the Godhead conducts with mankind;"[30] it knows that only the individual can be truly responsible. Yet its attitude is not that of atomistic individualism. Rather does it take its stand affirming community as against both individual self-sufficiency, in which the personality of one's neighbor is ignored or denied, and the collectivism in which all persons are swallowed up and engulfed in the mass. This double distinction has been well formulated by Martin Buber:

Individualism [he writes] understands only a part of man; collectivism understands man only as a part. Neither advances to
the wholeness of man, to man as a whole. Individualism sees
man only in relation to himself; but collectivism does not see
man at all—it sees only "society". . .The fundamental fact of
human existence is neither the individual as such nor the aggre-
gate as such. . .The fundamental fact of human existence is
man-with-man. . .Collectivity is based on an organized atrophy
of personal existence; community, on its increase and confirma-
tion in life lived towards the other. . .The person becomes questionable through being collectivized. . . Primacy is ascribed to
the collectivity. . .The collectivity becomes what really exists;
the person becomes derivatory. Thereby the immeasurable value
which constitutes man is imperilled; it is a doctrine of serfdom.[31]

The individual is in duty bound to serve the society of which he
is part and to respect its authority: "Separate not yourself from the
community," is a familiar rabbinic dictum.[32] Yet the individual transcends his society and all possible societies, for society has no jurisdiction over him in the things that matter most—his conscience and
his relation to his God. Standing on the divine law, he may judge
and even defy the merely relative justice of his society. "The example
of the Hebrew nation," Lord Acton states, "laid down [the line] on
which all freedom has been won—. . .the doctrine of the higher
law, . . .the principle that all political authorities must be tested and
reformed according to a code which was not made by man."[33] The
integration of the good within any actual social system can never be
more than provisional, for there is no temporal society in which the
human spirit can find final rest and which it may not judge from a
vantage point that transcends it. If kingdom there must be for our
ultimate ideals to find lodgment, that kingdom can be nothing short
of the Kingdom of Heaven. Of that society, and of that society alone,
man can regard himself as a citizen without reservation.

It therefore goes without saying that the totalitarian claim of society
or the state to control a man's entire life is utterly repugnant to Judaism. Neither society nor the state can make such absolute claims;
they are barred from doing so because, in the Jewish view, man is
totally subject only to God, and it is an affront to Heaven for man
either to claim or to acknowledge a right which is God's alone. Our

charter of freedom as against men is thus ultimately derived from the humble recognition of our total subjection to God.

Judaism long ago made the distinction between the "things that are God's" and the "things that are Caesar's."[34] But the "things that are God's" are not limited in Jewish tradition to the teaching and practice of religion in the narrower sense. God's law is relevant to all things and therefore in all things there are limits beyond which society or the state may not rightfully go. Rabbinic law specifically forbids the Jew to obey the state if the latter enjoins anything that involves idolatry, murder or sexual impurity—even if such disobedience costs one his life.[35] The areas in which the claims of the state must be questioned or denied are not fixed once and for all; they vary with circumstances and the changing conditions of social life. Ultimately, one's conscience must decide and we must recognize a man's right—nay, his duty—to follow his conscience even when his conscience seems to us to be wrong. But whatever the relativities of the situation, the principle is always the same: neither society nor the state has a total claim on man and when such claim is made, it must be categorically rejected.

Not only the individual person but the community of believers transcends the state and has rights against it as well as against society as a whole. Jewish tradition is one continuous story of the witness of faith against those who hold power in state and society. "The prophet," Buber writes, "is appointed to oppose the king and even more, history [i.e., the course of events]."[36] From prophet against king we go on to Hasidean against Hasmonean, to Pharisee against Sadducee and Herodian. In every case, it is the man or community of faith challenging the inordinate pretensions of official society in areas where its authority cannot be recognized. "In the eyes of [the Pharisees]," Leo Baeck reminds us, "the struggle for God and his commandments was often a struggle against the commandments of the state."[37]

It is hardly to be expected that any state, even the most democratic, or any society, even the most tolerant, will welcome this radical challenge to its authority, for all societies and all states have secret pretensions to absoluteness. Yet this challenge is the only condition upon which the precarious balance between freedom and order in society can be maintained and social authority prevented from lapsing into totalitarianism. It is, as Lord Acton has said, the line "on which all freedom has been won." It is the only effective principle that can be set against the powerful trend toward the enslavement of the human spirit that is the mark of our time.

This trend toward the enslavement of the human spirit is born out of the malady of the age. We may here recall what was said in an earlier chapter about the disintegration of life in modern industrial society. In an effort to refashion himself and the world in autonomous terms, modern man has disrupted the age-old continuities of life—religion, the family, the community—and has reduced the individual to a forlorn, fragmentary existence in which he is no more than an insignificant cog in the vast impersonal mechanism of society. Loneliness and anxiety pervade life in the wasteland of our "asocial society,"[38] our society without community. Totalitarianism comes forward to offer the semblance of the community we crave, the "togetherness of the whole" in race or party or nation, and all it asks is that we abandon our personal being and responsibility. No wonder that it has been able to work such enchantment upon scores of millions of forlorn and disoriented men of our time.

For totalitarianism, we must never permit ourselves to forget, comes not simply as the claim of an external power to total allegiance; there is something in the human spirit itself which drives man to total engulfment in the mass and idolatrous submission to a leader. Freedom is hard to bear, an intolerable burden for those who have lost their grounding in the divine. Freedom means responsibility; it means decision, and the responsibility of decision engenders that painful anxiety which Kierkegaard has called the "dizziness of freedom."[39] The urge to renounce one's freedom so as to relieve oneself of responsibility is an impulse deeply rooted in the human heart; in our own time, it has driven whole peoples to seek a self-annihilating security in the totalitarian herd. Anything is welcomed if it promises escape from the dreadful *anomie* of contemporary existence.[40]

From the viewpoint of Hebraic religion, surrender to the lure of totalitarianism is treason to God. For the renunciation of freedom and responsibility is the renunciation of human personality; it is the repudiation of the divine demand upon man to fulfil himself as the unique image of God. "Man," says J. P. Sartre, "is condemned to be free."[41] True, but it is precisely this "condemnation" to freedom that constitutes the grandeur of human existence, which no one may renounce and yet remain truly human. Totalitarianism therefore confronts us with a double responsibility: to reorganize social life so as to make possible the emergence of true community in freedom, and to strengthen within us our spiritual resources of personality and responsibility. Both tasks alike imply unswerving allegiance to the divine law as the law of our life.

All earthly rule is subject to the divine law; from this it follows that all actual politics must be secular. This is no paradox. It simply means that no course or policy of government can possibly claim to be the simple enactment of the divine will; no folkway or custom or social standard regulating human life can make pretensions to absoluteness. Theocracy—in which the ruler, whether king or priest, claims divine sanction and immunity for his actions on the ground that it is not he but God through him who is really ruling—is utterly contrary to the spirit of Hebraic religion. "The idea of theocracy as opposed to any other form of government was quite foreign to the Rabbis," Schechter says. "There is not the slightest hint in the whole Rabbinical literature that the Rabbis give any preference to a hierarchy with an ecclesiastical head who pretends to be the vice-regent of God . . . The high priests, Menelaus and Alcimus, were just as wicked . . . as the [lay rulers], Herod and Archelaus."[42] Every legitimate social power, in the opinion of the rabbis,[43] receives its authority from Heaven, but this "commission," so to speak, does not convert these powers into infallible instruments of the Deity. They, no more than ordinary folk, have the right to cover their entirely human activities with the mantle of divinity or to claim a divine sanction for their deeds. All, all are subject to the divine law, which is beyond the law of state or society, and all fall under divine judgment.

Emphasis on the secular and relative character of actual politics is so important because the conversion of a social purpose, no matter how meritorious, into a "holy cause" opens the door to the most destructive fanaticism. "Holy causes"—communism, fascism, nationalism, even democracy conceived as religion—are the curse of our time, which has witnessed an upsurge of fanaticism almost unparalleled in virulence and scope. When a cause becomes "holy," the means used to achieve it inevitably become vile; all dikes and barriers are swept aside and everything is permitted. The unshakable affirmation of the transcendence and holiness of God, which is at the heart of Hebraic religion, stands as a perpetual challenge to every earthly power that is tempted to make pretensions beyond its limited and creaturely authority.

The political thought that derives from Hebraic religion is built on a series of antitheses. Man free under God is confronted by the coercive state, the individual person by the claims of society, the community of believers by the authority of the secular world: at every point, there is a tension and polarity that cannot be resolved through any dialectic. Each side has its right and its necessity, even though the two can never be fully reconciled in this world. Every formula of adjustment, however useful, is but provisional and temporary; even democracy is no more than "a method of finding proximate solutions of insoluble problems."[44] The contradictions that crop up everywhere in social existence are contradictions inherent in the conditions of human life in history and cannot, therefore, be finally eliminated within history. In one way or another, they are all reducible to the crucial contradiction between power and justice. No historical society, no society of sinful men, is capable either of wielding power without corruption or of maintaining justice without power. It is the highest reach of human wisdom to maintain the tension between freedom and order as a living force, recognizing both the existence of the conflict and the fact that resolution of it is not possible within history.

Yet that cannot be our last word. For while Hebraic religion is ready to recognize, and in fact even to insist upon, the contradictions of human life in history, it cannot admit them to be final. It sees with the eyes of faith the resolution of the contradictions of human existence in the great fulfilment toward which all history is heading, where in the Kingdom of God freedom and order, power and justice, will become one in a love that dissolves all oppositions. It is this faith that enables one to find meaning in the partial and precarious achievements of history, while avoiding the pitfall of absolutizing the relative and of identifying the temporary balance we may have been able to establish with the final truth of life. The final truth of life is not within life and history but beyond it.

## NOTES TO CHAPTER 14

1. *M.* Sanh. 4.5.
2. J. Wellhausen, *Ein Gemeinwesen ohne Obrigkeit;* quoted by Martin Buber, *Moses* (East & West Library: London, 1946), p. 87.
3. "Then all the elders of Israel gathered together and came to Samuel at Ramah and they said to him: '. . . Now make us a king to judge us like all the nations.' But the thing was evil in the sight of Samuel . . . And Samuel prayed unto the Lord and the Lord said to Samuel: 'Hearken unto the voice of the people . . ., for they have not rejected you but they have rejected me from being king over them.' " I Sam. 8:4-7. "I gave them a king in mine anger." Hos. 13:11.
4. Of course, there is also a pro-monarchical strand in Scripture, but even this is much mitigated and circumscribed by the basic affirmation of the kingship of God. "The Hebrews . . . never thought that 'kingship descended from heaven.' Hence the Hebrew king did not become a necessary bond between the people and the divine powers. On the contrary, it was in the kingless period that the people had been singled out by Yahveh and that they had been bound, as a whole, by the Covenant of Sinai . . . Yahveh's covenant with the people antedated kingship." Henri Frankfort, *Kingship and the Gods* (University of Chicago: Chicago, 1948), pp. 339, 341. "In Israel, monarchy was a unique phenomenon. Elsewhere, the king was absolute; a limted monarchy is, to the Oriental, a contradiction in terms." T. H. Robinson, *Palestine in General History*, p. 42. "The monarchy endured on sufferance, never for one moment surviving or functioning in its own right." O. J. Baab, *The Theology of the Old Testament* (Abingdon-Cokesbury: Nashville, Tenn., 1949), p. 167. In rabbinical thought, the ancient Davidic kingship was already part of the sacred tradition and closely interwoven with the Messianic hope. It was not an operative concept in actual political life.
5. *B.* Baba Metzia 10a (*B.* Kiddushin 22a).
6. *M.* Abot 3.2.
7. Bronislaw Malinowski, *Freedom and Civilization* (Roy: New York, 1944), p. 244.
8. Thus, e.g., John Dewey: "For in the long run, democracy will stand or fall with the possibility of maintaining the faith [in human nature] and

justifying it by works." *Freedom and Culture* (Putnam's: New York, 1939), p. 126.

9. V. I. Lenin, *State and Revolution* (International Publishers: New York), chap. iv, sec. 6. Almost identical sentiments are expressed by William Godwin, *Political Justice*, Bk. VIII, chap. ix.

10. This is precisely Engels' argument, as Lenin points out. *State and Revolution*, chap. iv, secs. 3 and 6.

11. "In monarchy, the private interest [of the sovereign] is the same as the public interest." Thomas Hobbes, *Leviathan*, chap. xix.

12. "Now the sovereign, being formed only of the individuals that compose it, neither has nor can have any interest contrary to theirs; consequently, the sovereign power need give no guarantees to its subjects." Jean-Jacques Rousseau, *Social Contract*, Bk. I, chap, vii.

13. For the Stalinist use of this argument, see Sidney and Beatrice Webb, *Soviet Communism* (Scribner's: New York, 1936), particularly Vol. II, chap. viii.

14. Rosa Luxemburg, *Program Manifesto of the Spartacus League*, January 1919.

15. Buber makes a telling argument against this point of view in his polemic with Friedrich Gogarten. Gogarten finds man "radically and therefore irrevocably evil, that is, in the grip of evil." The ethical quality of the state, therefore, consists simply "in its warding off the evil to which men have fallen prey by its sovereign power and by its right over the life and property of its subjects." To which Buber replies: "The concept to which Gogarten refers, of the radical evil of man, his absolute sinfulness, is taken from the realm where man confronts God and is significant there alone. . . . Man, more precisely fallen man, considered as being unredeemed, is 'before God' sinful and depraved. Now I do not see how this concept of being evil can be translated from the realm of being 'before God' into that of being before earthly authorities, and yet retain its radical nature. In the sight of God, a state of radical evil can be ascribed to man because God is God and man is man and the distance between them is absolute . . . In the sight of his fellow-men, of human groups and orders, man, it seems to me, cannot be properly described as simply sinful, because the distance is lacking which alone is able to establish the unconditional." Buber, "The Question to the Single One," *Between Man and Man* (Kegan Paul: London, 1947), pp. 76-77.

16. Cf. Will Herberg, *"The Ethics of Power,"* Jewish Frontier, Vol. XII (March, 1945), No. 3.

17. Lord Acton, Letter to Mandell Creighton, April 5, 1887, *Essays on Freedom and Power*, ed. Gertrude Himmelfarb (Beacon: Boston, 1948), p. 364.

"The possession of power inevitably corrupts the untrammeled judgment of reason." I. Kant, "Perpetual Peace," *Critique of Practical Reason and Other Writings in Moral Philosophy*, ed. L. W. Beck (University of Chicago: Chicago, 1949), p. 330.

18. *B*. Pesahim 87b. "When man is appointed an official on earth, he becomes a man of evil above." Midrash Haserot ve-Yaterot 39.

19. *M*. Abot 1.10.

20. Bertrand Russell, *A History of Western Philosophy* (Simon & Schuster: New York, 1945), pp. 728-29. See also Russell, *The Impact of Science on Society* (Columbia University: New York, 1951).

21. Machiavelli himself was probably not a Machiavellian in this sense, if one goes not by *The Prince* alone but by his writings as a whole, particularly the *Discourses on Livy*, just as Marx was not a Marxian in the common acceptation of the term.

22. Hobbes, *Leviathan*, Part I, chap. x.

23. "Power abdicates only under stress of counter-power." Buber, *Paths in Utopia* (Macmillan: New York, 1950), p. 104.

24. Cf. Will Herberg, "Bureaucracy and Democracy in Labor Unions," *Antioch Review*, Vol. III (Spring, 1943), No. 3.

25. Some years ago, a distinguished social scientist told a convention of the Association for the Advancement of Psychoanalysis that "they held 'a refined scientific instrument for answering the question of who can be trusted with power.' He advocated that it be applied to decision-making public figures in the form of tests and interviews based on psychoanalytically procured data." *New York Times*, May 13, 1946.

   The messianic pretensions of the "new" anthropology are examined in a very interesting article by Robert Endelman, "The New Anthropology and its Ambitions." *Commentary*, Vol. VIII (September, 1949), No. 3.

26. "In the questions of power . . ., let no more be heard of confidence in man . . . Free government is founded in jealousy [i.e., suspicion], not in confidence." These are the words of Thomas Jefferson (Kentucky Resolutions, 1798), popularly regarded as America's greatest apostle of "faith in man."

27. "Sometimes it is said that man cannot be trusted with the government of himself. Can he, then, be trusted with the government of others? Or have we found angels in the form of kings to govern him?" Jefferson, *Messages and Papers*, ed. James D. Richardson (Bureau of National Art and Literature: Washington, 1910), I, 332.

28. "[The American Constitution] is the work of men who believed in original sin and were resolved to leave open for transgressors no door which they could possibly shut." James Bryce, *The American Commonwealth* (Macmillan: London, 1889), 2nd ed., revised, Part I, chap. XXVI, sec. viii.

29. Cf. Herberg, "Democracy and the Nature of Man," *Christianity and Society*, Vol. XI (Fall, 1946), No. 4.

30. Buber, "The Question to the Single One," *Between Man and Man*, p. 80.
31. Buber, "What is Man?" *Between Man and Man*, pp. 200, 202-3, 31, 80.
32. *M*. Abot 2.4.
33. Acton, "The History of Freedom in Antiquity," *Essays on Freedom and Power*, p. 33.
34. "They [the rabbis] tried 'to render unto Caesar the things that were Caesar's and unto God the things that were God's.' " Solomon Schechter, *Some Aspects of Rabbinic Theology* (Macmillan: New York, 1909), p. 107.
35. "R. Yohanan said in the name of R. Simon b. Yehozadak: A vote was taken in Lydda and it was decided: with regard to all sins of the Torah, if it is said to a man, transgress and you will not be killed, let him transgress—except for idolatry, sexual immorality and murder." *B* Sanh. 74a.
36. Buber, "Biblical Leadership," *Israel and the World* (Schocken: New York, 1948), p. 130.
37. Leo Baeck, "The Pharisees," *The Pharisees and Other Essays* (Schocken: New York, 1947), p. 48.
38. The phrase is Alex Comfort's. Comfort describes it as "a society of onlookers, congested but lonely, technically advanced but utterly insecure, subject to a complicated mechanism of order but personally irresponsible." *The Novel in Our Time* (Phoenix House: London, 1948), p. 12. See also Dr. Comfort's *Sexual Behavior in Society* (Duckworth: London, 1950), pp. 41ff.
39. Sören Kierkegaard, *The Concept of Dread* (Princeton University: Princeton, N. J., 1944), p. 55.
40. "Reduced to panic, industrial man joins the lemming migration, the convulsive mass escape from freedom to totalitarianism, hurling himself from the bleak and rocky cliffs into the deep, womb-dark sea below." A. M. Schlesinger, Jr., *The Vital Center* (Houghton Mifflin: Boston, 1949), p. 244. See also the brilliant analysis of totalitarianism and "totalitarian man" in chapters iv and v of the same work.
41. Jean-Paul Sartre, *Existentialism* (Philosophical Library: New York, 1947), p. 27.
42. Schechter, *Some Aspects, etc.*, pp. 92-93. "The Jewish theocracy, so-called, was an aberration from the true national genius and tradition." H. and H. A. Frankfort, *et al.*, *The Intellectual Adventure of Ancient Man* (University of Chicago: Chicago, 1946), p. 358.
43. *B*. Berakot 58a; *B*. Abodah Zarah 11a.
44. Reinhold Niebuhr, *The Children of Light and the Children of Darkness* (Scribner's: New York, 1944), p. 118.

# 15. HISTORY: IDEA AND MEANING

## I

All peoples have their history, recorded in written word or oral tradition. All have their records, their monuments, their tales of great deeds, their annals and chronicles. But the *sense* of history, the feeling for the full reality and significance of temporal events, is by no means universal. It is, in fact, the fruit of the Hebraic religious spirit and comes to us, directly or indirectly, from the Hebraic heritage of our civilization.

"An authentic conception of history," writes Berdyaev, "was foreign to Hellenic consciousness. Its origin must be sought rather in the the consciousness and spirit of ancient Israel. It was the Jews who contributed the concept of the 'historical' to world history."[1] Not only the Greeks but all ancient peoples uninfluenced by the Hebrews fell short of the idea of history. Nowhere did "they show [a] sense of the unfolding [of events] through the ages according to some fixed plan or temporal order."[2] The Hindus, indeed, committed as they were to an extreme spiritualism which saw the whole earthly scene as *maya*, a mist of illusion, even held temporal history to be devoid of reality. History was not something that the Eastern mind could take seriously.[3]

The Greeks had their historians, and great ones, too. But their his, torical insight was surprisingly limited. Herodotus wrote of the wonders of the world and the achievements of the Hellenes. Thucydides, with scrupulous care and critical intelligence, probed the motivations of men in politics so as to provide lessons for citizens and statesmen of the future. Polybius strove to account for the greatness of Rome in terms of national character and domestic institutions. Plutarch prepared his inspirational biographies as moral tracts. Livy celebrated the greatness of the past and Tacitus pilloried the corruptions of his day. But none of them—not even Polybius, not even Thucydides— showed any sign of believing that the doings of men in time were really important, were somehow significant for the destiny of mankind. To

193

the Greeks, mankind had no destiny. The strivings and doings of men, their enterprises, conflicts and achievements, led nowhere. All, all would be swallowed up in the cycle of eternal recurrence that was the law of the cosmos.

That is why Greek thought, in which the ancient mind outside of Israel reached its zenith, could develop no true idea of history. In addition to a strong strain of idealism, which led the Platonist to devaluate the empirical and mutable in comparison with the timeless, and the Aristotelian to brush aside the particular and individual as merely "accidental," there was the fatality of the recurrent cycle which gripped everyone from philosopher to the man in the street.[4] Everything moved in cycles: day and night, the seasons of the year, birth and death, generation and corruption. Whatever men did in time could have no lasting significance since it was all bound to be wiped out by the turn of the wheel. The Stoics even spoke of a cosmic fire in which the entire universe was periodically consumed, only to begin again anew: "And so there will be another Socrates and another Athenian jury which will again sentence him to death . . ." Under such circumstances, only the timeless, only the eternal idea, could retain any value; true historical consciousness was out of the question.[5]

"The concept of history is the product of Prophetism."[6] The prophet is pre-eminently the interpreter of history, in which he finds revealed God's will, judgment and redemptive purpose. The prophet, moreover, looks forward. The pagan world had no sense of time as creative and therefore no sense of the future. But in the prophetic vision, time is primarily future; past and present take on significance in terms of that toward which they are directed.

The prophets were the first authentic "philosophers of history."[7] "The Hebrews," writes Hyatt in his study of prophetic religion, "were the first people in the ancient world to have a sense of history. They were the first to conceive of God as a God of history, manifesting himself on the stage of time and controlling the destiny of men and nations. The Hebrews affirmed the reality and importance of time. To them, it was not an illusion, something from which man must escape, but something which must be redeemed."[8] In its realistic emphasis on the full authenticity of time, change and human action, Hebraic re-

ligion comes much closer to what is best in modern thought than does
the idealism of the Greek tradition.

The Hebraic mind, as we find it in Scripture, sees all history as a
great and meaningful process under the control of the God who is
the Lord of history. Already with Amos, the vision is universal. The
God of Israel is the Lord of men everywhere. Under his governance
stand all peoples of the earth, whether they know it or not: "Did I
not lead Israel from the land of Egypt, and the Philistines from Caph-
tor, and the Syrians from Kir?" (Amos 9:7). History is of one piece,
a single great drama, under one Lord: thus emerges the idea of the
unity of history as *world*-history.[9]

Because history is under the control of God, it has purpose. "The
Hebrews did not think of history as a series of cycles without ultimate
meaning . . . History was linear: the past itself showed purpose, and
the past contained promises which could be fulfilled only in the future."[10] God's ends are effected with time, in and through history;
the salvation that is promised as the ultimate validation of life lies
indeed beyond history but it lies beyond it as its fulfilment and consummation. It is conceived not as the negation of time but as a "new
time" in which historical life will be redeemed and transfigured. From
this point of view, earthly history takes on a meaning and seriousness
that are completely absent where the Hebraic influence has not been
felt.

But above all it is the sense of the future that creates authentic history. The pagan world was literally without hope: there was nothing
to look forward to, nothing to strive for beyond one's own day, nothing that time could bring but a turn of the wheel of fortune, a recurrence of the cycle. Hence the profound melancholy that pervades the
best of pagan spirituality and that leaves heavy traces even in the
book of Ecclesiastes.[11] Hence, too, the astonishing fact that all the
historical writing of the pagan world, even the most profound, is turned
entirely to the past, without any feeling for the forward thrust of historical time. "The classical historian," according to Löwith, "asks:
How did it come about? The modern historian: How shall we go
ahead?"[12] This attitude, which seems so obvious to us and which

would have been so incomprehensible to Tacitus and Thucydides, is the product of the Hebrew prophets for whom the past and the present were oriented to the future as the beginnings of a great work to its completion, or better, as the promise to its fulfilment. With this living, vital sense of the future, the true idea of history is born.

It is, therefore, no mere fancy or pious compliment to speak of the prophets as the creators of the idea of history. In the prophetic books and in all other parts of Scripture filled with the prophetic spirit, we get a glimpse of human history—the doings of men in time—as unified, real, significant, the medium and vehicle of the divine purpose. Human action in history is not mere moving in an endless circle; it gets somewhere, it accomplishes something, it has meaning to God and man alike. It is *serious,* the most serious thing conceivable for man, for it is in the course and context of history that, in the freedom of decision, he confronts God and works out his destiny.

This sense of history permeates Judaism and Christianity to the very core. It is true that with the rise of scholastic rationalism, rooted in a neo-Platonized version of Aristotle, history was denied any philosophic standing and the real and normative were again identified with the timeless. Maimonides, Baron tells us, "was frequently impatient with the accidental turns of historical events,"[13] and Thomas Aquinas certainly shared his impatience.[14] But even then, all was not lost. Both Maimonides and Thomas Aquinas were committed to a faith that was historical through and through, that looked to the future for the fulfilment of its goal and that no metaphyical speculations could turn into a system of timeless doctrine. The idea of history remained dormant within the elaborate structures of scholastic theology, but it was vital and operative in the faith of the believers who lived by the promise of the future—of the Messiah, of the "new heaven and new earth," foretold by the prophets. With the decay of scholasticism, the idea was released and began to work its tremendous effect upon the Western mind. "All modern attempts to delineate history as a meaningful . . . progress toward fulfilment," says Löwith, "depend upon this theological thought"[15] that came with the prophetic revelation. It is an idea that has transformed the world.[16]

II

The search for the meaning of history is, in a sense, the ultimate problem of life. For human life is not simply lived *in* history, in the context of social existence; it is lived *as* history, as a temporal process in which the fate of the individual is somehow related to his occurrence in time. Even those who see salvation as essentially an escape from history must first take account of history, if only to expose it as ultimately meaningless. History—temporal existence, temporal activity —is the stuff of life, and any inquiry into the meaning of life becomes, at some stage, an inquiry into the meaning of that ongoing process of life, individual and collective, which we call history.

History confronts us as a problem in meaning because events in themselves so obviously lack meaning. Taken in their bare particularity, the occurrences of life can never lay claim to a validity that will stand up against what the next wave of time will bring. While we are engaged in any enterprise—whether it be making love or making war or making money—it seems laden with ultimate significance and entirely self-justifying, but the slightest reflection is often enough to make us realize how deceptive such appearances are. Viewed in a somewhat larger perspective of interest and time, the enterprises that once seemed to us so tremendously significant quickly lose their meaning. Love frequently turns into indifference or hate; a revolution conceived in an enthusiasm for freedom is wiped out or else culminates in total slavery; even the mightiest empires are here today and gone tomorrow. All human existence is precarious and equivocal, because nothing in life is ever unambiguously good or evil and no human endeavor is exempt from what the future may bring. Taken in their own terms, the events of history add up to nothing. All effort, as the Preacher tells us, is a "striving after wind" (Eccles. 1:14); and in the end, death swallows up everything in the oblivion of nothingness.

Sometimes we believe we discern fragments of meaning in life and history beyond the events themselves. But these fragments of meaning, whether we think of them as partial judgments of God or as partial schemes of rational intelligibility, cannot maintain themselves as meaningful in a vast sea of chaos and absurdity. Some overall affirmation about the totality of life and history is necessary if life is to receive any validation and history any meaning. All men, whether they know it or not, make such overall affirmations. For men, unlike animal creation, cannot live out their lives in the fixed patterns of nature; in their freedom, they must live to some purpose—and that purpose, however inarticulate, however primitively conceived, is in effect one's "philosophy" of life and history. A "philosophy of history" in this sense is thus no theoretical question; it is quite literally a question of existence.

Man's first impulse in validating his existence is to take some partial value, some partial interest or activity, and exalt it to universal significance as the ultimate meaning of life. We are already familiar with this mechanism, for it is the device of absolutizing the relative which we have learned to know as idolatry. This is what men do who, as we say, "live for" their family, their business, their party, their nation, their cause. It is the dynamic of this universalized interest that keeps them going and gives significance to their lives.

For much of life, particularly in ordinary times, this may prove adequate, and yet ultimately it is not enough. These partial meanings, however desperately we try to universalize them, are, simply as such, never sufficient to sustain life. We "live for" our family, our business, our nation, but none of these is immortal; we can conceive of them as coming abruptly to an end, taking with them all the meaning of life. Causes and movements, however exalted, are, insofar as they enter into history, subject to all its vicissitudes. Something more is apparently needed if life is to be sustained.

Faced with this problem, we may take one of three ways: (a) we may assert that while any particular event or enterprise of history is equivocal, history itself as process is meaningful; (b) we may deny that history has any meaning and look for the meaning of human life in an escape from history, in a dimension of eternity far removed from the vicissitudes of senseless change; or finally (c) we may strongly affirm the reality and significance of history but insist that its meaning, both in part and in whole, is ultimately to be resolved not within history itself but in terms of an "end" which is beyond history and yet is directly relevant to it as final fulfilment and judgment. The first is the *this-worldly naturalism* that has become more or less normative in modern thought; the second is the *otherworldly idealism* of Greco-

Oriental spirituality and of almost all our philosophic tradition; the third is the *trans-worldly messianism* that is the answer of Hebraic religion to the ultimate problems of existence.

The this-worldly naturalism so characteristic of modern thought takes many forms, but they are all concerned with making history self-redemptive. Whatever problems arise in history, history will solve; whatever evils emerge in human existence, history, in its process, will eliminate. Taking history in its entirety, the meaninglessness that is undoubtedly inherent in particular events disappears, for each event is seen to be the result of a meaningful process. And while, of course, no man can claim to know the entire pattern of events, it is possible for us to master history by acquiring an insight into its inner "law of motion," which is always immanent. History is self-revealing in its true significance: this is the claim of every naturalistic philosophy of history and of some philosophies whose naturalistic premises are not so obvious at first sight.

Let us be clear from the beginning that whatever validity such claims may have, this validity is not that of empirical science. Science, no matter how far the term is stretched, reveals no ultimate meaning in anything, least of all in history. Every interpretation of history is ultimately grounded in an affirmation of faith about existence, and no amount of manipulation of scientific-sounding phrases can eliminate the presuppositions at the core. What we are discussing, therefore, is not the deliverances of the "science" of history but the constructions of the human mind in an effort to give rational form to one's central affirmation of faith. This is as true of the naturalist philosopher, who thinks he is talking science when he is discoursing on the meaning of history, as it is of the religious thinker, who knows that he is dealing with theology.

Naturalism has brought forth many different schemes of meaning to master the chaos of history. Their variety is due primarily to the difference in the aspect of "nature" that is taken as the principle of meaning. But whatever the type, all or almost all naturalistic schemes in modern times resolve themselves into some theory of evolution, more particularly into some doctrine of progress. The progressive process may be causal and mechanical, as in Spencer and orthodox

Darwinism; it may be organic and vitalistic, as with Bergson; it may be logico-dialectical, as with Hegel (who has his naturalistic aspects) and Marx; it may even be naively rationalistic, as with some of the eighteenth-century *philosophes*. It may proceed harmoniously or through conflict, gradually or by way of sudden "revolution." Through all variations, however, the upshot remains the same: history is self-redemptive, history is salvation. It possesses within itself the power to solve every problem and answer every question; given time, there is nothing it cannot accomplish. Spencer is not very popular these days; he is felt to be somehow too crass and crude, too self-assured in his sweeping assertions. And yet it is Spencer who has formulated the doctrine of redemption through progress with a conviction and force that remain unparalleled, and it is to Spencer that we must turn if we want to get an idea of what the gospel of progress really affirms.

> Progress [writes the English philosopher] is not an accident but a necessity. The modifications mankind have undergone and are still undergoing result from a law underlying the whole organic creation, and, provided the human race continues and the constitution of things remains the same, those modifications must end in completeness . . . As surely as there is any efficacy in educational culture or any meaning in such terms as habit, custom, practice, . . . so surely must things we call evil and immorality disappear; so surely must man become perfect.[17]

Does this sound incredibly naive, hopelessly mid-Victorian? Then listen to John Dewey, the dean of contemporary American philosophers and the honored spokesman of what regards itself as ultramodern naturalism. "Life," Dewey tells us, "travels upward in spirals.[18] . . . Social intelligence has found itself after millions of years of errancy as a method and it will not be lost forever in the darkness of night."[19] Is this so very different from Spencer? "Life," we are assured by both alike, "travels upward." Both see the past as hopelessly benighted— "millions of years of errancy" is Dewey's sweeping phrase—and our own time, the past three or four centuries, as the new age of enlightenment. Both see human reason, aided by more automatic forces, as the operative power in progress: "social intelligence," Dewey calls it; "educational culture" is Spencer's term. The only difference is that Spencer, writing in the full flush of mid-nineteenth-century optimism, knew nothing of the "darkness of night" to come. But although Dewey knows it—indeed, it was in the very midst of it that he composed the books from which I have quoted (1935, 1940)—it really means nothing to him so far as his philosophy is concerned. The resurgence of demonic evil in this century he sees simply as a passing event, a futile attempt to "set the clock back;" our enlightenment, he assures us, "will not be lost forever in the darkness of night." Why not? Obviously, since Dewey would not appeal to God, it must be because he has an unshakable faith in the redemptive power of history, exactly as Spencer has. Progress may meet its setbacks on occasion, but these are at worst only turns of the spiral; the real and decisive movement is ever upward and onward, toward "completeness" and "perfection." That stage may be far off—indeed, it may, strictly speaking, never be quite attainable—but, apart from a few temporary reverses here and there, we are constantly approaching nearer to it. Such is the normative doctrine of progress; it may be held wholeheartedly or with reservations and modifications, but as long as it is held at all, the central affirmation remains untouched: history is salvation.

It would be rather pointless in this day and age to attempt a detailed refutation of this conception. The events of the past generation have thoroughly discredited it, and its basic presuppositions have been challenged by the most significant thinkers of our time. "We delude ourselves," Arthur M. Schlesinger, Jr. concludes, "when we think that history teaches us that evil will be 'outmoded' by progress . . . [This] is to misconceive and grotestquely to sentimentalize the nature of history. For history is not a redeemer, promising to solve all human problems; nor is man capable of transcending the limitations of his being. Man generally is entangled in insoluble problems; history is consequently a tragedy in which we are all involved, whose keynote is anxiety and frustration, not progress and fulfilment."[20] With this judgment we can certainly agree. We need not deny that there has been notable progress made in various fields of human life and in various periods of human history, or that we always stand under the obligation to enhance human welfare on all fronts. But we must challenge any doctrine that transforms progress into a cosmic force capable of redeeming mankind and completing the meaning of history.

Much more important than engaging in a polemic with a doctrine so obviously untenable is to try to uncover the affirmation of faith in which it is grounded. This faith is faith in man, in his goodness, his omnipotence, his perfectibility. It is because man is held to be innately good that evil is written off as essentially superficial, the product of ignorance and bad institutions, and human perfection is hailed as a possibility or near-possibility within history. It is because man is held to be his own master in the universe that no limit is set to the "progress" which, in his virtue and intelligence, he is capable of attaining. Thus, at the heart of the gospel of progress we find the self-idolizing cult of man. Dewey himself is quite clear as to what is involved. "The question," he writes, "[is] whether there are adequate grounds for faith in the potentialities of human nature and whether they can be accompanied by the intensity and ardor once awakened by religious ideas upon a theological basis . . . The word *faith* is intentionally used."[21] To this we can but answer in the words of the Prophet: "Cursed is the man who trusts in man and makes flesh his arm of strength. . . . Blessed is the man who trust in the Lord. . . . [For] the heart [of man] is treacherous above all things and desperately sick—who can understand it?" (Jer. 17: 5, 7, 9). These words may not flatter human pride but they are far truer to the realities of life and history than the delusive self-worship of man.

Like all forms of idolatry, the self-idolizing cult of man at the heart of the doctrine of progess leads to confusion of mind and to an intellectual blindness that obscures the most obvious facts of life. What Louis Jaffe says of the late Justice Brandeis will serve to indicate the effects of this doctrine upon even the most intelligent of liberals: "He moved with such assurance in the realms of light that darkness had ceased to him to be a living reality. The demonic depths and vast violence of men's souls were part of the historical past rather than the smouldering basis of the present. . . . Nothing in his system prepared Brandeis for Hitler."[22] Nothing in the system of the devotee of the cult of progress and the faith in the simple rationality and goodness of man prepares him for anything history may bring.

If the this-worldly, naturalistic interpretation of history linked with the cult of progress is delusive in its optimism, naturalism stripped of its faith in progress becomes positively demonic. By a compulsive inner logic, it leads to a self-destructive adoration of the "wave of the future," of history as blind omnipotence that recks not of man or his works. This view, paradoxically enough, also reflects the self-worship of man as ultimate in the universe, only it is no longer the good in man that is absolutized and deified but the demonic power in him. The old-line "liberal" of the type of Spencer or Dewey sees man as unlimited in his capacity for goodness and rationality, and is therefore content to rest confidently in the expectation of what human progress will bring. The naturalists of more recent time see man as a being moved by obscure, nonrational forces that drive him into those terrible conflicts that make up the content of history; they, on their part, confront history either by identifying themselves with its ruthless power, by prostrating themselves in masochistic submission, or else by striking a pose of stoic endurance.[23] But they, no less than the optimists, are caught in the vicious circle of human self-absolutization; it is a blind alley from which naturalism in none of its forms can escape.

The otherworldly idealism that stands at the opposite pole in the interpretation of history is much older than naturalistic this-worldliness. It has dominated much of the religion and philosophy of mankind. In its basic affirmation, it denies the naturalistic premise that history is self-revealing and self-redeeming simply because it denies that there is any meaning or true reality to history at all.

We need not here repeat what was said above about the antihistorical orientation of Greek and Oriental spirituality and of idealistic philosophy in all its varieties. The actual world of events—indeed, everything that is involved in time—is regarded either as unreal, a mist of illusion, or else as hopelessly caught in an endless cycle of recurrence that leads nowhere. In either case, history, and life in the context of history, can yield no meaning. If human life is to have any significance at all, it must be sought outside of history, outside the dimension of time and change. "Both in thought and in feeling, even though time be real, to realize the unimportance of time," that strange Platonic "naturalist," Bertrand Russell, teaches us, "is the gate of wisdom."[24]

The realm of meaning for idealism is thus to be found in the eternal and immutable. This may be conceived as the Ultimate or All-Soul of Hindu mysticism, as the archetypal Ideas of Plato, as the "spirit-heaven" of a certain type of Jewish and Christian theology, or as the

ideal realities and values of Western philosophy. To enjoy the ideal
in mystic union or philosophic contemplation, and, for the more active
idealists at least, also to serve it, is held to be the ultimate aim of existence and the only meaning life is capable of yielding. The modern
idealist, who see his highest hopes and most cherished enterprises go
shipwreck in the course of history, is able to sustain himself by the
conviction that really it does not matter what history does to one's
ideals; it is the ideals themselves that count. This is not the same as
believing that history will come out all right in the end, for to the
genuine idealist, it is fidelity to his ideals as eternal truths and not
what history may or may not bring that gives meaning to life. History
may never bring anything but confusion and chaos, yet truth and
beauty and justice remain unaffected as the ultimate realities of existence. Serving and enjoying them is its own reward.

This is a noble faith—by human standards. It is the faith that sustained Socrates and Plato and the best of the Stoics. It is the faith
that sustained some of the finest men and women in recent centuries,
who did their duty like sentinels at the post even though the whole
world was being overwhelmed with darkness. It is a faith that appeals with particular force to men dedicated to philosophy, science,
art, or social service.

It is a noble faith and at first sight it seems to be indistinguishable
from the selfless service to God and fellow-man that is the highest
law of Hebraic religion. Is it not virtually identical with the celebrated
rabbinical injunction attributed to Antigonos of Socho: "Be not like
servants who serve the master on condition of receiving a reward, but
be like servants who serve the master without thought of reward?"[25]
Almost identical—yet worlds apart! It is this disparity, at first sight
hardly discernible, which provides the basis for a criticism of the
idealist attitude to life and history.

Let us note that when the idealist serves his ideals, it is these ideals
he is serving, not God, not even his fellow-men, except incidentally.
The idealist's attitude to the world, insofar as it is consistent and true
to itself, is negative and impersonal. The actual world is written off
as worthless. It does not matter what history may bring, says the idealist proudly, I will pursue truth, cherish beauty, fulfil my obligations.
*It does not matter what history may bring*: in other words, it does not

matter what happens to men! The idealist may, of course, regret the disasters of history, he may even be heartbroken at the sufferings of men, because, after all, he is human, and subject to the affections of men. But these are weaknesses, and, ultimately, unrealities. The one true reality is the timeless ideal, and the true meaning of life is single-minded devotion to it. No idealist today is likely to be so ascetic in his faith, because all of us today are more or less touched with the personalism of Hebraic spirituality, yet the celebrated Stoic maxim, "Let justice triumph though the heavens fall" (i.e., though mankind is destroyed), ought to give us some notion of what idealism in its pure form really implies.[26]

The fact of the matter is that the true idealist, even when he is serving man, sees not man but the ideal. Idealism knows nothing of the I-Thou communion of love; it knows nothing of *persons*. And if it does not see man, it sees God even less. Antigonos of Socho spoke of serving "the master," but what can the idealist say? True, the Stoics referred vaguely to some sort of pantheistic "Zeus," but that was hardly more than a figure of speech. Neither Plato nor the modern idealists can speak of anything but ideas, which, no matter how you objectify them, remain ideas, not persons. Personality is a category completely absent from the idealist view of things, and where personality is gone, there can be no true love of God or man. All that remains is self-love.

For the idealism we have described, whatever its forms, ends up, like naturalism, in a self-idolizing cult. It is "the best in man" that is absolutized and taken as the ideal to be worshiped and served. We have already seen what that means. Should we forget, the Stoics, with their self-righteousness, their spiritual arrogance, their cold-blooded equanimity and their ruthless devotion to their precious ideals, would be enough to remind us.

But there is another distinction that is perhaps even more fundamental. Antigonos of Socho warns against serving God for reward but he does not doubt for a moment that God has a purpose with the world and that man's actions in history can somehow contribute to the advancement of that purpose. Nor must we take him as denying that reward does await the man who serves God, insofar as he serves God. The reality of actual life and its fulfilment are thus his presupposition. But to the true idealist, this presupposition must seem mere foolishness, since nothing, as Fichte puts it, can be expected of the historical, neither promise nor meaning.

I have so far concerned myself almost entirely with idealism as a moral affirmation because it is this aspect of idealism that is operative today among so many as a principle of meaning in life and history. Yet moral idealism is but part of the larger idealistic worldview and hardly makes sense apart from it. This larger view, as we have noted several times already, is rooted in a matter-mind dualism, in which matter is devaluated as evil, intrinsically unreal and impotent, while mind is exalted as spiritual and eternal, the very heart of all that is real and good. Man—not real, existing man, but the reason or spirit, which is the "true" man—is credited with unlimited capacities of creativity and transcendence in the realm of the timeless. Man's thoughts, insofar as he thinks truly, are the thoughts of the Absolute Idea that is the ground of all. Man's deeds, insofar as he pursues the eternal ideals, are truly divine. In the end, man only too easily takes on the dimensions of God.

The universe of which self-deified man is lord in the pretensions of metaphysical idealism is, of course, a timeless universe. In Plato and in most Oriental systems, this is quite obvious. But even Hegel, who shows such a profound feeling for history and who incorporates many seminaturalistic elements in his philosophy, ends up with a universe from which temporal relations have been eliminated as part of ultimate being. History is merely a kind of shadow play of the timeless categories of the spirit. Philosophy is, at bottom, a means for dehistoricizing reality No more than naturalism, which at least tries to take time seriously, can idealism, whether of the Greek, Oriental or modern variety, serve as the key to the meaning of life and history.

Most contemporary philosophies of history are neither purely naturalistic nor purely idealistic; they are varying combinations of the two, with an admixture of a third element, the prophetic-eschatological vision of Hebraic religion. Such philosophies try to combine a naturalistic concern with time, a cyclical approach, borrowed from the Greeks, and the notion of a directed time-movement oriented toward a significant future, taken from Scripture. Spengler is one of the few

Religion and Society    207

moderns who categorically rejects eschatology: his succession of "cultures," arising, maturing and dying like organisms, has no direction or purpose. Yet even Spengler permits himself an attitude of stoic contempt for the decadence of contemporary civilization and a glimmer of hope at the heroic virtues that the early stages of the next cycle of culture will bring. Sorokin's two-phase sequence of ideational and sensate culture is saved from endless circularity by his recent gospel of mass salvation through the cultivation of "altruism."[27] Toynbee's earlier views were rather naturalistic in spirit and entirely cyclical in general conception; his mature thought, however, is an impressive effort to combine a carefully worked out cyclical pattern of civilizations with a rectilinear movement of religious or spiritual progress. "Religion," he says, "is, after all, the serious business of the human race," and it is the advancement of religion that the movement of history serves. But this view, too, cannot be regarded as ultimately satisfactory, for it denies history any intrinsic meaning whatever and grants it significance only insofar as it serves something outside of itself—"religion"—which Toynbee conceives in rather ecclesiastical-mystical sense. "Our. . . .precept, in studying history as a whole," he tells us, "should be to relegate economic and political history to a subordinate place and give religious history the primacy."[28] But in Scripture, there is no religious history in the proper sense at all—that is, there is no particular concern with the history of religious doctrines, institutions or practices as if they had some special primacy. The history with which the prophets are concerned is precisely the economic and political and military history of their time, which for them is real history, as real and important as anything can be. Their way of relating "religion" to history is to try to reveal the divine purpose in the very worldly history with which they deal. And this they do not only by indicating the partial judgments and fulfilments that occur within history but also by pointing to the *eschaton*, to the "end-time," in which history itself will be redeemed and its full meaning revealed in a great act of final judgment and fulfilment. But with such eschatology Toynbee shows little real concern.

The true eschatological passion through the nineteenth century and well into our own times burned not in the thinkers who proclaimed themselves Jewish or Christian, but in such official enemies of "religion" as Marx and Nietzsche. Their thought was permeated with the prophetic feeling of urgency and futurity, although the gospels they proclaimed were often demonic and the systems they laid down riddled with many of the vices and fallacies of their time. In most modern thinkers of the more conventional sort, the Hebraic eschatological element makes its appearance indirectly in a truncated and secularized form as the notion of progress. It is this notion of progress, whether conceived as inevitable or merely possible, that separates the modern thought of the West from the thought of all other times and peoples, the Hebrews alone excepted. As the ultimate principle of history, it is, as we have seen, utterly untenable, but it is not therefore to be discarded as worthless, any more than is the corrupted eschatology of Marx and Nietzsche. If we are to disengage the genuine element in these conceptions as well as to retrieve what is valid in idealism, we must understand and appropriate the authentic concept of Hebraic eschatology.

## NOTES TO CHAPTER 15

1. N. Berdyaev, *The Meaning of History* (Geoffrey Bles: London, 1934), p. 28.
2. M. R. Cohen, *The Meaning of Human History* (Open Court: La Salle, Ill., 1947), p. 9. Cohen is here referring specifically to the Chinese.
3. "When a cultivated Hindu reads of Israel's exodus from Egypt, he is apt to see in it only an allegory of the soul's separation from God. When I once urged on the Hindu philosopher Ramanathan that Dante, who recognized such an allegoric interpretation, also believed in the reality of the temporal event, I was rebuked by the remark that the eternal spiritual meaning is the only one worthy of serious attention, that only the carnal-minded are preoccupied with temporal events (Cohen, *op. cit.*, pp. 9-10).
4. "[In Greek thought], the temporal course of events was always treated as something merely secondary in which there was no real metaphysical interest. At the same time, Greek thought regarded not only the individual human being but also the whole human race, with all its destinies,

deeds and sufferings, as an episode, as a passing, transitory, particular phenomenon, of the cyclic world process, which takes place eternally according to the same laws. The question of a meaning for the history of humanity as a whole, a systematic plan behind the course of historical development, was never raised as such; still less did it occur to any of the ancient thinkers to regard this as the real nature of the world" (W. Windelband, *Lehrbuch der Geschichte der Philosophie* [Fisher: Freiburg, Germany, 1892], p. 212).

5. Greek thought viewed reality, including history, as nature involved in the cosmic process, and "where reality is viewed as nature, it is governed by the symbol of the circle that returns upon itself. . .On this basis, true historical thinking is impossible. . .Consequently, [for the Greeks], there is no view of the world as history, even though there is no lack of historiography as a report of the confusion of human movements and as an example for politicians" (Paul Tillich, *The Interpretation of History* [Scribner's: New York, 1936], p. 244).

6. Hermann Cohen, *Die Religion der Vernunft aus den Quellen des Judentums* (Kaufmann: Frankfort a. M., 1929), p. 307.

7. "The Hebrew Prophets are the first philosophers of history because they apprehend events as a significant whole, determined and fashioned by the eternal creative principle which,while transcending them, is active within them." Harold Knight, *The Hebrew Phophetic Consciousness* (Lutterworth: London, 1947), p. 162.

8. J. P. Hyatt, *Prophetic Religion* (Abingdon-Cokesbury: Nashville, Tenn., 1947), p. 76.

"For the Hindu, the historical is the illusory; for the Greek, it is the incidental, the evanescent; for the Hebrew, it is that which is real." William Robinson, *Whither Theology* (Lutterworth: London, 1947), p. 76.

9. "It was indeed from the Prophets and their successors, the apocalyptists, that the very conception of the unity of history was derived." H. Wheeler Robinson, *Inspiration and Revelation in the Old Testament* (Clarendon: Oxford, 1946), p. 197.

10. Hyatt, *op. cit.*, p. 89.

11. Eccles. 1:9; "That which has been is that which shall be, and that which has been done is that which shall be done; and there is nothing new under the sun."

12. Karl Löwith, *Meaning in History* (University of Chicago: Chicago, 1949), p. 17.

13. S. W. Baron, "The Historical Outlook of Maimonides," *Proceedings of the American Academy for Jewish Research*, VI (1934-35), 7.

14. Thomas Aquinas, in accord with the whole scholastic outlook, tended to resolve history into the nontemporal. According to him, "all events which have happened, which are happening or which ever will happen

## 210    *Judaism and Modern Man*

are caused by the same timeless act." Robert L. Patterson, *The Conception of God in the Philosophy of Thomas Aquinas* (Allen and Unwin: London, 1933), p. 144.

15. Löwith, *op. cit.*, p. 160.

16. "It is Jewish-Christian futurism which opened the future as the dynamic of all modern striving and thinking." Löwith, *op. cit.*, p. 111.

17. Herbert Spencer, *Social Statics* (Appleton: New York, 1865), p. 80.

18. This is Dewey's motto for his *Living Thoughts of Thomas Jefferson.* (Longmans: New York 1940).

19. John Dewey, *Liberalism and Social Action* (Putnam's: New York, 1935), p. 93.

20. A. M. Schlesinger, Jr., "The Causes of the Civil War: A Note on Historical Sentimentalism," *Partisan Review,* Vol. XVI (October, 1949), No. 10.

21. Dewey, *Freedom and Culture* (Putnam's: New York, 1939), p. 126.

22. Quoted in A. M. Schlesinger, Jr., *The Vital Center* (Houghton, Mifflin: Boston, 1949), pp. 162-3.

23. The first attitude—self-identification with the ruthless power of nature—is exemplified by Hitler and the Nazi leaders generally. "The fundamental basis of Hitler's *Mein Kampf,*" writes Hans Kohn, "is an interpretation of man according to which he is purely a natural being, biologically determined, and inescapably subject to the 'iron logic of nature,' which he has to obey as animals do if he wishes to preserve or increase his strength and to be true to his 'nature.' " *The Twentieth Century* (Macmillan: New York, 1949), p. 165. The second attitude—masochistic submission—is typical of the totalitarian mass-man, who "needs someone to give him orders" and who cannot live without feeling the "Party thong" on his back. A. M. Schlesinger, Jr., *The Vital Center* pp. 54-56. The third attitude—stoic endurance—is, at its best, exemplified by Jakob Burckhardt, who, in the middle of the last century, saw civilization about to be overwhelmed by a new wave of barbarism but felt that there was nothing that could be done but to endure. See J. H. Nichols' introductory essay in J. Burckhardt, *Force and Freedom: Reflections on History* (Pantheon: New York, 1943). With Burckhardt, however, this attitude was no mere pose but was deeply felt and lived.—Freud viewed what he considered the illusions and follies of mankind with the weary, understanding eye of the physician, but he, too, harbored the optimistic faith that in the end, progress would dissipate these illusions and complete the rational perfection of man. *The Future of an Illusion* (Liveright: New York, 1928), pp. 92-98.

24. Bertrand Russell, *Mysticism and Logic* (Norton: New York, 1929), pp. 21-22.

25. *M.* Abot 1.3.

26. The difference in temper between the impersonal rigorism of idealist ethics and the personalist ethic of rabbinic tradition is strikingly illus-

trated by comparing Kant's absolute prohibition of telling an untruth, even where it may prevent a murder ("On a Supposed Right to Lie from Altruistic Motives," *Critique of Practical Reason and Other Writings in Moral Philosophy*, ed. by L. W. Beck [University of Chicago: Chicago, 1949], pp. 346-50), with the view of Rabbi: "All kinds of lies are prohibited, but one may make a false statement in order to make peace between a man and his neighbor" (*Tosefta* Derek Eretz, Perek Shalom 5, ed. Higger, pp. 88, 253-54).
27. See Pitirim A. Sorokin, *The Reconstruction of Humanity* (Beacon: Boston, 1948).
28. Arnold J. Toynbee, "The Unification of the World," *Civilization on Trial* (Oxford: New York, 1948), p. 94. See also the final essay, "Christianity and Civilization."

# 16.   HISTORY: MEANING AND FULFILMENT

## I

As seen from the standpoint of Hebraic religion, history is neither self-subsistent nor self-revealing: it is but the middle phase of a three-phase process, and can be understood only in terms of a "beginning" and an "end," which are themselves not history but without which history would have no meaning. This "beginning" and "end" enter into history at every point and constitute the ultimate frame of reference within which it is to be interpreted.

The biblical account of the scheme of human destiny represents it as a temporal process with creation and the paradisal state at the beginning and redemption in the Kingdom of God at the end. In between is history, which despite its bewildering variety exhibits a singleness of pattern that makes it one. What the biblical narrative tells us may, and indeed must, be understood also in its existential, contemporaneous sense. History, individual and collective, as it takes place *now*, insistently points backward to a "prelude" and forward to a "postlude" without which it cannot lay claim to reality or significance. Every aspect of history, as well as history as a whole, acquires its meaning from its place in this total pattern.

The primal life in Paradise, according to the biblical picture, images the order of creation—what man is created as and for. This includes his existence as creature and person, and therefore his need for personal self-maintenance in loving obedience to God; his heterosexuality ("Male and female created he them. . ." [Gen. 1:27]), and thus the need for sexual union and companionship; and finally, his individual incompleteness and responsive "outgoingness" ("It is not good for man to be alone. . .[Gen. 2:18]), and therefore the need for community. But *how* these needs and aspects of man's essential nature are to be met, what the *concrete* and *particular* institutions through which they are implemented are to be, that is not in itself part of the eternal order of creation; it is the product of history and subject to all the contingencies and vicissitudes of the historical order. Marriage as such is part of the order of creation, but not any particular form of marriage. Community is part of the essential nature of man, but no particular structure of society is given in the scheme of creation. They are for man himself to work out within the relativities of history.

The "prelude" to history comes to an end with man's fall and expulsion from Paradise. History in the specific sense emerges only when man violates his essential nature and upsets the normative pattern of life through sin. In the biblical account, the first historical event is, significantly enough, Cain's murder of his brother Abel (Gen. 4:1-16). History is thus the concrete working out of man's sinful existence in collective life and reflects the radical ambiguity of that existence.

Basically, history reflects the fact that man is forever driven forward to self-transcending creative effort to give concrete embodiment to the order of creation and yet at the same time is forever tempted to make every enterprise of his a vehicle for the assertion of self. If the murder of Abel is the opening event in history according to Scripture, let us remember that in the biblical account Cain comes forward sincerely to sacrifice to God, and only in the chagrin of wounded pride does his pious act become an occasion to crime. No matter where we look or how far back we go, we find man engaged in great enterprises and we find him motivated by that passionate urge to self-aggrandizement that we have learned to know as the "evil impulse" (*yetzer ha-ra*). So impelled, he creates technology, brings forth institutions, establishes civilizations and engages in all that is characteristic of social life. "Were it not for the evil impulse," a profound rabbinic comment teaches us, "man would not build a house or take a wife or beget a child or engage in business, as it is said: 'All labor and work comes of a man's rivalry with his neighbor'."[1] Self-interest does not create society; the need and basis for that are given in creation. But within the order of creation, it is self-interest that supplies the movement of history.

But never self-interest simply as such. Man in his enterprises can never rest in the immediate. He builds a house, yet it is not merely a house he builds but a city and a nation with its laws and its loyalties. He takes a wife and begets children, but in doing this he does more: he establishes the family which soon becomes something greater than himself. He "engages in business," but that involves him in development of a vast structure of institutions that regulate his life. And beyond house and family and business, or rather in and through them, he creates culture—poetry, science, art, philosophy, religion. He establishes law and justice. He sets up states and systems of states, makes war and peace, launches empires and plans utopias. Behind it all is the push of the self—but it is the self extended, transformed, universalized. Every striving of the self is taken up into some larger concern in which the self is both expressed and overcome. The family includes but is more than its members, and the national state is never merely a handy instrument for its citizens to use in aggrandizing themselves. New interests and values emerge that transcend the narrow confines of the self, yet which the self is eager to recognize and serve since it is thereby, after all, serving itself. For paradoxically, it is precisely in these larger concerns that the self somehow finds itself again.

Man's creative work in history is thus complex and multidimensional. We pursue our interests and then, on another level, transcend them in ideals and higher loyalties. But this transcendence is itself neither complete nor final, for at the heart of our ideals we find the self again, acknowledging them indeed but ready to utilize them for its own glorification and advantage. Does not family devotion, which so transcends and absorbs the individual self-interest of its members, become in its turn an instrument of self-assertion on a higher level? Does not the solidarity of kinship easily pass over into the demonic force of racial pride, and the fellowship of national community become an aggressive nationalism? Do not even philosophies and religions serve for the mobilization of interests in which the self and what is beyond self are compounded past all possibility of discrimination? In everything man does, he strives to embody his ideals: that is the imperative of his essential nature given in creation. In everything he does, he strives to exalt the self: that is the compulsive of sin. Together they go to make up the movement of history. History is thus the implementation of the order of creation through social activities and institutions, but in such an ambiguous way that the order of creation is thereby both effectuated and thwarted, both realized and perverted.

From another point of view, history may be interpreted as the effort of men to build structures of security for themselves through the collective enterprises that constitute social life. In this respect, history is but the extension of individual existence. In both alike, in history and in individual life, security is never something static. Man is never content with what he has done; he has no sooner accomplished anything than he finds it inadequate. Why? Because no finite achievement can guarantee him any real security in the encirclement of self-centered existence. Self-centeredness converts every human being into an autonomous power arrayed against the world, uneasily concerned over the aggressions of others and desperately intent upon countering them with aggressions of one's own. The endeavor to achieve security thus becomes an endless struggle for differential advantage and preponderant power. The collective structures of society and even the ideal constructions of the mind become so many citadels to which the anxious self retires and from which it draws a sense of integrity and power. Institutions, interests and ideas with which we are identified are invested with inordinate significance and are converted into exclusive fixations, which, while they may unite us with some, bring us into conflict with others of our fellow-men. Thus arise the various groups, classes and alignments, whose interaction forms so much of the substance of history. They are all, or almost all, rooted in the necessary coherences of social life but they inevitably become vehicles for the exorbitant claims of those whose interests they serve. Family, race, party, nation, economic groups as well as social and spiritual movements are thus turned into instruments in the ceaseless struggle for security and power. Society is fragmented and mankind is divided against itself. All history is indeed the history of "class struggles" if by "class" we mean not simply the economic units which Marx had in mind but all the various and multiform groupings in which men enter in order to maintain themselves in a world that has lost its divine center.

The interests and loyalties that define our position in society in large measure define also the point of view from which we see things and the judgments through which we evaluate them. Self-centeredness has its effects, intellectual as well as moral. Each particular form of property, Marx says, generates "an entire superstructure of various and peculiarly formed sentiments, modes of thought and views of life."[2] Marx was wrong only in limiting the ideology-generating interests to the economic. The taint of ideology clings to all the activities of men in history. Every interest, every institution, every ideal even, because it is utilized in the struggle for security and power, distorts our vision and makes us see things in a way that will justify our claims and promote our purposes. The teachings of Marx and Freud, reinforced by the events of the past three decades, have made us all familiar with the notions of ideology and rationalization, but it would be well to realize that in these phenomena we have manifestations of the corruption of sin. It is sin—self-centeredness—that divides man against himself and turns him against his neighbor; it is sin that requires the elaborate structures of deception and self-deception that we develop to protect our self-seeking special interests.

But this is only one side of the picture. If ideology and rationalization are to serve their purpose in validating our pretensions to ourselves and to others, they must make their case in terms of universal principles above the self-interest of individual or group. We are, therefore, back to the other side of the human ambivalence: self-interest cannot be pursued simply as such; it must be taken up in some ideal or principle that transcends the self and yet at the same time serves to justify the self in its self-interest. This dialectic of sinful existence, the operations of which we have traced in individual life, pervades the entire texture of history.

We take another text from Marx, whose "materialist" dogma hides profound insights into the meaning of history: "Man makes his own history, but he does not make it out of the whole cloth; he does not make it out of conditions chosen by himself, but out of such as he finds at hand."[3]

Human freedom is the creative power of history. History is the sphere of decision. It is never merely the outworking of a biologic pattern determined by natural need; animals, too, struggle to survive but they have no history. It is when natural need is compounded with freedom, when the fixed patterns of nature are lost in the indeterminate possibilites of spirit, that genuine history emerges. The appreciation of this transcendent dimension of the historical movement is the first prerequisite for a serious understanding of history.[4]

But human freedom in history, while it is incalculable, is not infinite: man is not God. It is conditioned first by nature and then by society, or rather by a complex of factors in which both are fused. Man—the real individual human being, not the abstraction—is born into a given situation, into a system of social forces, institutions, customs and traditions, that set definite limits to his freedom and creativity. It is within these limits that his existential decisions must be made.

This sounds like a platitude, yet it raises some of the most profound questions about the nature of history. Why is it that, as we have noted more than once, man in actual life is confronted not so much with a choice between absolute good and absolute evil as with a choice among courses of action, all of which are to some degree infected with evil? Here is a man who wants to live by the divine law, the law of love. His country is at war. He is tending to his fields when suddenly he sees an enemy aviator on a mission to destroy his town. He has the opportunity of saving his town, but he can do so only by killing the airman. What shall he do? Taking the life of a fellow-man, even of an enemy at war, is surely no exemplification of the law of love. But neither is letting the enemy airman go on to destroy the town and its inhabitants. There are, in the situation, but two courses open to him and each of them is a violation of the law of love. Something he must do—inaction is also action—and he will no doubt do what seems to him to be the lesser evil under the circumstances, as judged from the point of view of the absolute imperative of the divine law. We are not here concerned with which of the two courses open to him he chooses or how he justifies his choice. What we are concerned with is the question: Why is it that he is *compelled* to violate the divine law? The compulsive factors are obviously not of the natural order; it is not any physical fact or natural power that prevents him from fulfilling the law he recognizes as binding. What, then, is it that has reduced his freedom to the point where no matter what he does he will involve himself in responsibility for the death of his fellow-men? The compulsive factor here is nothing short of the entire course of human history as that has culminated in the contemporary situation, in the "conditions at hand." The actions and decisions of men do not disappear with the generation that initiates them. No; the actions and decisions of men enter into the stream of history and live on in their consequences. No man faces the world as if it had just left the hand of the Creator. Each of us is caught up in a world that has been "spoiled" by sin, that has been overlaid and deformed by the sinful activities of men through the ages. If we really wanted to find out why it is that our farmer has no choice but to involve himself one way or another in responsibility for the death of his fellow-men, we would have to go back at least to the Thirty Years' War and trace the development of European and world history through the past three centuries.

The story of the farmer is a parable of the plight of the individual in history. We, who have just fought two world wars and are now facing a third, ought surely to recognize that. In every situation with which life confronts us, we are called upon to choose, to decide, under judgment of God, but we can choose only within the narrow confines permitted us by history. We are all caught in the solidarity of sin. Nothing could be more false to the facts of life or to the insights of biblical religion than the ultraindividualistic notion that sin begins and ends with the individual person who commits it. The sins of men coagulate into a vast collective deposit that permeates the structures, institutions and attitudes of society at every level of life. What men have done at other times and places, what men do elsewhere in our own time, what we ourselves have done in the past, enter into the conditions that compel us to take life, to live by exploitation, to eat while others go hungry—just as what we do now adds to the burden of sin that will beset the men of time to come and cruelly restrict their freedom of action. So subtly and yet so inescapably are we bound together by the fabric of our social humanity.

What I have been suggesting is said with shattering power in the Scriptural pronouncement that has caused so much scandal to men with a fine sense of individual moral responsibility: "The Lord visits the iniquity of the fathers upon the children and the children's children unto the third and fourth generations" (Exod. 20:5, 34:7; Num. 14:18; Deut. 5:9). We can now feel the force of this statement. The sins of the fathers are visited upon the children not merely in the sense that one generation has to bear the consequences of the deeds of another—"Our fathers have sinned. . .and we have borne their iniquities" (Lam. 5:7)—but in the far more important sense that the sins of the fathers create a situation in which the children, too, do evil, if only because, in the concrete circumstances, no course of action is open to them that is not to some degree infected with it. There is no escaping the solidarity of sin because there is no escaping the solidarity of mankind.

The far-reaching power of sin through its embodiment in the structures and institutions of society is a basic aspect of the influence of the past upon the present that makes for the continuity of history. It accounts for the plight in which men find themselves at any point in the course of events, but it does not relieve them of responsibility for their actions. Here Jeremiah and Ezekiel, who laid such stress upon individual responsibility, are right: "Every one shall die for his own iniquity; every one that eats the sour grape, his teeth shall be set on edge" (Jer. 31:29-30; cf. Ezek. 18:2-3). Each of us is responsible for what he chooses and does. The tragic predicament of men in history is that the iniquity which we do and for which we are responsible is only too often something we have had to choose because the historical situation offered us no course of action that was altogether free from evil.

Not evil alone, however, but the good that men do lives beyond them. "If one man sins," says Marmorstein, explaining the rabbinical doctrine of the "solidarity of Israel and the world," "the whole generation suffers on account of him. [And] if there is one righteous man, the whole world stands for his sake."[5] Every act of justice and lovingkindness, every action in which the self is transcended for what is genuinely (though perhaps not completely) beyond the self, enters into the stream of history as a power in its own right. In contrast to the effect of sin, the good that men do helps to keep open and even to extend the areas of freedom available in social life. Humanitarian effort and social reform, sacrificial service to others, the struggle against injustice and oppression wherever they show themselves, do not merely relieve the distress of those immediately affected; they serve also to enlarge the possibilities of life for other men and other generations. In this sense, we all live by the grace of God and the "merit of the fathers." But the cumulative power of sin in the historical life of mankind is not thereby dissolved, for self-interest soon finds a way of insinuating itself into and exploiting even the most idealistic achievements. Is there, then, no way in which this vicious circle of sin perpetuating itself from generation to generation in the institutions of society can be broken? To answer this question we will have to turn back and examine a little more closely the dialectic of creativity and sin in history.

If we read Scripture aright, we cannot fail to note that history is there understood as a divine-human encounter in which God calls to man, man in his pride defies God, and God in his judgment punishes sinful man. A brief glance at what actually happens in history should be enough to vindicate the relevance of this insight.

Human history, as we have seen, may be conceived as a movement in which man works to implement the order of creation by devising techniques and institutions to meet the needs of life. His creativity is therefore in itself by no means evil; indeed, it is through his creativity that he becomes a "co-worker with God" in the maintenance and reconstruction of the world. In rabbinic literature, man is pictured as "imitating" the divine power of creation and thus "sharing in the divine work".[6] The call of God in every situation is a call to creativity. But precisely because of its vast potentialities, human creativity is always in peril of being converted by the self into an instrument of pride and self-aggrandizement. The enterprises we set going are wrenched from their proper subordination to God in the order of creation, are identified with ourselves, and are then invested with a value and significance utterly out of proportion to their real place in the scheme of things. A particular status quo in which we are interested is held to be essential to the survival of civilization; a particular program of reform upon which we have set our hearts becomes identical in our minds with the future of mankind. Institutions arising out of some natural coherence or erected to serve some social purpose are exalted beyond their merely relative validity and are led to make pretensions to finality and absoluteness. They become vested interests, structures of human selfishness and instruments of injustice and oppression. As such they fall under the judgment of God.

We saw in an earlier chapter how this process by which the institutions of society are perverted to the advantage of those who control them operates in economic life. Very much the same is true of the "race problem." Distinctions of color, differences of ethnic origin and the natural ties of kinship are absolutized and made to serve the pride and pretensions of the dominant group at the expense not only of the oppressed minorities but of the nation at large. What is particularly poignant in these cases and in others that might be mentioned is that the process is so unconscious: the advocates of "laissez-faire" capitalism and of "white supremacy" are so sure of their disinterestedness, so certain that the views they profess are born out of a concern for the general welfare, so unaware of the ideological taint of self-interest! And with good reason, for it is usually not the narrow, crude, obvious self-interest that is involved but a kind of higher self-interest, in which the narrow self is merged into a larger whole through which it finds its vicarious expression. But it is not any the less dangerous for that.

This tendency of man to absolutize his works and thereby to absolutize himself in his collective existence is the source of the demonic in history. It is the force that blocks the harmonious development of society, that precipitates revolutions and destroys civilizations. Toynbee very aptly calls it the "idolization of the ephemeral" and holds it to be the "nemesis of creativity." The term "idolization" he uses with careful intent, for it is precisely the tendency toward the absolutization of the relative, ultimately self-absolutization, that proves so ruinous. "This infatuation is the sin of idolatry," Somervell explains in his abridgement of *A Study of History*. "It may take the form of an idolization of the idolator's own personality or society in some ephemeral phase. . .; or it may take the limited form of the idolization of some particular institution or technique which once stood the idolator in good stead. . ."[7] But whether it is the self or society or some institution or technique that is thus absolutized, the result is the same: creativity is paralyzed; the great achievements of the past are transformed into forces of destruction; institutions that once served as the forms of development of the historical process now turn into its fetters. The entrenched vested interests, who take their stand upon the "ephemeral" thus absolutized, raise up their own destroyers and thus call down upon themselves the judgment of God. Society is disrupted from within and without, and all of the calamities that accompany war, revolution and the downfall of civilizations overwhelm mankind. Historical crisis—let us now recall the original meaning of "crisis"—comes as divine judgment.

This theme of man's overweening pride and God's chastening judgment runs through every phase of the prophetic interpretation of history. Thus thunders Ezekiel, bringing the word of God against the prince of Tyre: "Because you are puffed up with pride and have said, 'I am a god, I sit in the seat of the gods,'. . .therefore behold, I will bring strangers against you, the most ruthless of nations. . . .You were puffed up with pride because of your beauty; you corrupted your wisdom by reason of your splendor; therefore I flung you to the ground and exposed you for kings to gaze at" (Ezek. 28:2-7, 17-18). And Isaiah pronounces the doom of Assyria, who, according to the Phophet, had been raised by God as the "rod of [his] anger" against Israel, in the following words: "Therefore it shall come to pass that when the Lord has performed his whole work on Mount Zion and on Jerusalem, he will punish the arrogant heart of the king of Assyria and his vainglorious pride. For he [i.e., Assyria] has said: 'By the strength of my hand I have done it, and by my wisdom, for I have understanding. . . ' Shall the axe boast over him that hews therewith, or the saw lord itself over him that plies it? As if a rod were to sway the man that wields it, or a staff were to lift up what is not wood! Therefore the Lord, the Lord of Hosts, will send a wasting sickness into his fat, and under his glory there shall be kindled a burning, a burning like the burning of fire" (Isa. 10:5-16). These passages point to a characteristic and extremely significant difference between the biblical view of the downfall of civilizations and the view that has come down to us from Greco-Roman moralism. Whereas the latter sees the decline of cultures as due primarily to luxury, dissoluteness and debauchery, the biblical writers trace the destruction of kingdoms and civilizations to insolent pride, insatiable greed and other manifestations of the self-absolutization of idolatry.

It is important to note that in the Scriptural view, the divine judgment under which sinful rulers and nations and institutions fall is generally executed through the regular operations of history. The proud prince of Tyre was brought low by the neighboring kings; the judgment against godless Israel was carried out by the King of Assyria, who had no notion that he was serving a divine purpose but who simply thought of himself as a great conqueror and the judgment against the arrogant Assyrian was, in its turn, to be executed by the Babylonians. In the dialectic of history, the judgment of God operates immanently through the nemesis that absolutistic pretensions inevitably raise against themselves. The agent of divine judgment may be an ambitious king, a rebellious peasantry, an insurgent working class, a revolutionary party, a nationalist movement. They do their work to serve their own purposes, impelled by their own motives compounded of idealism and self-interest; but the work they do executes the judgment of God upon the tyrant, the exploiter, the oppressor, who has forgotten the Lord of history and has exalted himself into the god of his own little universe.

The dialectic we have described is a succession of self-absolutizing pretensions and the divine punishment they bring in their wake. But the vicious circle of sin continues without abatement, for the instrument of divine justice today becomes the arrogant pretender of tomorrow. I do not mean to imply that great changes cannot come as a result of this movement of history: the facts show quite otherwise: every execution of the divine judgment at the hands of some historical agent shakes up the rigid structure of society, destroys obsolete institutions and wipes out entrenched vested interests. But, in the very process, new wrongs are brought into being, perhaps even worse than the old—new injustices, new vested interests, new oppressions. Even if one can detect a net gain in some period—and I would certainly insist that such a positive balance can be drawn in the case of a number of great revolutions in history—the circle of sin and evil is not broken through. *Can* it be broken through?. Is genuine repentance—the only way the vicious circle of sin is broken through in individual life—a real possibility for collectivities of men, for nations and cultures?

It would, at first glance, seem altogether out of the question. Repentance means a "change of heart," an abandonment of all pretensions to self-sufficiency, a contrite and humble "turning" to the divine source of our being. How is that possible for nations and cultures? They have no real personalities in the sense in which personality is given in the "image of God." Even the moral resources which individual men, for all their sinfulness, are able to muster up seem to be out of the reach of collectivities. Collectivities generally function at a much lower moral level than the individuals who go to make them up. "In every human group," Niebuhr writes, "there is less reason to guide and check impulse, less capacity for self-transcendence, less ability to comprehend the needs of others and therefore more unrestrained egoism, than the individuals who compose the group reveal in their personal relationships."[8] Common experience reveals the two levels of morality on which men live, the level of personal conduct and the level of social life; men who act on behalf of others in a collective capacity are generally ready to follow the dictates of corporate self-interest with a frankness and consistency impossible in their private affairs. No one expects a statesman or a trade union leader to sacrifice the interests of his people for the sake of other groups in the sense in which individuals are expected to place the welfare of others on a level with their own. The antithesis, "moral man and immoral society," may do too much credit to man but it certainly does not misrepresent society. How, then, can we speak of repentance in connection with society?

And yet something very like repentance does take place in history. The recent determination of the British people to carry through the dissolution of the Empire is a case in point. An historical development of such magnitude does not lend itself to simple analysis, but I think no one really acquainted with the situation would care to deny that behind it all there actually was some sort of "change of heart" on the part of the British people, a genuine revulsion of feeling against the unsavory record of colonial imperialism. Of course, the changed position of Britain in the world had something to do with bringing about this momentous decision, yet when all is said and done, it must be recognized that Britain has met the challenge of the new situation not by die-hard entrenchment and new pretensions but by an impressive effort to break through the age-old structure of vested interests and make a genuine "new beginning." That this strategy may, in the long run, strengthen the British position simply means that in the collective affairs of mankind, too, there are occasions when the wisdom of dying to the old self in order to live to the new proves itself even in worldly terms.

This, I think, is as far as repentance can go for nations and cultures. It is very far from being repentance in the profound and transforming sense in which we know it in personal life. Yet it does, after all, hold out the possibility that the divine judgment over nations may lead to reform and renovation rather than to disaster, that old structures and institutions may be renewed rather than destroyed by the violence of history. Such things do happen, and the British example is only the most recent. Peaceful change and the gradual disestablishment of privilege are not unknown, and although in every case it is possible to discover new forms of self-interest at work, the reality of the "change of heart" need not be challenged.

God's judgment in history, pronounced against the self-absolutizing pretensions of men, may thus lead either to repentance or to destruction. Is this not what we learn in the Book of Jonah about Nineveh, that most wicked of cities? But repentance for classes, nations and cultures is no more possible without divine grace than it is for individuals. The resources of divine grace in history are generally mediated through the works of God-fearing men, whose devoted service to their fellows is never without effect. The prophet and saint, the social reformer, the man genuinely concerned with the welfare of his neighbor, are the great assets of society. They are a leaven that works from within and helps dissolve the rigid structures of sinful self-interest that burden mankind from age to age. What they accomplish is not always visible on the surface, but it constitutes a fund, a treasure, upon which their own and subsequent generations may draw. It is almost a commonplace that the healthy development of the British labor-socialist movement, in comparison with its Continental counterparts, is due, to some extent at least, to the sound moral foundations laid by the devout men—many of them lay preachers and nonconformist ministers—who helped bring it into being. And in our own country, can we account for the astonishing development of social-welfare legislation in the course of the past fifteen years without mentioning the decades of patient agitation on the part of the dedicated men and women who first brought an understanding of social responsibility to the public mind? The ancient rabbinical doctrine of the "merit of the fathers" (*zekut abot*), according to which the good deeds of men in the past constitute a resource of redemption for our own time, may thus be seen to possess a far greater relevance to social reality than has usually been allowed.

History, then, is a process of dialectic interaction between the divine intent in creation and human self-will, or, on another level, between the self-transcending creativity of man and the corrupting self-interest that always invades it. But that cannot be the whole story, for if history were nothing more than that, it would be nothing at all. It would have no *eschaton*, no end—either in the sense of culmination or purpose. And if there is no *eschaton*, there is no future, for it is the *eschaton*, the end, that gives history its direction and makes it possible for us to speak of the future in any significant sense.

It is true that history, even in its succession of events, reveals something of judgment and fulfilment. We have seen how the blind arrogance of self-absolutization involved in the "idolization of the ephemeral" leads to destruction, and we have seen, too, how self-transcending goodness may achieve its results in history. Even so personal, so existential, an experience as repentance may, to a limited degree at least, enter into the historical process and open the way for new possibilities. But all such judgments and fulfilments are at best merely partial and provisional. In themselves, they lead nowhere, for they do not transform the character of history, which remains an ambiguous, two-sided process, taking away with one hand what it gives with the other. At the very most, such a dialectic may reveal the tension that underlies the movement of history, but it reveals it as apparently a movement without total purpose or direction.

That cannot be. If the Living God is the Lord of history, history *must* have a total purpose and direction: the divine intent must enforce itself in and through the doings of men, not only partially and provisionally but completely and finally. Without this ultimate reference, even the partial meanings discernible in the flux of events would not be able to sustain themselves. Partial judgments imply a final judgment, partial fulfilments a total fulfilment, partial redemptions the ultimate redemption of the entire historical process. The meaning of history must somehow be *completed* if there is to be any meaning at all.

## II

The problem of meaning is the problem of the completion of history. In itself, history is incomplete and fragmentary, not only in the obvious sense that no overall pattern seems to fit the particularity of events, but also in the more profound sense that, however comprehensive our view, we do not seem to be able to extract from history itself any indication of what it is all about. No immanent meaning emerges, even to the most penetrating insight. "The problem of history as a whole," Löwith concludes, "is unanswerable within its own perspective. Historical processes as such do not bear the least evidence of a comprehensive and ultimate meaning. History as such has no outcome. There never has been and never will be an immanent solution of the problem of history."[9] Otherworldly idealism eagerly acknowledges this fact and concludes therefrom that history is unreal and insignificant and that man can fulfil himself only in the timeless realm of the eternal. This-worldly philosophies deny the fact and attempt to give history meaning by completing it in its own terms. But this kind of completion is always bound to be a false completion, for it operates by selecting some one aspect of man and his works and making it the key to the whole. Such idolatrous absolutization leads necessarily to the distortion of historical existence and the conversion of any philosophy of history based upon it into an ideologizing system in which everything is sacrificed to the interests of the false absolute. Confusion inevitably follows upon man's effort to complete his life through his own power or to solve the mystery of existence by his own wisdom.

The problem thus becomes one of completing the meaning of history while avoiding the false and premature solutions involved in any attempt to do so in and through the historical process itself. The problem is solved in principle when it is recognized that all human completions are not only inadequate but contain positive contradictions to the true meaning, which can only be given to history by a power not man's. It is solved in practice when it is recognized that man's part in the making of history is of ultimate significance only when it is performed in service to the God who is the Lord of history. But whether in theory or in practice, it is a solution that will make sense only to those who approach history from the standpoint of faith.

The understanding of history in Hebraic religion is based on the presupposition that underlies the entire biblical faith: the affirmation of the Living God, of a transcendent Power who is active in life and history and whom man meets in personal encounter in the context of historical existence. Seen from the vantage point of this affirmation, history takes on a new significance. Its meaning is completed in terms beyond itself, yet integral to the full particularity of the historical process.

Hebraic eschatology[10] finds the completion of history in the Kingdom of God. The symbols of faith in which prophet and rabbi envisage the final outcome may seem strange to the modern mind, but, if properly understood, they illumine the problem of existence in a way that neither naturalism nor idealism is able to do.

All our enterprises within history remain unstable and ambiguous no matter how far the historical process is carried. More history can never redeem history from the chaos and irrationality that history itself brings forth. History may be the realm of meaning, but it is a meaning that history itself cannot confer. If meaning there is to be—and our faith in the Living God as Lord of history assures us that meaning there must be—it can only be meaning conferred in a culmination and by a power beyond history itself. History, in the biblical-rabbinic vision, is finally clarified, completed and redeemed through the Messiah and the Kingdom of God.

. Nowhere in Scripture or rabbinic tradition is there any suggestion that history itself brings mankind into the Kingdom of God slowly and gradually, through cumulative, unending progress. On the contrary, this notion, still so popular in "liberal" circles, is directly repudiated in Jewish tradition by the teaching concerning the "troubles" that are to usher in the Messianic Age. On the very eve of the fulfilment, we are told, the world will find itself not in a state of near-perfection but in the grip of terrible suffering, turmoil and conflict:

> Like the early Prophets and the later apocalyptic writers [Greenstone summarizes the Jewish doctrine on the subject], the Rabbis also taught that the Messianic period will be preceded by many tribulations, called "Messianic woes," not only for Israel but for all the nations of the earth as well. These trials preliminary to the advent of the Messianic era will be of all kinds, social and political both.[11]

This does not sound much like the "march of progress ever onward and upward." Whatever form the Messianic teaching may take in the rabbinic writings, however extravagant the imagery may sometimes be, the essential realism is never lost: history cannot redeem itself; on the contrary, it proceeds and ends in catastrophe from which it must be redeemed by the hand of God.

The coming of the Messiah "at the end of days" is this redeeming act of God. Not that redemption does not enter history at every point and endow it with the partial meanings and fulfilments which it reveals. But these partial meanings and fulfilments, as we have seen, can sustain themselves only in terms of an ultimate fulfilment to which we look forward in faith. The coming of the Messiah opens the "new age" of fulfilment.

The first phase of the Messianic act is presented to us as the final defeat of the powers of evil in history and the vindication at last of the divine intent in creation. That is why the Messiah means hope and why the pagans who know not the Messiah and do not await him are literally without hope. The Messianic hope of redemption in Jewish tradition has a double aspect: "particularist," relating to the reintegration of Israel and restoration to Zion; and universalist, proclaiming the redemption of all mankind and indeed of the cosmos as a whole. In a later chapter, we shall consider these two aspects in their relation and organic unity; for the present, we need not press this distinction within the larger vision of the Messianic fulfilment.

The advent and triumph of the Messiah leads, in normative Jewish tradition, to the next and culminating phase—the resurrection of the dead, the last judgment, and the inauguration of the "world-to-come" (*olam ha-ba*).[12] Perhaps nothing seems so outrageous to the modern mind as these eschatological symbols, and yet they are literally indispensable for any profound view of life and history.

The symbol, "resurrection of the dead," expresses the depth and dimensions of Hebraic religion in relation to the destiny of mankind more adequately perhaps than any other concept. This becomes clear if we contrast it with the essentially Greek belief in the immortality of the soul, with which it is so often confused. The teaching of the resurrection affirms, in the first place, that man's ultimate destiny is not something that is his by virtue of his own nature—by his possession of an "immortal soul," for example—but comes to him solely by the grace and mercy of God, who "wakes him from the dead." It thus emphasizes total dependence on God as against metaphysical self-reliance. It affirms, in the second place, that what is destined to fulfilment is not a disembodied soul that has sloughed off its body, but the *whole* man—body, soul and spirit—joined in an indissoluble unity. It affirms, in the third place, that the salvation promised of God is not a private, individual affair that each one acquires for himself upon his death, but the salvation of mankind, the corporate redemption of men in the full reality of their historical existence.[13] The whole point of the doctrine of the resurrection is that the life we live now, the life of the body, the life of empirical existence in society, has some measure of permanent worth in the eyes of God and will not vanish in the transmutation of things at the "last day." The fulfilment will be a fulfilment for the the *whole* man and for *all* men who have lived through the years and have entered into history and its making. This is the meaning of the doctrine of the resurrection of the dead; it is a doctrine with which we cannot dispense, no matter how impatient we may be with the literalistic pseudo-biological fantasies that have gathered around it through the centuries.

Following upon the resurrection of the dead, in the traditional picture, is the last judgment. For the completion of history is not merely fulfilment; it is fulfilment that is also judgment. In this last judgment, men and their enterprises come before God for the final clarification. Pride and oppression are brought low; the humble are raised and their tears wiped away.[14] That in men and their deeds which is found worthy in God's eyes is fulfilled and completed; that which is evil and contrary to the divine intent is purged and destroyed. Then, at last, does life lose its ambiguity and our deeds their equivocal character in the transfigured existence of the "world-to-come." The last judgment is the judgment at the "last day" and therefore always impending: it hangs over us and our enterprises at every moment of existence. It is thus, as in Amos, a fearful prospect that is shatteringly contemporaneous: "Woe unto you who desire the day of the Lord! . . . It is darkness and not light!" (Amos 5:18). But at the same time, it is the glad promise of life abundant and everlasting: "For behold, I create a new heaven and a new earth. . . . Be ye glad and rejoice forever in that which I create" (Isa. 65:17-18).

The culmination of the transfiguration promised in faith at the "last day" is the "world-to-come" (*olam ha-ba*). But the term in its English translation is misleading; it is not a new "place" that is promised, but a new *time*, a new *age*.[15] Just as the intermediate period that is history follows upon a primal age that is prelude, so it culminates in a new age that is both postlude and fulfilment. The distinction is not spatial, between one "world" and another ("this world" and the "world-to-come") but temporal, between one time or aeon and another ("this age" and the "age-to-come"). The difference is crucial, for only if it is understood in terms of time can the eschatological outcome be relevant to the historical process. The temporal terminology is, of course, symbolic, but the symbolism is not arbitrary; it is inherent in the reality of that which is symbolized. The historical process in time culminates in, is fulfilled and judged by, the "new time" of the Kingdom of God. In the Kingdom of God and the judgment that initiates it, the meaning of history is established and completed.

It must be obvious to the reader that this three-phase scheme, in which the meaning of the middle phase is given in part in relation to the beginning out of which it emerges, but primarily in terms of the end for which it is destined, bears a striking resemblance to the three-phase scheme of the Marxian dialectic of history. Marxism, too, begins with a primal state of innocence, "primitive communism," and proceeds by way of a "fall" into the middle period, the period of social evil, the period of private property and class society. But this phase is merely temporary and provisional; it is destined to be overcome and replaced by a "new age" of co-operation and uncoerced harmony, the "communist society" of the future. This culmination is preceded by social disturbances, conflicts and wars ("Messianic woes") and is ushered in by a great catastrophic act, the Revolution, which judges and purges and opens the way for renewal. But the Revolution and the "new society" are not simply promises of the future; they are that in terms of which every event in history, every enterprise of men in society, past and present, is evaluated and assigned its partial meaning, to be validated in the great fulfilment at the "end." The structural analogy could hardly be closer.[16]

And no wonder. For Marxism is, at bottom, a secularization of the Hebraic "philosophy" of history. This secularization—in which human existence is reduced to the two dimensions of nature and society and deprived of its transcendent dimension of spirit—preserves the formal structure of the Hebraic scheme, but drains it of its real power and significance. For in Marxist secularism, the beginning and the end are simply points *in* history, events like all other events in the historical process. Eschatology is thus reduced to utopia, and history is called upon to realize the perfect and unconditioned society in the natural course of its development. History is once more its own redeemer; indeed, the illusions of Marxism as to the redemptive powers of history are perhaps even more gross than those of "liberal" progressivism. But the original imprint of Hebraic eschatology still remains evident in Marxism, and a comparison of the two, in their resemblance and differences, should prove particularly instructive to the modern mind. To those who have lost the sense of the transcendental, it may help to illustrate, however inadequately, what is implied when we speak of the meaning of history being revealed and completed in a great fulfilment at the "end."

The fulfilment of history is the Kingdom of Heaven (*malkut shamayim*). But here again the usual translation is misleading. What is meant is not a kingdom in a kind of superworld called "Heaven," but a new age in which the *kingship* of God is revealed in its fullness and sovereignty. The locus of the Kingdom is the world ("heaven and earth") which came into being in the creation; even when later rabbinic thought develops the image of the "Heavenly Jerusalem," it is still the earthly Jerusalem to which it is related. But while the locus of the Kingdom is the world, it is the world redeemed, transfigured and renewed through the establishment of a new relation to God. It is "a new heaven and a new earth" because it is "heaven and earth" in a new time.[17]

In the great prophetic visions of the "end-time," what is common amidst the variety of imagery is the passionate conviction that the new age of redemption will mark the return of man and nature to theocentric existence, in which fellowship with God in love and obedience will be the very texture of life. Sin—the *yetzer ha-ra*—will be eliminated, the rabbis tell us,[18] and the law of love will be not merely regulative but actually constitutive of existence. All nature will be transformed and the primal harmonies of Paradise restored in an unimaginable way:

> But in the end of days it shall come to pass that the mountain of the Lord's house shall be established as the top of the mountains, and it shall be exalted above the hills; and the peoples shall stream unto it . . . And they shall beat their swords into ploughshares, and their spears into pruning-hooks; nation shall not lift up sword against nation, neither shall they learn war any more. But they shall sit every man under his vine and his fig-tree; and none shall make them afraid. For the mouth of the Lord of Hosts has spoken (Mic. 4:1-4).

> And there shall come forth a shoot out of the stock of Jesse, and a sprout shall grow forth out of his roots. And the spirit of the Lord shall rest upon him . . . With righteousness shall he judge the poor, and decide with equity for the meek of the land; . . . and with the breath of his lips shall he slay the wicked . . . And the wolf shall dwell with the lamb, and the leopard shall lie down with the kid; and the calf and the young lion shall graze together and a little child shall lead them. And the cow and the bear shall be friends, and their young ones shall lie down together: and the

lion shall eat straw like the ox. And the sucking child shall play
on the hole of the asp, and the weaned child shall put his hand
on the viper's den. They shall not hurt or destroy in all my holy
mountain; for the earth shall be full of the knowledge of the
Lord, as the waters cover the sea (Isa. 11:1-9).

The grandeur and poetic magnificence of these visions should not
make us lose sight of what it is the Prophets are saying. In his own
good time, they proclaim, God will take decisive action to redeem
Israel and the world. He will send his Messiah and bring the reign
of evil in history to an end by rooting out sin and hatred from the
hearts of men and by allaying the violence and conflict in nature. To
this grandiose picture of the "new age" rabbinic speculation has added
rich imagery intended to emphasize the incredible fertility of nature
and the radical transformation of all life.[19] But in prophet and rabbi
alike, the crucial point is that "the earth shall be full of the knowledge
of the Lord": man will once again be at one with God, and *therefore*
at one with himself, with his fellow-men, and with all creation. The
"new age" of the Kingdom of God may indeed mark the end of history as we know it, but it is the beginning of life everlasting in its
fulness and truth.[20]

The Kingdom of God is thus basically conceived as a restoration
of the primal harmonies of Paradise before the Fall, an annihilation
of the contradiction which sin has introduced into existence.[21] But it
is more than that. For, as Brunner emphasizes, "the end of time and
the beginning are not the same . . . Between these two points, the
start and the finish, something happens, which even for God is real
and significant. There is history, an individual and universal human
history. . . ."[22] The "new age" of the Kingdom is, in a sense, a return
to the primal harmonies of God's order of creation, but it is a return
enriched with all that history in its creativity has brought forth. The
teaching of the Kingdom offers no comfort to primitivistic utopianism,
which regards all history as a mistake to be rectified by a return to
Paradise. It is deeply aware of the ambiguities of history, but it
understands that since human existence is thoroughly historical in its
structure, the fulfilment of existence must be a fulfilment of history
or it is nothing at all.

The Kingdom of God, because it is fulfilment, is promise, norm and demand. It is promise because it proclaims the hope of a total realization of life after judgment. It is promise because it holds forth the assurance that those who suffer oppression and injustice in the world-as-it-is will inherit their reward in the world-as-it-will-be. The Jewish folk-imagination that sees the Messianic Age as one of endless feasting on the Leviathan and the Behemoth, like the Negro spiritual that joyfully proclaims that in Heaven all God's children have shoes. may outrage the fastidious mind by its crass "materialism," but it shows a genuine understanding of the promise of the Kingdom, which is that life shall be completed and fulfilled in all its dimensions.[23]

But if the Kingdom is promise, it is also norm. The Kingdom of God is the life of man as it should be. The law of the Kingdom— total love of God, with all its implications—is the law of our life here and now. It is therefore demand as well, for it places us under the obligation never to rest so long as our life is lived in violation of this law—which in history it always is.

The Kingdom of God is thus both here and to come. Since the "new age" of the Kingdom is the time of the fulness of the divine sovereignty in the life of the redeemed world, the Kingdom may be said to be in power in *this* age wherever and to the degree that men are transformed in love of God and the acknowledgment of his total sovereignty. In this sense, the Kingdom is already here; yet for its coming we pray:[24] but it is one and the same reality in two stages of self-manifestation.

The Kingdom of God is therefore not some far-off event in the indeterminate future; were it merely that, all talk about it would be idle speculation without relevance to reality. The Kingdom of God is a dynamic force within life and history, here and now. It upsets all human calculations. It confounds human complacency and despair alike. Against complacency, it has the word of judgment; to despair, it holds out the promise of fulfilment despite everything. It validates human existence by revealing its goal and direction and by sustaining the partial meanings, which, even in its incompleteness, life brings forth.[25] It places all life under criticism, for it calls into question all human values and institutions, allowing nothing in this world to parade as final or absolute. It fills life with hope, for in faith we are assured that in the "new age" of the Kingdom, our present life will not be dismissed as meaningless but will be completed and fulfilled. It endows life with power for action and generates that "passionate thirst for the future" which Renan found to be the mark of the "true Israelite." It stands at the "end" of history, yet enters into history at every point and drives it forward to its consummation.

Just because the eschatological reality is also existential, it is necessary to distinguish it clearly from the perfectionist utopianism with which it is frequently confused. Eschatological perfection is not a possibility of history, although it points to ever-new possibilities within it. Isaiah's or Micah's vision of peace is not something that can be realized by the United Nations. Even the most perfect world state could do no more than *enforce* peace throughout the world, just as the national state does today within its own borders. But the hatreds and conflicts among men would remain, though prevented from breaking out into open violence. The "peace" of the prophets is something very different: it is an inner harmony and love that needs no external sanctions. As such, it transcends the resources of history to achieve, although every achievement of history must be measured in its terms. To ignore this fact and to attempt to reduce the prophetic vision of perfection to the level of perfectionist utopianism is to throw confusion alike into practical politics and the ultimate insights of religion.

The Kingdom is here, yet for it we pray. It is the redemptive act of God, yet for it we work. What a man does, Jewish tradition assures us, has its effect on the coming of the Messiah, yet it is God who sends him.[26] "It is not as though man has to do this or that to 'hasten' the redemption of the world . . .; yet those who 'turn' cooperate in the redemption of the world."[27] The fulfilment of the "new age" is a fulfilment of history through the power of God, but it would be meaningless were there not history—that is, the actions of men— to fulfil. It is the same paradox of decision and grace projected on the screen of the "horizontal" movement of history. "The mystery is that, on the one hand, duty is demanded of us as if duty not done will never be done. On the other hand, faith declares that man would be undone if God did not complete what we have left incomplete and purify what we have corrupted."[28] If the Marxist or "liberal" secularist finds this paradox too "mystical" for his taste, let him remember that he, too, is involved in it, for he, too, affirms the need for human action

while looking to "progress" or the "dialectic of history" to bring fulfilment. The truth is that some such paradox is inherent in any philosophy that takes history seriously, but only the eschatology of Hebraic
religion can raise it beyond the plane of mere contradiction and give
it profound meaning in the total scheme of human destiny.

Hebraic eschatology thus solves the problem of history in the only
way it can be solved, by finding its meaning not in the premature
completions that man in his pretensions tries to force upon it, but
in the judgment and fulfilment toward which it is directed by the hand
of God. Hebraic eschatology thereby escapes the dilemmas with
which naturalism and idealism are beset. It can affirm the reality and
meaning of historical time without falling into the secularist delusion
that time and history fulfil themselves. It can deny the pretensions of
history to self-salvation and self-revelation without lapsing into idealistic "eternalism." It can do justice to the valid insights of Marxism,
of the doctrine of progress and of other conceptions of history without succumbing to their one-sided absolutizations and oversimplifica-
tions. That is why an increasing number of social and historical
thinkers are beginning to make a certain use of the eschatological
framework to give depth to their analyses, even though they may not
be able to bring themselves to the faith out of which it springs. Such
pragmatic appropriation is a significant tribute to the realism and
power of the biblical view of history, but in the last analysis it is untenable and has no saving virtue.

For when all is said and done, the biblical view of history is not a
philosophy of history but a gospel of salvation. It tells us how and
why we have gotten into this dreadful plight of sinful existence. It
brings to us a shattering sense of the human predicament, yet forbids
us to despair, for it assures us that in the very midst of the tragedy
and frustrations of the historical process, the divine power is at work,
redeeming temporal existence and leading it forward to fulfilment in
a "new age" in which life will at last realize all its potentialities and
be transfigured in the fulness of the love of God. Such is the word of
Hebraic eschatology; it is a word that can be really apprehended only
in faith.

## NOTES TO CHAPTER 16

1. Gen. r., chap. ix, No. 7. "Election, defection [fall] and return are the three periods in which history is seen running its course. . . . Election without defection would be an assumption of paradisal historylessness; the fall gives impulse to history. Fall without return, however, would mean history surrendered and planless. Between fall and return history completes its course." N. N. Glatzer, *Untersuchungen zur Geschichtslehre der Tannaiten* (Schocken: Berlin, 1933), pp. 35-36.
2. Karl Marx, *Eighteenth Brumaire of Louis Bonaparte* (International Publishers, New York, n. d.), chap. iii.
3. Marx, *op. cit.*, chap. i.
4. W. Windelband, *Lehrbuch der Geschichte der Philosophie* (Fischer: Freiburg, Germany, 1892), p. 213, contrasts the Greek view of history as "an eternal process of nature" with the Hebrew-Christian conception of "the drama of world-history as a temporal activity of free and active wills."
5. A. Marmorstein, *The Old Rabbinic Doctrine of God: the Names and Attributes of God* (Oxford University: London, 1927), p. 48. Cf. also Marmorstein, *The Doctrine of Merit* (Jews' College: London, 1920), pp. 185ff.
6. Abot d. R. N., version B. chap. 21. Solomon Schechter, *Studies in Judaism*, Third Series (Jewish Publication Society: Philadelphia, 1945), p. 271; Isadore Epstein, *The Jewish Way of Life* (Goldston: London, 1946), pp. 131-32.
7. A. J. Toynbee, *A Study of History*, abridgement by D. C. Somervell (Oxford: New York, 1947), pp. 307-10, 581-82.
8. Reinhold Niebuhr, *Moral Man and Immortal Society* (Scribner's: New York, 1934), pp. xi-xii.
9. Karl Löwith, *Meaning in History* (University of Chicago: Chicago, 1949), p. 191.
10. An excellent account of biblical-early rabbinic eschatology is to be found in G. F. Moore, *Judaism* (Harvard University: Cambridge, Mass., 1927), Vol. II, Part VII, "The Hereafter."
11. J. H. Greenstone, *The Messiah Idea in Jewish History* (Jewish Publication Society, Philadelphia, 1906), p. 94. Greenstone supplies documentation.
12. "The Messianic period is to precede the 'world-to-come'; at its end, the resurrection will take place and then the 'world-to-come' will begin. . . . According to semi-authoritative statements in the Talmud, the Messianic period proper will precede the 'world-to-come' and the two thus become distinguished from each other . . . The belief in the coming of the

238    Judaism and Modern Man

Messiah, a scion of David, who will gather the Jews from exile and restore them to Palestine, in the resurrection, and in *olam ha-ba*, became cardinal principles and dogmas in Judaism." M. Waxman, *A Handbook of Judaism* (Bloch: New York, 1947), pp. 163-65. See also Schechter, *Some Aspects of Rabbinic Theology* (Macmillan: New York, 1909), p. 102. The explicit affirmation of resurrection was a fairly late development in Jewish faith, very largely post-biblical. The earlier expectation was essentially corporate, looking toward the vindication of God's purpose with Israel and the fulfilment of its vocation.

13. "There can be no complete consummation for the individual until there is consummation also for society." John Baillie, *And the Life Everlasting* (Scribner's: New York, 1933) p. 249.

14. "For the Lord of Hosts has a day against all that is proud and high and against all that is lofty and tall . . . Then the haughtiness of man will be humbled, and the pride of man will be brought low; and the Lord alone will be exalted on that day." Isa. 2:12, 17. "So the Lord God will wipe away the tears from all the faces, and will remove from all the earth the reproach that lies on his people." Isa. 25:8.

15. Moore, *Judaism*, II, 378, note 1—"But the Day of Judgment shall be the end of this age and the beginning of the eternal age-to-come." IV Ezra 7:43.

16. See Will Herberg, "The Christian Mythology of Socialism," *Antioch Review*, Vol. III (Spring, 1943) No. 1.

17. "[Prophetic messianism] implies no mere negation of the world in which we live, but its purification and completion; a community not of disembodied spirits but of men; 'a new heaven and new earth,' indeed, but erected upon the renewal of the human heart. This is the legacy of the Jewish Prophets." Martin Buber, *Der heilige Weg* (Literarische Anstalt Rütten & Loening: Frankfort, 1920), p. 34.

"Man . . . will become a new creature." M. Higger, *The Jewish Utopia* (Lord Baltimore Press: Baltimore, 1932), p. 103.

18. *B.* Sukkah 52a; Gen. r. chap xlviii, No. 11; Exod. r. chap. xlvi, No. 4; Num. r. chap. xv, No. 16.

19. See the very interesting compilation in Higger, *op. cit.* Also A. Cohen, *Everyman's Talmud* (Dutton: New York, 1949), pp. 352 ff.

20. "He will destroy death forever." Isa. 25:8. Since death came in as the fruit of sin (Sifra 27a), the restoration of life to theocentric existence will mean the overcoming of death.

21. According to Jewish tradition, even in respect to the physical features of creation, "conditions [in the Messianic Age] will be the same as before the fall." L. Ginzberg, *Legends of the Jews* (Jewish Publication Society: Philadelphia, 1938), V, 142, 152.

22. Emil Brunner, *Christianity and Civilization* (Scribner's: New York, 1948), First Part, p. 49.

23. It is therefore pictured as a "perpetual Sabbath": "The symbolic description of the world-to-come as the 'great Sabbath' . . . is of frequent occurrence in Jewish as well as early Christian literature." Ginzberg, *Legends*, V, 128.

24. Cf. the prayer in the *Kaddish*, so central to Jewish liturgy: "May he establish his kingdom [kingship] in your lifetime and during your days and within the life of the entire house of Israel, speedily and soon." Yet every time we affirm that "God is King" we acknowledge his kingship as a *present* reality.

25. It is in terms of the biblical scheme of creation, sinful existence in history, and redemption in the "new age" of the Kingdom of God that Hebraic thinking, as Milton well understood, "justifies God's ways to men." Philosophical thiodicy is completely foreign to the Bible and very largely to rabbinic thought.

26. "As against the belief that God had determined the exact date for the dawn of the Messianic era," A. Cohen explains (*op. cit.*, p. 351), "there grew up another doctrine that the date was not fixed but would be affected by the conduct of the people. That thought was read into the words, 'I the Lord will hasten it in its time' (Isa. 60:22), which were explained in this sense: 'If you are worthy, I will hasten it; if you are not worthy, it will be in its time' (*B*. San. 98a)".

27. Buber, "The Two Foci of the Jewish Soul," *Israel and the World* (Schocken: New York, 1948), p. 37.

28. Reinhold Niebuhr, *Beyond Tragedy* (Scribner's: New York, 1937), p. 268.

"We are dependent upon grace; but we do not do God's will when we take it upon ourselves to begin with grace instead of beginning with ourselves." Buber, "The Two Foci of the Jewish Soul," *Israel and the World*, pp. 32-33.

"It would be completely senseless to try to measure how great is man's part in the redemption of the world. . . . It is senseless to ask how far my action reaches and where God's grace begins. . . . Man's action is enclosed in God's action, but it is still real action." Buber, "The Interpretation of Chassidism," *Mamre* (Melbourne University: Melbourne, 1946), p. 114.

# IV.

# THE MYSTERY OF ISRAEL

# 17. SCRIPTURE, REVELATION AND REASON

The view of the basic realities of existence developed in the fore-going chapters as the essential teaching of Jewish religion is not the work of reason or the finding of science. What Jewish religion has to say about God, man and the world has its rational import and empirical relevance in that it bears directly on human life and helps to illumine as nothing else can the problem and perplexities of human existence. But it does not consist of propositions that can be established as logically compelling by the operations of reason or as empirically probable by the procedures of science. "God, freedom and immortality" cannot be proved, as the rationalists contend, nor can they be inferred from the latest discoveries of physics or biology, as the latter-day "scientific" philosophers of religion assure us. We must agree with the positivists and skeptics, though on entirely different grounds, that these questions are, in the last analysis, beyond the competence of pure reason or scientific method and that every attempt to "establish religion" either philosophically or scientifically is involved in hopeless fallacy. We have seen why this should be so: the affirmations of religion all hinge upon a crucial presupposition and commitment that emerges on a level far deeper than the rational processes of philosophy or science. Reason has its uses in the religious life, but its function is not to excogitate the ultimate truth about existence.

This does not mean that science and philosophy have no bearing upon what Hebraic religion holds to be the ultimate truth about existence. On the contrary, the insight into reality that comes of faith deals with the same real world with which science and at least the better part of philosophy are concerned. History, anthropology, psychology, all the social sciences are of genuine significance to the religious thinker, for they all have something important to say about the human situation with which he is concerned, but the frame of reference in which he does his thinking and the categories with which he operates

243

possess a dimension of depth to which science, because of its naturalistic premises, cannot pretend. In the multidimensional perspective of religious faith, the findings of science have their place and indeed acquire a new significance, but the perspective itself is not drawn from science nor can it be validated by reason or philosophy. The outlook of Hebraic religion, to which we have so often referred, finds its source and validation on an altogether different level of reality.

That source and validation is to be found in the Bible and in the religious tradition stemming from it. Reason and science are necessary to apprehend and make relevant what Scripture tells us, but it is Scripture and not science or philosophy that, in the normative Jewish view, reveals the living truth about man and the world.

The affirmation that Scripture is in some sense revelation is common to all religious thinkers in the Hebraic tradition, but the sense in which this claim is interpreted varies widely, and it is necessary to examine it somewhat more closely if it is to be given any real meaning.

Most familiar, and yet remote from its true import, is the fundamentalist conception of revelation as the supernatural communication of information through a body of writings which are immune from error because they are quite literally the writings of God. Everything in Scripture is thus held to be equally inerrant and equally inspired, whether it be notions about the shape of the earth or insights into the nature of man and his relation to God. Every incident is considered equally historical and equally factual, for its recording is believed to be at the direct dictation of the divine power. No critical examination of texts from the point of view of sources or process of development is possible, for the source is always immediately God and process of development there has not been. In many cases, this rigid, scholastic scheme is supported by an equally rigid rationalistic argument which pretends to substantiate the claim of Scripture by the resources of reason.

This fundamentalist doctrine, though its origins are ancient, developed into a hard-and-fast closed system only in relatively modern times, in part at least as a measure of defense against heterodoxy. Jewish orthodox opinion, indeed, has even tended to extend this notion of Scriptural inspiration and infallibility to the Talmud and other rabbinical writings, especially those dealing with *halakah*. It is hardly necessary to point out that fundamentalism today, while still widely affirmed, is thoroughly discredited with every critical mind. Much in the biblical writings—the bits of astronomical, geographical and biological information contained in them, for example—is obviously at odds with some of the best authenticated scientific knowledge of our time. The earth is not flat, the sun does not make its daily transit over it from one edge to the other, and life on earth did not appear quite in the way or the order described in Genesis. Neither the chronology nor the history recorded in the Scriptural works can be taken simply at its face value, although they have shown themselves in many ways better founded than scholarly opinion only recently was willing to grant. From another direction, the sacred writings themselves have been critically analyzed, and while much of the work of critical scholarship is by no means secure, it can no longer be seriously questioned that the Bible in its various parts is a highly composite work, reflecting a long and immensely complicated process of literary construction, redaction and development. However it may be related to God, the Bible is obviously not simply a transcript from his dictation and therefore no seamless whole incapable of error. And to complete the case against fundamentalism, it has become increasingly clear that the rationalistic conception of revelation as the supernatural communication of infallible information is altogether out of line with the Bible itself and is not even in harmony with much of later tradition. Fundamentalism, in short, defends a view of revelation that not only runs counter to substantial fact but is also of dubious religious power and significance.

As against the fundamentalist, the modernist accepts the findings of science and critical scholarship, but he so interprets these findings as to render revelation nothing but a figure of speech. The Scriptural writers, he concedes, were "inspired," but this means little more than saying that a Shakespeare or a Plato or a Buddha was inspired; the "inspiration" of the prophet is identified with the imagination of the poet and the illumination of the mystic or philosopher. As to the biblical writings themselves, they are, to the modernist, interesting compilations of myth, legend and folklore, in which are embedded a number of high ethical teachings. They are a kind of primitive literature, important for us culturally and pedagogically, no doubt, but hardly to be taken seriously as God's word. After all, we are reminded, has not criticism shown that even the Pentateuch is a patchwork of documents from different times, sources and historical settings —in other words, a compilation made by men rather than a single whole dictated by God?

Both modernism and fundamentalism agree on insisting that it must be either one or the other. If you question the fundamentalist premises, you must necessarily proceed to dissolve revelation into a meaningless phrase; and if you question the modernist conclusions, you must necessarily lapse into a benighted fundamentalism. Thus each protects itself by brandishing the scarecrow of the other. But we need not take this strategy too seriously. There *is* a third way, not "between" modernism and fundamentalism but beyond and distinct from both. Franz Rosenzweig and Martin Buber, among Jews, and H. Richard Niebuhr and Emil Brunner, among Christians, have shown how one may take Scripture with the utmost seriousness as the record of revelation while avoiding the pitfalls of fundamentalism. They have also shown how the findings of science and scholarship may be accepted at the same time that one affirms Scripture to be truly the vehicle of God's word. This third conception of revelation makes the attempt to be thoroughly biblical and thoroughly realistic at the same time, in the conviction that no conception can be the one without also being the other.

In this view, a shift in the very meaning of the term "revelation" is involved. Revelation is not the communication of infallible information, as the fundamentalists claim, nor is it the outpouring of "inspired" sages and poets, as the modernists conceive it. Revelation is the *self-disclosure of God in his dealings with the world.* Scripture is thus not itself revelation but a humanly mediated record of revelation. It is a story composed of many strands and fragments, each arising in its own time, place and circumstances, yet it is essentially one, for it is throughout the story of the encounter of God and man in the history of Israel. Scripture as revelation is not a compendium of recondite information or metaphysical propositions; it is quite literally *Heilsgeschichte,* redemptive history.

"He has made known his ways to Moses, his acts to the children of Israel" (Ps. 103:7): it is in this way that the Bible itself refers to revelation. What is revealed is God himself in his dealings with men; what is revealed is God's will—demand, judgment and mercy—in the ever-changing context of events; what is revealed is the "true history of the world" because it is the history of the world in its ultimate dimension of relation to God, "according to which [it] has an origin and a goal."[1] But although God reveals himself and his will in history, the meaning of history as revelation is visible not to the detached eye of the observer but to the inner eye of faith. When Isaiah proclaimed the outcome of the Assyrian war to be a revelation of God's judgment ("O Assyria, the rod of mine anger. . ." [Isa. 10:5]), he was referring to concrete historical events, but no Thucydides could have detected the operations of God in the course of these events. Through Isaiah, God spoke, but in receiving and transmitting the word of God, Isaiah was himself existentially involved in the situation as actor not as spectator. The insider can see what to the outsider must remain forever hidden: "spectator and actor stand in different worlds, speak a different language, and are unable to convince each other."[2] Revelation in Scriptural history is not simply the course of events; it is the course of events apprehended in faith and disclosed in its meaning by prophetic interpretation which itself becomes a factor deeply involved in the making of the history it is engaged in interpreting. History is history, but only to the eyes of faith is the meaning of history disclosed in its redemptive significance. Faith, the existential involvement of faith, is at once the presupposition and the interpretive principle of the divine revelation to which Scripture bears witness.

Because "revelation is something that *happens*, the living history of God in his dealings with the human race,"[3] Scripture knows nothing of any metaphysical speculations about the nature or essence of deity or of any mystical illumination through union with the divine. One might even say that Scripture in this respect is ultrapragmatic: it tells us nothing about God except his ways and his acts. "What the Bible says God *is*," Professor Baab asserts, "really amounts to saying what he *does*. Terms of description are really terms of function and behavior."[4] "The Hebrew," Professor Snaith insists, "does not say that Jehovah *is*, . .but that he *does*."[5] What both are saying is what Maimonides long ago pointed out: "All attributes ascribed to God are attributes of His acts."[6] Scripture tells us nothing, and therefore we can know nothing significant, about the *being* of God.[7] The only positive assertions that we can meaningfully make about God are affirmations of the divine activity in relation to man and the world; we can make such assertions because Scripture tells us about God's "ways" and "acts"; it is by testifying to his "mighty deeds" of judgment and redemption that Scripture brings us the revelation of God.

We have been speaking about Scripture as of a unity and yet we know that it is a veritable patchwork of documents from the most varied sources and historical contexts. How then can we call it one? "It is really one book, for one basic theme unites all the stories and songs, sayings and prophecies contained within it. [That] theme is the encounter between a group of people and the Lord of the world in the course of history. . .Either openly or by implication, the stories are reports of [such] encounters."[8] It is this oneness of theme, running through it from beginning to end, that makes the Bible one book and the faith grounded in it one faith. The views of Abraham on the nature of things and even on the "nature" of the divine were presumably far more "primitive" than those of Isaiah so many centuries later, but their faith was the same, for they stood in the same crisis of confrontation with God, shared the same ultimate covenantal commitment, and recognized the same Lord and his absolute claim.[9] Before this superhistorical reality, all historicism—though not all history—loses. its significance.

The unity of Scripture as revelation is not only a unity of theme; it is also a unity of vision and purpose. The history which carries the meaning of Scriptural revelation is *redemptive* history. It is the account of God's dealings with men told from the point of view of his redemptive purpose. Everything is directed toward that goal of redemption; even the genealogies, if properly understood, have that significance. Whatever other uses Scripture may have, its use as revelation is to disclose God's ways and purposes in the redemption of mankind and to open up to us the possibility of becoming part of that process by making the redemptive history our own.

This inner unity of Scripture is reflected in and conveyed through the unity that emerges from all the bewildering complexity of its literary development. The very work of compilation and redaction is creative and revealing. Granted that the biblical writings are compilations from various times and sources, the meaning of Scripture, Rosenzweig points out, is to be found not merely in what the Bible "says" in its various parts but also in how these parts are put together, just as in a mosaic the meaning of the picture emerges from the way the separate tiles are arranged and put together, regardless of the source of the constituents themselves. It is the whole that counts, and Scripture is a whole, a unique and organic whole. Rosenzweig regards the Redactor—using this term as the name for the compilers and editors of the biblical books—as the key figure in the development of the Bible.

> Our difference with Orthodoxy [he explains to the Orthodox leader, Dr. Jacob Rosenheim, in a letter dated April 21, 1927] consists in this, that from our belief in the holiness and uniqueness of the Torah and its character as revelation, we cannot draw any conclusions as to its literary origins or the philological value of the received text. Should Wellhausen prove right in all his theories. . . , our faith would not be affected in the least. . .We too translate the Torah as a single book. For us, too, it is the work of one spirit. . .Among ourselves we call him by the symbol which critical science is accustomed to use to designate its assumed redactor: R. But this symbol R we expand not into Redactor but into *Rabbenu.* For he is our teacher; his theology is our teaching.[10]

This view, it should be noted, implies that the work of recording, compiling and redacting that has gone into the making of the Bible is itself an instrument of the divine intent in revelation. The redactor through his work, like the prophet or chronicler through his, is helping to communicate the word of God in Scripture. It is a view that at first sight must seem strange to both the critical scholar, who assigns the redactor an altogether minor role in the Scriptural process, and to the old-line fundamentalist, who simply denies his existence. But it is the only view that does justice alike to the findings of critical scholarship and to the overall unity of Scripture. It is the only view by which inner meaning and the external process of literary composition may be made to clarify and sustain each other.

Understanding revelation in this way, we can see how it is possible to take Scripture seriously as the communication of God's word and the ultimate truth about existence without necessarily regarding it as verbally inerrant oracles dictated by God. It is, in a real sense, a record of God's "mighty deeds" and therefore a revelation of his "ways," but it is a record made by man and therefore subject to all the relativities and contingencies of human experience. God reveals himself through his actions in life and history, and the Bible is preeminently an account of his dealings with Israel, in which he makes known his will and displays his judgments and mercies. But the books of the Bible were put together and edited by men in the course of centuries and therefore contain God's word only as it has passed through the medium of the human heart and mind. "The Torah speaks in the language of men,"[11] the Talmud tells us, and this profound dictum may be understood as a criticism of modernism and fundamentalism alike. As against fundamentalism, it is necessary to emphasize the "language of men," which implies that the men of the Bible, communicating to other men, tell of God's ways with the world in terms of their own "language," their own necessarily limited, historically conditioned knowledge and imagination: hence the factual inaccuracies (relative to our present knowledge) of which the Bible is full. As against the modernists, it is necessary to insist on the fact that, despite its speaking the "language of men," the Bible is "Torah" —that is, "teaching" about the ultimate truth. And yet while their inadequacies stand thus exposed, both fundamentalism and modernism have valuable insights that we cannot afford to ignore. Fundamentalism is right in stressing the unity of the Bible and its character as revelation; modernism is right in pointing to what may be called the human aspect of the Bible and hence to its relativities and fallibilities. An adequate understanding of revelation must take into account what both have to say and combine them into a higher and more pregnant synthesis. This, I think, is in a large measure achieved by the view here presented, following the ideas of Franz Rosenzweig and Martin Buber. The Bible is the word of God, but it is also the work of man: neither side of this double affirmation may be suppressed or ignored.

It is, however, necessary to define biblical revelation a little more closely from another direction. Biblical revelation, like the biblical world-view in general, is ineradicably particularistic. This particularism, exhibited so obviously in the quite exceptional significance of the history of Israel as revelation, is a scandal to the modern mind as it was to the mind of Greek antiquity, for to both, truth is somehow identified with the timeless and the universal. We shall have occasion in another connection to discuss this question in some detail. For the present, it is enough to indicate that the particularism of the biblical outlook insists not only that God's dealings with Israel as recorded in Scripture reveal his will and ways in a uniquely significant manner, but that certain events within that history are uniquely significant as revelation. In Jewish faith, as we shall see in the next chapter, this crucial event is the "event at Sinai," understanding by this term the whole complex of events beginning with the call of Moses and culminating in the "reception of the Torah." It is this "Sinai-event," which, in Jewish thinking, constitutes "that part of our inner history which illumines the rest of it. . . , the intelligible event which makes all other events intelligible. . .[Through this event], we understand what we remember, remember what we have forgotten, and appropriate as our own past much that seemed alien to us."[12] Exodus-Sinai is, for the Jew, the interpretive center of redemptive history, as Calvary is for the Christian. Revelation is thus *einmalig*, "once and for all," not in the sense, of course, that God thereafter no longer reveals himself in his encounter with men, but in the sense that all other "visitations" of God, both before and after, yield their meaning only when seen with the eyes of faith from the perspective of this central event. The widespread notion of "continuous revelation," according to which all human thinking and all human events are in principle equally revelatory of God's truth, is in fact a dissolution of revelation into idealistic speculation, historical relativism or mystical illumination. Any turn of events which history may bring—the rise to power of national-socialism or communism, for example—may be interpreted as the latest and therefore the most authoritative revelation of ultimate truth. But no one really committed to Scripture as the revelation of God's will could for one moment think of accepting the idolatrous pretensions of a Hitler or a Stalin. In the biblical view, nothing that confronts man with a claim to authority as living truth can stand unless justified in terms of the central revelatory event. The particularity of Scriptural revelation, however offensive to the modern mind, reflects the inexpugnable particularity of existence and stands as a protection against the pressures and deceptions of the world.

Revelation is of the past, but it has no meaning unless and until it becomes existentially operative in the contemporaneous present. If, to use a figure that must not be pressed too hard, Scripture is conceived as a recording of God's word, man-made but an authentic recording nevertheless, then we must remember that a recording is inert and silent until it is played and listened to: the Bible is simply a closed book until it is read with an open heart and a ready will. Scripture is not a body of abstract propositions that can be apprehended in intellectual detachment. It is God's summons to man, and only when it is heard in the context of present experience can it become an active force in life once more and impel men to make themselves the means whereby the redemptive history which it records is carried one step further according to the purposes of God. Revelation is a call to present decision and a guide to present action.[18] So appropriated, it becomes an existential power because it transmutes the past into the present and thus drives it to the future. "When the past is made to function as a project for the future, tradition itself becomes a form of prophecy. Past and future are welded into one on the forge of life."[14]

Revelation, as we have so far discussed it, is obviously "special" revelation: it is understanding derived from God's self-disclosure to, and in the history of, Israel. But is there not a more "general" revelation, a knowledge of God freed from all particular contexts and accessible to *all* men simply as men? Do not the heavens declare the glory of God to all alike? Is there not something in the human reason, conscience or imagination that can, if only he is willing to follow up the clue, lead man to God? And if there is such a "general" revelation, of what ultimate need or significance is the very different kind of revelation to which Scripture testifies?

These questions are extraordinarily hard to answer, for a distinction must be made between man in his essential nature and man in his "fallen" existential condition, and if this distinction is but for a moment lost sight of, everything is in danger of collapsing into utter confusion.

Taking man in his essential nature as he leaves the hand of his Creator—let us think of man in Paradise—it cannot be denied that he possesses the capacity, simply as man, somehow to know God and his ways. For man is made for loving fellowship with God, and such fellowship implies the direct knowledge of personal relation. Hence Scripture depicts Adam in familiar intercourse with the Deity and enjoying full knowledge of his environment.[15] Yet it is a notorious fact that men, in their actual existence, do not of their own wisdom know the Living God and that even their efforts to prove the existence of a "supreme being" seem to lead nowhere. What is the source of this defect in actual human reason that somehow bars it from independent knowledge of ultimate reality?

The defects of reason, which are felt in all its operations, seem to be of two orders, relating respectively to man's creatureliness and to his sinful existence in the world. As a result of his creatureliness, his view of things is irremediably conditioned by his particular position in the universe, so that everything he sees he sees from his special perspective. Even if he could, as the idealist philosophers pretend, rethink God's thoughts, these thoughts would necessarily be relativized, and hence to some degree falsified, by his creaturely particularity. But much more important are the factors of the second order—the effects of sin. Our sinful egocentricity distorts and perverts everything in the interests of the self and its idols. Schechter refers to the rabbinical teaching that "it [was] sin which made Israel deaf so that they could not hear the words of the Torah and blind so that they could not see the glory of the Shechinah."[16] Sin blinds and makes deaf; it ideologizes and falsifies. These effects of sin on the human mind are pervasive; nothing in thought or experience is immune. If it were to their compelling self-interest to think of twice two as five, Hobbes says, men would very soon come to do so, and we, who are familiar with Marx and Freud, can appreciate the point of this remark. Yet while the effects of sin are pervasive, they do not touch all aspects of human thought alike. "The competence of reason," Brunner writes, "is a graduated one: the reason is more competent to know the world than to know man; it is better able to discern the bodily than the spiritual quality of man. . ."[17] This is not due simply to the allegedly greater complexity of the subject matter; it is due primarily to the fact that the "objective" human reason becomes increasingly obscured and perverted by sin as it approaches closer and closer to the inner "subjective" core of existence. When it becomes a matter of authentic knowledge' of God, and therefore of authentic knowledge of man, the incapacity of the unaided human reason is only too obvious.

Yet since man's essential nature, however obscured, is never entirely destroyed by sin, man remains *homo religiosus,* always "searching" for God in the sense of constantly striving to relate his being to something ultimate beyond himself. But when he tries to find God through his own powers, he invariably lapses into idolatry, for his sinful egocentricity impels him to set up and "discover" gods after his own heart. His natural religiosity leads man not to the Living God but at best to some sort of pantheism in which the totality of being, with which one's own being is somehow merged, is felt to be suffused with divinity and therefore identified with God. On this level, the "natural light" of human reason is not merely insufficient; it is actually delusive.

Idealism, which claims for man a knowledge of God through reason, overlooks both the creatureliness and the sinful perversion of the human mind. In the idealist view, man not only retains unmarred his perfection of before the fall, but he is even somehow able to free himself, at least in thought, from his creaturely limitations. Philosophy thus becomes, as Jaspers points out, "the way of man's self-assertion through thinking."[18] In its extreme form, this type of spiritual pretension easily passes over into mysticism, in which all distinction between the human and the divine is wiped out.

Skepticism and positivism, on the other hand, tend to take the existential limitations of human reason for its essential nature. It has "some perception of the truth that man cannot know God by his own efforts, that all rational knowledge of God is in the highest degree hypothetical and uncertain. . .The positivist is not prejudiced or 'crazy' about any metaphysical system. . .He has a feeling for the arrogance of all rational metaphysical systems, and he has something of the modesty of one who is aware that he is not sufficient for these things."[19] But since he has no inkling of man's true origin or destiny, the positivist, too, soon converts his critical reserve into a "way of self-assertion through thinking" by erecting it into an absolute dogma from the vantage point of which he wages war upon all those who dare go beyond his doctrinaire bounds. Where the idealist cannot concede that any aspect of reality is inaccessible to human reason, the positivist, confronted with the incompetence of the usual methods of empirical science in dealing with the ultimate realities of existence, simply denies that they are realities. Neither understands the full complexity of the human situation and hence neither is capable of grasping the actual problem of religious knowledge.

While, therefore, we cannot deny "general" revelation in principle, we must emphatically reject its possibility in fact, for though God is everywhere to be discerned in his person, activity and works, the mind of sinful man is incapable of finding him through its own un-aided powers. The heavens do indeed declare the glory of God, but only to those who have eyes to see. To those whose eyes are blinded by sin and unbelief—and what is sin but unbelief?—the heavens say nothing but what is already in their mind and heart.

Reinhold Niebuhr, it seems to me, has pushed the possibility of "general" revelation just about as far as it will go without losing its biblical basis, and it is instructive to see what this "general" revelation becomes in his thinking. It is reflected, he says, both in philosophical speculation about the world and in "the sense of being confronted with a 'wholly other' at the edge of human consciousness," which latter he calls "private revelation" and which he finds to be "not so much a separate experience as an overtone implied in all experience." "Private revelation" in this sense possesses three aspects: "the sense of reverence for a majesty and of dependence upon an ultimate source of being;" "the sense of moral obligation laid upon one from beyond oneself and of moral unworthiness before a judge;" and "the longing for forgiveness."[20] In each of these aspects, the mind points to something beyond, but it is utterly incapable of discovering for itself what it is to which it points. It is only in the "special" revelation of biblical faith that the " 'wholly other' at the edge of human consciousness" is recognized as the Living God and is seen to be related to the three aspects of "private revelation" as Creator, Judge and Redeemer. Without the light afforded in Scripture, however, man's effort to transcend self and reach what is beyond inevitably results in the conversion of the "wholly other" into an idolatrous god after his own heart.

Yet though human reason cannot find God or think out the ultimate truth about existence, it has its indispensable uses in the religious life. Our capacity to receive the word of God in revelation—our "capacity of the word"—is grounded in reason, which is one of the aspects of the divine image in which we are made. Our very ability to formulate our insights is a power of reason. But however necessary, reason in the religious life remains subsidiary to revelation. The saving truth is not the excogitation of our rational powers but the self-disclosure of God.

"The Torah speaks in the language of men." What the Torah speaks about transcends nature and experience, but the "language of men" is a language borrowed from nature and experience. We are compelled to speak of a multidimensional reality in the vocabulary of our limited understanding. Every statement we make is therefore necessarily going to be symbolic—conveying truth, but false if taken literally. "The eternal is revealed and expressed in the temporal," Niebuhr reminds us, "but is not exhausted in it. . .The temporal process is like a painter's flat canvas. It is one dimension upon which two dimensions must be recorded. This can be done only by symbols which deceive for the sake of the truth."[21] Religious thinking, therefore, is inherently paradoxical since it can express its insights only in a form that must appear to self-consistent reason as contradictory and "absurd." The rabbinical pronouncement, "All is foreseen but freedom of choice is given,"[22] tells the truth about existence, but it tells it necessarily in a way that is offensive to simple rationality. And yet paradox itself is at bottom a device of reason, for paradox reflects "a rational understanding of the limits of rationality, an expression of faith that a rationally irresolvable contradiction may point to a truth which logic cannot contain."[23]

Is biblical revelation, then, rational or is it contrary to reason?

If reason as it appears in sinful (idolatrous) man is absolutized and made the ultimate criterion of truth, then, of course, the biblical revelation is irrational. But this very self-absolutization of reason is in another sense itself irrational, for it refuses to see that this kind of reason is totally inadequate to do justice to the depth and complexity of human existence. On the other hand, biblical revelation, for all its paradox, and precisely because of its paradox, may well be said to represent a higher rationality in the sense that "it acknowledges a center and source of meaning beyond the limits of rational intelligibility, partly because it 'rationally' senses the inadequacy or idolatrous character of centers and sources of meaning which are within the limits of rational intelligibility."[24] From the standpoint of a reason unspoiled by sin and idolatry, the paradox and "absurdity" of revelation might well appear to be the height of rationality, although even in this case, the creaturely limitations of the human mind would preclude it from a comprehensive grasp of ultimate truth and always leave something beyond its range of intelligibility.

Why is it that modern man finds it so difficult to "accept" revelation? Is it simply because there is so much bad science in the Bible, or that our intellectual sophistication does not permit us to "believe" so many of the things the Bible tells us? Perhaps; but let us remember that modern man has shown himself quite capable of believing the most extraordinary "unscientific" absurdities when they have come to him as part of the gospel of communism or nazism or secular humanism. There is nothing men will not believe in support of what they want to believe, and the man of today, for all his alleged sophistication, is no exception. As a matter of fact, resistance to the word of God is no monopoly of the modern mind. Men have always been impelled to reject it, as the Bible itself bears striking witness. And in rejecting it, they have always employed arguments and justifications that have seemed conclusive in terms of the culture of the time. The Greeks had their philosophy and we have our science, and even when, as in the Middle Ages, conformity was the rule, human ingenuity had its devices—was not a certain type of legalistic or scholastic theology precisely such a device?—by which the impact of the biblical word could be blunted and turned aside. No, we need not be too much im-

pressed by the protestations of intellectual scrupulosity on the part of
the modern unbeliever.

The fact of the matter seems to be that the modern unbeliever refuses to believe for the same basic reason that the unbelievers of all
ages have refused: the biblical word is a decisive challenge to his
pretensions to self-sufficiency and to all the strategies that he has devised to sustain them. Modern man is ready to "accept" revelation
if that revelation is identified with his own intellectual discovery or
poetical intuition. But with the revelation that comes from beyond
to shatter his self-sufficiency, to expose the dereliction of his life and
to call him to a radical transformation of heart, with that revelation
he will have nothing to do.

The resistance to revelation is a resistance to the exposure of the
idolatries by which we live. It is resistance to a truth which is not
after our heart, because our heart is turned inward in sinful egocentricity. It is, in a sense, true that man is always searching for God—
in the sense that he is always trying to relate his limited being to
something beyond. But it is also and perhaps even more importantly
true that man is always fleeing from God, from the Living God who
demands everything and will brook no idolatrous self-absolutization.
In fleeing from God, he naturally flees from the revelation that is the
word of God.

The standard device by which men in all ages have protected themselves against the word of God in revelation is "objectivity." They
declare themselves ready to examine the claims of revelation "objectively," and having put themselves in that relation to it, inevitably
reject it. "There are objects," Tillich points out, "for which the so-
called 'objective' approach is the least objective of all because it is
based on a misunderstanding of the nature of its object. This is especially true of religion. Unconcerned detachment in matters of religion (if it is more than a methodological self-restriction) implies an
a priori rejection of the religious demand to be ultimately concerned.
It denies the object which it is supposed to approach objectively."[25]
Only those ready to "hear and obey" can understand. The power
and truth of revelation are known only in the decision of faith.

For in the end, revelation, faith and repentance converge. Only
the repentant heart renewed in faith can receive the word of God in

revelation. Only the grace of God working within can overcome the resistance of idolatrous unbelief and open the mind to the saving truth of Scripture. To those still lost in the devices of their own hearts, the Bible can mean nothing, however frequently it is read and however assiduously it is studied. Biblical truth, despite the rationalist theologians, carries no external "objective" proofs; it must prove itself in the life of the believer or it cannot prove itself at all. The authenticity of revelation is existentially guaranteed by the Living God who is encountered within it. When thus inwardly appropriated, it discloses a significance for human existence that neither science nor philosophy of itself can achieve.

But science and philosophy, too, are not left untouched. They also are transformed. By a shift in basic presuppositions, in which the distortion of human self-centeredness is set right, the findings of philosophy and science—here we have the so-called "human" or social sciences primarily in mind—are seen in a new perspective and are interpreted in a new and more profound way. Through this change of perspective, we are enabled to integrate the knowledge that science gives us about man into a total framework that encompasses a vision of his origin, his nature and his destiny. Our thinking is no longer held down to the flat plane of naturalism or idealism to which everything is reduced when, in one form or the other, man is made ultimate in the universe. A new dimension of reality and meaning—a vertical dimension of relation to God—is disclosed. Because faith itself implies the reorientation of life toward God, so the new insight into reality gained through faith results in the reconstruction of all knowledge on a theonomous basis. It is not new information about empirical things that revelation brings—that is not its purpose—but a new center and a new perspective in terms of which whatever knowledge we have may be related to the ultimate truth about existence.

## NOTES TO CHAPTER 17

1. Martin Buber, "The Man of Today and the Jewish Bible," *Israel and the World* (Schocken: New York, 1948), p. 94.

2. Paul S. Minear, *Eyes of Faith: A Study in the Biblical Point of View* (Lutterworth: London, 1948), p. 59.

3. Emil Brunner, *Revelation and Reason* (Westminster: Philadelphia, 1946), p. 8.

4. Otto J. Baab, *The Theology of the Old Testament* (Abingdon-Cokesbury: Nashville, Tenn., 1949), p. 120.

5. Norman H. Snaith, *The Distinctive Ideas of the Old Testament* (Westminster: Philadelphia, 1946), p. 48.

6. Maimonides, *Guide for the Perplexed* tr. by Friedländer (Dutton: New York, 1904), Part I, chap. liv, p. 75.

7. "Since the Prophets realized the exaltation of God over creation, the faith had in it the element of reverential agnosticism." W. A. L. Elmslie, *How Came our Faith* (Cambridge University: Cambridge, 1948), p. 377.

8. Buber, "The Man of Today and the Jewish Bible," *Israel and the World*, p. 89.

9. This is the thesis of Buber's *The Prophetic Faith*.

10. Franz Rosenzweig, *Briefe* (Schocken: Berlin, 1935), pp. 581-82.

11. *B.* Kidd. 17b, and elsewhere. This statement is generally found in a halakic context to support a principle of interpretation.

12. H. Richard Niebuhr, *The Meaning of Revelation* (MacMillan: New York, 1946), pp. 93, 110.

13. "Revelation is inseparable from demand for immediate decision." Minear, *op. cit.*, p. 132.

14. Fritz Kaufmann, "The World as Will and Representation," *Philosophy and Phenomenological Research*, Vol. IV (March, 1944), No. 3.

15. This is suggested by Adam's "naming" the animals (Gen. 2:19-20), for the "name" means knowledge and power.

16. Solomon Schechter, *Some Aspects of Rabbinic Theology* (Macmillan; New York, 1909), p. 238.

17. Brunner, *Man in Revolt* (Westminster: Philadelphia, 1947), p. 529.

18. Karl Jaspers, "Philosophy and Science," *Partisan Review*, Vol. XVI (September, 1949), No. 9.

19. Brunner, Revelation and Reason, pp. 356-57.

20. Reinhold Niebuhr, *The Nature and Destiny of Man* (Scribner's: New York, 1941), I, 127, 131.

21. Reinhold Niebuhr, *Beyond Tragedy* (Scribner's: New York, 1937). pp. 4, 5.

22. *M.* Abot 3.19.

23. Reinhold Niebuhr, *The Nature and Destiny of Man,* I, 262.

24. Reinhold Niebuhr, *Faith and History* (Scribner's: New York, 1949), p. 119.

"If human knowledge refuses to understand that there is something which it cannot understand, or more accurately, something about which it clearly understands that it can *not* understand it, then all is confusion."

Sören Kierkegaard, *Journals,* tr. by Dru (Oxford: New York, 1938), No. 633.
25. Paul Tillich, *The Protestant Era* (University of Chicago: Chicago, 1948), p. xi.

# 18. THE NATURE AND DESTINY OF ISRAEL

"In Israel, all religion is history."[1] Hebraic religion is not a system of abstract propositions to be apprehended intellectually or some esoteric wisdom to be received in mystic illumination. Hebraic religion is history, or rather it is faith enacted as history, not to be experienced, understood or communicated apart from that history. There is no Judaism without Abraham and Moses, without Egypt and Sinai; there is no Christianity without these and without Jesus and Calvary in addition. The saving truth of Buddhism can be put in the form of a set of timeless statements about the source of human misery and the way to liberation; in Hebraic religion, the saving truth is the history of God's dealings with men in pursuit of his redemptive purpose. Hebraic religion is thus in essence *Heilsgeschichte*—redemptive history, which is at one and the same time the history of redemption and the history which redeems. Only by making ourselves part of this redemptive history, by making it our own, can we be saved. If salvation is by faith, it is because faith, from this point of view, is precisely the appropriation of redemptive history as one's own.

The redemptive history which is Hebraic religion is the history of Israel interpreted as *Heilsgeschichte.* But though it is history of Israel, it is not merely history *for* Israel, as so much of modern nationalistic history is history for the favored nation. It is history for the world; indeed, in a sense, it is history of the world—the "true history of the world," Buber calls it.[2] If this history is Israel-centered, as of course it is, this is because at the very heart of Hebraic religion is the conviction that, in a special and unique way, Israel is God's instrument for the redemption of the world. Mankind is the ultimate concern of redemptive history, and to that concern everything that relates to Israel, however large it may loom in Scripture and the rabbinical writings, is entirely subsidiary. The redemptive history of Israel is history for the world because it is through that history that the world is to be redeemed.

This is a bold—indeed, some would say, brazen—affirmation. All mankind, the entire universe, dependent for its salvation upon some particular history and upon the history of an obscure, insignificant people at that! Is not God equally the Father of all mankind? How then can it be claimed that he plays favorites among men and makes his grace available not in the form of rational truths or spiritual insights accessible to all, but in the form of a history embodying his dealings with a strange small folk stemming from a corner in the Near East? Would it not better agree with the universal character of deity if divine salvation were itself universal in the sense of being equally related to all men without regard to the trivial accidental divisions among mankind, which surely must mean nothing or less than nothing in the sight of God?

This is the "scandal of particularity" which has offended high-minded men of all ages and has moved them to bitterness and ridicule in rejecting the "absurd" pretensions of Hebraic religion. Some eighteen hundred years ago, the pagan philosopher Celsus inveighed against the "irrational" claims of Jews and Christians in terms that awaken a distinct echo in the modern mind:

> Jews and Christians appear to me like a host of bats or ants who come out of their hiding places, or like frogs who sit in a swamp, or like worms who hold a meeting in the corner of a manure pile, and say to one another: "To us God reveals and proclaims everything. He does not trouble himself with the rest of the world; we are the only beings with whom he has dealings. . .To us is subjected everything: the earth, the water, the air, the stars. Because it has happened that some among us have sinned, God himself will come or will send his own Son in order to destroy the wicked with fire and to give us a share in eternal life.[3]

Of course, there is some unfairness and misunderstanding in this picture: it is not, for example, because "some of us" have sinned but all mankind that God must judge and redeem. Yet, on the whole, we must admit that what Celsus in his invective charges to Jews and Christians is more or less what Judaism and Christianity in their authentic forms have affirmed. What sense can we make of so unintelligible an affirmation?

Let us note that the "scandal of particularity," as it strikes the philosophic mind, contains two aspects: first, that the universal, "timeless" God should reveal himself and his redemptive purpose through time and history, which is particularity; and secondly, that the God of all mankind should arbitrarily select a particular group as the recipient of his revelation and the instrument of his redemptive purpose. Both assertions seem absurd and incredible to the philosophic mind but on rather different grounds and on rather different levels.

The philosophic mind boggles at the notion of a universal God acting through the particularities of history because, on the one hand, as we have seen, it devaluates time and history, and, because, on the other, it conceives of the divine in essentially impersonal, intellectual terms. Universal ideas are impersonal, and if salvation is through ideas, then of course the particularistic claims of Hebraic religion are absurd on the face of it. But if salvation is through personal relation and action, as both Judaism and Christianity affirm, the matter takes on an altogether different aspect. Truly personal relations are never universal; they are always concrete and particular. And while an idea or a doctrine may be made available to all men universally and timelessly, action must necessarily be particular in the sense that it is action here and now, in reference to this particular person or group rather than to another. The Hebraic insistence on historical particularity is thus seen to be an essential aspect of what has been called the "Abrahamic postulate," the affirmation of a *Living* God operative in life and history, who meets man in *personal* encounter in the context of life and history. Properly understood, the "scandal of particularity" is a scandal only to those for whom ultimate reality is necessarily timeless and impersonal. The rejection of particularity is at bottom a rejection of time and history and personality.

If God is a Living God, operative in and through the particularities of history, then it no longer seems so strange that he should effect his purposes through particular groups of people or even that he should "create" particular groups for his special purposes. To ask the philosopher's question, "Why this group rather than that?" is to demand a universal rule by which the time-bound particularities of history may be rendered rationally intelligible and the will and purposes of God justified before the court of human reason. The idealistic rejection of history and personality is thus supplemented by a rationalistic arrogance that would make reason, human reason, into the final law of the universe. To a mind consumed with such pretensions, particularity, emphasizing the irreducible priority of God's will and the severe limitations placed upon human reason, must indeed seem intolerable. Celsus, who thought it almost obscene for Jews and Christians to speak about being "God's people" in some special way, is at one with Fichte, who insisted that "the metaphysical only and not the historical can give blessedness,"[4] with Lessing, who in his inaugural address at Jena, confessed that for him "the particular facts of history cannot establish eternal truths,"[5] and thus also with all the high-minded idealists of our time who spurn the biblical doctrines of revelation and election as a scandalous example of Jewish "ethnocentrism." This is the stand of self-sufficient human reason, impatient of history and personality. Biblical faith, on the other hand, permeated with the inexpugnable particularity of existence, takes its stand on the affirmation: "Salvation is of the Jews."[6]

"Salvation is of the Jews" because the history of Israel, biblically understood, is the history of God's redemptive purpose with mankind. It is not history totally distinct from "general" or "secular" history and yet it is not identical with it. The difference is not so much in the events themselves, which, in large part, belong to both. The difference is primarily in the point of view and interpretation. "Secular" history, even the most positivistic, has its schemes of redemption in terms of which it is written. These schemes—I have in mind nationalism, progress, Marxism, humanism—are not always explicit, but they are there. They are, as we saw in an earlier chapter, the exaltation of some fragmentary meaning to ultimate significance. The redemptive scheme of Hebraic religion, on the other hand, is a transcendent scheme, allowing no self-absolutization and keeping all partial truths, even those represented by the elect community, under constant criticism and the judgment of God. That is why redemptive history claims to be "true history" in the fullest sense and to reveal the meaning of all history. It sees things from its own perspective, of course, and estimates them from its own scale of values, but this perspective and these values are not just one set among many. In a real sense, they include as a component something that emerges from the self-disclosure of God, and therefore they constitute a framework of ultimate meaning for all history.

Redemptive history, and thus the existentially meaningful history of mankind, has its beginning in creation and its "end" in the final judgment and fulfilment to come. But both beginning and end as well as the entire course of history are themselves interpreted, as we noted in the last chapter, in terms of a crucial event, which may very justly be called the *center* of history. In Jewish faith, this event, or rather complex of events, is Exodus-Sinai. Exodus-Sinai, for Jewish faith, is the divine-human encounter par excellence, illumining and setting the pattern for all other encounters before and after. Exodus-Sinai is the crisis of crises in the history of Israel, the focal point in terms of which all earlier redemptive events are understood and from which all subsequent divine disclosures take their orientation. "I am the Lord thy God who brought thee out of the land of Egypt. . ." (Exod. 20:2; Deut. 5:6) is the introductory formula in the proclamation of the Torah in which God makes his demands upon and reveals his gracious promises to Israel, and it remains henceforth the keystone of the entire structure of Jewish self-understanding.

The Exodus [writes Rylaarsdam] was basic in the consciousness of Israel . . . [It] was of existential significance. . . For Israel, reality was laid bare in that bit of history. God revealed himself in it. It is the normative event. . .Yahweh redeemed Israel. . . This is the people by which he will fulfill his intention for all mankind. . .This is the perspective in terms of which the Exodus becomes the formative and guiding "event" in Israel's religious tradition. When we read, on to the end of the Old Testament, we find that all of it—with the possible exception of such items as Proverbs and Ecclesiastes, which omit reference to our historical locus of revelation—is written as testimony to this perspective that emerges from the Exodus event.[7]

In the view of Maimonides, as Baron points out, "the greatest event. . .was the 'giving of the Torah' [at Sinai], and the period preceding it represents a kind of human prehistory."⁸ So it is in the entire rabbinic literature. "The labor of Israel in seeking to understand [its history] has never been completed, being continued by the rabbis of an earlier and the present day; but the revelatory occasion and idea have remained constant";⁹ that "occasion and idea" has always been recognized as Exodus-Sinai.

What is it that Exodus-Sinai signifies in redemptive history? In the first place, it shows forth, for the Jew, God's supreme act of redemptive love, the paradigm of all of God's redemptive activity. It therefore establishes God's claim upon Israel,¹⁰ and, at the same time, calls forth responsive love, for love, as Judah Halevi points out, originally comes from God, not from us.¹¹ We love with the love wherewith we are loved. In the second place, and directly as a consequence of God's redeeming act, Exodus-Sinai means the creation of the People Israel as God's covenant-folk. At Sinai, we are shown God by a mighty act of his providence forming a people which should be the bearer of his redemptive purpose. Second Isaiah represents God as the "creator" of Israel in a very special sense that refers not to the general act of creation at the beginning but to the bringing of Israel into being as an elect, a "gathered" community: "I the Lord am your Holy One, I the Creator of Israel am your King . . ." (Isa. 43:15). And, according to Maimonides, the individual Israelites leaving Egypt had to be circumcised, baptized and brought to offer sacrifice—had to be *"newly born" like proselytes*—before they could come forth as truly the people of God.¹² All testimony and tradition converge to the same conclusion: "The Jews became a people by act of the Sinaitic revelation"¹³—"Our people are only a people by virtue of its Torah."¹⁴ Whatever the Israelites may have been when they came down as a family to Egypt, it was only Exodus-Sinai that created the People Israel.

The formation of Israel as people is represented to us as the consequence of the gathering and binding power of the divine covenant into which God entered with Israel at Sinai. In this covenant, God "called" Israel by its "name"—that is, chose it—and made it his "portion" (Isa. 43:1); but he also gave Israel its Torah—its Way and its Law—and laid upon it its vocation as his instrument in the divine scheme of redemption. Scripture and rabbinic tradition never tire of returning to the theme of Israel's election,[15] but there is little suggestion that the election came to Israel through any merits of its own: on the contrary, it "attributes the election to a mere act of grace or love on the part of God."[16] If there are tales in tradition which imply that Israel more or less willingly accepted the Torah and the covenantal obligations, there are also tales which state emphatically that Israel had to be threatened with extinction in order to make it yield to the demand of God.[17] Just as there is no flattering of the corporate vanity of Israel in its election, so is there none in what the election comes to mean in later teaching. The prophets use the election and covenant to bring down judgment upon Israel and to call it to unconditional obedience—"You only have I known among all the families of the earth; *therefore* will I visit upon you all your iniquities" (Amos 3:2)—and the rabbis draw the conclusion from Israel's special relation to God that "there is no quality becoming Israel more than poverty" and suffering.[18] Biblical particularism may be Israel-centered, but it is poles apart from the mere projection of ethnic self-esteem. The election and vocation of Israel give it a unique role in world-history, but it is the role of Suffering Servant rather than of world conqueror. And yet, for all that, the covenant in which this vocation is grounded is a covenant of glory and salvation, for it promises ultimate vindication and fulfilment to all within the elect community who remain true to its obligations.

Such is the central event in the redemptive history of Jewish faith. Everything before and everything after is interpreted in terms of this crucial event. Looking back, we find the people-creating covenant at Sinai foreshadowed in the calling of Abraham and the covenant with him and his descendants. And beyond the patriarchs, there are Noah and even Adam, with whom, too, in biblical-rabbinic tradition God formed his covenants covering all mankind. The covenant, indeed, becomes in biblical thought the paradigm for the interpretation of all experience. What we call the laws of nature are understood in the Bible as God's covenant with his creation, inanimate as well as animate. The stars move in their courses, day follows night and night day, the beasts of the field obey their masters, all in fulfilment of their covenants.[19] The covenant of election at Sinai is but the hub of a larger system of divine covenants by which nature, life and history are maintained in their appointed ways.

Forward beyond Sinai, too, the Exodus event and its covenant are normative in Jewish faith. The chroniclers recount the history of the tribes and kingdoms as a succession of revolts against the covenant and of returns under divine judgment. For the prophets, "the Exodus from Egypt is . . . a decisive act of the living God in history and makes a kind of fixed point of reference for all discussions of his ways with his people."[20] In Amos, there is already a beginning of the prophetic emphasis on the deliverance from Egypt as the real point of departure in the career of Israel. Hosea, indeed, goes back to the patriarchal period, but for him this period is essentially a kind of "prenatal" anticipation; Israel was really born in the exodus from Egypt: "When Israel was a child, I loved him, and from Egypt I called my son . . ." (Hos. 11:1). We find the same note in Jeremiah, where the deliverance from Egypt becomes the prototype of the coming redemption.[21] But it is surely in the latter part of Isaiah that this theme receives its most exalted treatment. Second Isaiah goes back in his vision of history to the creation of the world and the very beginning of time. He mentions Noah as well as Abraham. But the crucial event in God's dealings with his people is defined as the deliverance from Egypt. The entire destiny of Israel is reinterpreted by this great prophet in terms of the covenant promises and the world-redemptive vocation of the covenant-people. In the eschatological visions of the prophets and later teachers, the great fulfilment at the "end" is seen not only as the restoration of the primal harmonies of creation but also as the realization of the promises of the covenant with Israel.

This covenant expresses as no conceptual formula can the unity and tension of the universalistic and particularistic elements in the vocation of Israel: it is a covenant *with* Israel and *for* Israel, yet for Israel only because, *through* Israel, it is destined for the world. "As the Rabbis expressed it, it is only 'with the redemption of Israel that the Kingdom of Heaven will be complete.' Israel is the microcosm in which all the conditions of the Kingdom are to find concrete expression."[22] Yet when the vocation of Israel is finally and completely fulfilled in the Kingdom of God at the "end," Israel will lose its reason for existence and all mankind will again be one.[23] "The election of Israel was never meant to be a thing in itself, but as a first step toward the realization of the Kingdom of God on this earth. Israel is only 'the first fruit of his increase' (Jer. 2:3). Thus Jewish existence is indissolubly linked with that final goal. Its meaning lies in, and its justification derives from, the never-ceasing work of preparation for . . . the *malkut shamayim* (Kingdom of Heaven)."[24] All this is comprehended as in potentiality and promise in the covenant at Sinai.[25]

Apart from the context of its redemptive history, the very being of Israel is a blank mystery and its history an anomaly without sense or meaning. For if we consider Jewish existence in its full concreteness, it is impossible to deny Carl Mayer's conclusion that "the Jewish people represent a sociologically *unique* phenomenon and defy all attempts at general definition."[26] "The existence of Israel," Buber agrees, "is something unique, unclassifiable. This name . . . marks the community as one that cannot be grasped in the categories of sociology or ethnology."[27] Being a Jew does not in itself mean belonging to a particular race or to a particular nation or to a particular culture or even to a particular religious denomination. Many and diverse "racial" strains are to be found among Jews; Jews have the most varied national origins, allegiances and cultures; and even those Jews who renounce the Jewish religion, or religion in general, somehow remain Jews. Yet though we must recognize that Jewishness is neither a racial nor a national nor a cultural nor a religious fact, we cannot deny that somehow each of these factors is in some way relevant to it. But what Jewish existence is does not emerge from any of them singly, nor from any combination of them, nor even from all of them taken together. The "secret" of Jewish existence is obviously something that transcends these or any other categories which the social scientist is able to devise. "The continued existence of the Jews . . . has been called a contradiction in terms. At any rate, the phenomenon does not fit into any of the usual patterns—idealistic or positivistic—by which we try to read the pages of history."[28]

Calling the Jews a "people" does not in itself illumine the problem. For if "people" is used in the familiar sense in which we speak of the "American people" or the "French people," it obviously does not apply to the Jews: one may be a Jew and a Frenchman or American at the same time, which would be impossible were the term "people" used in the same sense in both contexts. And if the term as it applies to Jews is used in a different and unique sense, it does not in itself tell us anything about the nature of Jewish existence. The term "people" may, of course, be employed, but it has to be defined in some fundamental way or else it will possess no meaning and merely serve to confuse and obscure the real problem.

Nor does it get us very far to speak of the "plural sources" of Jewishness, as do so many secular "survivalists" of our day. Granted that one or another aspect of Jewish existence may be most prominent in Jewish life in a particular time or situation, the question still remains as to what unites all the varied forms of existence under the one category of "Jewishness" and permits us to speak of phenomena that apparently have nothing in common, as if they were all manifestations of a single reality. If Jewish existence is really and irreducibly plural, then it is not one, and the term "Jewish existence" or "Jewishness" is meaningless. If, on the other hand, this term is held to possess meaning, it must point to a reality that transcends and underlies all "plural" manifestations.

What is this reality? It is clearly not something that can be indicated or defined in purely naturalistic, purely scientific terms. Every attempt to give meaning to the concept of Jewishness in such terms must necessarily end in failure and lead to the conclusion that the concept is empty of intrinsic content and really refers to a "nothing" generated out of a persistent and rather malignant delusion on the part of Jew and non-Jew alike. This, in essence, is Sartre's view and Koestler's, too,[29] and it has been held, in more or less sophisticated forms, by a considerable number of people in modern times. It is essentially the conclusion reached by the anthropologist, Melville J. Herskovits, in his study, "Who Are the Jews":

> It is apparent that it is neither race, nor such an aspect of physical type as nasality, nor a "Jewish look," that affords terms in which the question, "Who are the Jews?" is to be answered. . . .In like manner, language, culture, belief all exhibit so great a range of variation that no definition cast in terms of these concepts can be more than partial. Yet the Jews do

represent a historic continuum, have survived as an identifiable, yet constantly shifting series of groups. *Is there any least common denominator other than the designation "Jew" that can be found to mark the historical* fait accompli *that the Jew, however defined, seems to be? It is seriously to be questioned*[30] (my emphasis.—W. H.).

On a naturalistic basis, no other conclusion is possible.

Jewish existence acquires meaning only in terms of the categories that emerge from the biblical-rabbinic faith. In the normative biblical-rabbinic view, as we have seen, Israel is not a "natural" nation; indeed, it is not a nation at all like the "nations of the world." It is a *supernatural* community, called into being by God to serve his eternal purposes in history. It is a community created by God's special act of covenant, first with Abraham, whom he "called" out of the heathen world and then, supremely, with Israel corporately at Sinai. Jewish tradition emphasizes the unimportant and heterogeneous character of the People Israel apart from God's gracious act of election, which gives it the significance it possesses in the scheme of world destiny. The covenant of election is what brought Israel into existence and keeps it in being; apart from that covenant, Israel is as nothing and Jewish existence a mere delusion. The covenant is at the very heart of the Jewish self-understanding of its own reality.

We miss the entire meaning of the covenant as understood in biblical-rabbinic thought if we imagine it as something that depends for its power and reality upon the voluntary adherence of the individual Jew. The covenant, in biblical-rabbinic faith, is not a private act of agreement and affiliation; it is not a contract that becomes valid only when the individual Jew signs it. Indeed, the individual Jew would not be a Jew at all in any intelligible sense were he not *already* under the covenant. The covenant is an objective supernatural fact; it is God's act of creating and maintaining Israel for his purposes in history.

What are these purposes? What is the vocation of the covenant-folk? These questions bring us to the heart of the "mystery of Israel."

"You shall be unto me a kingdom of priests and a holy nation" (Exod. 19:6): that is the basic formula in which the election and vocation of Israel are defined. Taken in its fulness, as it is developed in subsequent thought, this commission may be seen to imply a triple task: to receive and to cherish the Torah of God; to hear and to obey his voice in loving service and thus to live a holy life in a holy community under his kingship; and to be a "light to the gentiles" by showing forth God's greatness and goodness as well as by an active effort to bring the peoples of the world to acknowledge the Holy One of Israel. In a word, in inward life, corporate existence and outgoing service, to "sanctify the Name" and to stand witness to the Living God amidst the idolatries of the world.

This is hardly the place to undertake an examination of the vast and crucial subject of the significance of Christianity from the Jewish point of view and its relation to Judaism. In the context of our discussion, we may, however, note that Christianity arose, at a great crisis in Israel's history, as an outgoing movement to bring the God of Israel to the gentiles by bringing the gentiles into the covenant. What Solomon Grayzel defines as Paul's intention may very properly be extended to cover the basic intention of Christianity: "He so broadened the term 'Jew' as to include in it, as an honorable fellowship, all those who transformed their lives by being faithful Christians."[31] The "divine role" of Christianity as "Israel's apostle" and carrier of the "divine truth to the nations of the world" is emphasized by A. A. Neuman in his description of the age-old "Jewish dream for the future of humanity."[32] But it is perhaps Franz Rosenzweig whose thought on this subject is most profound and fruitful. Israel—so his position has been summarized[33]—"can bring the world to God only through Christianity. [But] Christianity. . . could not long remain an effective force for redemption if Israel did not remain in its midst."[34] And in the following pregnant words, he defines the twin vocations of Israel and the Church as covenant-communities: "Israel to represent in time the eternal Kingdom of God, Christianity to bring itself and the world toward that goal."[35] So defined, the functions of Judaism and Christianity in the divine economy are seen to be organically related[36]—part of one vocation—and yet irreducibly different in their orientations: Judaism looking *inward* to the Jews; Christianity looking ever *outward* to the gentiles, who, through it, are brought to the God of Israel.[37]

Fundamentally, therefore, the vocation of the People Israel continues the same, for all the change, after the emergence of Christianity as it was before. Even for the outgoing function of the conversion of the gentiles, Israel remains indispensable, though now indirectly so. The primary and basic aspects of the vocation, the heart of the divine purpose in the calling of Israel—the "sanctification of the Name"—remains pre-eminently and irreplaceably the responsibility of Israel. To receive and to cherish the Torah of God, to live a holy life under his ever-present kingship, to stand witness to his word against the idolatries of the world: these are the functions for which Israel is appointed. That this vocation involves suffering and martyrdom all history testifies; how could it be otherwise? "[God] chose Israel"—so Dr. Finkelstein defines the Jewish teaching—"to be his suffering servant, to bear persecution with patience, and by precept and example to bring his word to all the peoples of the world."[38] Such remains the God-appointed vocation of Israel until the "last day."

Anti-Semitism is the other side of the election and vocation of Israel. However it may express itself on the social, economic, cultural and political levels, whatever may be its involvement with other factors in the ongoing life of society, anti-Semitism is, at the bottom, the revolt of the pagan against the God of Israel and his absolute demand. This was obvious in pre-Christian anti-Semitism, but it is equally true of anti-Semitism in the Christian world, where "hatred of Judaism is at bottom hatred for Christianity."[39] That is how Rosenzweig understood anti-Semitism—"Whenever the pagan within the Christian soul rises in revolt against the yoke of the Cross, he vents his fury on the Jew"[40]—and that is how the most penetrating modern thinkers, Jewish and Christian, have understood it. "It is of Christ that the [anti-Semites] are afraid . . .Therefore they. . . make their assault on those who are responsible for the birth and spread of Christianity. They spit on the Jews as Christ-killers because they long to spit on them as Christ-givers."[41] "We reject the Jews in order to reject Jesus as the Christ. Hatred of the Jews is a result of our hatred of Christ."[42] "Hatred of Jews and hatred of Christians spring from a common source, from the same recalcitrance of the world. . . That is why the bitter zeal of anti-Semitism always turns in the end into bitter zeal against Christianity itself."⁴³ "Western civilization, which represents the wedding of Greco-Roman culture with Hebraic culture, has ever since been trying to effect a divorce. Hebraism, as a prophetic and transcendent view of history, has made it difficult for our Western civilization to rest lightly in its protensions. Anti-Semitism is our answer. . . . Destroy the symbol of Hebraic culture, and the uncertainty of our conscience as well as the reality of our guilt are obliterated. Resisting our destiny, we must destroy those who call that destiny to mind. Until we surrender to that destiny, the Jew will not be safe. . . .The Jew is always the enemy of an idolatrous culture."⁴⁴ But it is Houston Stewart Chamberlain, the forerunner of modern neo-pagan anti-Semitism, who, in a burst of self-disclosure, puts the whole thing in one illuminating phrase: "The Jew came into our gay world and spoiled everything with his ominous concept of sin, with his Law and his Cross."⁴⁵

Anti-Semitism is thus as "mysterious" as Israel itself, and like Israel it manifests itself in various changing historical forms. It is one of the ways—the typical, symbolic way—in which the pagan "gods of space" revenge themselves on the people of the "Lord of time" (Tillich). It stems from a tension, which, however much it may be reduced, diverted or suppressed, can never be entirely overcome until all history is overcome at the "end of days."

Israel as covenant-folk is a superhistorical⁴⁶ community running through history but also transcending it. Baron well describes the prophetic conception of Israel as "the idea of a Jewish people beyond state and territory, a divine instrument in man's overcoming of 'nature' through a supernatural process in the course of 'history.' "⁴⁷ It is this duality in time and in eternity that is responsible both for the tension of "abnormality" in Jewish life and for its spiritual creativity. To try to overcome this tension, to try to "normalize" Jewish existence in any fundamental sense, means to try to make the People Israel "like unto the nations" and thus to rob it of its reason for existence. However much confusion such efforts may produce, they cannot succeed, for they run counter to the divine purpose in the creation and election of Israel.⁴⁸

Israel lives in both time and eternity. The People Israel, eternal and superhistorical though it is, because it lives and acts *in* history must always find some concrete embodiment in some particular historical form. Or rather it would be more accurate to say, various sections of the covenant-folk find particular historical embodiments depending on time, place and circumstance—sometimes as a nation, as once and now again in Palestine; sometimes as a national minority, as in eastern Europe for many centuries; sometimes as a self-contained cultural group, as formerly in the United States; sometimes as a religious "denomination," though paradoxically including nonreligious Jews as well, as in this country today.[49] But whatever be the particular forms of Jewish existence—and I have, of course, mentioned only some—they are all merely relative, transient and localized; underlying and yet transcending them is Israel as covenant-folk. Were it not for the continuing self-identity of Israel as covenant-folk, there would be no basis of existence for any of these particular communities as Jewish communities and no bond of unity among them. Beyond all historical communities with their particular histories, there is Israel and its redemptive history, without which Jewish existence is nothing at all.

The concept of the covenant governs Israel's relations to Zion as well. As covenant-folk Israel has no native land. The individual Jew, of course, has his nation and his land, whether it be France, America or the new State of Israel; but Israel as covenant-folk is bound to no land, not even to the Holy Land. As Ignaz Maybaum points out,[50] when in the Wilderness the Israelites were told to place the Ark, the visible symbol of the divine Presence and covenant, in a tabernacle, they were forbidden to remove the staves that were used to carry it: "The staves shall be in the rings of the Ark; they shall not be taken out" (Exod. 25:15). Even after Canaan had been conquered, and a great empire established under David and Solomon, even after a magnificent Temple had been erected in which the Ark was to be "permanently" lodged, the staves were still not to be removed (I Kings 8:8). Israel was indeed in possession of the Land, but it was not *fixed* to it: it stood ever ready to take up the Ark and begin its wanderings anew. Under judgment of the Lord of history and in loyalty to him, it could make no concessions to the "gods of space."

Yet Zion *is* the Land of Israel, not its native but its promised land. The bond between Israel and Zion, despite all dispersion and separation, is a theme that runs through the entire body of Scriptural and rabbinic writings. The destiny of Israel *begins* and *ends* with Zion: it is the land to which, in the beginning, God called Abraham and to which he led the children of Israel from out of Egypt; it is also the land to which, in the final fulfilment of the Messianic Age, the People Israel will be restored. But *between* the beginning and the end, there is the "great parenthesis" when Jewish existence and Jewish destiny are irremediably dual, centering around *both* Zion *and* the *Galut*. These two aspects are to be related as two poles or foci in dialectic tension with each other, each functioning as a norm and balance for the other. Each has its own characteristic strength and weakness, its own peculiar needs and resources. In a sense, the two complement each other, but the tension between them can never be resolved in history.

This duality of existence is naturally reflected in a differentiation of the vocation of Israel in the Land and in the *Galut*. In the Land, the Jews are called upon to establish their national life so that the opportunity may be given to build toward the "true community" enjoined by the divine law, a community in which what Moore describes as the "ideal of the religion of Israel"—"a society where all the relations of men to their fellows [are] governed by the principle, 'Thou shalt love thy neighbor as thyself, '"[51]—can be given some measure of concrete embodiment. For that, political independence, or at least a high degree of autonomy, is obviously required. Here Buber finds the reason and justification for the kind of Zionism he espouses, which he believes to be in full harmony with Jewish religious tradition. "At that time," he writes, in an open letter to Gandhi vindicating the Zionst idea, "we did not carry out that which was imposed upon us; we went into exile with our task unperformed; but the command [to set up a just way of life] remained with us and it has become more urgent than ever. We need our own soil in order to fulfill it; we need the freedom to order our own life. . ."[52] This may be granted, with a small warning perhaps against the dangers of utopianism. But it is necessary also to remember what even Buber sometimes tends to forget, that there is an "unperformed task" for the Jew in the *Galut* as well, and will continue to be throughout history. The Dispersion came not only as a judgment upon Israel but also as a new way and a new field of service to God.[53] In the lands of the Diaspora, it is for the Jew by his word and deed, by his conduct as a man and a citizen, by his very being as a Jew, to "sanctify the Name" and to help redeem the evil time. It is for him to stand witness to the Living God against the dominant idolatries of the age wherever they may appear, in secular or religious life, in his own community first of all. The testimony in life which the Jew by his very existence is called upon to give— "Hear, O Israel, the Lord is our God, the Lord is One"—is testimony that the world needs and must have, now more than ever—and will never cease to need until all life is redeemed in the final fulfillment. And by the same token, "Jewish existence, in its ambiguity, strangeness and inconceivability, must be understood as the most powerful expression of the fact that the world is not yet the kingdom of God."[54]

The Jew who is faithful to his calling must always be at odds with the life around him because the life around him is always making claims and pretensions that bring it into conflict with God. The Jew faithful to his calling is always "in a minority. . .He can hardly avoid putting a note of interrogation after every dogma or convention. . . ."[55] This is basically as true for Palestine as for the rest of the world. The widely held view that a "full Jewish life" is possible only in the State of Israel seems to me to be radically false on two grounds. In the first place, it involves a drastic devaluation of some of the most significant periods of Jewish history, from the age of the Babylonian Talmud to the time of the Gaon of Vilna. But perhaps even more crucially, it seems to imply the notion that now at last in Palestine, since a "Jewish State" has been established, all "abnormalities" have been overcome and all tensions dissolved. This notion is utterly delusive; it does not reckon with the full dimensions of Jewish existence. The tensions and "abnormalities" of Jewish existence are due not merely to life in the *Galut*; they are due also and more basically to the life of the Jew in the world, which is necessarily on two levels: on the *supernatural* level of the covenant-folk and on the *natural* level of the nation and society to which he belongs, whether it be the United States or the State of Israel. It is this antithesis between the Jew as

Son of the Covenant and the Jew as citizen of his secular community
that gives rise to the peculiar tension of Jewish existence. And this
antithesis is basically no more overcome for the Jew in the State of
Israel than in the United States, for the secular society of the State
of Israel is no more to be simply identified with the covenant-com-
munity than is any group of Jews elsewhere in the world. Not even
in the state of Israel can the "self-alienation" of the Jew be finally
overcome, for the State of Israel, however highly we may regard it,
is, after all, but another communty of this world, whereas Israel transcends all historical communities of whatever sort. Even in the State
of Israel, the Jew, insofar as he remains a true Son of the Covenant,
must remain a man of two souls, a citizen of his community and an
"alien of uneasy feet."⁵⁶ No institutional change or inner reconstruction of the state in one direction or another can alter this fact. The
Jew lives "more in time than in space"; he is "always on the way."⁵⁷
Never in history can he settle down to rest, never can he be at ease
in this world—not even in Zion.

Most American Jews feel, and I think very justly, that their bond
with the State of Israel and its Jewish community is of unique and
profound significance. But why? What is this bond? It is certainly
not "racial" or national. Nor is it in any important sense cultural if
that term is used with any precision. Just as little is it "religious" in
the sense of adherence to the same religious denomination, for large
numbers of the Jews of Israel have fallen away from the Jewish faith
and are even its acknowledged opponents, and yet with them, too,
we feel the tie that binds us to the others. The bond that unites us with
the Jews of Israel and their national community goes far deeper. It
is compounded, I think, of the solidarity which every Jew, whether
he knows it or not, feels with his fellows under the covenant and of
the deep and utterly nonnationalistic "love of Zion" that is so ingrained in Jewish spirituality and is itself an aspect of covenant-
existence. These factors are operative in the lives of many Jews who
make no conscious religious affirmation and in whom they come to
expression in strange and often distorted and contradictory forms.
But they are there, and it is out of them that, at bottom, is generated
the tie, as unmistakable in its workings as it is hard to define, which
binds the American Jew to the State of Israel and its Jewish com-

munity. It is perhaps fortunate that this tie should be grounded so deeply in Jewish existence, for it will certainly, in future days, have to stand the strain of diverging cultures and of different, perhaps conflicting national concerns and interests.

In all biblical and rabbinic visions of the "end," from the earliest to the last, Zion stands in the very center of the eschatological picture. "In the end of days it shall come to pass that the mountain of the Lord's house shall be established as the top of the mountains and it shall be exalted above the hills, and the peoples shall stream unto it, and many nations shall come and say: Come let us go up to the mountain of the Lord, to the house of the God of Jacob, that he may instruct us in his ways and that we may walk in his paths; for out of Zion shall come forth Torah, the word of the Lord from Jerusalem" (Mic. 4:1-2; Isa. 2:1-3).[58] And from the first beginnings of dispersion, the "return" of Israel to Zion was made part of the fulfilment. Both, however, must be understood in their Messianic context; both the exaltation of Zion and the restoration of Israel are part of the "last things." "The idea of the kingdom [of God]," Schechter writes, "is so often closely connected with the redemption of Israel from exile, the advent of the Messiah and the restoration of the Temple as to be inseparable from it."[59] To interpret the establishment of the State of Israel as the beginning of the final "ingathering of the exiles" and the definitive dissolution of the *Galut,* as so many have done, seems to me to be but little short of false messianism and completely out of line with the tradition of faith. Yet while the Zion that is to be exalted as the "top of the mountains" to which all the peoples shall stream, is the Zion of the "new age" and thus a transfigured Zion, it is nevertheless the Zion we know, the Zion of the earth, that is to be thus transfigured. For Jewish faith is not only enacted historically; it is also, so to speak, oriented geographically. Jerusalem, an earthly city, is proclaimed to be the center of the Kingdom of Heaven: that is another aspect of the biblical particularity that is so hard and yet so indispensable for us to accept.

While the vision of the "end" thus remains irreducibly particularistic, it is also universal. For "on that day," *all* peoples shall stream to Zion, and the word of the Lord that shall go forth from Jerusalem shall come to *all* alike. The Torah—which, when it was given to Israel, the rabbis tell us, was given in the wilderness, so that Israel might not think of it as its own "national" property[60]—will "on that day" become in fact the possession of all mankind, redeemed and transfigured in a world itself redeemed and transfigured. Then at last will Israel disappear, its vocation fulfilled. For "in this world, men, through the promptings of the evil *yetzer,* have divided themselves into various tongues (peoples). But in the world-to-come, they will agree with one accord to call on his name alone, as it is said: 'For then will I restore the speech of the peoples to a purified speech that they may all call upon the name of the Lord and serve him with one accord' (Zeph. 3:9)."[61] Thus the day of vindication and triumph of Israel is but the prelude to its dissolution into a redeemed mankind, at last at one with itself because it is at one with God.

Such is the picture of the nature and destiny of Israel as seen from the perspective of biblical-rabbinic faith. It is the picture of a redemptive process set in a context of historical movement with a beginning, center and end. Each of us who makes this history his own is always at some point of the movement, looking back at the beginning, orienting himself toward the center, and looking forward to the end—not as to some dim and distant event but as to the absolute future confronting him at every moment of existence with its promise and demand. It is a picture of a redemptive history transcending and yet including the "secular" history of mankind.

The history of salvation, which is the authentic form of Hebraic faith, is the story of the gracious effort of God to bring a perverse and rebellious world back to the intent of creation through an elect community set apart for that purpose. The operative instrumentality of salvation is the covenant with the elect community through which men may be restored to God and become heirs of the divine promises. Anyone may reach God to whom the grace of God goes out, but if it is truly the Holy One of Israel whom he reaches, it is in some way in and through the covenant with Israel. "The individual Israelite," says Richardson, "approaches God in virtue of his membership in the holy people. . .In the whole of the Bible, . . .there is no such thing as a private personal relationship between the individual and God apart from his membership in the covenant-folk."[62] The rabbinical writings and the liturgy are full of appeals to the covenanted grace of God as the only hope of salvation.

> Sovereign of all the worlds, [so runs a memorable passage in the Morning Prayer] not because of our righteous acts do we lay our supplications before thee, but because of thine abundant mercies. What are we? What is our life? What is our piety? What is our righteousness? What is our power? . . . What can we say in thy presence, O Lord our God and God of our fathers? . . . *Nevertheless, we are thy people, the sons of thy covenant, the children of Abraham thy friend, to whom thou didst promise on Mount Moriah. . ."*[63]

The dynamic of the redemptive process thus proceeds in and through the covenant, through its inward realization and its outward extension until it covers all mankind. For this work, Jew and Christian have been appointed to co-operate—in unity and in tension—for the glory of the Living God to whom both owe their ultimate allegiance. Of course, the covenanted community in its mass is always sinning, always rebelling, but where many fall, there is always a remnant. God never leaves himself without those who will bear witness to his Name and perform representatively, as it were, the redemptive function of the entire community.[64] Who it is that at any time compose this saving remnant, we do not know; perhaps they do not themselves know, for where is there the saint who is conscious of his own saintliness? Everything remains hidden until the final clarification. But that they are there and at work, this we do know, for it is by them that we are sustained, the time is redeemed, and the world driven forward to that great day when the "peace of God" will reign here below as it does in heaven.[65]

## NOTES TO CHAPTER 18

1. Martin Buber, "Hasidism in Religion," *Hasidism* (Philosophical Library: New York, 1948), p. 199.
2. Buber, "The Man of Today and the Jewish Bible." *Israel and the World* (Schocken: New York, 1948), p. 94.

3. Origen *Against Celsus,* iv 23.

4. Quoted by H. R. Mackintosh, *Types of Modern Theology* (Nisbet: London, 1937), p. 110.

5. Quoted by Sören Kierkegaard, *Concluding Unscientific Postscript* (Princeton University: Princeton, N. J., 1944), p. 86.

6. These are the words of Jesus to the Samaritan woman (John 4:22). They represent, of course, the universal conviction of Jewish tradition.

7. J. Coert Rylaarsdam, "Preface to Hermeneutics," *Journal of Religion,* Vol. XXX (April, 1950), No. 2.

"The Exodus, or deliverance from Egypt, is the central or focal point in Israelite history and faith." G. Ernest Wright, *The Old Testament Against its Environment* (SCM: London, 1950), pp. 49-50.

8. S. W. Baron, "The Historical Outlook of Maimonides," *Proceedings of the American Academy of Jewish Research,* Vol. VI (1934-35), p. 103.

9. H. Richard Niebuhr, *The Meaning of Revelation* (Macmillan: New York, 1946), p. 111.

10. The deliverance from Egypt, the rabbis remind us, is mentioned as sanction in connection with every single commandment (Sifre, Num., Shelah, 115, 35a). He who violates a commandment is "as if he denied the going out of Egypt." Sifra 109c.

11. "It has been taught us. . ., 'With eternal love thou lovest us,' so that we should bear in mind that it originally came from him, not from us." Judah Halevi, *Kitab al Khazari,* tr. by Hirshfeld (Richards: New York, 1927), p. 115.

12. Baron, *op. cit.,* p. 25.

13. Carl Mayer, "Religious and Political Aspects of Anti-Judaism," *Jews in a Gentile World,* ed. by Graebner and Britt (Macmillan: New York, 1942), p. 314.

14. Saadia Gaon, *The Book of Beliefs and Opinions* (Yale University: New Haven, Conn., 1948). Treatise III, chap. vii, p. 158.

"If it had not been for the Torah, they [Israel] would not have differed from the nations of the world." Sifra 112c.

15. "The notion of election always maintained in Jewish consciousness the character at least of an unformulated dogma. . . .There was hardly any necessity for the Rabbis to give any reasons for their belief in this doctrine, resting as it does on ample Biblical authority." Solomon Schechter, *Some Aspects of Rabbinic Theology* (Macmillan: New York, 1909), pp. 57-58.

16. Schechter, *op. cit.,* p. 61.

17. *B.* Shabbat 88a; *B.* Abod. Zar. 2b, and elsewhere.

18. Schechter, *op. cit.,* pp. 110, 309ff.

19. "My covenant with the day and my covenant with the night." Jer. 33:25. See also Jer. 8:7 and Isa. 1:3.

20. C. H. Dodd, *The Bible Today* (Macmillan: New York, 1947), p. 54 See also J. P. Hyatt, *Prophetic Religion* (Abingdon-Cokesbury: Nashville Tenn., 1947), pp. 80-85.
21. Jer. 16:14-15 (23:7-8). See also Isa. 43:2, 18-21; 51:10.
22. Schechter, *op. cit.*, p. 144.
23. Schechter, *op. cit.*, p. 64.
24. Mayer, *op. cit.*, p. 321.
25. See Hayim Greenberg, "The Universalism of the Chosen People," *Jewish Frontier*, Vol. XII (Oct., Nov., Dec., 1945), Nos. 10, 11, 12.
26. Mayer, *op. cit.*, p. 312.
27. Discussion in Stuttgart, January 14, 1933, reported in *Theologische Blätter*, September, 1933.
28. Mayer, *op. cit.*, p. 316.
29. See Jean-Paul Sartre, *Anti-Semite and Jew;* Arthur Koestler, *Thieves in The Night* and various magazine articles.
30. Melville J. Herskovits, "Who Are the Jews?" *The Jews*, ed. Finkelstein (Jewish Publication Society: Philadelphia, 1949), p. 1168.
31. Solomon Grayzel, "Christian-Jewish Relations in the First Millennium," *Essays on Antisemitism*, ed. by Pinson (Conference on Jewish Relations: New York, 1942), p. 27.
The incorporation of the gentiles into Israel through Christianity is graphically expressed by H. Richard Niebuhr: "Through Jesus Christ, Christians of all races recognize the Hebrews as their fathers; they build into their lives as Englishmen or as Americans, as Italians or Germans, the memories of Abraham's loyalty, of Moses' heroic leadership, of prophetic denunciations and comfortings. All that has happened to the strange and wandering people of God becomes a part of their own past." *Op. cit.*, pp. 115-16.
32. A. A. Neuman, "Judaism," *The Great Religions of the Modern World*, ed. by Jurji (Princeton University: Princeton, N. J.), pp. 228-29.
33. Jacob Agus, *Modern Philosophies of Judaism* (Behrmans: New York, 1941), pp. 191-94.
34. "Can the Christian Church supersede the synagogue in the struggle against paganism?" asks the Christian theologian, A. Roy Eckardt. "No, because the Church is itself subject to pagan distortions. . . .Against all idolatries, Judaism protests: 'Hear, O. Israel, the Lord our God is one Lord.' " *Christianity and the Children of Israel* (Columbia University: New York, 1948), pp. 146-47.
"It is important that there always be Judaism. It is the corrective against the paganism that goes along with Christianity." Paul Tillich, quoted by Eckardt, *op. cit.*, pp. 146-47.
35. Franz Rosenzweig, *Briefe* (Schocken: Berlin, 1935), p. 100.
36. "The Judeo-Christian tradition is one system, of which Judaism is the core and Christianity the periphery." Louis Finkelstein, *Tradition in*

284    *Judaism and Modern Man*

*the Making* (Jewish Theological Seminary: New York, 1937), p. 12. That is how the unity of Judaism and Christianity must appear to the Jew from his position, although the same relation will necessarily appear rather different to the Christian from where he stands.

37. "Church and Synagogue, conscious of their election, know the difference between their places in the world. . . .The mission of Judaism is to endure till the end of the world as the people of the King to whom one day all the nations will bow down. The mission of Christianity is to preach to the heathen, to Christianize the countries of the world and the souls of the people." Ignaz Maybaum, *Synagogue and Society* (James Clark: London, 1944), pp. 154-56.

38. Finkelstein, *The Beliefs and Practices of Judaism* (Devin-Adair: New York, 1941), p. 25.

39. Sigmund Freud, *Moses and Monotheism* (Knopf: New York, 1939), p. 145. The context is worth quoting: "One might say they [the anti-Semitic peoples] are 'badly christened'; under the thin veneer of Christianity, they have remained what their ancestors were, barbarically polytheistic. They have not yet overcome their grudge against the new religion which was forced upon them and they have projected it on the source from which Christianity came to them. . . The hatred of Judaism is at bottom hatred for Christianity."

40. Agus, *op. cit.,* p. 193. See also Rosenzweig, *op. cit.,* p. 100

41. Maurice Samuel, *The Great Hatred* (Knopf: New York, 1940), pp. 127-28.

42. Eckardt, *op. cit.,* p. 55.

43. Jacques Maritain, *A Christian Looks at the Jewish Question* (Longmans Green: New York, 1939), pp. 29-30, 42.

44. Fred Denbeaux, "The Roots of Anti-Semitism," *Christianity and Society,* Vol. X (Fall, 1945), No. 4.

45. "Anti-Semitism is Europe's revenge on the Prophets. . . .It is because the Jew brought ethics, the conception of sin into the western world. . . .The European Christian cannot forgive the Jew for giving him Christianity. . . .It is not because. . .they are 'good Christians' that the Europeans are instinctively antisemites. It is because they are bad Christians, in reality repressed. . .pagans." H. Sacher, "Revenge on the Prophets: A Psychoanalysis of Anti-Semitism," *Menorah Journal,* Vol. XXVIII (Fall, 1940) No. 3. Following Freud, a number of psychologists and sociologists have approached anti-Semitism in a way that in part at least agrees with the findings of the theologians. See especially *Anti-Semitism. A Social Disease,* ed. Ernst Simmel (International Universities Press: New York, 1946). Simmel himself writes: "The Jew must take over the role of innocent lamb, carrying the load of hate which up to now has not been absorbed in the process of Christian civilization. The anti-Semite who tortures and kills the Jew actually re-enacts the crucifixion of his Savior. . . . God. . . was transformed [by the Jews] into a spiritual

collective superego. . . . In choosing the Jew as the object of his hatred [the anti-Semite's] ego takes upon itself the privilege of attacking this superego, to punish it, instead of being punished by it. It will therefore not evoke surprise if we assert that the Jew, as the object of anti-Semitism, represents the bad conscience of Christian civilization." *Op. cit.*, pp. 61, 62, 65.

46. I use the term "superhistorical" to suggest permanence underlying the changes of empirical history without any suggestion of timelessness in the larger scheme of redemptive history. Israel arises in history and will disappear with the "end" of history, but *within* empirical history its reality as covenant-folk remains unchanged.

47. S. W. Baron, *A Social and Religious History of the Jews* (Columbia University: New York), I, 83-84.

48. See Will Herberg, "Assimilation in Militant Dress: Should the Jews be 'Like Unto the Nations'?" *Commentary*, Vol. IV (July 1947), No. 1.

49. See the very interesting article by Jacob Agus, "The Status of American Israel," *Conservative Judaism*, Vol. II (February, 1946), No. 2.

50. Maybaum, *op. cit.*, pp. 159-60.

51. G. F. Moore, *Judaism* (Harvard University: Cambridge, Mass., 1927), II, 156.

52. Buber, "The Land and its Possessors," *Israel and the World*, p. 229.

53. "The Holy One scattered Israel over the earth so that proselytes might be added to them." *B.* Pesahim 87b.

54. Mayer, *op. cit., p.* 322.

55. Sacher, *op. cit.*, p. 248.

56. "He becomes a disturber of the intellectual peace but only at the cost of becoming an intellectual wayfaring man, a wanderer in the intellectual No Man's Land, seeking another place to rest, further along the road, somewhere over the horizon. They are neither complaisant nor a contented lot, these aliens of uneasy feet. . . ." Thorstein Veblen, "The Intellectual Preëminence of Jews in Modern Europe," *Essays in Our Changing Order*, ed. by Ardzrooni (Viking: New York, 1934), p. 227.

57. These phrases, used in somewhat different connection, are from A. J. Heschel, *The Earth is the Lord's* (Schuman: New York, 1950), p. 15.

58. For the rabbinic teachings, see M. Higger, *The Jewish Utopia* (Lord Baltimore Press: Baltimore, 1932), chap vi, "The Holy Land," and chap. vii, "The Holy City,"

59. Schechter, *Some Aspects*, p. 98. The liturgy fully bears out Schechter's assertion.

60. See Schechter, *op. cit.*, p. 131, and C. G. Montefiore and H. Loewe, *A Rabbinic Anthology* (Macmillan: London, 1938), p. 166.

61. Tanh. Noah 19; Schechter, *op. cit.*, p. 64. Another way of indicating the final unity and the completion of the vocation of Israel is found in Isaiah: "On that day, Israel will be a third with Egypt and Assyria as a blessing in the midst of the earth, which the Lord of Hosts has blessed

in these terms: 'Blessed be Egypt my people and Assyria the work of my
hands and Israel mine inheritance' " (19:24-25).
62. Alan Richardson, "Instrument of God," *Interpretation*, Vol. III (July,
1949), No. 3.
63. Cf. also: "Our Father, our King, even though we are without righteousness and good deeds, *remember in our favor the covenant of our
fathers* and our daily testimony, The Lord is One. . ."; "Have mercy
upon us *for the sake of thy covenant.* . ."; "O gracious and merciful
King, *remember thy covenant with Abraham;* let the binding of his only
son appear before thee for Israel's sake. . ."—The familiar combination,
"Our God and the God of our fathers," relates to the same conviction,
for the "God of our fathers" is the God of the covenant who becomes
"our" God by virtue of our relation to the "fathers" (Abraham, Isaac
and Jacob) and to the covenant-people.
64. For the rabbinic doctrine of the "remnant," see Schechter, *op. cit.,*
pp. 88-89, and Montefiore and Loewe, *op. cit.,* pp. 231-32.
65. From the *Kaddish*: "He who establishes peace in his heights above,
may he establish peace for us and for all Israel."

# 19.   TORAH: TEACHING, LAW AND WAY

No word in Jewish religion is so indefinable and yet so indispensable
as the word *Torah*. It is Law, yet more than Law, for it is also Teaching and Way. It is a book, an idea, a quality of life. It is the Pentateuch; the Bible in all its parts; the Bible and the rabbinical writings;
all writings dealing with revelation; all reflection and tradition dealing
with God, man and the world.[1] It is represented as a bride, the
daughter of God, as a crown, a jewel, a sword; as fire and water; as
life, but to those who are unworthy, as poison and death.[2] It is the
pre-existent Wisdom or Word of God, present at creation and acting
as the "architect" of the creative work. It preserves the world from
destruction; without it all creation would lapse into chaos: it is the
harmony and law of the universe. It is all this and much more, for
the exaltation of the Torah in Jewish tradition is a theme which no
words can exhaust. But what, after all, is Torah, and what does it
mean to the living Jew, here and now?

Perhaps it would be well to approach this problem from the point of view of *Heilsgeschichte* developed in the last chapter. What is the meaning of Torah in terms of the redemptive history which is Jewish religion?

Redemptive history is not merely history of redemption; it is also redeeming history, history with the power to save. The Jew achieves salvation not through purely individual, mystical exercises which somehow bring him into union with God. The Jew becomes a "true Jew" and makes available to himself the resources of divine grace under the covenant by making Israel's past his own, its sacred history the "background" of his own life.[3] It is by this process of *existential identification* that the Jew becomes a Jew-in-faith, that his existence becomes authentically Jewish existence and he is enabled to encounter God as a Son of the Covenant, within the framework of the divine election. This existential self-integration into the sacred history of Israel gives the individual Jew a grounding in the past, a place of standing in the present, a hope for the future. It gives a context of ultimate significance to life, and that is itself redemption from the blank meaninglessness of self-contained existence. The authentic I-Thou relation between man and God, which we saw to be the existential content of salvation, emerges for the Jew within the framework of his personally appropriated redemptive history.

From this point of view, and this is the point of view most congenial to biblical thought, Jewish faith is the affirmation of the sacred history of Israel as one's own particular history, as one's own "true past." It is the way by which the power of redemptive history becomes effectual *for us*. Idolatry is false redemptive history and therefore false faith. It is easy to see this if we think of the demonic idolatries rampant in the modern world. Totalistic nationalism, communism, fascism, each has its own special *Heilsgeschichte*, cutting across and challenging those of Judaism and Christianity. Each has its own redemptive pattern of history, its own sacred calendar of holy days, in which this redemptive history is proclaimed and enacted; each has its own great redeeming event in the past which gives promise of still greater redemption to come. Each offers the believer a significant context of life, a significant past, in terms of which his existence is given larger meaning and his future made to yield the promise of salvation. Each, in short, parodies the authentic redemptive history of mankind as expressed in Hebraic religion. In this sense, our idolatries are spurious, man-created redemptive histories, just as the gods of idolatry are spurious, man-created idols. Each of us has many contexts of life which strive to serve, partially at least, as redemptive histories—the family, the nation, the labor movement, social and political causes, etc. These all tend to give some fragmentary meaning to certain aspects of life. They become idolatrous only when they claim to provide the full and ultimate meaning of existence. It is then that they must be broken by repentance—that is, by return to one's true *Heilsgeschichte* in which is encountered the Living God in his "mighty deeds" of judgment and mercy.

The true redemptive history for the Jew—and in a rather different sense for the Christian as well—is the sacred history of Israel. One becomes a Jew-in-faith by becoming an "Israelite," by *re-enacting* in *his own life* the redemptive career of Israel. Hebraic religion is historical religion, above all in the sense that the believer must himself appropriate it in his own life as his own history. Every believing Jew *in his own life* stands in the place of Abraham our father and *in his own life* re-enacts the historical encounter between Israel and God. The three great festivals of Judaism—*Pesah* (Passover), *Shabuot* (Pentecost) and *Sukkot* (Tabernacles)—whatever may be their original roots in "nature," gain their religious significance through the fact that they are *history festivals*.[4] They are the liturgical pattern in which the crucial event in the redemptive history of Israel—Exodus-Sinai—is re-enacted and through which the individual Jew integrates himself into that redemptive history. These festivals are not mere commemorations. They are decisive moments in which eternity enters time, in which the temporal takes on the dimensions of the eternal. They are moments when sacred history is repeated in our own lives. In the Passover ritual, every Jew, insofar as he participates in it existentially, becomes an Israelite contemporary with Moses, whom God is drawing out of Egypt, the house of bondage, to bring to the foot of Sinai to receive the Torah. "All this I do," the Passover *Haggadah* represents the Jew as saying in explanation of the order of service, "all this I do because of what God did for *me* in bringing me forth from Egypt."⁵ For *me*, not for my ancestors or for someone else, but for me in exactly the same way as *he* did for Moses and the Israelite slaves of the time. *Shabuot* is the reception of the Torah at Sinai, and he for whom this festival has its authentic existential significance, *himself* goes to Sinai in fear and trembling to receive the Torah. He knows that what Moses told the Israelites "when they had come out of Egypt beyond the Jordan, in the valley opposite Beth-Peor" applies to him just as truly, for he, too, is one of the children of Israel whom God has delivered: "Hear, O Israel . . . the Lord our God made not his covenant with our fathers, but with *us,* even *us,* who are all of us here alive this day" (Deut. 5:5). And what is true of *Pesah* and *Shabuot* is also true of *Sukkot,* which relates to the wandering in the Wilderness. These three festivals are for us the living re-enactment of the formative events in the redemptive history of Israel. Just as Israel became Israel through the events to which they refer, so the individual Jew becomes a Jew-in-faith by "repeating" these events in his own life. It is neither past time nor timeless eternity in which we live in faith, but *contemporaneity.*⁶ "He who does not *himself* remember that God led him out of Egypt," says Martin Buber, "he who does not *himself* await the Messiah, is no longer a true Jew."⁷

To be a Jew means not only to stand in Abraham's place and answer "Here am I" to God's call when and where it comes; it means also to stand at the foot of Sinai and receive the Torah, not figuratively, but actually, through existential "repetition." "On this day, Israel came to Mount Sinai," we read in Scripture (Exod. 19:1). "Why on *this* day rather than on *that* day?" ask the rabbis. "So that you may regard it," they answer, "as though the Torah were given *this day,*⁸ . . . as a *new* proclamation which all run to read."⁹ Yet, although each of us stands at the foot of Sinai and receives the Torah as did the children of Israel in days of old, we stand *now,* not then. It is not so much that we stand at a different time; rather it is that we stand in a different context of life. It is the same Torah, yet different, because we who receive it are different and we hear it in a different way.

What is this Torah which each of us receives at Sinai as God's truth and yet which each of us must "make true" for himself?

Torah, in the first place, is *Teaching,* and its acquisition, in the familiar term, is "learning." In this sense, we may take Torah to represent the entire biblical-rabbinic tradition of "religious" wisdom, remembering, however, that for the rabbis, "if religion is anything, it is everything."[10] Torah starts with the Bible. From the very beginning, however, it is not the Bible simply as written, but the Bible as read and understood. And yet what is thus "added" to the Bible is not really added, for can the Bible have any living significance except as read and understood and therefore as "added to"? This is the truth in the orthodox contention that the Oral Torah (tradition) was given to Moses along with the Written Torah (Bible) on Sinai and is therefore just as truly revelation. Here, too, I think Franz Rosenzweig has put the matter in a more striking and existentially truer way than orthodox fundamentalism is willing to do. "[To the orthodox]," he writes, "the Oral Torah is a stream parallel to the Written Torah and sprung from the same source. For us, it is the completion of the unity of the Book-as-written through the unity of the Book-as-read. Both unities are equally wonderful. The historical view discovers multiplicity in the Book-as-written as well as in the Book-as-read: multiplicity of centuries, multiplicity of writers and readers. The eye that sees the Book not from the outside but in its inner coherence sees it not merely as written but as read. In the former, it sees the unity of teaching; in the latter, it finds the unity of learning, one's own learning together with the learning of centuries. Tradition, halakic and haggadic, itself becomes an element in [understanding and] translation.[11] Thus, the Torah is "from Sinai," and yet the "Torah from Sinai" includes, as the Talmud assures us, everything that the earnest and sincere spirit propounds in trying to understand it and make it vital for life.[12] All is Torah as Teaching.

The Rosenzweigian distinction between the Book-as-written and the Book-as-read applies not only to the Bible but to all the "religious" literature of Israel as soon as that is given the permanence and authority of writing. Once, the Mishnah and Talmud were Oral Torah, "completing" the unity of the Bible as Written Torah. But soon the Mishnah and Talmud themselves became Written Torah and were themselves "completed" in a continuing tradition of Oral Torah. That is why he who wants to appropriate for himself the Torah in its fulness must appropriate it as total living tradition. We cannot start with any external criterion of value, whether it be the distinction between the biblical and the extra-biblical, the "essential" and the "nonessential," the religiously "inspiring" and the religiously "uninspiring." Whatever distinctions and discriminations have to be made must come from *within* the total living tradition of Torah as distinctions and discriminations of parts in terms of the whole; but it is the whole that is the Teaching and must be acquired as "learning." The continuity of Torah, as written and as read, was well understood by the rabbis, who affirmed, to use Schechter's words, that "prophecy [is] the 'word of God' and the continuation of his voice heard on Mount Sinai, a voice which will cease only with the Messianic times—perhaps because the earth will be full of the knowledge of God and all the people of the Lord will be prophets."[13] Let us remember, however, that this "voice," like the word of God at Sinai, reaches us only as mediated through the minds and hearts of men and therefore in a relativized and fallible form. To discover the word of God in the words of the writings is the effort of all "learning," and is a task never done.

Since Torah is Teaching and its acquisition "learning," the study of Torah has from early time been the great and absorbing concern of the believing Jew. It is equivalent to the Temple sacrifices, we are told;[14] indeed, it is that for which man is created.[15] It would be utterly wrong to conclude from this emphasis on study that Jewish spirituality runs dry in the sands of intellectualism and scholasticism. Study of the Torah is something very different in Jewish reality: it is a genuine spiritual exercise, the characteristic and authentic Jewish equivalent of mystical communion with God. Indeed, it is rather more likely to run over into mysticism than into intellectualism, although neither excess is intrinsic to it. Certainly, the coachmen of Warsaw who— as reported by the scholar mentioned by Dr. Heschel[16]—were wont to seize a few moments from their work to gather in a group to con a page of the Talmud, were no intellectuals concerned only with the intricacies of scholastic dialectics. They were deeply earnest men thirsting for spiritual refreshment, for communion with the Living God, and they found it, as countless generations of Jews before them had found it, in the study of Torah. "Oh, how I love thy Torah; it is my meditation all day long" (Ps. 119:97): with Torah understood

in its fullest, this may be taken as the authentic attitude of the believing
Jew to Torah as Teaching.

Yet the study of Torah is as nothing or worse than nothing if it is
not associated with doing. Indeed, it is held to be of such transcendent
value precisely because it is relevant to life and action.[17] This leads
us to a consideration of Torah as Law.

Torah is not in itself identical with law, as the usual translation
would make it.[18] But it is Law, or *halakah*, in one of its aspects. Torah
as Law reflects the fact that the Jew, in his covenant-existence, lives
"under the Law," which is the constitution, so to speak, of the elect
community, the "holiness-code" of the covenant-folk. That this conviction of living "under the Law" need not entail a graceless legalism
or the notion of self-salvation through good works the slightest acquaintance with genuine Jewish spirituality or the most cursory reference to the Prayer Book—which, as Schechter points out,[19] is the best
witness to authentic Jewish belief—is enough to prove. Certainly the
countless generations of Jews who have prayed daily, "Our Father,
our King, be gracious unto us, for we have no merits. . . . Our Father,
our King, if thou shouldst take account of iniquities, who could stand?
. . . We know we have no merits, so deal with us graciously for thy
Name's sake. As a father has compassion on his children, so, O Lord,
have compassion upon us. . . . Righteousness is thine, O Lord, and
confusion is ours. How can we complain? What can we say? How
can we justify ourselves? . . . Save us because of thy grace, O Lord"—
the people who uttered these prayers were under no illusion that they
could save themselves through the accumulation of merit. Nor can the
rabbis—who, for all their circumstantial enumeration of commandments, taught that all were ultimately "compressed" or reduced to one,
"The righteous shall live by his faith"[20]—be charged with the fragmentation and trivialization of the divine imperative. Yet, though it does
not succumb to legalism, normative Jewish faith is halakic through
and through in the sense that it is oriented to the Torah as Law as
well as to the Torah as Teaching.

Torah as Law, like Torah as Teaching, is not merely the Pentateuch,
not merely the Bible, not merely these plus the Talmud. It is the en-

The Mystery of Israel    293

tire living body of tradition that confronts us with its claim, and its
claim is to the totality of life.

Torah as Law is the divine imperative in all its unity and absolute
demand. It "derives its authority from the Kingdom [of God]," as
Schechter points out.²¹ It is not merely an aggregation of particular
commandments; it is in the first place, the affirmation of the total kingship of God, and to this everything else is subordinated. "Why," asks
R. Joshua b. Karha, "does the section [of the *Shema*] *Hear, O Israel*
precede *And it shall come to pass if ye shall hearken?* So that a man
may first take upon him the yoke of the Kingdom of Heaven and after-
ward take upon him the yoke of the commandments."²² *First*, the yoke
of the Kingdom; *then*, the yoke of the commandments. Just as sin,
rebellion against God and his kingship, is the source and origin of particular sins, so the acknowledgment of the divine kingship is the
source, basis and sanction of the particular commandments. But just
as, on the other hand, no man can be merely sinful in the abstract
without engaging in particular sinful activities, so no man can truly
acknowledge the kingship of God without subjecting himself to his
Law in its particularity as commandments.

The commandments (*mitzvot*) that follow upon the acknowledgment of the divine sovereignty are in themselves neither absolute nor
unchangeable, however much they may appear to be so in the conventional formulation. They are, in fact, generally recognized, though
not always explicitly, to be changing and relative to the human situation. No commandment is conceived as absolute in the sense of being
automatically applicable without regard to circumstances. Even the
Sabbath, the rabbis teach, "is delivered into the hand of man (to break
it when necessary), and not man into the power of the Sabbath."²³
"Danger to life annuls the Sabbath . . .,"²⁴ and one Sabbath may be violated to save many.²⁵ And what is true of the Sabbath is, of course,
equally or even more true of other commandments. The general principle is, "that a man shall live by them—*live*, not die."²⁶ This principle
provides not only a criterion for the application, suspension and, where
necessary, the violation of particular commandments, but also a rule,
though by no means the only one, by which orderly change and development are made possible. To take a famous example, biblical law

requires the cancellation of all debts in the sabbatical year (Deut. 15:1-3). However this law of *shemittah* may have worked in very ancient days, by the time of Hillel, circumstances had so changed as to make it a serious threat to economic and social life. In the Mishnah, we are told that when Hillel saw that people were refusing to make loans for fear that they would be canceled on the seventh year and were thus offending against a commandment (to help those in need), he devised a procedure (*prosbul*) by which the biblical requirement could be avoided and lenders could grant loans without fear of cancellation.[27] Thus was a solemn Scriptural injunction annulled on the grounds of economic necessity (the need for an extensive credit system). The fact that the annulment was not explicitly recognized as such but was presented under cover of a legal fiction as an interpretation of the Scriptural provision casts important light on the methods and devices by which change was effected; it does not alter the fact that change there was, and radical change at that. Interpretation, reinterpretation, enactments both positive and negative, emergence of the new and obsolescence of what has become meaningless: all of these processes find plentiful illustration in the development of the halakah through the centuries.[28] Torah as Law is very far indeed from being a fixed and rigid legalistic system without concern for human needs and changing requirements. It recognizes, by implication and act and sometimes even in so many words, the essential relativity of the commandments and their susceptibility to change in response to changing conditions. The lifeless rigidity that characterizes a certain type of contemporary orthodoxy is very far indeed from the classical conception and practice.

Jewish thought has made a variety of distinctions among the *mitzvot* —"heavy" and light," moral and ceremonial, rational and nonrational, those relating to God and those relating to one's neighbor. While under Torah as Law, all commandments are the same in nature and sanction, there are purposes for which such distinctions, properly qualified, can be of use.

For most Jews today, the existential significance of the various kinds of commandments is by no means the same. A good many— those dealing with political, criminal and civil law, for example—have lost all practical meaning since they have been superseded by the law of the state, and, according to the ancient rabbinical maxim, "The law of the state is the law."[29] Others, such as those relating to the Temple sacrifices, are obviously of no contemporary relevance. There are, in fact, left but two kinds of commandments that are of direct concern: the moral prescriptions, on the one side, and the "ritual" or "ceremonial" observances, on the other.

Most people today, as did some of the rabbis of former times, consider the moral commandments to be essentially grounded in reason or natural law, so that "these things, if they had not been written [by God] would have had to be written [by man]."[30] We have seen that there is good reason to doubt this notion. But however that may be, it is obviously not the ethical laws included in halakah that perplex the modern Jew; it is the so-called "ritual observances"—*kashrut,* Sabbath, circumcision—that perplex him. Not that he usually insists on being supplied with a "reason" for each particular observance.[31] What he is concerned with is something more serious and more basic. What are observances *as such* for? What is their religious meaning? What part do they play in religious life?

These questions, in the acute practical form in which they are put, are essentially new, for rarely before modern times did such a problem arise for masses of Jews. The necessity and binding power of the *mitzvot* were always taken for granted, and while there were always plenty of "sinners in Israel," the principle itself was never seriously challenged. This, of course, is no longer the case today. The principle *is* challenged, both in theory and in practice. And so the contemporary Jew requires an answer in essentially new terms; the conventional formulas, however much truth they may contain, will no longer do.

But conventional formulas are all that the spokesmen of orthodoxy, even of its modern branches, seem able to supply. The ritual observances are the direct command of God and therefore must be obeyed: that is virtually all they have to say. If it is pointed out that these ritual observances have changed in many important respects through the centuries, so that they cannot possibly be the eternal and unchanging word of God, we are assured that such change, emergence and obsolescence are only apparent. All the *mitzvot* comprising the Oral

Law were given to Moses on Sinai along with the written Torah; sub sequent generations have simply "uncovered" the *mitzvot* through the use of certain canonical rules of interpretation. This type of fundamentalism runs counter to the plain evidence of the facts[32] and can obviously have but little appeal to the contemporary Jew who is existentially concerned with making the special observances of his faith religiously available to himself.

At the opposite pole is the position of "classical" or old-line Reform Judaism. In this view, the traditional ritual observances are written off as largely obsolete, religiously peripheral and unnecessary to Judaism in its "pure" creedal form. Recently there has been some shift within American Reform toward a greater measure of observance, but this has been due, in part at least, to a growing cultural nationalism with only a remote religious reference. In any case, no new conception has been developed in Reform circles to replace the obviously untenable position of old-line Reform.

Under the influence of secular Jewish nationalism, a new regard for certain traditional holidays and observances has emerged. These are approved because they seem to be the most significant and enduring aspect of "Jewish culture" and thus very useful to stimulate folk solidarity and promote folk survival. Often these secular survivalist arguments are presented under religious guise, but sometimes their nonreligious character is frankly avowed. In any case, this approach is not one that is likely to appeal to those who take Jewish faith seriously. It involves not only the idolatrous exaltation of folk or national values, but also a deliberate exploitation of sacred things that must appear very close to sacrilege to the religious mind. It bears an uncomfortable resemblance to the postion once adopted by Charles Maurras, leader of the ultranationalist L'Action Française, in relation to the Catholic Church. Himself an unbelieving positivist of the Comtean school, Maurras strongly urged support of the Church and its ceremonies. "Differing on the truth," he explained, "we have come to agree on the useful. Divergencies of speculation persist but we have reached a practical accord on the value of Catholicism to the nation."[33] Sincere Catholics were outraged at this overture, and I do not think its Jewish counterpart is likely to commend itself any more favorably to the believing Jew.

Reconstructionism has attempted to develop a philosophy of ritual observance which would avoid the pitfalls of all of these positions. It regards observances not as halakah (binding law) but simply as traditional Jewish folkways which should be pruned, modified, but on the whole preserved for their functional utility. This is defined as the twofold purpose of contributing simultaneously to "Jewish survival" and the "enrichment of Jewish spiritual life." But "Jewish survival," without the conviction of Israel's election and vocation—and this teaching Reconstructionism rejects—is simply a narrow ethnocentrism indistinguishable from secular "folkism," while "enrichment of spiritual life," in the context of Reconstructionist thinking, easily falls into subjectivism and a kind of religio-aesthetic sentimentality which searches for psychological devices to make one "feel spiritual." In the end, the observances lose all compelling religious power and become mere "folkish" trimmings of a subjective "religious experience."[34]

Yet although fundamentalism, modernism, secularism and Reconstructionism must all be rejected insofar as they attempt to provide an adequate answer to the problem of religious observance, they all have something significant to say. Orthodoxy contains the crucial emphasis on the centrality and unique importance to Jewish faith of ritual observance as halakah, while modernism places a valid stress on free inquiry and historical criticism. Reconstructionism deserves recognition for its insistence on the interplay of historical continuity and change in the tradition. Even secular "folkism" is in order when it points to the undeniable socio-cultural role of religious observances. There is some degree of partial truth, greater or less, in each of these positions but none of them is adequate. It is necessary to find a new approach that will preserve the valid emphasis of tradition and yet make that emphasis intelligible to the contemporary believing Jew.

Let us note, in the first place, that all religious observance, existentially considered, is the *acting-out* of one's religious convictions. Our convictions if they are truly existential and involve the entire being, operate along all three dimensions of the personality: thinking, feeling and doing. Of these, the aspect of doing is perhaps as important in religion as either of the others. Not only early religion, but religion in general, seems to be in a basic sense a dromenon, a pattern of *doing,*[35] at least as much as a way of thinking and feeling. We need not agree entirely with Rosenzweig, who commends "the Pharisees and the saints of the Church" for knowing that "man's understanding extends *only* as far as his doing"[36]—this probably goes too far—to appreciate the fact that a man's understanding *involves* his doing. Man being the unitary creature he is, no one can be said really to hold any conviction if it does not somehow find expression in a pattern of doing. Jewish religious thought is particularly sensitive to this truth, for, as Dr. Finkelstein points out, "the ultimate expression of Jewish doctrine remains to this day that of 'propositions in action.' "[37]

Religious observance is, then, in effect the *doing* of one's religious convictions. Now, among Jewish observances, there are two kinds: those that are of a *general-religious* type, more or less common to all religions (prayer, communal worship, consecration of birth, marriage and death), and those of the *special-Jewish* type, that are held to apply to Jews and to Jews only (circumcision, *kashrut*, Sabbath, etc.). A believing Jew will feel that his Christian neighbor ought to pray, attend church and give his children a religious training, but no Jew, not even the most orthodox, will feel that a Christian ought to observe *kashrut* or light the Sabbath candles. These things are somehow meant for Jews alone. It is with observances of this latter kind that we are here primarily concerned.

What is the religious significance of these observances? Is it not obvious that they are, in effect, the *acting-out* of the Jew's affirmation of the election of Israel and its "separation" as "priest-people?" "You shall be holy unto me, for I have separated you from among the nations that you should be mine" (Lev. 20:26): in this proclamation lies the meaning of Israel's existence and the ultimate grounding of the halakic code of ritual observance. The Jew, who, in existential "repetition," stands at the foot of Sinai and receives the Torah, receives it not only as a teaching about the election of Israel but also as a code, a "holiness-code," in terms of which he is to enact that teaching into the pattern of his life.[38] "Law, lived and experienced, is expression and justification of the divine election of Israel. Both belong together."[39]

In this view, Jewish ritual observance is halakah, for the Jew lives "under the Law," and the special discipline to which the halakah subjects him is the commandment of God involved in the election of

Israel. But this is a far cry from asserting, as do the fundamentalists, that the particular, detailed observances confronting the Jew at any time are the eternal prescriptions of God, communicated to Moses on Mount Sinai. Nor, on the other hand, are they "mere" human inventions. As with Scripture, so with halakah, it is fruitless, even meaningless, to attempt a simple and definitive differentiation between the "human" and the "divine." One cannot accept the "general principle" of election as divine but relegate the particular commandments to the rank of the peripheral and "merely human." The "general principle" cannot be really *understood* unless particular commandments are *observed*. "The truth of the theological connection between Chosenness and Law becomes evident when we actually fulfill the command. Only the 'living reality,' the unmediated experience of the single law, leads to a conception of the objective theological fact."[40] Observances have their history; they have arisen, changed and many of them lost their effectiveness with the passage of time. The commandments, like the Bible, are immediately the products of human life, as the modernists claim. But they are not therefore any the less the commandments of God. God operates in and through history, and the history of Israel certainly cannot be dissociated from the divine intent for Israel. It is the historical belief and practice of the community of Israel—*kelal Yisrael*[41]—that provides us with the contents of halakah. In the tradition of Israel, we find the unique and inseparable combination of the divine and the human that constitutes the Torah as Teaching and Law.

Buber has objected to the "ritualistic" emphasis of the halakic tradition on the ground that it "hampers the striving for realization." "The will to the covenant with God through the perfected reality of life in true community," he explains, "can only emerge in power where one does not believe that the covenant with God is already fulfilled in essence through the observance of prescribed forms."[42] This is a basic argument against the halakic concept, and it cannot be denied that it has its force. Were the "observance of prescribed forms" held to be in itself sufficient for the fulfilment of the covenant, then it would deserve all the denunciation that the prophets heaped upon "burnt-offerings" and "sacrifices," and insofar as halakic observance is sometimes so conceived, it deserves such condemnation. But the halakic concept is in itself very far from legalistic ritualism. The election and vocation of Israel mean more, much more, than fixed ritual observance; they include the entire moral law, and no area of life is unaffected by their transforming power. Buber, moreover, himself speaks of the "mysteries whose meaning no one learns who does not himself join in the dance."[43] The halakic pattern is the "dance" in which the Jew learns the "mystery" of the election of Israel.

But in order to have this significance, the ritual observances performed must be not just halakah, but halakah-*for-me*. Rosenzweig deals with this problem—which is a problem particularly, though not exclusively, for those Jews of our time who "return" to Judaism and have to begin "acquiring" the halakah—in a profound essay, *"Die Bauleute."*[44] He stresses the necessity of an existential appropriation of the Torah as Law by each individual Jew standing face to face with God. Unless a *mitzvah* is really made one's own, unless it can be and is performed with true inwardness, it has no effective power. The entire body of halakic tradition, ever changing in its historical conditionedness, yet ever the same, confronts the individual Jew as *Gesetz* ("law" in the external sense, mere "substance"). To become operative, it must be turned into *Gebot* ("commandment" in the inner sense, an inward compulsion to deed). "In the realm of Law, as in the realm of Teaching, contents and material must cease to be mere substance and must be transformed into inner power. *Gesetz* [must] . . . become *Gebot,* which, in the very moment it is heard, turns into deed. The living reality (*Heutigkeit*) is the purpose of the law. This aim, however, is not to be achieved by obedience to the paragraphs of a code. Only personal ability to fulfill the precept can decide. We choose; but it is a choice based on high responsibility."[45] Thus, through responsible personal appropriation, halakah-as-such is transformed into halakah-for-me and becomes operative as the way in which I as a Jew *live out* in ritual pattern my existential affirmation of faith. No man can decide for another what he can or cannot make his own; each must decide for himself, in responsible recognition of the claim that the tradition of the Law has upon him, but for himself nevertheless. In the end, the appropriation of Torah as Law is an existential decision made in divine-human encounter as at Sinai. In the end, too, everyone who has taken upon himself the yoke of the Kingdom and the commandments is vindicated before God for what he does in the full consciousness of responsibility, according to the saying of R. Zedekiah b. Abraham: "Every man receives reward from God for what he is convinced is right, if this conviction has no other motive but the love of God."[46]

Torah as Law is the active side of Torah as Teaching. It embraces not merely ritual observance, but in a sense everything the Jew does, for it recognizes no ultimate distinctions in the totality of life, which is all subject to God and his Law. Law and Teaching constitute two aspects of the same reality, and that reality, in unity and synthesis, is Torah as Way.

The conception of Torah as Way has exercised the imagination of Jewish mystics through the ages. In their visions, it has become virtually the Way, or *Tao,* of the universe—the premundane Word and Wisdom of God operative as the Logos in the creation and maintenance of the cosmos. But if we desire to avoid such theosophical speculation, so alien to the "reverential agnosticism"[47] that characterizes the prophetic faith, we will think of Torah as the Way for the Jew in his life under the covenant.

Here, too, everything depends on decision. Every Jew is under the covenant, whether by birth or adoption; and once under the covenant, his covenant-existence is an objective fact independent of his will. He can no more help it than he can help being a man of the twentieth century or the son of his father. The son is indeed confronted with a crucial decision: to be a good son or a bad son, to live up to or to repudiate the responsibilities of sonship, but no matter what he does or desires to do, he cannot make himself not the son of his father. So too the Jew. He is confronted with a crucial, life-determining choice: to acknowledge and try to live up to or to repudiate the responsibilities of his Jewish covenant-existence, but no matter what he does, he cannot remove himself from under the covenant and its obligations.[48] The fateful decision confronting every Jew is therefore not: Shall I or shall I not come under the covenant? but: Shall I affirm my covenant-existence and live an *authentic* life or shall I deny it and as a consequence live an *inauthentic* one? Judaism is the living out of the affirmative decision. It is the decision to take the Way of the Torah.

The consequences of this decision, both in its individual and collective aspects, are vast and far-reaching. Covenant-existence for the Jew is not a mere figure of speech; it is an objective though supernatural fact. It enters into the Jew's very being, and the attempt to deny it or to repudiate its responsibilities must lead to deep inner division which may manifest itself disastrously in various psychological, social and cultural forms. Ezekiel's thunderous words against the faithless community of his time apply with equal force to the Jewish individual and Jewish community of all times: "And that which comes into your minds shall not be at all, in that you say, We will be as the nations, the races of the lands, to serve wood and stone. As I live, says the Lord God, with a mighty hand, with an outstretched arm and an outpoured fury, will I be king over you" (Ezek. 20:32-33). This is the same "mighty hand and outstretched arm" that delivered Israel from Egypt;[49] but now it no longer delivers, it destroys. Against those who repudiate it in word or deed, the divine election under the covenant turns into the wrath of God. For what they are doing is to deny their true redemptive history and seek salvation elsewhere, by worshiping other gods, which are mere "wood and stone" even though they be compounded of the best that science and philosophy can provide.

But if the repudiation of his true redemptive history is so destructive to the Jew, his wholehearted affirmation of the covenant brings with it the divine blessing of authenticity. Authentic Jewish covenant-existence made operative in life: that is the Torah in its totality as Way.

Because of this ambivalence, the Torah is decision and judgment. It is decision, for it confronts every Jew with the demand for recognition and appropriation, not only once for all but at every moment of existence: "Choose you this day whom you will serve" (Jos. 24:15). It is judgment because, upon this decision, depends the Jew's existence as Jew: "It is not a trifling thing for you; it is your life" (Deut. 32:47). Or, as the rabbis put it, Torah may be either balm or poison. "For him who deals rightly with it, it is a drug for life; but for him who deals wrongly with it, it is a drug for death."[50] Torah is for the Jew the permanent *crisis* of his life, for it is demand, decision and judgment. But it is also *joy,* for it is the testimony of the election, the abiding expression of God's mighty act of redemption in the past and the promise of the greater and final redemption to come. It is at once the symbol and the embodiment of Israel's redemptive history. Torah as Way is the totality of everything that has meaning for the Jew in his religious existence. To live a Torah-true life is, for him, to live a life that is true to his inmost being because it is true to the God who is the source and law of that being.

## NOTES TO CHAPTER 19

1. "The comprehensive name for the divine revelation, written and oral, in which the Jews possessed the sole standard and norm of their religion, is *Torah*. It is a source of manifold misconception that the word is customarily translated 'Law,' though it is not easy to suggest any one English word by which it would be rendered. 'Law' must, however, not be understood in the restricted sense of legislation, but it must be taken to include the whole of revelation—all that God has made known of his nature, character and purpose, of what he would have man be and do. . . . In a word, Torah in one aspect is the vehicle; in another and deeper view, it is the whole content of revelation." G. F. Moore, *Judaism* (Harvard University: Cambridge, Mass., 1927), I, 263.
2. See C. G. Montefiore and H. Loewe, *A Rabbinic Anthology* (Macmillan: London, 1938), chap. v, "The Law"; also Solomon Schechter, *Some Aspects of Rabbinic Theology* (Macmillan: New York, 1909), chaps. viii, "The 'Law,' " and ix, "The Law as Personified in the Literature."
3. "[In the history of Israel] we see the prehistory of our own life, each of us the prehistory of his own life." Martin Buber, *Drei Reden über das Judentum* (Literarische Anstalt Rütten & Loening: Frankfort, 1920), p. 28.
4. The transformation in rabbinic tradition of these "nature" festivals into history festivals expresses better than anything else the true genius of the Jewish religion. Those who today are trying to convert them back into "nature" festivals are, wittingly or unwittingly, trying to undo the work of the rabbis and to paganize Jewish observance. — "It is well known that the ancient Israelitic festivals were taken over from the previous oriental cultures of Canaan and Babylonia. But in each case, ancient Judaism changed the fundamental meaning of the festival first by adding to it, then by substituting for its natural a historical interpretation.

Thus, the *shalosh regalim*, the three great holidays of the year, originally natural holidays of agricultural production, became, for the Jews, holidays commemorating great historical events. Passover, the ancient spring festival, became and remained the festival of the Exodus from Egypt, or of the origin of the Jewish nation. Pentecost, still 'the day of the first fruits' in the Old Testament, was transformed by the early Pharisees into a memorial chiefly of the giving of the Torah, i.e., of the foundation of the Jewish religion. The Feast of Tabernacles celebrates chiefly the migration through the desert. . . ." S. W. Baron, *A Social and Religious History of the Jews* (Columbia University: New York), I, 5.

5. "In every generation, one should regard himself as personally having come out of Egypt." *M*. Pesahim 10.5.

6. Cf. Will Herberg, "Beyond Time and Eternity: Reflections on Passover and Easter," *Christianity and Crisis*, Vol. IX (April 18, 1949), No. 6.

7. Buber, "Der Preis," *Der Jude*, Vol. II (October, 1917), No. 8; *Die jüdische Bewegung*, (Jüdischer Verlog: Berlin, 1916), II, 123-24.

8. Tanh. B. Yitro, 38b.

9. Pesik. K. 102a. "To the Rabbis and their followers, the Revelation at Sinai and all that it implies was not a mere reminiscence or tradition. . . . Through their intense faith, they rewitnessed it in their own souls, so that it became to them a personal experience." Schechter, *Some Aspects of Rabbinic Theology*, p. 24.

10. Schechter, *op. cit.*, p. 142.

11. Franz Rosenzweig, *Briefe* (Schocken: Berlin, 1935), pp. 582-83.

12. "Whatever a discerning disciple will one day proclaim before his teacher was already said by Moses on Sinai." *J*. Peah 9b.

"Rabbi Isaac said: The Prophets drew from Sinai all their future utterances. . . . Not only to the Prophets alone does this apply but to all the sages that are destined to arise in after days." Tanh. Yitro, 11, 124. Note, however, that Sinai is taken as the criterion of all that is valid as future Torah.

13. Schechter, *op. cit.*, p. 123.

14. Tanh. B., Ahare Mot, 35a.

15. *M*. Abot 2.9.

16. A. J. Heschel, *The Earth is the Lord's* (Schuman: New York, 1950), p. 46.

17. The question was discussed: Is study the greater thing or doing? R. Tarfon said doing, but Rabbi Akiba insisted on study on the ground that "study leads to doing." *B*. Kidd. 40b. To this all agreed. See also Sifre, Deut. 48:84b. "One who studies with an intent other than to act, it were better for him had he never been created." *J*. Shabbat 3b.

18. "It must be stated that the term *Law* or *Nomos* is not a correct rendering of the Hebrew word *Torah*. The legalist element, which might rightly be called the Law, represents only one side of the Torah. To the

Jew, the word Torah means a teaching or instruction of any kind. It may be either a general principle or a specific injunction, whether it be found in the Pentateuch or in other parts of Scripture, or even outside the canon. The juxtaposition in which *Torah* and *Mitzvot*, Teaching and Commandments, are to be found in the Rabbinic literature, implies already that the former means something more than merely the Law." Schechter, *op. cit.*, p. 117.

19. Schechter, *op. cit.*, pp. 9-11.

20. *B.* Makk. 23b-24a. The biblical quotation. is from Hab. 2:4.

21. Schechter, *op. cit.*, p. 116.

The total claim of God upon Israel is, as we have seen, related to the divine act of deliverance from Egypt: "We were Pharaoh's slaves in Egypt, and the Lord brought us out of Egypt with a mighty hand. . . . And the Lord commanded us to observe all these statutes and fear the Lord our God, for our good always. . . ." Deut. 6:20-24.

22. *M.* Ber. 2.2.

23. Schechter, *op. cit.*, p. 152. See Mekilta on Exod. 31:13.

24. Tanh. B., Massee, 81a.

25. Mekilta, Shabb. 1.

26. Sifra 86b. Three commandments, however—the prohibition of idolatry, murder and sexual "impurity"—are to be observed even at the risk of death. *B.* Sanh. 74a.

27. *M.* Shebiit 10.3-7.

28. See the extremely informative and illuminating article by Robert Gordis. "The Nature of Jewish Tradition," *Jewish Frontier,* Vol. XIV (November, 1947), No. 11.

29. *B.* Gittin 10b and parallels.

30. *B.* Yoma 67b.

31. Maimonides has some interesting remarks, cast in a rather modern anthropological vein, on the origins of some of the biblical prohibitions. See Leon Roth, *The Guide for the Perplexed: Moses Maimonides* (Hutchinson's University Library: London, 1948), pp. 75-76. In general, however, the rabbis discourage speculation on these matters as vain and confusing.

32. See the study by Robert Gordis referred to above.

33. Quoted by Carlton J. H. Hayes, *The Historical Evolution of Modern Nationalism* (Smith: New York, 1931), p. 209.

34. "Toward a Guide for Jewish Ritual Usage," Reconstructionist Pamphlet No. 4, pp. 7 and 8. Particularly revealing is this passage: "A satisfactory rationale for Jewish [ritual] usage is one that would recognize in it both a method of group survival and a means to the personal self-fulfilment or salvation of the individual Jew. Through it, the individual Jew will know the exhilaration of fully identifying himself with his people and thereby saving his own life from dullness, drabness, and triviality."

306    *Judaism and Modern Man*

Thus, even the "personal" aspect is reduced to the "folkish."
35. Jane Harrison, *Ancient Art and Ritual* (Oxford: New York, 1948), pp. 35-38.
"The ritual is a symbolic expression of thoughts and feelings by action." Erich Fromm, *Psychoanalysis and Religion* (Yale University: New Haven, Conn., 1950), p. 109.
36. Rosenzweig, "Das neue Denken, "Kleinere Schriften (Schocken: Gerlin, 1937), p. 374.
37. Louis Finkelstein, "The Role of Dogma in Judaism," *The Thomist: Maritain Volume* (Sheed & Ward: New York, 1943), Vol. V, January, 1943.
38. It is not without significance that, according to some scholars, most of the biblical "purity" regulations were originally binding upon the priestly group alone. As all Israel became a "kingdom of priests," these observances were extended to the entire people.
39. So N. N. Glatzer ("Franz Rosenzweig," *Yivo Annual of Jewish Social Science: I*, p. 125) summarizes the position taken by Franz Rosenzweig in his essay "Göttlich und Menschlich" (*Briefe*, pp. 518-21).
40. Glatzer, *op. cit.*, p. 124: Rosenzweig, *op. cit.*, p. 519.
41. Schechter uses the term, "Catholic Israel." *Studies in Judaism* (Jewish Publication Society: Philadelphia, 1945), First Series, pp. xviii-xix.
42. Buber, *Der heilige Weg* (Literarische Anstalt Rütten & Loening: Frankfort, 1920), p. 53. A somewhat more *heilsgeschichtliche* formulation of the same argument is to be found in Buber's "The Two Foci of the Jewish Soul," *Israel and the World* (Schocken: New York, 1948), pp. 28-29: "My point of view with regard to this subject [Law] diverges from the traditional. It is not a-nomistic, but neither is it entirely nomistic. . . . The teaching of Judaism comes from Sinai; it is Moses' teaching. But the soul of Judaism is pre-Sinaitic; it is the soul which' approached Sinai and there received what it did receive; it is older than Moses; it is patriarchal, Abraham's soul, or more truly, since it concerns the product of a primordial age, it is Jacob's soul. The Law put on the soul, and the soul can never again be understood outside of the Law; yet the soul itself is not of the Law." This is to be associated with Buber's denial that Exodus-Sinai constitutes the "center" of Israel's redemptive history: "The Bible does not set a past event as midpoint between origin and goal. It interposes a movable, circling midpoint which cannot be pinned to any set time, for it is the moment when I . . . catch through the words of the Bible the voice which from the earliest beginnings has been speaking in the direction of the goal. . . . The revelation at Sinai is not this midpoint itself, but the perceiving of it, and such perception is possible at any time." "The Man of Today and the Jewish Bible," *Israel and the World*, p. 94.
43. Buber, "What is Man," *Between Man and Man* (Kegan Paul: London, 1947), p. 192. Cf. Finkelstein: "Vivid enough for those who are sen-

sitive to them, such propositions expressed in action or commandments have little or no meaning for anyone outside the group which practices them." "The Role of Dogma in Judaism," *op. cit.*, p. 106. Also Rosenzweig: "No single commandment can be made intelligible as a 'religious' demand to anyone who stands outside." *Briefe*, p. 519.
44. Rosenzweig, *Kleinere Schriften*, pp. 106-21.
45. Glatzer, *op. cit.*, p. 124; Rosenzweig, *op. cit.*, pp. 116, 120.
46. Schechter, *Studies*, First Series, p. 325.
47. See above, chap. 17, note 7.
48. "The Israelites have been chosen by God to be his sons and servants. There is no escape. God will use them for his purpose, whether they will or no." Thus do Montefiore and Loewe formulate the normative rabbinical view. *A Rabbinic Anthology*, p. 123.
49. "And brought forth Israel from the midst of them [the Egyptians] . . . with a mighty hand and outstretched arm." Ps. 136:11-12.
50. *B.* Shab. 88b; *B.* Yoma 72b.

# 20. CONCLUSION: FAITH FOR LIVING

The problem of religion is the problem of existence, for "religion *is* man's life insofar as it is defined by his supreme loyalty or devotion."[1] The problem of religion is precisely the problem of one's "supreme loyalty or devotion."

It is a problem at once theological and anthropological in character, for it is a problem both of man and of God. Man, as we have seen, stands at the juncture of finitude and infinity. He is a creature, but he knows himself to be such and is therefore anxious and uneasy in his creatureliness. The very dynamic of his existence drives him beyond himself. His existence, in other words, is self-transcending; it points beyond to something "other," something larger, in which the self attempts to ground itself and establish its security. Man, we may say, is always searching for a "god."

But—and this is the testimony of all Hebraic religion—the "god" that man finds as long as he relies simply on himself is never the true God; it is always some idol constructed after his own heart. It may be a crude fetish (a "golden calf"), a natural power, an ethical system, a cosmic principle or a social utopia, but no matter how refined or elevated, it remains an idol—something devised or possessed by man, the product if not of his hands than of his mind or spirit. And because it is an idol, it cannot save; the attempt to establish one's life upon what is after all the self projected, objectified and worshiped only deepens and extends the chaos, the confusion and fragmentariness of existence.

The tragedy of human life would thus seem to be utterly without hope, for apparently man's every effort to save himself from the misery of existence only tends to increase his perplexities and multiply the possibilities of chaos. And indeed there is no hope so long as man continues to believe that he can *save himself*. But it is the glad word of Hebraic religion that what man cannot do, God will do if only we turn to him. For as the misery of existence is, at bottom, due to our alienation from God, so our "return" to him opens the way for the validation of life, individual and collective. The "return" to God is faith; it is faith that restores the wholeness of life and reorients our total existence in a new direction, toward the Living God who is the source and end of our being.

Faith overcomes despair by bringing us through and beyond it. In faith, we see that the tragedy of life is neither the first not the last word about it. It is not the first word because we know that evil is not inherent in existence but is the consequence of its spoiling through sin. It is not the last because in faith we know that the God who is the Lord of history has his purpose with the world and that purpose shall prevail. The evil in existence, from which no human enterprise, no matter how exalted, is ever free, is thus finally brought under the dominion of God, the true and universal good. To the degree that we make this perspective and this conviction operative in our existence, to that degree is life lifted beyond the plane of fear and tragedy. A living faith banishes fear.

This faith is an active faith because it is a faith of personal commitment and decision. It takes a firm stand against the flight from freedom and responsibility that is so characteristic of our time. To renounce freedom or to try to escape responsibility is, indeed, to repudiate our allegiance to God, for the very first thing God requires of us in Hebraic religion is that we confront reality, decide and act. "Choose you this day" is the demand that comes to us at every moment and in every situation of life. We serve a Master who calls upon us to be free and who assures us that if we act like free men, in truth and responsibility, we will be acting in obedience to his law and in accordance with his will. We may not evade responsibility, but we need not fear it either. For if God be with us, and God *is* with us to the degree that we put ourselves in his service, who can be against us?

For the Jew, the faith that saves is the faith that becomes concrete in the redemptive history of Israel. The God of Jewish faith is no abstract principle but is the Lord who "led us out of Egypt," the God of Abraham, Isaac and Jacob, the God at Sinai, the God who in the "end" will send his Messiah to redeem Israel and the world. For the Jew to "believe in" this God means to affirm with his whole being, in thought, feeling and action, that this entire story is quite literally the substance of his personal biography. Thus is established the *Heilsgeschichtliche* context of faith that gives ultimate meaning to our existence, that defines our signficant past, illumines our present, and proclaims the hope that creates our future. For the Jew, the redemption of life comes in and through his self-integration into the redemptive history of Israel.

On this level, too, faith is won through a never-ending struggle against idolatry. For every loyalty and concern of life—family, profession, social interest or nation—has, so to speak, its own *Heilsgeschichte* which makes its total claim upon the individual as the context of ultimate meaning. And each *Heilsgeschichte* has its own "god," its own absolute. Idolatry, as we have emphasized, is false *Heilsgeschichte*. Amidst the competing claims of "redemptive histories," Hebraic *Heilsgeschichte* stands alone in affirming a God who is not to be identified with anything of this world, who transcends the world and all its power and vitalities as Creator, Judge and Redeemer. Utter loyalty to this God, in which alone lies salvation, means the uncompromising affirmation of the redemptive history of Israel as the ultimate context of existence. Each of us stands in Abraham's place, each of us confronts God and receives the Torah at Sinai, each of us looks forward in the tension of expectation to the coming of the Messiah: that is the meaning of Jewish faith.

Hebraic religion is thus, on every level, a declaration of permanent resistance to idolatry. It is a declaration of total and unreserved allegiance to the Living God who alone is absolute and to whom all other powers, concerns and allegiances are subject. It answers the ultimate question of existence, "Whom shall I serve?" with an unqualified "Fear the Lord your God, walk in all his ways, love him and serve him with all your heart and all your soul" (Deut. 10:12).

Everywhere today we hear that what mankind needs is a "philosophy" capable of coping with the perils and compulsions of modern social existence. We possess such a "philosophy," if philosophy it can be called: it is the biblical faith to which Judaism stands witness. It is for us today, in this crisis of mankind, to lay hold of this faith and make it a vital power in our lives and the life of society.

NOTES TO CHAPTER 20

1. Robert S. Calhoun, *What is Man* (Association Press: New York, 1929), p. 76.

# INDEX

311

# Spirituality

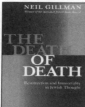

## THE DEATH OF DEATH
### Resurrection and Immortality in Jewish Thought
by *Neil Gillman*

Noted theologian Neil Gillman explores the original and compelling argument that Judaism, a religion often thought to pay little attention to the afterlife, not only offers us rich ideas on the subject—but delivers a deathblow to death itself. By exploring Jewish thought about death and the afterlife, this fascinating work presents us with challenging new ideas about our lives.

"Enables us to recover our tradition's understanding of the afterlife and breaks through the silence of modern Jewish thought on immortality.... A work of major significance."
—*Rabbi Sheldon Zimmerman, President, Hebrew Union College–Jewish Institute of Religion*

6" x 9", 336 pp, Hardcover, ISBN 1-879045-61-3 **$23.95**

## HOW TO BE A PERFECT STRANGER, In 2 Volumes
### A Guide to Etiquette in Other People's
### Religious Ceremonies
*Edited by Stuart M. Matlins & Arthur J. Magida*

BEST REFERENCE BOOK OF THE YEAR

*"A book that belongs in every living room, library and office!"*

Explains the rituals and celebrations of America's major religions/denominations, helping an interested guest to feel comfortable, participate to the fullest extent possible, and avoid violating anyone's religious principles. Answers practical questions from the perspective of *any* other faith.

### VOL. 1: America's Largest Faiths

VOL. 1 COVERS: Assemblies of God • Baptist • Buddhist • Christian Science • Churches of Christ • Disciples of Christ • Episcopalian • Greek Orthodox • Hindu • Islam • Jehovah's Witnesses • Jewish • Lutheran • Methodist • Mormon • Presbyterian • Quaker • Roman Catholic • Seventh-day Adventist • United Church of Christ

6" x 9", 432 pp. Hardcover, ISBN 1-879045-39-7 **$24.95**

### VOL. 2: Other Faiths in America

VOL. 2 COVERS: African American Methodist Churches • Baha'i • Christian and Missionary Alliance • Christian Congregation • Church of the Brethren • Church of the Nazarene • Evangelical Free Church of America • International Church of the Foursquare Gospel • International Pentecostal Holiness Church • Mennonite/Amish • Native American • Orthodox Churches • Pentecostal Church of God • Reformed Church of America • Sikh • Unitarian Universalist • Wesleyan

6" x 9", 416 pp. Hardcover, ISBN 1-879045-63-X **$24.95**

## SPIRITUALITY...OTHER BOOKS:

*Being God's Partner: Finding the Hidden Link Between Spirituality and Your Work* by Jeffrey K. Salkin. 6 x 9, 192 pp, HC, ISBN 1-879045-37-0 $19.95; PB ISBN -65-6 $16.95

*The Empty Chair: Finding Hope & Joy—Timeless Wisdom from a Hasidic Master, Rebbe Nachman of Breslov* Adapted by Moshe Mykoff & The Breslov Research Institute. 4 x 6, 128 pp, Deluxe PB, ISBN 1-879045-67-2 $9.95

*Finding Joy: A Practical Spiritual Guide to Happiness* by Dannel Schwartz with Mark Hass. 6 x 9, 192 pp, HC, ISBN 1-879045-53-2 $19.95

*Minding the Temple of the Soul: Balancing Body, Mind & Soul through Traditional Jewish Prayer, Movement & Meditation* by Dr. Tamar Frankiel & Judy Greenfeld. 7 x 10, 184 pp, Quality PB, illus., ISBN 1-879045-64-8 $15.95

*Tormented Master: The Life and Spiritual Quest of Rabbi Nahman of Bratslav* by Arthur Green. 6 x 9, 408 pp, Quality Pb, ISBN 1-879045-11-7 $18.95

*Your Word Is Fire: The Hasidic Masters on Contemplative Prayer* Edited & transl. by Arthur Green & Barry W. Holtz. 6 x 9, 152 pp, Quality Pb, ISBN 1-879045-25-7 $14.95

# Spirituality

## MEDITATION FROM THE HEART OF JUDAISM
### Today's Teachers Share Their Practices, Techniques, and Faith
Ed. by *Avram Davis*

Techniques explained by the masters, giving readers an inspiring yet very practical introduction to *Jewish* meditation.

Meditation has been practiced for centuries in the Jewish community. In their own individual voices, 22 experts—teachers, scholars, rabbis—explain why meditation is a Jewish spiritual resource for today. Includes a compendium of the experts' "Best Practices."

6" x 9", 224 pp. (est.) HC, ISBN 1-879045-77-X **$21.95**

---

## SELF, STRUGGLE & CHANGE
### Family Conflict Stories in Genesis and Their Healing Insights for Our Lives
by *Norman J. Cohen*

*How do I find greater wholeness in my life and in my family's life?*

The stress of late-20th century living only brings new variations to timeless personal struggles. The people described by the biblical writers of Genesis were in situations and relationships very much like our own. We identify with them. Their stories still speak to us because they are about the same problems we deal with every day.

A modern master of biblical interpretation brings us greater understanding of the ancient text and of ourselves in this intriguing re-telling of conflict between husband and wife, father and son, brothers, and sisters.

"Delightfully written ... rare erudition, sensitivity and insight."
— *Elie Wiesel*

6" x 9", 224 pp. Quality Paperback, ISBN 1-879045-66-4 **$16.95**; Hardcover, ISBN -19-2 **$21.95**

---

## ECOLOGY & THE JEWISH SPIRIT
### Where Nature and the Sacred Meet
Ed. by *Ellen Bernstein*

What is our place in nature? How can we protect what is sacred?

Brings to light environmental themes that are native to Jewish tradition—themes woven through ancient Jewish texts, the biblical creation story, Jewish law, the cycles of holidays and festivals, *mitzvot* (good deeds), and more.

This, the first book in the emerging field of religion and environment to reflect a *Jewish* ecological perspective, awakens us to the Jewish tradition's resources for creating a modern ecological vision.

6" x 9", 250 pp. (est.), HC, ISBN 1-879045-88-5 **$21.95**

# Spiritual Inspiration for Daily Living...

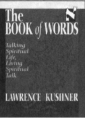

# ...The Kushner Series

## GOD WAS IN THIS PLACE & I, i DID NOT KNOW
### Finding Self, Spirituality & Ultimate Meaning
by *Lawrence Kushner*

Who am I? Who is God? Kushner creates inspiring interpretations of Jacob's dream in Genesis, opening a window into Jewish spirituality for people of all faiths and backgrounds.

In a fascinating blend of scholarship, imagination, psychology and history, seven Jewish spiritual masters ask and answer fundamental questions of human experience.

"A brilliant fabric of classic rabbinic interpretations, Hasidic insights and literary criticism which warms us and sustains us."
—*Dr. Norman J. Cohen, Provost, Hebrew Union College*

"Rich and intriguing." —*M. Scott Peck, M.D., author of* The Road Less Traveled *and other books*

6 x 9, 192 pp. Quality Paperback, ISBN 1-879045-33-8 **$16.95**
6 x 9, 192 pp. Hardcover, ISBN 1-879045-05-2 **$21.95**

## HONEY FROM THE ROCK
by *Lawrence Kushner*

**"Quite simply the easiest introduction to Jewish mysticism you can read."**

An introduction to the ten gates of Jewish mysticism and how it applies to daily life.

*"Honey from the Rock* captures the flavor and spark of Jewish mysticism. . . . Read it and be rewarded." —*Elie Wiesel*

"A work of love, lyrical beauty, and prophetic insight. "
—*Father Malcolm Boyd*, The Christian Century

6 x 9, 168 pp. Quality Paperback, ISBN 1-879045-02-8 **$14.95**

## THE RIVER OF LIGHT
### Spirituality, Judaism, Consciousness
by *Lawrence Kushner*

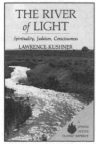

A "manual" for all spiritual travelers who would attempt a spiritual journey in our times. Taking us step by step, Kushner allows us to discover the meaning of our own quest: "to allow the river of light—the deepest currents of consciousness—to rise to the surface and animate our lives."

"Philosophy and mystical fantasy...exhilarating speculative flights launched from the Bible....Anybody—Jewish, Christian, or otherwise...will find this book an intriguing experience."
—*The Kirkus Reviews*

"A very important book."—*Rabbi Adin Steinsaltz*

6 x 9, 180 pp. Quality Paperback, ISBN 1-879045-03-6 **$14.95**

# Spirituality

## MY PEOPLE'S PRAYER BOOK
### Traditional Prayers, Modern Commentaries
Vol. 1—The Sh'ma and Its Blessings
Ed. by *Rabbi Lawrence A. Hoffman*

*My People's Prayer Book* provides a diverse and exciting commentary to the traditional liturgy, written by 10 of today's most respected scholars and teachers from all perspectives of the Jewish world.

The groundbreaking first volume examines the oldest and best-known of Jewish prayers. Often the first prayer memorized by children and the last prayer recited on a deathbed, the *Sh'ma* frames a Jewish life.

7" x 10", 180 pp. (est.) HC, ISBN 1-879045-79-6 **$19.95**

## GOD & THE BIG BANG
### Discovering Harmony Between Science & Spirituality
by *Daniel C. Matt*

Mysticism and science: What do they have in common? How can one enlighten the other? By drawing on modern cosmology and ancient Kabbalah, Matt shows how science and religion can together enrich our spiritual awareness and help us recover a sense of wonder and find our place in the universe.

"This poetic new book...helps us to understand the human meaning of creation."

—*Joel Primack, leading cosmologist, Professor of Physics, University of California, Santa Cruz*

6" x 9", 216 pp. Hardcover, ISBN 1-879045-48-6 **$21.95**

## THEOLOGY & PHILOSOPHY

*Aspects of Rabbinic Theology*
by Solomon Schechter. 6 x 9, 440 pp, Quality Paperback, ISBN 1-879045-24-9 $18.95

*The Earth Is the Lord's: The Inner World of the Jew in Eastern Europe*
by Abraham Joshua Heschel. 5.5 x 8, 112 pp, Quality Paperback, ISBN 1-879045-42-7 $13.95

*Godwrestling—Round 2: Ancient Wisdom, Future Paths*
by Arthur Waskow. 6 x 9, 352 pp, HC, ISBN 1-879045-45-1 $23.95

*Judaism & Modern Man: An Interpretation of Jewish Religion*
by Will Herberg. 5.5 x 8.5, 336 pp, Quality Paperback, ISBN 1-879045-87-7 $18.95

*Israel: An Echo of Eternity*
by Abraham Joshua Heschel. 5.5 x 8, 272 pp, Quality Paperback, ISBN 1-879045-70-2 $18.95

*The Last Trial: On the Legends and Lore of the Command to Abraham to Offer Isaac as a Sacrifice*
by Shalom Spiegel. 6 x 9, 208 pp, Quality Paperback, ISBN 1-879045-29-X $17.95

*A Passion for Truth: Despair and Hope in Hasidism*
by Abraham Joshua Heschel. 5.5 x 8, 352 pp, Quality Paperback, ISBN 1-879045-41-9 $18.95

*Seeking the Path to Life: Theological Meditations on God and the Nature of People, Love, Life and Death*
by Rabbi Ira F. Stone 6 x 9, 132 pp, Quality Paperback, ISBN 1-879045-47-8 $14.95; HC, ISBN -17-6 $19.95

*The Spirit of Renewal: Finding Faith After the Holocaust*
by Edward Feld 6 x 9, 224 pp, Quality Paperback, ISBN 1-879045-40-0 $16.95; HC, ISBN -06-0 $22.95

# Healing/Recovery/Wellness

*Healing of Soul, Healing of Body: Spiritual Leaders Unfold the Strength & Solace in Psalms*
Edited by Rabbi Simkha Y. Weintraub, CSW for the Jewish Healing Center. 6 x 9, 2-color text, 128 pp,
Quality Paperback, ISBN 1-879045-31-1 $14.95

*Twelve Jewish Steps to Recovery: A Personal Guide to Turning from Alcoholism & Other Addictions*
by Dr. Kerry M. Olitzky & Stuart A. Copans, M.D. 6 x 9, 136 pp,
Quality Paperback, ISBN 1-879045-09-5 $13.95   HC, ISBN 1-879045-08-7 $19.95

*Recovery from Codependence: A Jewish Twelve Steps Guide to Healing Your Soul*
by Dr. Kerry M. Olitzky. 6 x 9, 160 pp,
Quality Paperback, ISBN 1-879045-32-X $13.95   HC, ISBN 1-879045-27-3 $21.95

*Renewed Each Day: Daily Twelve Step Recovery Meditations Based on the Bible*
by Dr. Kerry M. Olitzky & Aaron Z. Vol. I, Genesis & Exodus, 224 pp; Vol. II, Leviticus, Numbers &
Deuteronomy, 280 pp; Two-Volume Set, Quality Paperback, ISBN 1-879045-21-4 $27.90

*One Hundred Blessings Every Day: Daily Twelve Step Recovery Affirmations, Exercises for Personal
Growth & Renewal Reflecting Seasons of the Jewish Year*
by Dr. Kerry M. Olitzky. 4.5 x 6.5, 432 pp, Quality Paperback, ISBN 1-879045-30-3 $14.95

# Lifecycle

*Bar/Bat Mitzvah Basics: A Practical Family Guide to Coming of Age Together*
Edited by Cantor Helen Leneman. 6 x 9, 224 pp,
HC, ISBN 1-879045-51-6 $24.95   Quality Pb, ISBN 1-879045-54-0 $16.95

*Embracing the Covenant: Converts to Judaism Talk About Why & How*
Edited by Rabbi Allan Berkowitz and Patti Moskovitz. 6 x 9, 192 pp, Quality Pb,
ISBN 1-879045-50-8 $15.95

*Grief in Our Seasons: A Mourner's Kaddish Companion*
by Rabbi Kerry M. Olitzky. 4 x 6, 400 pp (est), Deluxe PB, ISBN 1-879045-55-9 $18.95

*A Heart of Wisdom: Making the Jewish Journey from Midlife through the Aging Years*
Ed. by Susan Berrin; Foreword by Harold Kushner. 6 x 9, 384 pp, HC, ISBN 1-879045-73-7 $24.95

*Lifecycles, Vol. 1: Jewish Women on Life Passages & Personal Milestones*
Edited by Rabbi Debra Orenstein. 6 x 9, 480 pp, HC, ISBN 1-879045-14-1 $24.95

*Lifecycles, Vol. 2: Jewish Women on Biblical & Contemporary Life Themes*
Ed. by Rabbi Debra Orenstein & Rabbi Jane Litman.
6 x 9, 464 pp, HC, ISBN 1-879045-15-X $24.95

*Mourning & Mitzvah: A Guided Journal to Walking the Mourner's Path Through Grief to Healing*
by Anne Brener. 7.5 x 9, 288 pp, Quality Paperback, ISBN 1-879045-23-0 $19.95

*The New Jewish Baby Book: Names, Ceremonies, Customs—A Guide for Today's Families*
by Anita Diamant. 6 x 9, 328 pp, Quality Paperback, ISBN 1-879045-28-1 $16.95

*Putting God on the Guest List, 2nd Edition: How to Reclaim the Spiritual Meaning of Your Child's
Bar or Bat Mitzvah* by Jeffrey K. Salkin. 6 x 9, 232 pp,
Quality Paperback ISBN 1-879045-59-1 $16.95  HC ISBN 1-879045-58-3 $24.95

*So That Your Values Live On: Ethical Wills & How to Prepare Them*
Edited by Jack Riemer & Nathaniel Stampfer. 6 x 9, 272 pp,
Quality Paperback, ISBN 1-879045-34-6 $16.95   HC, ISBN 1-879045-07-9 $23.95

*A Time to Mourn, A Time to Comfort: A Guide to Jewish Bereavement and Comfort*
by Dr. Ron Wolfson. 7 x 9, 320 pp, Quality Paperback, ISBN 1-879045-96-6 $16.95

*When a Grandparent Dies: A Kid's Own Remembering Workbook for
Dealing with Shiva and the Year Beyond* by Nechama Liss-Levinson, Ph.D. 8 x 10, 2-color text, 48 pp,
HC, ISBN 1-879045-44-3 $14.95

# Art of Jewish Living Series for Holiday Observance

## THE SHABBAT SEDER
by Dr. Ron Wolfson

*The Shabbat Seder* is a concise step-by-step guide designed to teach people the meaning and importance of this weekly celebration, as well as its practices.

Each chapter corresponds to one of ten steps which together comprise the Shabbat dinner ritual, and looks at the *concepts, objects,* and *meanings* behind the specific activity or ritual act. The blessings that accompany the meal are written in both Hebrew and English, and accompanied by English transliteration. Also included are craft projects, recipes, discussion ideas and other creative suggestions for enriching the Shabbat experience.

"A how-to book in the best sense...."
— *Dr. David Lieber, President, University of Judaism, Los Angeles*

7" x 9", 272 pp. Quality Paperback, ISBN 1-879045-90-7 **$16.95**

---

Also available are these helpful companions to *The Shabbat Seder*:
- •Booklet of the Blessings and Songs    ISBN 1-879045-91-5   $5.00
- •Audiocassette of the Blessings    DNO3   $6.00
- •Teacher's Guide    ISBN 1-879045-92-3   $4.95

---

## HANUKKAH
by Dr. Ron Wolfson
Edited by *Joel Lurie Grishaver*

Designed to help celebrate and enrich the holiday season, *Hanukkah* discusses the holiday's origins, explores the reasons for the Hanukkah candles and customs, and provides everything from recipes to family activities.

There are songs, recipes, useful information on the arts and crafts of Hanukkah, the calendar and its relationship to Christmas time, and games played at Hanukkah. Putting the holiday in a larger, timely context, "December Dilemmas" deals with ways in which a Jewish family can cope with Christmas.

"This book is helpful for the family that strives to induct its members into the spirituality and joys of Jewishness and Judaism...a significant text in the neglected art of Jewish family education."
— *Rabbi Harold M. Schulweis, Cong. Valley Beth Shalom, Encino, CA*

7" x 9", 192 pp. Quality Paperback, ISBN 1-879045-97-4 **$16.95**

---

## THE PASSOVER SEDER
by Dr. Ron Wolfson

Explains the concepts behind Passover ritual and ceremony in clear, easy-to-understand language, and offers step-by-step procedures for Passover observance and preparing the home for the holiday.

**Easy-to-Follow Format**: Using an innovative photo-documentary technique, real families describe in vivid images their own experiences with the Passover holiday. **Easy-to-Read Hebrew Texts**: The Haggadah texts in Hebrew, English, and transliteration are presented in a three-column format designed to help celebrants learn the meaning of the prayers and how to read them. **An Abundance of Useful Information**: A detailed description of how to perform the rituals is included, along with practical questions and answers, and imaginative ideas for Seder celebration.

"A creative 'how-to' for making the Seder a more meaningful experience."
— *Michael Strassfeld, co-author of* The Jewish Catalog

7" x 9", 336 pp. Quality Paperback, ISBN 1-879045-93-1 **$16.95**

---

Also available are these helpful companions to *The Passover Seder*:
- •Passover Workbook    ISBN 1-879045-94-X   $6.95
- •Audiocassette of the Blessings    DNO4   $6.00
- •Teacher's Guide    ISBN 1-879045-95-8   $4.95

# Children's

## IN GOD'S NAME

AWARD WINNER

Selected by
Parent Council Ltd.™

by *Sandy Eisenberg Sasso*
Full color illustrations by *Phoebe Stone*          **For ages 4-8**

MULTICULTURAL, NONSECTARIAN, NONDENOMINATIONAL. This modern fable about the search for God's name celebrates the diversity and, at the same time, the unity of all the people of the world. "What a lovely, healing book!" —*Madeleine L'Engle*

9 x 12, 32 pp. Hardcover, Full color illus., ISBN 1-879045-26-5  **$16.95**

AWARD WINNER

## GOD'S PAINTBRUSH

by *Sandy Eisenberg Sasso*
**For ages 4-8**     Full color illustrations by *Annette Compton*

MULTICULTURAL, NONSECTARIAN, NONDENOMINATIONAL. Invites children of all faiths and backgrounds to encounter God openly in their own lives. Wonderfully interactive, provides questions adult and child can explore together at the end of each episode. "An excellent way to honor the imaginative breadth and depth of the spiritual life of the young." —*Dr. Robert Coles, Harvard University*

11x 8½, 32 pp. Hardcover, Full color illus., ISBN 1-879045-22-2  **$16.95**

## SHARING BLESSINGS
### Children's Stories for Exploring the Spirit of the Jewish Holidays
by *Rahel Musleah* and *Rabbi Michael Klayman*
Full color illustrations by *Mary O'Keefe Young*          **For ages 6-10**

What is the spiritual message of each of the Jewish holidays? How do we teach it to our children? Many books tell children about the historical significance and customs of the holidays. Now, through engaging, creative stories about one family's spiritual preparation, *Sharing Blessings* explores ways to get into the spirit of the holidays all year long.

"A beguiling introduction to important Jewish values by way of the holidays."
—*Rabbi Harold Kushner*

7 x 10, 64 pp. Hardcover, Full color illus., ISBN 1-879045-71-0  **$18.95**

## A PRAYER FOR THE EARTH: The Story of Naamah, Noah's Wife
by *Sandy Eisenberg Sasso*
Full color illustrations by *Bethanne Andersen*          **For ages 4-8**

9 x 12, 32 pp. HC, Full color illus., ISBN 1-879045-60-5  **$16.95**

## BUT GOD REMEMBERED:
### Stories of Women from Creation to the Promised Land
by *Sandy Eisenberg Sasso*
Full color illustrations by *Bethanne Andersen*          **For ages 8 and up**

9 x 12, 32 pp. HC, Full color illus., ISBN 1-879045-43-5  **$16.95**

## THE 11TH COMMANDMENT: Wisdom from Our Children
by *The Children of America*          **For all ages**

8 x 10, 48 pp. HC, Full color illus., ISBN 1-879045-46-X  **$16.95**

## THE BOOK OF MIRACLES: A Young Person's Guide to Jewish Spiritual Awareness
by *Lawrence Kushner*          **For ages 9-12**

6 x 9, 96 pp. (est.), HC, 2-color illus., ISBN 1-879045-78-8  **$16.95**

### Order Information

| # of Copies | Book Title / ISBN (Last 3 digits) | $ Amount |
|---|---|---|
| _____ | _____ | _____ |
| _____ | _____ | _____ |
| _____ | _____ | _____ |
| _____ | _____ | _____ |
| _____ | _____ | _____ |
| _____ | _____ | _____ |
| _____ | _____ | _____ |
| _____ | _____ | _____ |
| _____ | _____ | _____ |
| _____ | _____ | _____ |
| _____ | _____ | _____ |
| _____ | _____ | _____ |
| _____ | _____ | _____ |

For s/h, add $3.50 for the first book, $2.00 each add'l book
(to a max of $15.00)     $ S/H _____

TOTAL _____

Check enclosed for $_____ *payable to:* JEWISH LIGHTS Publishing

Charge my credit card:     ❐ MasterCard     ❐ Visa

Credit Card #_____Expires _____

Signature _____Phone (_____)_____

Your Name _____

Street_____

City / State / Zip _____

**Ship To:**

Name _____

Street_____

City / State / Zip _____

*Phone, fax or mail to:* **JEWISH LIGHTS Publishing**
P.O. Box 237 • Sunset Farm Offices, Route 4 • Woodstock, Vermont 05091
Tel (802) 457-4000   Fax (802) 457-4004   www.jewishlights.com
**Credit card orders (800) 962-4544** (9AM–5PM ET Monday–Friday)
*Generous discounts on quantity orders. SATISFACTION GUARANTEED. Prices subject to change.*